Memory, Thought, a

Memory, Thought, and Behavior

Robert W. Weisberg
Department of Psychology
Temple University

New York • Oxford
OXFORD UNIVERSITY PRESS
1980

Copyright © 1980 by Oxford University Press, Inc.

Library of Congress Cataloging in Publication Data
Weisberg, Robert W
  Memory, thought, and behavior.
  Bibliography: p.
  Includes index.
  1. Thought and thinking. 2. Memory. 3. Psycholinguistics. I. Title. [DNLM: 1. Memory. 2. Thinking. 3. Behavior. BF455 W426m]
BF455.W38   153   79-56
ISBN O-19-502583-0

Since this page cannot accommodate all the copyright notices, the pages 457–458 constitute an extension of the copyright page.

Printed in the United States of America

To Nancy and Michael
and to
Michael's grandparents

Preface

Recent books on cognitive processes have generally taken one of two orientations. First, there is the position originally taken by Neisser (1967) and subsequently adopted by many authors. Information is followed as it moves into the system and is processed or transformed until it is permanently stored. The processed information can then be used as needed. This viewpoint entails a consideration of such topics as pattern recognition, attention, sensory information store, short-term memory, and long-term memory, more or less in that order. One problem with this point of view is that, while information may be acquired, it is never used. For example, in these books there is often no chapter on problem solving; or if there is, it is tacked on at the end, with little or no connection to the concepts that have been developed earlier. In the same way, their discussion of language is concerned mainly with speech recognition, and little is said about using language as a communication device. Thus, if one is interested in complex processes, these books leave one disappointed.

The second popular point of view begins with a description of the knowledge that humans have acquired, and then attempts to outline how this knowledge is put to use in various situations. These theorists have constructed network models of various sorts to represent the structure of human concepts, and have developed computer programs to apply these networks to various specific domains. However, there are problems with this approach also. First, and probably most serious, is the question of whether these models are adequate as descriptions of human concepts. Network models are based on certain assumptions about what concepts "are," and as will be shown several times in later chapters, these assumptions can be called into question. In addition, this general orientation toward cognitive functioning is based on the "symbolist" conception of thinking (Price, 1953, Chapter 10). This theory argues that thinking is a mental act of a special sort, which involves the manipulation of special sorts of objects, called concepts. This assumption can also be questioned, as we shall see later. In addition to these logical problems, these models have also been limited in their areas of application. For example, network models have generally not been applied to the areas of practical problem solving, language development, or cognitive development. ("Practical" problems are defined by Duncker, 1945, p. 1, as problems in which the subject must bring about the solution through action. These sorts of problems are also called "insight" problems. There has been much interest recently in problem solving, but the interest centers on the "move" type of problems studied by Newell and Simon and others.) Also, network models have not been applied to much of the recent work in memory, with some exceptions in the work of Anderson, Bower, and Wickelgren. Once again, someone with a broad interest in complex processes will be somewhat disappointed by network models of cognition.

The present book is also concerned with the acquisition and use of knowledge, but in a way different from the two viewpoints just discussed. Our central concern will be with what could be called the higher mental processes—memory, problem solving, language use and language development, the development of thought, and the question of the medium of thought. The whole enterprise was motivated from the first by the need to deal with these sorts of phenomena in their complexity. The general position that directs the present work is that cognitive functioning in many different situations are special cases of a more general process: selective retrieval of information from memory. That is, it will be argued that in order to understand and explain the things that people do in various situations, we must take into account what information people have available about these situations, and how this information is retrieved and applied to the situation at hand.

This point of view obviously also brings with it an interest in how information is stored in memory in the first place. Accordingly, we begin in part One with an analysis of memory processes themselves, because there has

Preface

been a great deal of knowledge accumulated over recent years by memory researchers concerned with just these sorts of questions. Once this has been done, this analysis will serve to elucidate cognitive functioning in other areas. There are four chapters in part One. Chapter 1 presents an outline of a model of memory based on a detailed analysis of the Peterson and Peterson (1959) task as a microcosm of memory functioning. Several processes are pointed out, and their generality in other memory situations is discussed. Chapters 2–4 go into detail in more specified areas, such as the process of storing information and the form of the information that is stored (chapter 2); the nature of recall—specifically, the question of the reconstructive nature of recall (chapter 3); and the basis for our ability to order events in time, which may be a phenomenon with broad ramifications (chapter 4).

Part Two deals with pattern recognition and attention (chapters 5 and 6), and could also be considered as the end of part One. These chapters bridge the gap between research in memory and questions concerning the medium of thought, an issue that has recently had a rebirth in psychology. Part Three includes discussions of imagery (chapter 7), abstract concepts (chapter 8), and language (chapter 9) as possible media of thought. The conclusion from part Three is that there is no medium of thought, in the traditional sense, although imagery and language play a role in thinking.

Parts Four and Five are similar in orientation, although different in subject matter. Both sections are built around the argument that one must take into account a person's knowledge before drawing any conclusions about the explanation of a given behavioral act. Part Four examines research in problem solving, with an emphasis on practical problem solving, an area that has a long history in psychology, but which recently has been almost totally ignored. One reason for this is because Gestalt-influenced psychologists have been prone to employ esoteric concepts in their explanations of practical problem solving, and these concepts have been adopted by cognitively oriented theorists. Perhaps because of this, this area is fragmented, with no overriding principles to organize the literature. The purpose of part Four is to demonstrate that practical problem solving can be understood as a special case of retrieval of information from memory, making it unnecessary to introduce such terms as *insight* and *spontaneous restructuring* in explanations of problem solving. The basic argument in part Four is that one can explain the solutions produced by problem solvers to various problems if one knows the information available to the problem solver, and if one knows what the problem solver is trying to do.

It is argued that previous work in practical problem solving was inadequate because researchers failed to take into account one or both of these factors. Other recent work in problem solving is also considered in this section.

Part Five deals with some important issues in cognitive development. In recent years, questions have been raised concerning discontinuity in cognitive development, mainly through the influence of Piaget's work. As is well known, Piaget argues that qualitative changes occur in thought processes from infancy to childhood, and from childhood to adolescence. We shall argue that, contrary to the Piagetian point of view, there are no qualitative changes in thought processes as humans develop. Chapter 13 is concerned with Piaget's analysis of development in infancy. It will be argued that the phenomena discovered by Piaget are the result of inefficiency in processing and storing information on the part of the infant, rather than qualitative differences in thought processes. Chapter 14 is concerned with the development of concrete operations, and it is argued that the phenomena that Piaget took as evidence for "pre-operational" thought are the result of simple ignorance on the part of the child. Once again, the processes are not different, but the knowledge is.

Chapter 15 is concerned with language development, another area that has seen some controversy in recent years, especially the debate over whether language could be learned by humans. The present discussion builds on recent work that indicates that cognitive factors are important here also. The chapter will emphasize the role of memory, pattern recognition, and attention in language development. It is argued that the changes that occur in children's linguistic output are due mainly to the children's increased efficiency in processing the speech that they hear around them. This increased efficiency is due to experience in hearing others talk, and the basic mechanisms involved are those discussed in parts One and Two. The final chapter, chapter 16, concerns the mechanisms of thought—the question of interest is how thought becomes internalized. The discussion will center on an old idea—Sechenov's notion that thought is the first two-thirds of a reflex. In more modern terms, we shall consider the idea that thinking is behavior with inhibition of output. The discussion will build on the concepts developed earlier.

In sum, the present book presents a framework for analyzing human thought processes. The general orientation could be called traditional, although sometimes old ideas appear new when presented in a contemporary context.

Acknowledgments

Many people deserve thanks for their help in bringing this book to completion. Sam Glucksberg introduced me to the study of human cognition, and he has remained a good friend and a good critic. My colleagues David Goldstein and Lynn Hasher have been a constant source of stimulating ideas, cogent criticism, and encouragement. Many students have responded to the ideas presented in the book, and have had great effects on my thinking. Among these people are Walter Chromiak, Marie DiCamillo, Tom Fink, Marianne Lono, Louis Scavo, and Frances Wren. The preparation of the manuscript itself could not have been completed without the efforts of Dorothy Mewha and her staff at the Temple Word Processing Center. Finally, Marc Boggs and Nancy Amy at Oxford helped to make the actual birth relatively painless.

R. W. W.

Philadelphia
July 1979

Contents

Part One Memory
  Chapter 1. Outline of a model of memory
    1.0   Introduction 3
    1.1   The short-term memory experiment: a microcosm 4
    1.2   The processes underlying short-term recall: three possible models 8
    1.3   Summary of preliminary model 11
    1.4   Recall on the basis of recency 12
    1.5   Summary cues 14
    1.6   Subjective organization of "random" lists 16
    1.7   Organization and the use of knowledge in recall 18
    1.8   Generality of proactive interference effects 19
    1.9   Retroactive interference 21
    1.10 Summary 23

  Chapter 2. Storing information in memory: encoding and thinking
    2.0   Introduction 24
    2.1   The dual-process hypothesis 25
    2.2   Recognition-recall differences 27
    2.3   How good is recognition memory? 28

- 2.4 An encoding as the memory for a word   32
- 2.5 Encoding operations examined through recognition tests   34
- 2.6 Encoding and recall   37
- 2.7 Encoding and thinking   41
- 2.8 Summary   43

Chapter 3. Reconstruction and recall
- 3.0 Introduction   45
- 3.1 Bartlett's reconstructive theory of recall   46
- 3.2 Memory for sentences   48
- 3.3 More than meaning   50
- 3.4 Topics and contexts: scripts   53
- 3.5 Recall and reconstruction: summary   59
- 3.6 Interpretation and nothing else?   60
- 3.7 Knowledge and reconstruction in recall   62
- 3.8 On the function of retrieval cues   67
- 3.9 Summary and conclusions   68

Chapter 4. Time and some related issues
- 4.0 Introduction   71
- 4.1 Models of temporal order in memory   72
- 4.2 The psychological present—the psychological state   75
- 4.3 Background information, retrieval, and associations   77
- 4.4 Developing general knowledge from specific experiences: episodic versus semantic memory   79
- 4.5 Summary   83
- 4.6 Summary of part One   83

Part Two   Pattern recognition and attention

Chapter 5. Pattern recognition
- 5.0 Introduction to part Two   87
- 5.1 Introduction to recent theorizing   88
- 5.2 Sequential processing in pattern recognition   91
- 5.3 Parallel processing within fixations   95
- 5.4 Orientation and recognition of patterns   99
- 5.5 Expectations and perception   101
- 5.6 Pattern maps and novel patterns   103
- 5.7 Pattern maps within pattern maps: recognition of more complex patterns   105

Contents

- 5.8 Hierarchical structure of knowledge 106
- 5.9 Ease of recognition 107
- 5.10 A related question: abstract pattern maps? 109
- 5.11 Pattern recognition, concepts, and internal representations 114
- 5.12 "Top down" versus "bottom up" 114
- 5.13 Summary and conclusions 115

Chapter 6. Selective attention
- 6.0 Introduction 116
- 6.1 Shadowing: the basic data 117
- 6.2 Broadbent's filter model 118
- 6.3 Processing the meaning of the rejected message: problems for the filter 119
- 6.4 Kahneman's limited-capacity model 121
- 6.5 Neisser's synthesis model 122
- 6.6 Top-down models of pattern recognition as models of attention 123
- 6.7 On hearing and attending to one's name 128
- 6.8 Conclusions from recent models of selective attention 132
- 6.9 On "analyzing the meaning" of a message 132
- 6.10 Consciousness and attention 134
- 6.11 Summary 138
- 6.12 Summary of part Two 139

Part Three The medium of thought

Chapter 7. Mental imagery as the medium of thought
- 7.0 Introduction to part Three 143
- 7.1 The imagist theory of thinking in philosophy 146
- 7.2 Images and abstract ideas 147
- 7.3 Imagery in early psychology 151
- 7.4 Imagery in memory 153
- 7.5 Interactive imagery and recall 154
- 7.6 How does imagining assist memorizing? 156
- 7.7 Imagination and knowledge 158
- 7.8 Imagining and perceiving 159
- 7.9 Pattern maps and sequential processes in visual imagery 162

7.10 Scanning rooms versus "scanning" images   165
7.11 Consciousness, symbolization, and imagery   171
7.12 Summary and conclusions   173

Chapter 8. Concepts, internal objects, and thinking
8.0 Introduction   175
8.1 Constructing semantic representations: concepts and sentences   176
8.2 Concepts: philosophical background   184
8.3 Studies of family resemblances   191
8.4 What does one have when one has a concept?   194
8.5 A critical examination of arguments in support of abstract conceptual models   195
8.6 What do network models describe?   198
8.7 Recognizing sentences   200
8.8 Abstract grammatical classes   203
8.9 Meaning and use: sentence-to-sentence moves in language games   204
8.10 Summary   206

Chapter 9. Language as the medium of thought
9.0 Introduction   208
9.1 Russian theorizing   210
9.2 Brief history of the study of speech and thought in the United States   213
9.3 Language learning as the source of concepts   217
9.4 Language as the basis for "nonapparent" concepts   219
9.5 Language and concepts: conclusions   221
9.6 Use of speech muscles in thinking   222
9.7 The role of speech in problem solving   226
9.8 On "self-direction"   230
9.9 Moving in language games, verbalization, and consciousness   232
9.10 Several possible functions for overt speech during problem solving   235
9.11 An overflow model for production of speech-for-self   237
9.12 Summary   241
9.13 Summary of part Three: Is there a medium of thought?   242

Contents

Part Four Problem solving

Chapter 10. Problem solving as selective recall and imagination: outline of a model of solution of practical problems

- 10.0 Introduction to part Four 247
- 10.1 Problem solving: some general considerations 250
- 10.2 The candle problem 251
- 10.3 Recognizing familiar problems 252
- 10.4 Similar problems 254
- 10.5 New problems: making past experience relevant 254
- 10.6 Producing a solution 255
- 10.7 Thinking out a solution: stopping and thinking 258
- 10.8 Summary and conclusions concerning the candle problem 259
- 10.9 Chess playing as problem solving 260
- 10.10 Perception and memory in chess 262
- 10.11 Rayner's analysis of pegity (Gomoku) 264
- 10.12 Selz's Theory of Productive Thinking 265
- 10.13 Problem solving without problem-specific past experience and without planning: recent research on simple move problems 266
- 10.14 Summary 272

Chapter 11. Task-specific knowledge and more general knowledge: a consideration of hypothesis-testing models of problem solving

- 11.0 Introduction 274
- 11.1 A model of classification based on hypotheses 276
- 11.2 Formulating hypotheses 278
- 11.3 Complicated solution rules 279
- 11.4 Retaining and relinquishing hypotheses 282
- 11.5 Summary and conclusions 286

Chapter 12. "Insight" and "fixation" in problem solving

- 12.0 Introduction 287
- 12.1 Trial-and-error 289
- 12.2 Insight as sudden illumination 293
- 12.3 Water-jar problems 294

12.4 The subject's interpretation of the experiment: math test scripts 296
12.5 Extinction of a set 298
12.6 Relevant data 299
12.7 Direct solutions by control subjects: what does the subject bring to the experiment? 301
12.8 Levine's research on unsolvable problems 303
12.9 Problem solving set: summary 305
12.10 Insight problems and fixation 305
12.11 The two-string problem 306
12.12 Hat rack problem 309
12.13 Scheerer's studies of fixation 310
12.14 Duncker's radiation problem 312
12.15 Functional fixation 314
12.16 Summary 316
12.17 Summary of part Four 317

Part Five   Cognitive development
Chapter 13.   Cognitive development I: Thinking in Infancy
13.0 Introduction to part Five 321
13.1 A brief outline of Piaget's theory 322
13.2 Sensorimotor development: the major phenomena 324
13.3 The object concept 328
13.4 Development of visual tracking 331
13.5 Objects and movements 332
13.6 Adult visual tracking and the object concept 333
13.7 Manual search and the object concept I: out of sight, out of mind 335
13.8 Manual search and the object concept II: perseverative search 340
13.9 Summary and conclusions 343

Chapter 14.   Cognitive development II: Thinking in childhood
14.0 Introduction 345
14.1 Schemas to operations 346
14.2 The child's understanding of relations 347

Contents

- 14.3 The child's thinking about reality 348
- 14.4 Mathematical and logical reasoning 351
- 14.5 The development of concrete operations: summary 353
- 14.6 Egocentrism and ignorance 354
- 14.7 The development of conservation 359
- 14.8 Changing the child's mind: learning about being the same while looking different 361
- 14.9 Some relevant data: conservation of number and conservation of quantity 363
- 14.10 Memory problems in concrete-operational tasks 365
- 14.11 Summary and conclusions: do young children think differently than adults do? 366

Chapter 15. Cognitive factors in language development
- 15.0 Introduction 368
- 15.1 The first words: semantic features 369
- 15.2 Nelson's analysis of first-word acquisition: functional concepts 374
- 15.3 Expressing semantic relations in two-word utterances 378
- 15.4 Communication and context 381
- 15.5 The development of communication skills 383
- 15.6 The creativity of language: creating new utterances as problem solving I: words 385
- 15.7 Creating new utterances II: sentences 389
- 15.8 Why are young children's sentences telegraphic? 390
- 15.9 Why does child speech become more complex? 394
- 15.10 Summary 396

Chapter 16. Internalization of overt responses: outline of a model of thinking
- 16.0 Introduction 398
- 16.1 Initiation and selectivity of reactions 402
- 16.2 Generalization of reflexes 404
- 16.3 The waning of responsiveness 407
- 16.4 Internalization, habituation, and thinking 409
- 16.5 Behavior in knowledgeable organisms 411
- 16.6 Thoughts as the cause of actions 414

16.7 Summary 417
16.8 Summary of part Five 417
16.9 Memory, thought, and behavior—summary and conclusions 419

References 422
Index 442

You can't always take the easy way out.
Sometimes you have to leave the easy way in.

>   Michael Weisberg

ONE
Memory

1
Outline of a model of memory

1.0 Introduction

This book will examine many different situations in which human thought occurs. It will consider recent research in memory, imagery, language comprehension and the development of the ability to speak, and problem solving. It will also consider some changes that occur in thinking as humans develop. There are two general themes which will serve to organize the various discussions in the chapters that follow. First, we shall examine these various situations as special cases of selective retrieval of information from memory. In order to understand what people do in situations involving thinking, it is necessary to know the information which people have available about that situation, and it is necessary to know how people can recall this information and use it as needed. That is why this book on thinking begins with a discussion of memory.

The second general organizing theme of the book involves a conception of the nature of the thinking process. Most people, both psychologists and nonpsychologists, hold a common conception of what the activity called thinking entails. According to this view, thinking is an internal activity, which involves operations on mental objects of some sort. These objects can be called ideas, thoughts, concepts, or images, but they function as the object of thought. This mental object is called a mental representation by psychologists.

Here is how two recent books in cognitive psychology describe thought:

What is the nature of human thinking and what is its content? A carpenter knows that his task is to shape wood. At a superficial level, at least, the qualities of the wood are simple to grasp. But what is the object with which the thinker deals and how does he alter its form? (Posner, 1973, p.1)

An enduring problem of great psychological significance is this: How does the external world come to be represented in one's mind? (Reynolds & Flagg, 1977, p.2)

These quotes make clear the main points of the typical view of thinking: It is an activity that involves actions on mental objects, and these mental objects stand for, or represent, or symbolize, objects in the real world. This view could be called the "symbolist" conception of thought (Price, 1953, chap. X), because it argues that thought is an activity carried out on symbols.

The second issue which will serve to organize the book is whether this common sense conception of thinking, this "symbolist" point of view, is helpful in developing a scientific understanding of human thought. We shall see at several points that there are strong reasons for questioning the notion that thinking entails constructing and manipulating mental representations of objects in the world. Given that this common sense notion can be questioned, we shall spend some time considering alternative conceptions of human thinking.

This is enough in the way of abstract introduction. We can now begin to examine the basic processes involved in memory, which will serve as the core around which the rest of the book will be organized. The discussion in this chapter will be organized as follows. We shall first spend some time considering one deceptively simple experimental situation used by psychologists who study memory. We shall find that two general principles are important in determining recall in this situation. These two principles will then be shown to have wider relevance to other experiments involving memory.

The purposes of this chapter are three: First, to introduce recent research in memory, which is the focus of part 1. Second, some of the phenomena to be introduced in this chapter will be relevant throughout the remainder of the book. Finally, the chapter will introduce the reader to the sort of analysis to be carried out throughout the book.

1.1 The short-term memory experiment: a microcosm

The experiment which will be the basis for discussion is by Peterson and Peterson (1959) on short-term memory for verbal materials. We shall con-

Outline of a model of memory

sider this experiment to be representative of situations in which memory is used, and we shall try to derive some general principles from an analysis of this situation.

The basic data. The procedure of the Peterson and Peterson study was this: The experimenter read a string of three consonants (a consonant-consonant-consonant string, or CCC), which the subject was to remember. Immediately after the CCC, the experimenter read a three-digit number, and the subject began to count backwards by threes from that number. After a specified retention interval, which lasted up to 18 seconds, the subject tried to recall the CCC. The counting backwards is referred to as a distractor task, because it distracts the subject from rehearsing. After attempting to recall the CCC, another CCC was presented, followed by additional counting backwards, and so on, for several trials.

Table 1.1. Summary of recall data from Peterson & Peterson (1959).

Retention interval (sec.)	3	6	9	12	15	18
Percent recall	.80	.60	.40	.25	.10	.08

The basic results of the study are summarized in Table 1.1. Recall decreased as the retention interval increased, and there was almost total forgetting of the CCC after 18 seconds of the distractor task. There are several likely causes of this forgetting. First, the 18-second interval itself might cause the forgetting. Alternatively, perhaps the distractor task interferes in some way with the CCC which the subject is trying to recall, in much the same way as typing one letter directly over another makes it impossible to read either of the letters.

Proactive interference. Keppel and Underwood (1962) demonstrated that neither of these explanations is correct. They measured recall performance for only the first trial of a short-term memory experiment. If either of the above explanations were correct, then recall should be poor after 18 seconds of the distractor task on the very first trial. However, they found that recall on the first trial was essentially perfect, even with 18 seconds of counting. This one result indicates that neither time alone, nor the distractor alone, nor the simple combination of the two of them, produces the forgetting found by the Petersons.

Keppel and Underwood hypothesized that the forgetting found by Peterson and Peterson came about because the CCCs from earlier trials were interfering with recall on later trials, since the Petersons's subjects were given many trials. This is proactive interference, because when the earlier CCCs interfere with the later ones, the interference works forward in time, or proactively. If earlier items do interfere with recall on a given trial, then recall should be very good if there are no other items to bring about interference. As already mentioned, Keppel and Underwood eliminated interfering items by looking at recall on the very first trial. Recall then was essentially perfect, even with 18 seconds of the distractor task. A second prediction from this point of view is that recall should get worse on the second trial, because there is now the CCC from the first trial to interfere with recall. On the third trial, recall should be still worse, because there are now two earlier items to produce interference. This was found to be the case by Keppel and Underwood, as was the fact that recall barely decreased over trials with a 3-second retention interval, in contrast to the

Table 1.2. Summary of trial-by-trial analysis of Keppel & Underwood (1962). (proportion correct)

Retention interval	Trial number					
	1	2	3	4	5	6
3 sec.	.91	.80	.80	.80	.88	.83
18 sec.	.92	.68	.57	.57	.45	.43

large amount of forgetting that occurred over a series of trials with an 18-second retention interval. The results of this study are summarized in Table 1.2. The short retention interval may somehow prevent the earlier items from interfering.

Thus short-term forgetting seems to be the result of proactive interference, as the subject is given a series of trials with very similar items within an experimental session. Further, this interference is related to the retention interval, in that it does not occur (or is greatly decreased) with very short retention intervals.

Further studies of proactive interference in short-term memory. The study by Keppel and Underwood stimulated much research. One important finding was that the similarity among the to-be-recalled items was of great importance in determining the amount of interference that occurred. If the same type of material (e.g., bird names) was given on several consecutive trials, then recall decreased greatly over trials. However, if the type of to-be-recalled material was changed (e.g., to foods), then there was little or no forgetting on the first trial with the new material. Proactive interference would then build up if more of this new material was presented for additional trials, and recall would decrease. A change to still another type of material would result in high recall again, and so on. Thus, changing the type of material produces a "release from proactive interference" (Wickens, 1970).

In addition to the similarity of the to-be-recalled items on a series of trials, temporal factors are also important in determining the amount of proactive interference which develops over a series of trials. First, as already mentioned, Keppel and Underwood found little or no build-up of proactive interference with a 3-second retention interval. Thus, if the to-be-recalled items were very recently presented, recall stays high. Secondly, Loess and Waugh (1967) found that if 120 seconds elapsed between consecutive trials, recall stayed high. That is, there was no proactive interference found from earlier items, even though the items were all consonant-vowel-consonant strings (CVCs). In the usual study, the time between trials is only a matter of a few seconds, in contrast to the 120 seconds used by Loess and Waugh.

A question which immediately arises from this is whether it is the 120 seconds alone that reduces the proactive interference, and several recent studies have shown that this is not so (Goggin & Riley, 1974; Wickens & Gittis, 1974). For example, in the Goggin and Riley study, some subjects sat quietly between trials with bird names as the to-be-recalled items, while other subjects were given other experimental trials with other types of materials. In both cases, the same amount of time intervened between the trials with the bird names. The subjects who simply sat between trials showed little or no proactive interference from the earlier similar items, while the subjects who continuously worked on memory trials did show proactive interference. It seems that the subjects who simply sat between trials could easily differentiate the earlier bird names from the most recent ones, because each trial was isolated from the others due to the rest intervals between them. However, the subjects who were continuously working had the trials with bird names intermingled among a lot of other trials. Thus, the most recent trial with bird names became much more difficult to differentiate, and proactive interference occurred.

Summary. The data with which we shall begin our examination of memory can now be outlined as follows:

1. On the first trial of a short-term memory experiment, recall is essentially perfect, even with a relatively long retention interval filled with a distractor task. (This perfect recall on the first trial does not occur if

there are five or six to-be-recalled items. In the present discussion we shall concentrate on the situation in which perfect or near-perfect recall does occur on the first trial. It should be noted, however, that even with five or six items, recall gets worse over trails, indicating that proactive interference still plays a role.)
2. If additional trials with the same type of to-be-recalled materials are presented, recall quickly decreases to a low level. This is proactive interference.
3. Proactive interference will not be found, however, if the recall interval is very short.
4. Proactive interference will also not be found if the intertrial interval is long and empty.
5. Proactive interference will not be found if a new class of material is presented. However, if this class of material is now repeated, proactive interference will occur within this new class.

1.2 The processes underlying short-term recall: three possible models

Let us now consider three simplified models of what might be happening as a subject goes through several trials of a short-term memory experiment. We shall begin by centering on the distractor. There are two general assumptions that one could make concerning what the subject is doing while counting backwards: (a) the subject could also be thinking about, or rehearsing, the items which were presented, even though we have asked that this not be done; or (b) the subject could be concentrating solely on the distractor task, as instructed. Each of these assumptions produces several unambiguous predictions, which can be tested by reexamining the results which have already been considered.

Rehearsing items during the retention interval. According to this idea, correct recall occurs because the subject has been able to do two things at once during the retention interval: count backwards and rehearse the items. There is evidence that subjects do carry out some rehearsal during the retention interval (e.g., Crowder, 1968), but this model will not account for the data which we have already considered. If recall came about only because the item was being rehearsed, we could not explain the fact that recall gets consistently worse when several trials with the same material are presented.

Concentration on the distractor alone. Let us now consider the possibility that the subject does not rehearse anything at all during the retention interval, but instead concentrates solely on the distractor. Assume that a subject is working through a series of trials, all with the same sort of materials, say CCCs. On any trial in this series, when we ask for recall, we are asking for the most recent CCC. If a subject has concentrated solely on the distractor, then at recall this subject will have no other basis for recall of the correct items than the fact that they were most recent. Thus, the question of interest becomes: if the subject is simply using recency as the basis for recall, will performance look like the data in the summary above?

The answer to this question seems to be no: if recall were based on relative recency, we could not account for the finding that proactive interference can be eliminated by simply changing the type of items which are presented. Consider first a control group, which is given four trials with letters, and then a fifth trial, again with letters. Recall gets worse because more and more letters are available, and the subject can't tell which are most recent. Now consider the experimental group. They get four trials with letters, and a fifth trial with a number-number-number string (NNN). Since the control group can't tell which letters were most recent, the experimental group should not be able to recall that the numbers were most recent either, since all the other aspects of the experiment are the same for the two groups. However, as we have seen, a large increase in recall is produced in the experimental group by a category switch. Since the experimental group can't be using recency to tell that the numbers were the most recent items, they must be using something else. Therefore, the notion that the subject concentrates totally on the distractor task during the retention interval, and uses only relative recency of items as the basis for recall, is not completely correct.

Summary cues and recall. If it is assumed that the subject must use some other information about the items, in addition to their recency, to cue recall, then all the results concerning proactive interference can be accommodated. Let us call this additional information a summary cue.

The elaborated model is then as follows. When the items are presented, the subject attends to them and at the same time notes some relevant information about them, such as the fact that they are letters or numbers (Wickens, 1970). At recall, the subject tries to "find" the most recent members of that summarized category, and these are produced as responses (Atkinson & Shiffrin, 1968). According to this model, recall is good on trial one because the only items from the summarized category are those from trial one, so the subject can't go wrong. On the second trial, if the same class of items is presented, and if the retention interval is long, recall should decrease, because the subject cannot tell which items were most recent, and the summary cue alone doesn't give enough information for the subject to differentiate the item from trial one from that from trial 2. With a short retention interval, however, recency alone can serve to produce the correct items. When the category is changed, perhaps to NNN, a new summary cue is produced by the subject, and recall should then increase, because there is only one NNN to be recalled. However, when a second NNN is presented, there should now be interference within that category as well. Thus, if we assume that subjects use two cues, recency and type of item, to direct their recall, we can deal with the data discussed earlier. A similar point of view has recently been put forward by Loftus and Patterson (1975), and Watkins and Watkins (1975).

In summary, we come to the conclusion that in order to remember some specific item of information out of a number of similar items, some additional information must be used as a cue for the recall of the specific item. This information could be based on temporal factors alone, such as relative recency, but is more often based on the meaning of the item in question along with its recency. If a cue is relevant to more than one item, the subjects will have difficulty in recalling because they won't be able to decide on the correct item. These two types of information, recency information and summary information, are usually referred to as retrieval cues, because they aid in retrieving information from memory. These two sorts of information have been discussed separately here, and it will be argued in chapter 4 that recall based on recency depends on a different type of information than recall based on a summary cue. The term "summary cue" is not as accurate as it could be, perhaps, because many different sorts of information can serve as a cue for the recall of a word. For example, one word can sometimes serve to cue another, even though one doesn't serve to "summarize" the other (e.g., *bread* can sometimes be an effective cue for *butter*). Also, a visual image can serve to cue recall of a word. Therefore, the reader should keep in mind that the term *summary cue* refers to many sorts of information.

There is a very important point to be made concerning these summary cues—they arise from the interaction of the person's knowledge with the to-be-recalled words. That is, the person realizes that the list contains flowers, say, because he or she knows that rose, tulip, and lily are flowers. Thus, one "thinks of" a cue because the to-be-recalled material matches some bit of our knowledge. A person's knowledge plays an important role in memory, perception, attention, creation of images, comprehension of language, and problem solving, and this use of knowledge will be discussed many times in the chapters that follow.

Storage versus retrieval effects in interference. The model discussed so far bases all forgetting on confusion among potential responses. This idea is given support from a study by Gardiner, Craik, and Birtwhistle (1972). Subjects were given groups of wild-flower names as the to-be-recalled items for three trials in a short-term memory experiment. On trial 1, all subjects also saw the word "flowers" as a summary cue just before the trial. On trials 2 and 3, wild-flower names were presented, and no summary cues were presented. On the fourth trial, all the subjects were presented with the names of three *garden* flowers, and the subjects were divided into three groups, depending on how these words were presented. The control group saw only the names of the garden flowers. A second group was shown the summary cue *garden flowers* just before the names were presented. A third group saw only the flower names at the beginning of the trial, but when they were told to recall, they were also shown the summary cue *garden flowers*. The group which received the *garden flower* summary cue at presentation showed a significant increase in recall on trial 4, relative to the control group which was told nothing. However, the garden flowers cue was also effective when it was given only at recall, which indicates that all the groups probably stored the same information at presentation. The correct items were adequately represented, but the control subjects just didn't know which items they were. The garden-flowers cue was specific enough to give the other groups this information, and so facilitated recall. Thus, proactive interference seems to come about because there are too many potentially correct items around, not because the correct item is not there. Several other recent studies have also demonstrated that proactive interference in a short-term memory situation does not come about because later items are more poorly stored in memory (Loftus & Patterson, 1975; Watkins & Watkins, 1975).

1.3 Summary of preliminary model

When we attend to some material and are specifically trying to remember it for later recall, several things seem to occur. First of all, information concerning the item itself is stored in memory, along with some additional information which enables the subject to determine that the item occurred recently in a memory experiment. Second, if there are many items which have occurred at about the same time, and the subject wishes to recall only a subset of them, then some additional information, which we have called the *summary* of the item, must be available. At recall, the summary cue and recency information are used to retrieve the correct items from memory. Under certain circumstances, the recency cue alone may not be effective, because the correct item is no longer "recent enough." By the same token, the summary cue may not be helpful under certain circumstances, because it may not be specific enough to help the subject choose among possible items. If the cue which the subject is using results in several possible items for recall, then the subject may draw a blank.

1.4 Recall on the basis of recency

There is much evidence from other sorts of situations that the recency of an item can be a powerful retrieval cue in and of itself. Furthermore, the "loss of recency" by an item results in the item being nonrecallable if no other cues have been developed.

The serial position curve of free recall. One of the most thoroughly investigated phenomena in recent memory research has been the serial position curve for single-trial free recall. In single-trial free recall, subjects are given a list of words, one at a time, and are asked to recall the words in any order. After the first list is recalled, a second list of new words is presented once, and so on. The serial position curve summarizes the recall for each word as a function of its position in the series—its position in its own list. For instance, in Figure 1.1, the curve summarizes recall for a group of subjects for a set of several different lists, with each list presented only once. So, from Figure 1.1 we can see that the last few words in each list were recalled very well, on the average. In this way, the curve represents the average performance of a group of subjects on a group of lists.

The typical serial position curve for single-trial free recall has three important characteristics, as shown in Figure 1.1. First of all, the best recall is of the last few words in each list (the recency effect). Second, the words at the beginning of each list are also recalled well, although not as well as the words at the end of the list (the primacy effect). Finally, if one excludes the primacy and recency portions of the list, the probability of recalling any of the remaining words is about equal for all of them, producing the flat portion of the curve.

Interfering with recency. If it is true that the most recent words in a free-recall list can be recalled simply because they are most recent, then it ought to be possible to interfere with recall of these words by "displacing them

Outline of a model of memory

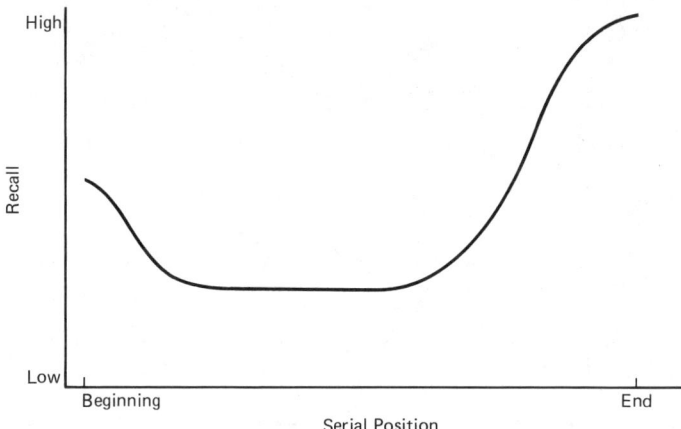

Figure 1.1. Typical serial position curve. Recall of each of a list words as a function of its position in the series (position in the list).

into the past." Two studies have demonstrated that presentation of a distractor task after the last word in a free-recall list, but before recall is attempted, has a disruptive effect on the recency portion of the serial position curve (Glanzer & Cunitz, 1966; Postman & Phillips, 1965). These results indicate that words at the end of the list are recallable only if the subject can keep rehearsing them, which keeps them "recent."

Negative recency. If a subject is given a series of free-recall lists and is asked to recall each list once, the results summarized over all the lists produce a standard serial position curve. If it is true that the recall of the last items in each list is due to their recency, then consider what would happen if we unexpectedly ask the subject at the end of the experiment to recall the words from all the lists once again. Since the recent words in each list are no longer recent, then the subject shouldn't be able to recall them on the surprise test. The results of an experiment of this sort by Craik (1970) are presented in Figure 1.2. The summary curve for the initial free recall on each list looks like the standard free-recall curve, but the summary curve for the final, surprise, free recall looks very different: the final words are now hardly recalled at all. The steady decrease over the last four or five serial positions has been called the *negative recency* effect. Thus, presentation of additional lists disrupts the recency of the last items in each list, so there is no basis for recalling them on the surprise test. Similar results using different materials and procedures have been reported by Madigan and McCabe (1971) and Jacoby (1973).

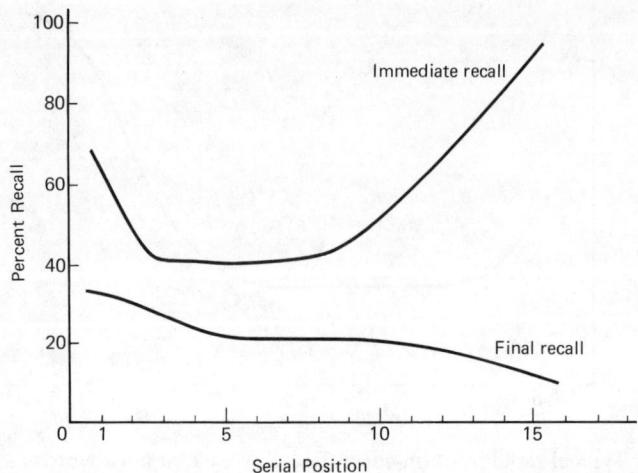

Figure 1.2. Comparison of immediate and delayed tree recall. (From Craik, 1970.)

Summary. These various studies have indicated that recent items are particularly easy to recall. However, if the subject must deal with other material, recall of these recent items decreases greatly. At its most extreme, recall can be perfect immediately after presentation and zero after other material has been presented. It seems that if an item can be effortlessly recalled because it was just presented, the item won't be recallable at all at a later time.

1.5 Summary cues

Let us now consider in more detail some of the predictions which the model makes about the use of summary cues. The points to be discussed in these sections are a synthesis and extension of the work of a number of investigators, the most prominent of whom are Mandler (e.g., 1967, 1968) and Tulving (e.g., 1968).

Cued recall: efficiency of cuing. The basic function of summary cues is to permit the recaller to differentiate among all the items which have been presented, and which cannot be differentiated on the basis of recency. Based on this, one would predict that the most efficient recall would occur if there was only one item that was related to each cue. Earhard (1967) presented lists of 24 words to subjects in a cued-recall experiment. The subjects were told to use the first letter of the word as a cue, and at recall the letters were presented to help the subjects recall the words. The number of words having the same first letter was varied. In one condition, all 24 words began with a different letter. In intermediate conditions, two, three, four, six, or eight words began with the same letter. Earhard found that recall was best when each cue was related to only one word, and that recall decreased systematically as the number of words per cue increased. A study by Tulving and Pearlstone (1966) had similar results. Based on these studies, if cues are presented at recall, they are most helpful when each cue is related to a very small number of words.

Non-cued recall: number of items versus number of cues. In the experiments just discussed, the cues were presented to the subject at recall. However if the cues aren't presented at recall, and if recall depends on the cues, then the subject must first recall the cues in order to recall the words. Let's say a subject was given a long list of words to recall, and the words are taken from 25 categories. We know from the last section that if there were 25 *words* to recall, the subject would need cues in order to recall them. Therefore, with 25 *cues* (category names) which must be recalled, the subject must run into exactly the same problem. There must be some other cues available to help in the recall of the 25 category cues.

Let us call the cues used to retrieve words first-order cues. If the number of first-order cues is larger than some small number that can be differentiated without cues (perhaps two or three), then second-order cues must be developed in order to make the recall of the first-order cues possible. In the same way, if there are too many second-order cues, then third-order cues must be developed, and so on (Mandler, 1968).

Therefore, all other things being equal, if a group of items naturally forms a hierarchical arrangement, then recall of these items should be very good. Bower, Clark, Lesgold, and Winzenz (1969) presented subjects with four sets of 28 words, with the words in each set forming a natural hierarchy. An example of one of these sets is presented in Figure 1.3. A control group received the same 28 words, but the words were randomly placed in the slots in the hierarchy, so that no organization was obvious. A total of four hierarchies was presented to each subject, with about a minute given to study each hierarchy. Each subject therefore saw a total of 112 words (28×4). The experimental group recalled all 112 words just about perfectly after *only two presentations,* while the control group was recalling only about one-third of the words after two presentations. Thus the hierarchical structure greatly facilitated recall.

Clustering in recall. When a subject recalls a cue, the cue then makes

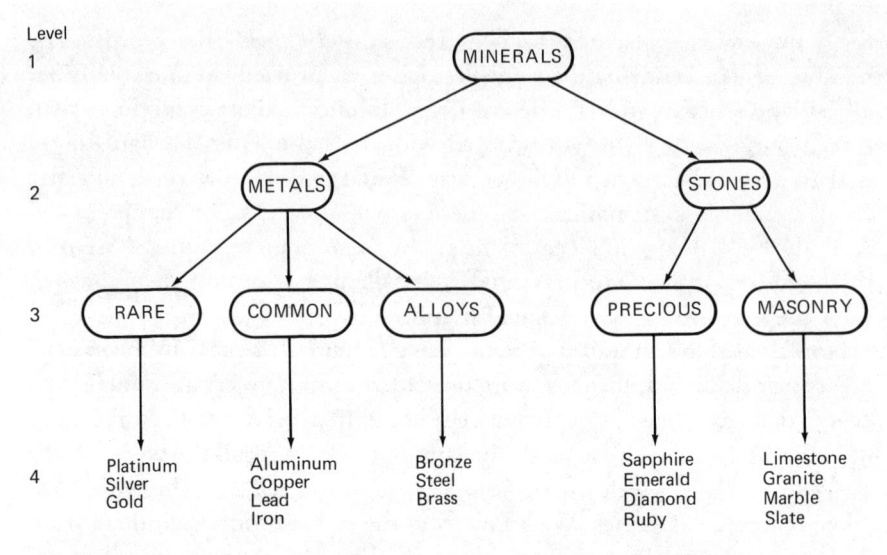

```
Level
 1                          MINERALS

 2              METALS                    STONES

 3       RARE   COMMON   ALLOYS    PRECIOUS   MASONRY

 4    Platinum  Aluminum  Bronze   Sapphire   Limestone
      Silver    Copper    Steel    Emerald    Granite
      Gold      Lead      Brass    Diamond    Marble
                Iron               Ruby       Slate
```

Figure 1.3. Hierarchically structured list. (From Bower et al., 1969.)

available a small number of specific items from the list. Therefore, recall should be organized so that all the members of a given group are recalled or "clustered" together. Many studies have reported that clustering by category occurs in the recall of categorized lists, one of the earliest and most influential being that of Bousfield (1953).

In summary, studies using categorized lists provide support for the summary cues assumptions of the model. First, presenting category names as recall cues facilitates recall. Second, there is a limit on how many cues a subject can use without further elaboration. Third, presenting material in an already organized manner greatly facilitates recall. Finally, recall is organized on the basis of the organization in the material.

1.6 Subjective organization of "random" lists

The discussion in the last section concerned a specific sort of material: categorized lists. There remains a question of generality. The model which we have been considering makes a simple prediction as far as *any* recall situation is concerned: if there are items to be recalled, and recency cannot be used as a cue, then some additional cues must be used. This prediction was supported by Tulving (1962), who demonstrated in a multitrial free-recall task that random lists of words are organized by subjects as the words are recalled over several trials. Multitrial free recall differs from single-trial free recall in that the same list of words is presented for several trials, so that the people get several tries at recalling the same list, and so recall improves over trials. The presentation order of the words varies randomly from trial to trial, and the subjects can recall the words in any order that they like. Using such a task, Tulving found that groups of words consistently appeared together in a given subject's recall, even though the presentation order of the words was changed from trial to trial. This was taken as evidence for organization of the material by the subject-subjective organization.

Since Tulving's initial demonstration, much research has been concerned with the relationship between subjective organization and recall. First, it has been demonstrated that organization is causally related to recall. For example, Bower, Lesgold, and Tieman (1969) showed that disrupting the subject's organization of a list of words retards recall, even though the words are presented several times for study. A list of 24 randomly selected words was arbitrarily divided into six quartets of words. Each quartet was presented separately, and the subjects were instructed to form an image containing the items represented by the four words. For one group of subjects, the same quartets were presented for three recall trials, while for a second group of subjects, the quartets were changed from trial to trial. The same 24 words were presented, but the way they were grouped was changed. Recall with varying quartets hardly improved at all over three trials. Therefore, simply studying the same words for three trials did not produce an improvement in recall, if the grouping of the words wasn't the same. The subjects with the same groupings over trials recalled very well. This supports the assumption that grouping or organization is necessary for recall.

Other research has demonstrated a parallel between subjective organization and the categorical organization discussed in the last section. Mandler (1967) has found that recall is related to the number of subjective groups used by a subject. If the subject uses too few groups, then there are too many words per group, and recall is hindered. Furthermore, if subjects are asked to give names for their subjective groups, these names can then be given to the subjects later as retrieval cues (Dong & Kintsch, 1968). This results in increased recall, comparable to that found by Tulving and Pearlstone (1966) with categorized lists.

To summarize, there is support for the assumption that organization must occur whenever large amounts of material are to be recalled. If such organization is not built in by the experimenter, it will be manufactured by the subject. Once again, this organization comes about because of the match between the person's knowledge and the to-be-recalled material. We cannot understand how recall comes about without taking into account the knowledge of the person doing the recalling.

1.7 Organization and the use of knowledge in recall

Much of the evidence discussed so far supports the notion that recall of large amounts of information depends on the person's ability to organize the information into smaller groups, so that the number of groups is kept within manageable limits. As mentioned several times already, this organization depends on the interaction of the to-be-recalled material and the person's knowledge. More specifically, the degree of organization in the material depends upon the match between that material and the knowledge of the person studying that material. As we have already seen in section 1.5, if the to-be-recalled material matches the person's knowledge closly, then recall is very good indeed.

It would be valuable at this time to discuss in more detail how one's knowledge is used in recall, because similar phenomena will be seen many times in later chapters.

A number of theorists have proposed similar models of how knowledge is used in recalling an organized list of words (e.g., Bower, 1970; Mandler, 1968; Tulving, 1968), and this brief discussion summarizes this point of view. Let us take the simplest situation and assume that someone is presented with a list made up of four categories, with five words in each category. Also, the members of each category are presented one after the other. When the first word is presented, the person presumably does little more than rehearse it, in whatever way he or she wishes. When the second word is presented, however, the subject will note that the first two words are members of the same category, say, *animals*. When the next three words come along, they will also be recognized as animals, so in addition to any rehearsal of the words, the person has also rehearsed *animals* several times, and the person has probably also noted something like "This list is made up of words from the same category."

When the sixth word appears, it is not the name of an animal; let us say that it is *rose*. The person now studies that word, but also notes that it is a flower, and probably now also expects other flowers to appear. Given the

Outline of a model of memory

way that the list is structured, this expectation will be confirmed. The same thing will happen when the last two categories are presented: the person will study the words, note the category name, and also note further that the list is highly structured.

At recall, the person now has several different sorts of information available. First, each of the individual words has been studied and rehearsed. However, there are too many words in total for them all to be recalled on the basis of their recency. In addition, the person knows that the list was made up of categories, and it is highly likely that this information will be available at recall, because the person may have kept it in mind throughout the list. This information would serve to retrieve the category names, since there is only a small number of them. The small number of category names, plus their relative recency because the person has just thought of them repeatedly, plus the fact that the person remembers that the list was made up of categories, combine to make it highly likely that the category names will be recalled.

When each category name is recalled, we now have a new set of cues available, the words which typically belong in that category. That is, the members of the category can now serve to "cue themselves." Since some of the members have been seen very recently, because they were in the just-presented list, it should be possible to recall them.

In summary, we have here a plausible outline of how one's knowledge is used at input and output in order to recall an organized list of words. We shall examine this phenomenon in more detail in later chapters, especially chapter 3.

1.8 Generality of proactive interference effects

Let us now consider a more general aspect of the model, the notion that proactive interference is the crucial factor in forgetting.

General importance of proactive interference in forgetting. In the history of the psychological study of memory, one of the most influential theoretical papers was one by McGeoch (1932), concerning the role of time in bringing about forgetting. When McGeoch wrote, one principle theoretical notion was the law of disuse, which said that unused material will simply be forgotten with the natural passage of time. McGeoch argue that *events*, rather than time alone, should be considered the cause of forgetting. McGeoch specifically proposed that forgetting was brought about by events which occurred after a given item had been learned. That is, new learning works retroactively to interfere with old learning. Thus, McGeoch placed emphasis on retroactive interference as the primary source of forgetting. Proactive interference was essentially not considered.

This point of view was questioned by Underwood (1957) as the result of an interesting analysis of many studies of recall. Underwood examined the results of several studies which tested the recall of a list of CVCs after 24 hours. The studies found that, on the average, 75 percent of the CVCs had been forgotten when the subject came back the next day to be tested. Underwood found it very hard to believe that the subjects could have learned material similar enough to the CVCs in the 24 hours to provide the retroactive interference necessary to bring about all this forgetting.

Underwood therefore hypothesized that those studies which found 75 percent forgetting of a single list of CVCs after 24 hours must have been testing subjects who received many lists in the same experimental session. Based on this hunch, Underwood examined many studies which tested the recall of a single list of items after the subjects had learned varying numbers of other lists before that critical last list. The results, when summarized across many studies, were clear. If subjects learned 20 lists, then after 24 hours they could recall about 15 percent of the last of these lists. In contrast, subjects who had only learned one list could recall 75 percent of it the next day. Thus, with no earlier lists to interfere with the to-be-recalled list, forgetting is greatly reduced. Proactive interference seems to be the main cause of forgetting in the studies reviewed by Underwood.

Temporal factors in proactive interference. The second conclusion of potential generality based on the analysis of short-term memory was that the separation in time of the to-be-recalled items and the interfering items seemed to play an important role in the amount of proactive interference that was found. This conclusion is also supported by studies using paired associates. In the typical experiment, subjects learn two lists of word pairs, one after the other. The first list of pairs can be represented as A-B, the second list A-D, and the design is an A-B, A-D design. The two items in a paired associate are called the stimulus and the response, because it was originally felt that an S-R association was being learned in such a situation. This no longer seems to be true, but the paradigm is still extensively used to investigate memory. In the A-B, A-D design, the same stimulus items are present in the two lists (the A terms), but the responses change from the first list (B items) to the second (D items). As an example, if table-finger was an A-B pair, then table-moon might be an A-D pair. The A-B

Outline of a model of memory

list would first be presented until all the pairs can be recalled, and the A-D list would then be presented until those pairs can be recalled. One can then test recall of the A-B pairs or the A-D pairs.

In the A-B, A-D design, if one tests for recall of A-D, one finds more forgetting than for a control group which also learns A-D, but does not learn A-B first. This is proactive interference: the A-B list interferes proactively with recall of the A-D list, which was learned later.

For the present discussion, the interesting question concerns the separation in time between the A-B and A-D tasks. In a study by Underwood and Freund (1968), one group of subjects learned A-B and A-D on the same day, while a second group learned A-D three days after they had learned A-B. Underwood and Freund found that approximately twice as much interference occurred when the two lists had been learned on the same day.

It was also found in short-term memory studies that proactive interference increased as the to-be-recalled items became less and less recent. That is, proactive interference increased with an increasing retention interval. A study by Underwood (1948) reported a similar finding with paired associates. An A-B, A-D design was used, and recall of A-D was tested either 5 hours or 48 hours after it was learned. Recall of A-D was worse after 48 hours than after 5 hours, which supports the assumption that proactive interference increases with the passage of time. A study by Postman (1962) also found that proactive interference increased with an increase in the retention interval.

1.9 Retroactive interference

So far, we have considered how previously-learned material can interfere with the recall of newer material. This comes about because the new material becomes less discriminable on the basis of recency. However, if it is true that the older information can interfere proactively with the recall of the newer information, then it also ought to be true that the newer information can interfere retroactively with the recall of the older information.

Retroactive interference in short-term memory. Retroactive interference in short-term memory, like proactive interference, is a function of the similarity of the items involved. Wickelgren (1965) examined the role of retroactive interference in forgetting in a short-term memory experiment using recall of letters as the task. The subject heard a set of four to-be-recalled consonants, followed by eight interference letters, which were not to be recalled. In order to examine the possibility of interference, Wickelgren varied the phonetic similarity of the to-be-recalled letters and the interfering letters. The results indicated that recall decreased as the number of similar-sounding interference items increased.

Recall that in the original Peterson and Peterson short-term memory experiment, retroactive interference by the distractor was ruled out as a source of forgetting. The present emphasis on retroactive interference seems to contradict that conclusion. However, in the Peterson and Peterson (1959) task, the to-be-recalled items were CCCs, and the distractor task was counting backward. Since the distractor material is so different from the to-be-recalled material, little or no interference occurs. Given this explanation, though, if the Peterson task had used *numbers* as the to-be-recalled items, then the counting backwards task should produce retroactive interference. A study by Pollack (1963) reported that with numbers to be recalled, and a numerical distractor task, more distractor items produced greater forgetting. In sum, the similarity of the distractor task influences forgetting in a short-term memory experiment.

Generality of retroactive interference. The studies which have demonstrated retroactive interference in other memory taks are legion. As one example, let us consider a study which examined the role of similarity in producing retroactive interference using paired associates. If one tests for A-B recall after both lists are learned, then one is testing for retroactive interference from A-D. Friedman and Reynolds (1965) had five groups of subjects learn the same eight-pair A-B list, which had CVCs as responses. Four of the five groups then were given 20 trials of A-D learning. One group had other CVCs as the second-list responses, a second group had CCCs, a third group had CVs, and the last group had NNNs. A control group filled out a personality inventory for the same amount of time as was needed to present the 20 A-D trials. All five groups were then asked to recall the eight first-list pairs. The recall scores were Control–7.7; NNN–6.7; CVs–5.1; CCCs–5.0; CVCs–3.4 This is evidence for the importance of similarity in the development of retroactive interference in paired associates. Similar results have been presented by Shuell (1968) using a free-recall design.

To summarize, retroactive interference is also an important factor in forgetting, and has been demonstrated to produce forgetting in many different studies. As was the case with proactive interference, the similarity of the to-be-recalled and interfering items is important.

1.10 Summary

This chapter began with a consideration of one experiment, and used it as the basis for a sketch of a model of recall and forgetting. An analysis of the short-term memory experiment by Peterson and Peterson (1959) indicated that proactive interference was the main source of forgetting (Keppel & Underwood, 1962). Two factors are important in determining whether or not such interference will occur, and whether or not the required information will be recalled. The first factor is the discriminability of the to-be-recalled information in time. Very recent information can be recalled effortlessly, even though it has not been studied in great detail, and even though there are many potentially interfering items available. In the case of very recent information, to perceive is to be able to recall, so long as recall is asked for very soon after perception.

The second factor which influences recall is the availability of additional information, called summary cues, which can serve to differentiate the to-be-recalled material from other material which might interfere with its recall. In order to recall some specific item, one must have available enough information to pick that item out from all the other information in memory.

These two factors were shown to have general relevance in a variety of situations in which memory has been studied. For example, recency has been found to be an important determinant of recall in experiments using both free recall and paired-associate procedures. Much research has also made clear the relevance of summary cues and organization of material for the recall of both organized and unorganized lists of words. The general relevance of interference notions to other situations was also pointed out.

2
Storing information in memory: encoding and thinking

2.0 Introduction

We have now spent some time considering the factors that influence a person's ability to recall an item. As yet, however, little or nothing has been said about the items themselves. What happens during a memory experiment to enable a person to report that such and such a word was presented? In essence, when one is asking this sort of question, one is asking about the "medium" of thought, or the "stuff" in which thinking is carried out. This issue has been of interest to philosophers and psychologists for many years, and is currently at the forefront of cognitive psychology. Recent research on memory can shed some light on this issue, as will be seen later in this chapter. The question of the medium of thought will also be discussed in part 3 of the book.

This chapter explores two hypotheses: the dual process hypothesis of recognition and recall, and the "encoding" hypothesis. The first assumes that there are simple representations for words in memory, and that these representations serve as the basis for our ability to recognize and recall words on memory tests. Some evidence to support this view, based on differences between recognition and recall, will be discussed. However, other evidence, especially evidence concerning "recognition failure," indicates that words don't have simple representations in memory. The second hypothesis, then, assumes that an "encoding" is the basis for recall. Based on this point of view, recall of a word does not depend on some specific internal representation of the word. Rather, the ability to recall a word depends on the activities which are carried out when the word is presented.

2.1 The dual-process hypothesis

When one considers the factors involved in recalling a word, there is one important point which must be made clear. When a human is presented with a list of words to try to recall, the person obviously does not have to learn the words. All the relevant words are known before the subject enters the laboratory (Tulving, 1968). Therefore, when one hears "subjects were given a list of common English words to learn," the description is not quite adequate. The words were already learned. Rather, new information is added to the subject's knowledge about some of the words already in memory. The new information is that just those words were presented in the experiment.

Some theorists have tried to explain how this information is added by starting with the assumption that words are more or less separate objects in our memories. In order for a subject to know which words were presented in an experiment, the appropriate words must be marked in some way. This notion of marking an item in human memory is derived from computer memories, in which it is possible to mark an item by adding more information to the item's location in the computer's memory. This section and the next present evidence to support this view, the following two present contrary evidence.

Words as nodes in memory. As an example of this sort of theorizing, Kintsch (1970) assumes that each word we know is represented in memory by a "bundle" of information that has been acquired through past experience. This information includes what the word sounds like (phonetic features), what it looks like (graphic features), what it means (semantic features), and perhaps associated images (image features) among other things. The interconnection among the sets of features means that the sight or sound of a word can make one think of the meaning of the word, and the object to which the word refers can make one think of the sound of the word, and so on. Activation of information by the sound pattern is what is usually meant when it is said that someone recognizes a word. Let us call this bundle of interconnected features in memory the *memory node*, or simply the *node*, which represents the word. Thus, this view argues that words are represented as more or less static items in memory.

According to Kintsch's model, the first step in a memory experiment is the activation of the node which corresponds to the first word on the list. This activation comes about because the appropriate set of features is heard or seen by the subject.

Marking nodes. Given that the representation of a word has been activated, the next step entails adding information to the memory node (Kintsch, 1970; Anderson & Bower, 1972). Anderson and Bower assume that information corresponding to the experimental context is added to the node. In addition to everything else about a word, the subject then would know that the word was presented in such-and-such a context. In the present case, the context is that of a psychology experiment. This information is added as follows: when the node corresponding to a word is activated, there is a whole set of other nodes also active, corresponding to the physical and psychological context that the word is presented in. For example, the subject is attending to the furniture in the room, noises from outside, and so on. Anderson and Bower assume that part of all this information is added to the memory node of the word as a context marker. When the subject is asked to recall the words which were just presented, the subject first examines the present context, both psychological and physical. The subject then searches memory for nodes which have contextual markers associated to them which correspond to the present context. These words will be produced by the subject.

Dual-process model. These ideas concerning markers can be combined with a retrieval model to produce a model of recognition and recall (Bower, 1970; Kintsch, 1970). First, some cue or cues must be used to retrieve items from memory. Second, each item which has been retrieved is tested to determine if it is marked appropriately. If so, then the item is produced by the subject as a response. This has been called a dual process model of recall because it assumes that two processes are involved in the act of recall: retrieval of "candidate" items, and testing the candidates for appropriate markers. This sort of a model is also sometimes called a *generate and test* model, because one could say that the two processes are (a) generating candidate items, and then (b) testing each of the candidates for the appropriate marking.

A dual-process model of recall also implies that recognition of an item involves only one of these two processes. When a word is presented on a recognition test, its node is automatically activated. If the node is marked appropriately, then the word was presented in the experiment. Thus, according to this model, the retrieval problem is bypassed with recognition, because the test itself retrieves the item from memory. Therefore, one way to test the notion that memories for words are marked nodes is to see if recognition does indeed bypass retrieval.

2.2 Recognition-recall differences

A number of important differences have been found between recognition and recall, and the differences seem to be consistent with the dual-process model. Many variables which have large effects on recall have little or no effect on recognition, which is almost always easier than recall. This would be expected if marking a word in memory occurred relatively automatically when the word was presented, and if a recognition test bypassed retrieval problems.

Rehearsal strategies. Several experiments have shown that having a subject simply repeat words a number of times does not guarantee long-term recall of the words (e.g., Bower, 1970; Jacoby, 1973). However, in both these studies, as well as others, recognition of these same items is very high, even though they cannot be recalled. Thus, if recognition implies earlier storage, then relatively complete storage may occur simply because the subject looked at the word, as predicted by marker models.

Directed forgetting. One interesting recent experimental innovation in the study of memory has been a design in which subjects are told to forget (Bjork, 1970). For example, in one study (Block, 1971), two six-word lists were presented, one after the other. After the first list, the subject was told whether or not it was to be recalled. When the subject was instructed to recall both lists, then recall of the second list was worse than that of control subjects who saw only the second list. However, when the first list was not to be recalled, performance on the second list was as good as when there was only one list presented, indicating a strong influence of the forgetting signal.

It is also possible to assess the subject's ability to recall the material that was to be forgotten. Assume that we present five CVC-word pairs to a subject. We can test any item for recall by presenting the CVC and asking the subject to give us the word that was paired with it. We now signal the subject that the first two pairs will not be tested, so they can be forgotten. We give the subject many trials, and whenever a forget signal is presented, we never test the items. The subject now believes that the forget cue is indeed that, since recall has never been tested when the forget cue was present. We can now test recall for one of the pairs that the subject was instructed to forget, without saying anything to the subject. Under these conditions, recall is almost zero, indicating that subjects don't do the work necessary to produce later recall when they believe that they won't have to recall the items.

However, in a number of cases it has been shown that *recognition* of the to-be-forgotten items is as good as of the to-be-recalled items (Block, 1971; Elmes, Adams and Roediger, 1970; Gross, Baresi, and Smith, 1970), even though *recall* of the to-be-forgotten items is very poor. This could be looked at as the activation of an item in memory without the further processing which produces the information needed for later recall.

Summary and conclusions. There seem to be some important differences between recognition and recall. A subject may not be able to recall much at all, but recognition may be very good. This supports the dual-process model, because if presentation of a word results in its node being marked in memory, then recognition ought to be reasonably good under almost any circumstances. However, before accepting the idea that memory for a word depends upon a marked node, consider further how good recognition memory really is.

2.3 How good is recognition memory?

A number of recent studies of recognition seem to indicate that the information needed for perfect recognition is acquired effortlessly, as argued by the dual-process model. We shall briefly review these positive results, then consider some evidence to the contrary.

One study supporting the notion of effortless recognition was performed by Shepard (1967). In each of three experiments, subjects were presented with a long series of over five hundred visual stimuli on cards. They were instructed to go through the items at whatever pace they wished. After the items, a series of pairs was presented, and for each pair the subject had to choose the item which had been in the series. Printed words were presented in one experiment, sentences were used in the second, and colored pictures for the third. In all cases recognition was remarkably good. Even after 7 days, almost 90 percent of the pictures were recognized correctly. These data are particularly striking when one thinks of how few of the items the subjects probably could have recalled. On the basis of these results, Shepard stated: "Evidently, after 20 or more years of absorbing visual information, subjects are still able to take in as many as 612 further pictures without any particular effort and, then, discriminate these from pictures not previously seen with (median) accuracy of over 98 percent" (p.160). This leads easily to the conclusion that there may be something like near-perfect storage for such a series of items, although very few of them could be recalled.

Shepard's findings were quickly supported by other researchers. Standing, Conezio, and Haber (1970) presented 2560 pictures to subjects, and they also found that recognition accuracy was better than 90 percent. A study by Standing (1973) used 10,000 pictures, and found good recognition performance. These sorts of findings led Haber (1970) to conclude that "These experiments . . . suggest that recognition memory for pictures is essentially perfect. . . . Recognition is based on some kind of representation in memory that is maintained without labels, words, or the need for rehearsal" (p.105).

This statement would seem to imply that when a subject examines a picture, some sort of "photographic" replica of the picture is effortlessly established, simply by the subject's inspecting the picture.

Storing pictures. There is some evidence available, however, which indicates that subjects must carry out some relatively complicated processing before near-perfect recognition of pictures can occur. In an important study, Loftus (1972) presented a series of pictures to subjects for varying lengths of time, and tested for recognition. He also measured and counted the subjects' eye movements while they were examining each picture, and he found that recognition improved as a function of the number of fixations that the subject gave to a specific picture. The overall result was that a 3-second presentation resulted in better recognition than a 2-second presentation. However, in some cases the same number of fixations was made during the 2-second and 3-second exposure times. When number of fixations was held constant, there was no effect of exposure duration.

So far, these results support the notion that the subjects are "taking a picture" of the stimulus. More fixations are needed to take a more complete picture, because one can only see a small portion of the stimulus clearly at any one time. However, Loftus also examined an additional condition, in which subjects were required to count backwards while viewing the pictures. This condition also produced a close relationship between number of fixations and recognition, but the overall level of recognition was far below that in the comparable normal viewing conditions, even with number of fixations held constant. This means that the distractor task did more than just cut down the number of fixations; it also reduced the amount of information "pulled out" of each fixation. Freund (1971, cited by Loftus, 1972) reported similar results. What this may mean is that in order to recognize the objects later, the subjects must be "thinking" about the objects that they are looking at. When they are counting backward, they are kept too busy to be able to do much thinking, so recognition is interfered with. From this one might argue that recognition is not based on the simple registration of the stimulus. Rather, the ability to recognize an object is the result of some processing that was carried out when the object was presented. Thus, the distinction between recognition and recall may not be as hard and fast as the dual-process model assumes.

The uniqueness of pictures. Loftus (1972) also reported one additional result which may shed some light on why recognition is so good in experiments with pictures. In one test condition, subjects first said whether a test picture had been presented before or not, and then gave one of two reasons for their choice: (1) there was some particular object or attribute that was memorable in the picture, or (2) there was nothing particularly memorable about the picture but the picture as a whole "looked familiar." In analyzing these results, Loftus found that when subjects said that they recognized one particular object in the picture, they had indeed spent much time looking at one particular object when the picture had originally been presented. This finding may help us to understand why recognition for pictures is so very good. A complex picture has many objects in it, and even a small sample of these could probably serve to differentiate this picture from all the others in the series. For example, if one picture has a fire hydrant in it, and none of the others do, then merely remembering the fire hydrant would enable the subject to recognize this picture perfectly. It should also be noted that in some of the picture-recognition studies, the pictures were purposely chosen to be as distinctive as possible (e.g., Shepard, 1967). Thus, one reason that recognition performance is so good with pictures may be because the recognition tests have been easy. In one study by Nickerson (1965), an attempt was made to make picture recognition more difficult by making the stimuli very similar to each other. Under these circumstances, recognition accuracy is reduced, as would be expected from the present arguments. However, it should also be noted that recognition for similar pictures was still better than recognition for the names of these pictures. The reason for this is not apparent, but in any case the main conclusion for the present discussion is that recognition can be made much more difficult if similar items are used as old and new items on a recognition test.

More stringent tests of recognition. There has been some recent research concerning recognition for verbal material which also supports the notion that recognition can be based on only partial information. If so, one must guard against a situation in which a subject performs well on a recognition test while remembering only a minimal amount of information. For example, assume that a subject is given a list of words to study. We then present a series of pairs, one of which is a word and the other of which is a CVC. We tell the subject to pick the item in each pair that was on the study list. Obviously, the subject would do very well simply by picking the word in each pair. One could perform perfectly in this situation without having stored anything about each item, other than that it was a word.

If recognition performance is considered in this way, then there is evidence that subjects do not have perfect records of the words they saw. In the first place, if the subject's memory were detailed enough to specify each word precisely, then it should not matter what test items were presented. Since each word that we know is different from every other word, a complete record should produce perfect recognition. However, there are many studies which have shown that recognition performance varies as a function of the number and type of test items (e.g., Murdock, 1963), which indicates that the subjects must not have had complete records available.

A study by Postman, Jenkins, and Postman (1948) examined the influence of the type of distractor (the incorrect items) on recognition performance. The study list consisted of forty-eight CVCs, which was then followed by a recognition test. One CVC from the original list was presented for recognition accompanied by three distractors. One of the distractors was the same as the correct CVC, except that one letter had been changed. The other two items were different from the correct CVC in all letters. It was found that the distractor item that was similar to the correct CVC was chosen more frequently than either of the other distractors. This is evidence that the information that the subjects were using for recognition was not complete. These results were supported by a study by McNulty (1965).

Different strategies for recognition and recall. This evidence leads to the conclusion that the ability to remember something entails work on the part of the subject. Recognition is possible, at least in part, because the subject did whatever is necessary to bring it about. This sort of an idea is well known to students, who like to know in advance the type of examination they will receive so they can study accordingly. Multiple choice exams, based on recognition, are prepared for differently than exams based on recall. If it is true that people can study to improve their recognition, then recognition would not seem to be based on simple activation of a word in memory, because that would not require a study strategy at all. A number of studies have shown that there are indeed different methods of preparing for different types of tests (Bernbach, 1973; Jacoby, 1973). The basic procedure in these studies is to give subjects some experience with one sort of test, recognition or recall, and then give the other sort of test without warning. In such a situation, subjects who were expecting recall do worse on recognition than subjects who were expecting recognition, and vice versa.

This is a very important result, because it tells us something about the way in which words are represented in memory. This discussion started with the dual-process model, which assumes that there is some chunk of information stored in memory to stand for each word that we know. This information was assumed to be the basis for our abilities to read a word and understand it, to hear a word and understand it, and to use the word correctly. However, it seems to be true that the information used to recall a word is not simply the information used to recognize the word plus appropriate retrieval cues. This means that there is not some specific bit of information which is used in all situations in which a given word is used. Therefore, in order to understand how subjects can answer correctly on memory tests, we must examine what it is that subjects do when they are presented with words.

2.4 An encoding as the memory for a word

There has been much recent research demonstrating that people do not simply take in information from the world, store this information, and bring the information back at a later time. It seems that people actively deal with the stimulus that is presented, or encode it. We have already considered examples of this in chapter 1 in the discussion of role of knowledge and organization in recall. The results of this encoding activity are very important in determining how the subject will behave at a later time.

Recognition failure. One bit of evidence for this conclusion comes from a study by Thomson and Tulving (1970). Words were presented either singly or paired with another word, followed by a recognition test. There were several different recognition conditions. A word which had originally been presented alone could be tested either alone or in a pair. If a word had been in a pair on the training list, then it could also be tested in a pair or alone.

The most important finding of the study was that recognition was interfered with if the context in which a word was tested was different from the context in which the word was originally presented. When two words which had originally been presented in a pair were presented separately on the recognition test, recognition was worse than if they were tested together in the same pair. By the same token, a word which had been alone on the training list was recognized less well if it was presented in a pair for recognition. These results indicate that something else besides the memory node is involved in recognition. If presentation of a single word on the training list simply resulted in the node being marked, then later recognition should not be interfered with by presenting this word in a pair. On the other hand, if presentation of a pair of words simply resulted in the two nodes being marked, then breaking up the pair at testing should not interfere with recognition. Since recognition is interfered with in both these cases, it seems reasonable to assume that recognition is based on something more than marked nodes.

Encoding. As an alternative notion, let us consider the extreme assumption that the subject may not store specific information about the word at all. Rather, let us assume that a subject does things when a word is presented, and recall depends on these activities. For example, if a pair of words such as *black-white* is presented, a subject may think of a checkerboard. Thus, presentation of a pair of words results in the subject's imagining various things, and later recall may depend on these activities, among others. Let us call these activities, when they take place in a memory experiment, *encoding operations*. The pair of words *black-white* would be *encoded* by the subject's thinking of a checkerboard, say, while the pair of words is presented. The imagined checkerboard could be called the *encoding* of the pair (Tulving and Thomson, 1973; Thomson & Tulving, 1970). We can now examine how encoding operations can result in recognition failure.

We have just discussed how a subject might encode the pair *black-white* during study. On the later recognition test, *black* is presented by itself. The subject now has a group of encodings in memory, all of which occurred during the recent experiment, and the subject must decide if one of these encodings could have been produced by *black*. It seems reasonable that this is done by first determining how this word might have been encoded, and then determining if this encoding is indeed one of those stored from the experiment. (This parallels the discussion of recall in section 1.9.) Since it seems probable that *black* alone could produce a different encoding than *black-white*, then there is a good chance that the subject won't recognize the word.

Thus, presentation of a list of words in an experiment serves to stimulate the person to do things, if "thinking of" something can be considered a case of doing something. (This point of view will be argued further in parts 2, 3, and 4). Therefore, when a list of words is presented, one goes through a series of "episodes" (Tulving, 1972), with each episode consisting of the things that one did when a given word was presented. The question to be considered in the remainder of this chapter is: What sort of things do subjects do when they study words? For the time being, we shall consider the mental events that occur when words are presented. However, as we shall see later, the subject's examination of the word itself is also part of the encoding of the word.

2.5 Encoding operations examined through recognition tests

This model of encoding predicts that the main basis for recognition is the similarity between the encoding stored in memory and the encoding given the test stimulus (Flexser & Tulving, 1978). Therefore, if two very different stimuli produce the same encoding, then subjects ought to confuse the two, saying that one had been presented earlier when in reality the other had been.

Implicit associative responses. An early study in this line of research is that of Underwood (1965). He argued that when a word is presented to a subject in an experiment, the subject can respond to it by covertly saying other words which are strongly associated to the presented word. Thus, words can be encoded through "implicit associative responses" (IARs). One way to test for the occurrence of IARs is through the use of a recognition test. The basic prediction is that if an IAR occurred when a specific word was presented, then there should be a tendency for the subject to mistakenly identify the IAR as actually having been presented in the list. Underwood tested this prediction by carefully selecting the words which were presented to subjects in a recognition experiment. A number of the words in the list had been chosen because subjects gave strong associations to them on word association tests. The expected IARs for these words were presented as test words on the recognition tests, and the hypothesized IARs were indeed incorrectly recognized more frequently than control words were.

Storing information in memory

On the basis of his results, Underwood concluded that subjects make associative responses to the presented word, and these responses may be included as part of the encoding of the word. Many investigators have found similar results (e.g., Cramer, 1970; Wallace, 1968).

Referential encoding. Underwood assumed that the sole determining factor in whether an IAR was produced was the "associative strength" between the word presented on the list and the response word, as determined by word association norms. Other studies have demonstrated that other factors can influence false recognition independently of the association between words. For example, a synonym of a word on the memory list will be incorrectly recognized as being on the list, even if it is not associatively related to the word on the list (Anisfeld & Knapp, 1968; Fillenbaum, 1969). The false recognitions produced by nonassociated synonyms indicate that encodings probably entail more than production of IARs.

Similar results concerning false recognitions of synonyms were presented by Anisfeld (1970). In one condition, Anisfeld presented a list of adjective-noun phrases as the material to be memorized. He then tested for false recognitions to synonymous, antonymous (opposite), and control phrases. As an example, if *back door* was the phrase on the list, then *rear door* would be a synonymous phrase, *front door* would be an antonymous phrase, and *screen door* would be a control phrase. The antonymous phrases were more strongly associated to the original phrases, but Anisfeld found that there were no more false recognition responses to them than to the control phrases. On the other hand, synonymous phrases were falsely recognized significantly more often than either the antonym or control phrases.

Anisfeld explained these results with what he called a referential encoding model. He assumed that when a phrase was presented on the study list, the subject responded to the meaning of the phrase by thinking of the object to which the phrase refers or its referent. Since synonymous phrases, such as *back door* and *rear door,* refer to essentially the same things, there would be a greater chance of false recognition here than with *back door* and *front door,* even though the latter phrases are associatively related. A number of other studies have found similar results, using different designs (e.g., Bobrow, 1970; Perfetti & Goodman, 1970). In summary, the results support the assumption that information based on the referent of a word or phrase can be included in the encoding. One point that needs clarification here is what it means to think of a referent of a phrase. An answer that immediately comes to mind is that one forms an image of an object that would be a referent of the phrase in question, such as the rear door of one's house. We shall talk more about imagery as an encoding device in chapter 7.

Verbal encodings for nonverbal stimuli. We have not yet considered how nonverbal stimuli are encoded. Bower and Holyoak (1973) presented subjects with various sounds and tested for later recognition by presenting the old sounds along with some new ones. The original stimuli were chosen because they were ambiguous; that is, when they were presented over a tape recorder, more than one description could be used for them. For example, one sound could be identified as a heartbeat or a bouncing rubber ball, and another could be identified as soldiers clumping down stairs or horses trotting through the streets. When the stimuli were presented on the training list, they were labeled (i.e., verbally encoded). Some subjects were asked to produce their own labels; for other subjects, each sound was labeled by the experimenter.

When the recognition test was given, the sounds were also labeled. Some sounds were labeled by the experimenter with the same label as they were given during training. Other sounds were given the other possible label during the recognition test. Still other sounds were labeled by the subject: the subject tried to recall the original label and if this couldn't be done then the subject simply produced a label. After the sound had been labeled, the subject judged whether or not it had been on the original study list. Half the sounds on the recognition list had been on the original list and half were new.

The most important result was that when an *old* stimulus was labeled differently on the recognition list, recognition dropped from 80 percent to 20 percent. The fact that the stimulus was identical was much less important than the fact that the label was the same. In addition, if the subject gave a *new* stimulus a label that had been used for one of the training stimuli, then the new stimulus was called "old" 72 percent of the time. New stimuli that received labels that hadn't been used before were judged to be old only 27 percent of the time.

Thus, these results show that if a new stimulus is verbally encoded in the same way as one of the training stimuli, then it will be called old almost as frequently as one of the old stimuli will be called old. These data show the importance of the encoding given the item. However, it was also found that, all other things being equal, there was a greater chance that an old stimulus given an old label would be recognized as old, compared to a new stimulus given an old label (see above data), indicating that some specific information about the old stimuli could also be remembered. This is an important point, and will be discussed further in the next chapter. It seems to mean that encodings, in the sense of associations and the like, are not all that influences one's memory for a word.

Summary. Several sorts of evidence support the notion that at least part of one's memory for an item consists of mental events which occur when the item is experienced, or mental actions carried out when the item is presented. This information has been referred to as the encoding given an item. Experiments using recognition have indicated that encodings can be manipulated, with subsequent effects on performance.

2.6 Encoding and recall

The discussion so far has considered three types of encoding operations: production of IARs, referential encoding, and verbal labels. However, it is obvious that subjects can do many things when a word is presented. In recent years there has been much research concerned with how different sorts of encoding operations influence the subject's ability to recall words at a later time.

Structural versus semantic encoding. Jenkins and his associates (Jenkins, 1974; Hyde & Jenkins, 1973; Till & Jenkins, 1973; Walsh & Jenkins, 1973) have carried out a number of studies in which subjects are instructed to respond to a list of words in different ways. One group of subjects is told to prepare for a recall test on the words. Other groups are given different tasks to perform when they hear the words, and are told nothing about the later recall test. The tasks are of two general types. *Structural* tasks require that the subject deal with some nonmeaningful aspect of the word. Examples of this would be estimating the number of letters in the word, or determining if the word contained an e or a g. *Semantic* tasks, on the other hand, require the subject to consider the meaning of the word. An example of this would be rating the word on a scale of pleasantness-unpleasantness. After the list is presented once, the subjects are asked to try to recall as many of the words as they can. This recall comes as a surprise to all the subjects except the group that was told to study the words.

Jenkins and his colleagues have consistently demonstrated that, in this sort of situation, semantic orienting tasks produce just as good recall as instructions to study the words, while the structural tasks produce lower levels of recall.

According to Jenkins, a semantic orienting task produces good recall because it results in information about the meaning of the word being activated, but that explanation leaves many important questions unanswered. For example, we are not told what happens when information about the meaning of a word is "activated" in memory, and how this results in good recall. In addition, the distinction between semantic and structural orienting tasks is not totally clear. Hyde and Jenkins found that estimating the frequency of usage of a word produced good recall, but it is really not clear what this task has to do with the meaning of a word. Several authors have recently argued that the semantic-structural distinction is really circular, because the only way the tasks are classified is by their effect on recall. However, if we say that a task is semantic because it produces good recall, then we have said nothing about why semantic tasks produce good recall (T. O. Nelson, 1977; Baddeley, 1978). Another question comes from the retrieval model outlined in the last chapter. It was argued that developing a set of retrieval cues is crucial if a large number of words is to be recalled. If that argument is correct, then in order for recall to be possible after the semantic orienting task, a set of retrieval cues must have been developed while the subjects were studying the words, as discussed in section 1.9. However, in these experiments, since the subjects are not trying to recall the words, they would probably make no conscious attempt to organize the words. Therefore, where would the retrieval cues come from? This will be considered further in section 2.7.

These are some of the questions that remain, but they should not obscure the importance of these results for the present discussion. First, it is possible to produce good recall by simply having a subject encode a word in a specific way, even though the subject does not intentionally try to remember the words. Second, under certain circumstances recall is as good as if the subject actively tries to recall the material.

"Depth" or "breadth" or "elaborateness" of encoding. One of the most important recent theoretical developments has been concerned with why different sorts of encodings produce different levels of recall. Craik and Lockhart (1972) have argued that the crucial factor in determining the strength of the memory for an item is the "depth" of processing that the item receives when it is presented. They conceive of the processing of an item to consist of a series of levels. (This position has been elaborated and changed somewhat in subsequent papers [e.g., Craik & Tulving, 1975; Lockhart, Craik, & Jacoby, 1975]. However, the basic aspects of the model, including the postulated differences in traces, are still present.) The most primitive analysis of an item consists of registration of the stimulus and extraction of its physical features. Higher levels of processing are concerned with matching these features with information in memory. Still-higher levels entail the recall of related information, as when one thinks of a referent of a word. Craik and Lockhart assume that the trace laid down in memory depends upon the analysis given the stimulus, and that the usefulness of the memory trace at recall depends upon the depth of processing which an input has received. According to Lockhart et al., items that are processed more deeply receive more unique encodings, since deeper processing means more elaborate processing. This means that deeper processing should produce better recall, all other things being equal.

It should be noted that this analysis is not limited to words; one can argue that all sensory patterns are analyzed in this way. For example, if a whistle sounds but the person hardly notes it, there will not be a lasting memory for it. If one recognizes the sound as a whistle, and it reminds one of trains that used to pass near home, then the memory for the event will be much longer-lasting. This is directly comparable to what is assumed to happen with words.

In summary, this position argues that the various tasks used by Jenkins and his associates produce differential recall because the various tasks result in different sorts of encodings. Some of these encodings produce better recall than others do.

The notion of levels of processing has also been recently criticized, on several grounds (T. O. Nelson, 1977; Baddeley, 1978). First, it has been demonstrated that memory performance can sometimes be better after a structural task than after a semantic task (e.g., Morris, Bransford, & Franks, 1977), which goes against the notion that deeper levels of processing simply produce "better" memory traces. Also, it has been found that learning can occur if subjects are given repeated structural tasks with the same words. That is, if one group of subjects simply goes through a word list once, checking for the presence of an e or g in each word, while a second group does this twice, the second group will recall more of the words than the first group. This means that learning can occur with structural encodings, which also raises questions for the levels of processing notion.

Given these difficulties, let us consider if the point of view developed so far in this book can say anything about why "semantic" tasks produce better performance on an unexpected recall test than do "structural" tasks.

Differential recall after different encoding operations. Suppose that a subject is to determine if a word contains an e. Perhaps it is possible to search for a single letter in such a way that one doesn't read the word

(Neisser, 1967). If so, then if a subject were unexpectedly asked to identify the word from memory, *even immediately after looking for the e,* the subject might not be able to do this. The same could be true of estimating the length of a word. One might selectively be able to consider only the overall shape of the word, and thereby ignore the letters. This too would result in inadequate information being stored as far as recalling the word is concerned. One could examine this by training a subject to do one of these tasks efficiently, and then giving a surprise test on a single word just after the subject has responded to it. Inadequate registration of the word would be evidenced by recall problems on this sort of a test.

On the other hand, with a semantic-type task, at the very least the subject must know the word that is being rated. So here is one potential difference between these two sorts of tasks, based on the kind of information that must be used to carry them out. However, there is another potential difference between structural and semantic tasks which Craik and Lockhart and their associates do not explicitly consider, and which bears mentioning.

Problems with retrieval cues. After a list of some two dozen words, as used by Jenkins and his associates, there are too many encodings available for the subject to retrieve them on the basis of recency alone. Therefore, according to the discussion in the last chapter, there must have been some retrieval cues developed when the word list was studied. This is a second potential difference between structural and semantic tasks. With the structural tasks, there may not be any relevant cues available. The subject did not think of any summary information when the words were presented, so there is nothing available after the list is finished. For example, if a subject has checked for the letter e in the words, then after the task is finished, the only possible information to use as cues would be "words with e" and "words with no e." Even if these are potentially useful cues, with a reasonably long list of words, there will be too many words of each sort for effective retrieval to occur. The situation would be comparable to one in which all the words in a twenty-four-word list start with the same letter, and we give the letter as a cue. If so, then it might be possible to produce better recall by using several structural-type tasks, with only a few words being used for each task. This should reduce interference, and it might increase recall. Such results have been obtained (Weisberg & Fish, 1979).

It should also be noted that the discussion in the last paragraph has been concerned with why structural tasks produce poor recall. Little has been said about why semantic tasks produce good recall, except a brief mention of the fact that the semantic tasks probably get adequate information into memory about the word itself. There is still the question of where the cues come from to retrieve this adequate encoding at recall. Perhaps when semantic-type encoding occurs, then earlier related words in the list are recalled when a given word is encoded. This could occur more or less automatically and could produce organization and higher-order cues. There is some evidence that this does occur (Hintzman & Block, 1973). Exactly *why* this automatic organization occurs with semantic tasks is not clear. In addition, Postman and Kruesi (1977) have recently argued that the subject may have to keep referring to earlier words simply to carry out the semantic task. For example, in order to rate the pleasantness of a word, one may have to keep referring back to what one rated other words, to keep the scale reasonable. Such activity is not necessary either for e checking or for most if not all of the structural tasks. The structural tasks can be carried out by dealing with each word individually, but, if Postman and Kruesi are correct, the semantic tasks cannot be carried out in this way. Thus, we have here a plausible mechanism whereby words could be interrelated during semantic tasks.

In conclusion, there are a number of possible reasons as to why different sorts of tasks produce differential recall. There may be differences in the adequacy of the information stored originally. There may also be a lack of adequate cues in some cases. This in turn could be due to the large number of words related to the few cues that could be used. An example of this is using the type of task as a retrieval cue, when only one task has been used for many words.

2.7 Encoding and thinking

We have now seen that what subjects remember may be based on the whole complex of events which occurs when a word is presented. Therefore, a word which a subject hears or sees in an experiment should be looked upon as a stimulus to do something, in the broad sense of "do." Subjects may think of associatively related words, or words that sound like the presented word, or events that the word in question refers to. These things that subjects think of could be looked upon as things that subjects do. That is, "thinking of a related word" may entail saying the word to oneself; "thinking of events" may entail imagining those events, and so on.

In all of this, it is important to note that there is nothing corresponding to a mental representation of the word in and of itself. There is no need to argue that there is some specific node at which is stored various sets of related features, such as phonological features, semantic features, and image features, as some theorists do. All that we need to assume is that seeing a certain collection of letters, or hearing a certain pattern of sounds, can make one do various things, ranging from saying something to oneself to imagining some event.

When the same word is presented two different times to the same person, the person may think of something different each time. This is the same as saying that the word is encoded differently each time. We have seen that this may result in the person's not recognizing the word as having been presented before. It is sometimes argued that the reason that a word can be encoded in more than one way is because not all of the features related to the word need be activated each time the word is presented. That is, if one assumes that each word is related to many features, then some of them may be activated the first time the word is presented, and others may be activated the second time the word is presented (e.g., Anderson & Bower, 1972; Flexser & Tulving, 1978).

It is true that if one thinks of an event when a word is presented, then the presented word has in a sense resulted in the activation of features. However, it is important to emphasize that the word does not simply activate a random subset of all the features that are related to it. Rather, the word activates a very specific subset of features, those which correspond to hearing oneself say some other word, for example. This is not simply a random set of features.

Storing information in memory. An additional conclusion that comes from this discussion is that one should not speak about "storing information in memory." This phrase is commonly used, both in psychological theorizing and in ordinary language. The phrase comes originally from computer models of cognition, or *information-processing* models. However, the same notion had been expressed by earlier students of memory by the phrase *memory trace*. The trace of an item is the information that the item leaves behind in memory after it is no longer present. However, based on the present discussion, when humans are under consideration, we might be better off if we did not refer to information or traces being stored in memory, for several reasons. First, there is no separate quantity, called information, that is being stored. Rather, a person can do any of several things during an event, and what the person does will in part determine if the event can be recalled at a later time. There is no specific act which involves storing information. Secondly, there is a problem with the notion that things are stored in memory. The notion of a separate memory store, like a closet, may have some usefulness, but if the present discussion is on the right track, then there is also no separate place where storage occurs. Most psychologists use the term "memory store" simply as a convenient shorthand; but it is only a convenience, not a strict definition.

In summary, a word is encoded, or a word *encodes itself,* to the extent that the word can make us carry out some act, in thought or in the world. Words should be looked upon as instigators of action, and this is what encoding a word entails. This conclusion has implications for theories of thinking, because such theories are concerned with the "representations" of events in thought. These representations are mental things that stand for external objects when we think about them (Price, 1953, chap. X). However, the discussion in this chapter leads to the conclusion that words do not have representations that stand for them in memory. We can recall having seen a word because we did certain things when the word was presented, but this does not mean that we have any specific representation of the word. It is also argued by some theorists that there are representations of all concepts in our memories, not only words (see chap. 8). As we shall see later, the negative conclusion drawn in this chapter about the mental representations of words may also be relevant to the mental representations of other things.

2.8 Summary

This chapter has been concerned with the form of the information stored in memory when an item is studied. We began with a review of the dual-process hypothesis, which argues that words are represented in memory as bundles of features. When a person perceives a word, the corresponding memory node is activated and "marked." At recall, cues are used in order to retrieve nodes, which are then checked for an appropriate marker. Nodes appropriately marked are produced as words. Thus, the two processes involved in recall are retrieval of nodes and checking for appropriate markers.

According to this hypothesis, recognition depends only on appropriately marked nodes. No retrieval is necessary, since presentation of the word on the recognition test gets the person to the relevant node. Evidence to support this aspect of the dual-process hypothesis comes from studies which have shown that recognition can be effortless under conditions in which recall is very difficult. This supposedly occurs because nodes are more or less automatically marked in situations in which no retrieval cues are available. Under such conditions, recall would be very poor, while recognition would be very good.

However, a close examination of this evidence raises questions concerning the marked-nodes aspect of the dual-process hypothesis. There are a number of situations in which recognition performance can be interfered with, although the dual-process hypothesis predicts that recognition should be quite easy in these situations. Therefore, the conception of words as nodes was rejected.

The remainder of the chapter was concerned with the notion that memory depends upon the encoding which is carried out when a word is presented. The encoding for a word consists of those things that a person does when the word is presented. There is evidence that people spontaneously produce implicit associative responses to words, and that people spontaneously think of the referents of words in an experiment. There is also evidence that the type of encoding given a word can affect how recallable the word will be.

Based on this, words are not static items in memory. Rather, words are cues to action, including "mental actions," and the action can vary greatly depending upon the situation that the person is in.

If "storing a word in memory" entails encoding the word, then "recalling the word" becomes a bit complicated. Based on the conclusions from this chapter, retrieval cues are used not to retrieve words, but rather to retrieve encodings, or episodes. There is now one additional step which we must consider: How does the person get from retrieving an encoding to recalling a word? That is, given that a person recalls a given episode, how is a specific word produced?

3
Reconstruction and recall

3.0 Introduction

In the last chapter, it was argued that recall of a word depends on the encoding given the word. An encoding consists of those acts that a person carries out when a word is presented. If this is so, then recalling a word becomes a complicated phenomenon, because retrieval cues now function to retrieve encodings, not words. That is, a retrieval cue serves to remind the person of a whole episode (Tulving, 1972). In order to produce a word, one further step is needed. The subject must decide what word could have been part of that episode: the subject must decode the encoding. Another way of putting this would be to say that the original stimulus word must be reconstructed from the encoding. We saw some evidence for this in the last chapter, where it was shown that subjects sometimes mistakenly "recognize" words that are associated to the words actually on the list. The present chapter will mainly be concerned with the recall of more complex materials than single words. However, we shall see that the same factors are at work here as in the recall of the word lists that were discussed in chapters 1 and 2. Thus, the differences in materials may not bring about different processes.

Bartlett (1932) was one of the first to argue that our ability to remember something is really the result of an act of reconstruction, in which the event is reconstructed from what it had left behind. Therefore, according to Bartlett, we do not recall an experience, in the sense of getting back the original experience as it was. Rather, we use what we have to reconstruct the original experience as it must have been. This point of view is usually contrasted with a "reproductive" view, which would state that recall entails reproducing the earlier event from the stored trace of that event. This reproductive view is what present-day followers of Bartlett feel they are arguing against. However, as we shall see later, Bartlett might not have totally agreed with present-day interpretations of his theorizing.

There has been much interest recently in the reconstructive nature of recall, and much recent evidence has been used to support the claim that events, per se, are never stored. All we have, according to this view, are our cognitive constructions, or encodings, and what we can reconstruct from them. The present chapter will be concerned with this issue, beginning with a discussion of Bartlett's research, and more recent research that has come from the same point of view. As just mentioned, it is argued from these results that one never stores specific information about an event. Rather, one reconstructs the event from the encoding which it leaves behind. However, we shall then consider other evidence that supports the view that very specific aspects of an event can also be remembered. It seems most reasonable to conclude that recall depends on multiple sources of information, both specific and general, and that recall is never exclusively a pure reconstruction or a pure reproduction. The chapter concludes with a specific example of how one's knowledge is used in recall.

3.1 Bartlett's reconstructive theory of recall

Bartlett (1932) proposed a theory of recall which argued that when we are presented with any sort of material, the first thing that we do is try to make sense out of it. This "effort after meaning" (p. 20) is carried out by applying our knowledge to the material, to try to relate the new material to something that we already know. We saw examples of this in the first two chapters, when we discussed the role of hierarchical structure and other sorts of organization in the recall of word lists. In these cases, too, new material is related to what we already know, and recall based on categories would be one specific instance of this. This aspect of Bartlett's theorizing is relevant to much recent work in memory.

A well-known story used by Bartlett is presented in Box 3.1. This story is the translation of an American Indian folktale, and it seems strange in content and style to a modern reader. Bartlett expressly chose it as stimulus material because it came from a cultural and social environment very

Reconstruction and recall

Box 3.1. The War of the Ghosts

> One night two young men from Egulac went down to the river to hunt seals, and while they were there it became foggy and calm. Then they heard war-cries, and they thought: "Maybe this is a war-party." They escaped to the shore, and hid behind a log. Now canoes came up, and they heard the noise of paddles, and saw one canoe coming up to them. There were five men in the canoe, and they said:
> "What do you think? We wish to take you along. We are going up the river to make war on the people."
> One of the young men said: "I have no arrows."
> "Arrows are in the canoe," they said.
> "I will not go along. I might be killed. My relatives do not know where I have gone. But you," he said, turning to the other, "may go with them."
> So one of the young men went, but the other returned home.
> And the warriors went on up the river to a town on the other side of Kalama. The people came down to the water, and they began to fight, and many were killed. But presently the young man heard one of the warriors say: "Quick, let us go home: that Indian has been hit." Now he thought: "Oh, they are ghosts." He did not feel sick, but they said he had been shot.
> So the canoes went back to Egulac, and the young man went ashore to his house, and made a fire. And he told everybody and said: "Behold I accompanied the ghosts, and we went to fight. Many of our fellows were killed, and many of those who attacked us were killed. They said I was hit, and I did not feel sick."
> He told it all, and then he became quiet. When the sun rose he fell down. Something black came out of his mouth. His face became contorted. The people jumped up and cried. He was dead.
>
> From Bartlett, 1932

different from that of his subjects, who were British students. The subject read the story once, and then tried to recall it a number of times, at varying intervals. The most impressive finding was that the content of the story changed in the retelling. Events that had little or no meaning to Bartlett's subjects were changed into more familiar events. For example, that black something that issued from the young man's mouth at the end was recalled as the soul leaving the body by some subjects, and one subject recalled the young man foaming at the mouth. Also, the seal-hunting expedition became a fishing trip.

These are just some of the distortions introduced by the subjects when they recalled the story. Bartlett argued that when the story is recalled, all we have available are bits and pieces of information which came out of the initial interpretation. This information can be in the form of images or words. At recall, we take this information and try to reconstruct a story that we think would have left those bits and pieces of information with us. For example, if we recall an image of the young man on the ground with something coming out of his mouth, and we also remember that we thought about convulsions, then we will recall that the young man was foaming at the mouth. Again, this point of view is consistent with the conclusions of many other psychologists, as discussed in chapters 1 and 2.

In summary, Bartlett (1932, chap. X) argued that when the story is presented, it is processed by the listener on the basis of the *schemas* that the person has available. The story is processed through the activation of some of the knowledge that the reader brings to it. At recall, the schemas that have been activated, in conjunction with some specific bits of information that are remembered, are used to reconstruct the story.

Although we have seen that Bartlett's theorizing is not very radical in the context of present-day work in memory, some investigators have chosen to emphasize one specific aspect of his theorizing. These theorists (e.g., Bransford & Franks, 1971) emphasize the reconstructive nature of recall, and they put almost no emphasis on Bartlett's claim that reconstruction is based on bits and pieces remembered from the original event. According to Bransford and Franks (and like-minded psychologists), recall of an event depends solely on the schemas which have been activated when the event occurred. Support for this view comes from research on memory for sentences and prose passages. Some early studies indicated that the meaning of verbal material was the most important factor in determining the later recall of the material. In some cases, it seemed that subjects could remember little or nothing about the actual stimulus, all they could remember was the meaning. This was taken as evidence that recall of a specific sentence must be reconstruction based on meaning.

We shall now follow the recent evolution of this point of view, and then criticize its most extreme form. Bartlett's original formulation, however, that recall depends on the interaction of specific information and general knowledge, will be seen to be closer to the truth.

3.2 Memory for sentences

One of the most often cited studies of memory for sentences is that of Sachs (1967). A number of passages were presented to subjects, and after

Reconstruction and recall

each passage, one sentence was tested for recognition. The subject indicated whether or not the test sentence had been in the passage. The test sentence was one of four types:

1. *Original sentence.* The test sentence was presented just as it had been in the passage.
2. *Semantic change.* The test sentence differed in meaning from the original sentence. This was done not by introducing new words, but by changing the order of the words in the original sentence.
3. *Passive/active change.* The grammatical form of the original sentence was changed, but the meaning was left intact. This was done by changing the verb from the active form to the passive form, or vice versa.
4. *Formal.* The words of the sentence were rearranged to form a new sentence which was synonymous with the original.

As concrete examples, here is one sentence used by Sachs, and the test sentences derived from it.

1. Original sentence:

He sent a letter about it to Galileo, the great Italian scientist.

2. Semantic change:

Galileo, the great Italian scientist, sent him a letter about it.

3. Passive/action change:

A letter about it was sent to Galileo, the great Italian scientist.

4. Formal:

He sent a letter about it to the great Italian scientist, Galileo.

In addition to the different types of test sentences, a second variable which was manipulated was the amount of material which intervened between the presentation of the original sentence and the test. The test occurred either immediately after the original sentence, or after 80 syllables of intervening material, or after 160 syllables of intervening material.

The recognition results indicated that subjects were able to recognize all the changes on the immediate test. On the two delayed tests, performance stayed relatively high for the semantic changes, but the subjects had difficulty in recognizing whether the other sorts of test sentences were new or not. This indicates that the important aspect determining recognition was not the exact string of words that had been presented, but the meaning that the string of words conveyed. Since only the semantic-change test sentences didn't fit the original meaning, they were the only ones that were rejected easily. The other types of sentences all fit the meaning of the original sentence, so the subjects weren't sure whether they were the original sentences or not. Thus, Sachs's results support the notion that comprehension of a sentence requires the use of the words to get to the meaning, and once that occurs, the specific words are not stored. In order to recall the sentence, then, the words would have to be reconstructed from the meaning.

A study by Bock and Brewer (1974) produced a similar conclusion. They carried out a recall experiment with sentences as the to-be-recalled items. The sentences consisted of pairs of related sentences, such as "The hi-fi fanatic turned up the volume" and "The hi-fi fanatic turned the volume up." The two sentences are two ways of saying the same thing, with the choice of one or the other being more or less a matter of taste. Some subjects were asked to rate the pairs of sentences as to which sentence sounded more natural. Other subjects were then given the sentences to recall, with a given subject seeing only one member from each pair of sentences. Bock and Brewer found that the recall of the preferred (more natural) member of the pair was better than recall of the nonpreferred one, because there was a strong tendency to recall the nonpreferred member in the preferred form. Bock and Brewer argued that this occurred because the subjects had stored the meanings of the sentences and had generated the surface forms of the sentences from the meaning. Because they used the more preferred forms in generating the surface forms, their recall of the nonpreferred forms was not exactly right.

In summary, these two studies seem to support the claim that recall of sentences is a reconstruction based on the stored meaning. At the most extreme, these data could be taken as support for the notion that the specific event isn't stored at all, that memory is a total reconstruction.

3.3 More than meaning

In recent years, there have been many studies of sentence storage, and some of the new findings have confirmed and extended these conclusions. Perhaps the most exciting findings come from several experiments on recognition for sentences, conducted by Bransford and Franks and their associates (e.g., Bransford & Franks, 1971; Johnson, Bransford & Solomon, 1973). Bransford and Franks took four complex sentences (or complex ideas) such as "The ants ate the sweet jelly on the kitchen table," and "The tall tree in the front yard shaded the man who was smoking his pipe." Each of the four-idea complex sentences was broken down into one-idea sentences ("The man was smoking his pipe" and "The tree was tall"), two-idea sentences ("The tall tree shaded the man"), and three-idea sentences ("The tall tree in the front yard shaded the man"). A number of sentences from each four-idea group was selected, and they were randomized to produce a study list. A test list was made up of several different sorts of sentences. First, there were old sentences, which had been presented on the acquisition list. Second, there were new sentences which came from the various idea groups, but which had not been presented during acquisition. Finally, there were noncase sentences, which were formed by combining ideas from different idea groups. An example of a noncase sentence would be: "The tall tree in the front yard shaded the man eating the jelly."

The subject's task was to indicate which sentences had been on the study list. The subjects were most confident that the four-idea sentences had been on the acquisition list, even though *none* of the four-idea sentences had actually been presented during study. In addition, the overall recognition scores depended not so much on whether the sentences were old or new, but on the number of ideas that they contained. That is, four-idea sentences were rated higher than three-idea sentences, and so on. Whether or not the sentence had actually been seen before was much less important than the number of ideas which the sentence contained.

In order to explain these results, it has been argued that the subjects did not simply store the meanings of the separate sentences, but rather integrated the material from all the separate sentences that referred to the same situation (Bransford & Franks, 1971, p. 348). Thus if the subjects heard "The tall tree in the front yard shaded the man" and "The man was smoking his pipe," they would integrate the information from the two sentences into one "wholistic idea" of the form: "The tall tree in the front yard shaded the man who was smoking his pipe." Therefore, after the acquisition list is completed, the subjects have available only the four wholistic ideas. When the recognition sentences are given, the subjects match them against the wholistic ideas that they have in memory. The sentence that matches best will produce highest recognition scores. There has been some controversy recently over this work. Questions have been raised concerning whether or not one needs to assume that the information from the various component sentences is actually integrated into one complete idea (Flagg, 1976; Reitman & Bower, 1973), and whether the integration phenomenon is limited to linguistic material (Katz, 1973). However, the outcomes of these controversies will not materially affect the conclusions to be drawn in this chapter, so we shall accept the Bransford and Franks results.

We have now gone another step from the actual sentence that was presented. Sachs's study showed that the surface form serves to convey the meaning; now Bransford and Franks indicate that meanings of individual sentences can be combined into larger units.

Although we are now at least two steps removed from the item presented originally, there is evidence that there is at least one more step. Other studies have shown that while people are studying sentences, they may bring in information that wasn't even in the sentence, and they may then think that this additional information was in the sentence. Consider the following two passages from Johnson, Bransford, and Solomon (1973).

A.
The river was narrow. A beaver hit the log that a turtle was sitting beside and the log flipped over from the shock. The turtle was very surprised by the event.

B.
The river was narrow. A beaver hit the log that a turtle was sitting on and the log flipped over from the shock. The turtle was very surprised by the event.

The only difference between the two passages is that passage A. contains the word *beside,* while passage B. contains the word *on.* After groups of subjects heard one of these two passages, they were given a test list of recognition sentences. One of the test sentences was: "A beaver hit the log and knocked the turtle into the water." Subjects who originally heard passage A. did not think that they had heard this test sentence, but subjects who heard passage B. thought they had heard the test sentence, even though the sentence was in neither passage.

The reason that the subjects who heard passage B. might think they heard the test sentence is because the sentence fits the passage, in a sense. If the turtle was on the log, and the beaver flipped the log over, then the turtle was knocked into the water. However, the passage contained nothing explicit about the turtle being knocked off the log. All that was said was that the turtle was on the log and that beaver flipped the log over. The subjects' knowledge enables them to infer that the turtle was knocked off, but it is not explicitly stated in the passage. This means that at some point the subjects made the inference, and the reason that the test sentence was incorrectly recognized was because it fit that inference.

To summarize, the studies of Bransford and Franks and their associates indicate that recall of sentences is related to comprehension of the sentences. The results also indicate that comprehending utterances entails doing more than simply extracting the meaning from each sentence as it is heard or read. First, the information from several sentences can be combined into a more detailed and complete structure than that conveyed by any single sentence individually. Second, the information in sentences may serve as the basis for the production of additional information by the hearer, as when an inference is made from the information. In some cases, the subject will mistakenly assume that this additional information was in the original sentence. These results are therefore supportive of the notion that recall depends upon reconstruction. The specific event is lost, and recall depends on the encoding that remains.

3.4 Topics and contexts: scripts

The studies just reviewed have indicated that during comprehension, one can add one's own knowledge to the information provided by an utterance. Furthermore, other research has shown that full comprehension of an utterance may require a much greater use of outside information than we have seen so far. It has been argued that an utterance is comprehended by placing it in a context. If the context is not obvious from the situation, then the hearer must construct a context in order to comprehend the utterance.

Scripts and comprehension. If one comprehends a message, then one can answer questions about the message, paraphrase the message, recall the meaning of the message (which may be the same as paraphrasing), and summarize the gist of the message for someone else. If these sorts of activities are taken as a rough operational definition of comprehension, then verbal messages can only be comprehended by someone with detailed knowledge of the topic being talked about.

The importance of knowledge in comprehension can be made clear by examining the recent work of Schank and his colleagues concerning the development of a computer program which can comprehend verbal material (e.g., Schank, 1975; Schank & Abelson, 1975). The following brief story can be comprehended by Schank's program:

John went to a restaurant. The hostess seated John. The hostess gave John a menu. John ordered lobster. He was served quickly. He left a large tip. He left the restaurant.

If an adult heard this story, he or she would probably be able to answer the question: Why did John leave a big tip? However, the answer to the question is not expressly mentioned in the story. Therefore, in order to answer such a question, one must make an inference from the information presented in the story. Given what one knows about people in restaurants, one could infer that John may have left a large tip because he was served quickly, and perhaps because he was pleased with the food. The first of these inferences is more strongly suggested by the passage than is the other, but neither is explicitly stated. Without some detailed knowledge about behavior in restaurants, one would be at a loss concerning why John left a large tip.

Furthermore, consider what would be required if one were asked to paraphrase the story. Again, it would seem that extensive knowledge would be necessary for any reasonably sophisticated paraphrase to occur. Given that so much is left for the reader to fill in in the restaurant story, paraphrase would be crucially dependent on knowledge. Recalling the story would also be based on knowledge, because even though the story is short, it still contains enough words so that one probably couldn't simply parrot it back. Therefore, some organizational scheme is necessary to break the story into fewer units, as we saw in chapter 1.

On several grounds it seems reasonable to conclude that comprehension depends upon knowledge. This then leads us to the question of the form of this knowledge. Schank and Abelson (1975) have argued that comprehension of a given class of events depends upon having a schema or a script for that event. (For the present discussion, we shall use the term *script* to refer to this organized knowledge about a class of events, since *schema* has already been used in several different ways in psychology.) A script for eating in a restaurant, for example, serves to summarize the typical phenomena which occur during such an event, and the types of people involved, and so on. Such a script is outlined in Box 3.2. Schank argues that computer "comprehension" of a story must also depend on an appropriate script, and his work is concerned in part with devising scripts such as that in Box 3.2, and developing a computer program which can use these scripts in understanding stories.

According to this point of view, when the beginning of the restaurant story is read, the words and concepts involved serve to activate the appro-

Box 3.2. Restaurant schema.

---

schema: Restaurant.
characters: Customer, hostess, waiter, chef, cashier.
Scene 1: Entering.
    Customer goes into restaurant.
    Customer finds a place to sit.
        He may find it himself.
        He may be seated by a hostess.
            He asks the hostess for a table.
            She gives him permission to go to the table.
    Customer goes and sits at the table.
Scene 2: Ordering.
    Customer receives a menu.
    Customer reads it.
    Customer decides what to order.
    Waiter takes the order.
        Waiter sees the customer.
        Waiter goes to the customer.
        Customer orders what he wants
    Chef cooks the meal.
Scene 3: Eating.
    After some time the waiter brings the meal from the chef.
    Customer eats the meal.
Scene 4: Exiting.
    Customer asks the waiter for the check.
    Waiter gives the check to the customer.
    Customer leaves a tip.
        The size of the tip depends on the goodness of the service.
    Customer pays the cashier.
    Customer leaves the restaurant.

---

priate script in the computer's memory. Comprehension of the story then entails matching up the descriptions in the story with the events outlined in the script. Once this occurs, then the program is able to make inferences by means of the information in the script. For example, it is obvious from the script in Box 3.2 how the program would be able to answer the question about a large tip even though nothing explicit is said about it in the story. Furthermore, given this script, one can also see where the ability to paraphrase the story would come from. According to Schank, both people and computer programs comprehend linguistic messages through the use of scripts.

Schank (1975) gives several examples of how important scripts are in human comprehension. Consider the following sets of sentences:

John went to a restaurant.
He asked the waitress to tell the chef to cook him a hot dog.

John went to a birthday party.
First Bill opened the presents and then they ate the cake.

John went to a birthday party.
He asked the waitress to tell the chef to cook him a hot dog.

In the first two sets, one has no trouble understanding the *the's* and the phrases that follow them. However, in the third set, these same words make one think, in order to figure out why they would be there. In English, when one introduces a phrase with *the*, one is assuming that the listener knows what the phrase refers to. In the first two sets, the relevant scripts make these phrases perfectly clear to the listener. However, in the third set, things get more complicated. Most birthday parties do not have waitresses, so the listener must actively search for a reason for a waitress being referred to. Thus, it seems that the script is being used all the time, even though we are not aware of it until things break down.

In summary, this important work with computers emphasizes the active use of knowledge in comprehending verbal material. There are several further points which bear mentioning here. First, this use of scripts in comprehension is the same as the use of one's knowledge to organize a list of words, as discussed in chapter 1. Based on the present discussion, one could say that recall of a long list of words depends on one's "comprehension" of the list, or one's "script" for the list. Second, this same active use of knowledge will be seen several times in future chapters. Third, there are one or two questions about inferences during comprehension which will be pursued further later in this chapter. Finally, it is important to note that a script can also serve as the basis for one's overt behavior, as when one uses a script in a restaurant. That is, the same knowledge would be used to determine what to do at what time, and it would also be used to understand what other people would be doing at various times. This point will also be discussed later in this chapter, as well as in chapters 5, 6, and 7. Let us now briefly turn to some work with humans which supports the same conclusions concerning the important role of scripts in the comprehension and recall of verbal material.

Scripts, comprehension, and recall. Consider the two passages in Box 3.3. The material is not particularly difficult: the words are relatively

Reconstruction and recall 57

concrete, they are all familiar, the sentence structure is simple enough, and yet the passages are very hard to understand. In a series of studies, Bransford and Johnson (1972) examined the comprehension and recall of passages of this sort. Subjects heard the passages, rated them for comprehensibility, and then tried to recall them. Control subjects were not told anything about the passages. Some experimental subjects were given a con-

Box 3.3.

Passage 1.
The procedure is actually quite simple. First you arrange things into different groups. Of course, one pile may be sufficient depending on how much there is to do. If you have to go somewhere else due to lack of facilities that is the next step, otherwise you are pretty well set. It is important not to overdo things. That is, it is better to do too few things at once than too many. In the short run this may not seem important but complications can easily arise. A mistake can be expensive as well. At first the whole procedure will seem complicated. Soon, however, it will become just another facet of life. It is difficult to foresee any end to the necessity for this task in the immediate future, but then one never can tell. After the procedure is completed one arranges the materials into different groups again. Then they can be put into their appropriate places. Eventually they will be used once more and the whole cycle will then have to be repeated. However, that is part of life.

From Bransford & Johnson, 1972

Context 1.
This passage is about washing clothes.

Passage 2.
If the balloons popped the sound wouldn't be able to carry since everything would be too far away from the correct floor. A closed window would also prevent the sound from carrying, since most buildings tend to be well insulated. Since the whole operation depends on the steady flow of electricity, a break in the middle of the wire would also cause problems. Of course, the fellow could shout, but the human voice is not loud enough to carry that far. An additional problem is that the string could break on the instrument. Then there would be no accompaniment to the message. It is clear that the best situation would involve less distance. Then there would be fewer potential problems. With face-to-face contact, the least number of things could go wrong.

Context 2.

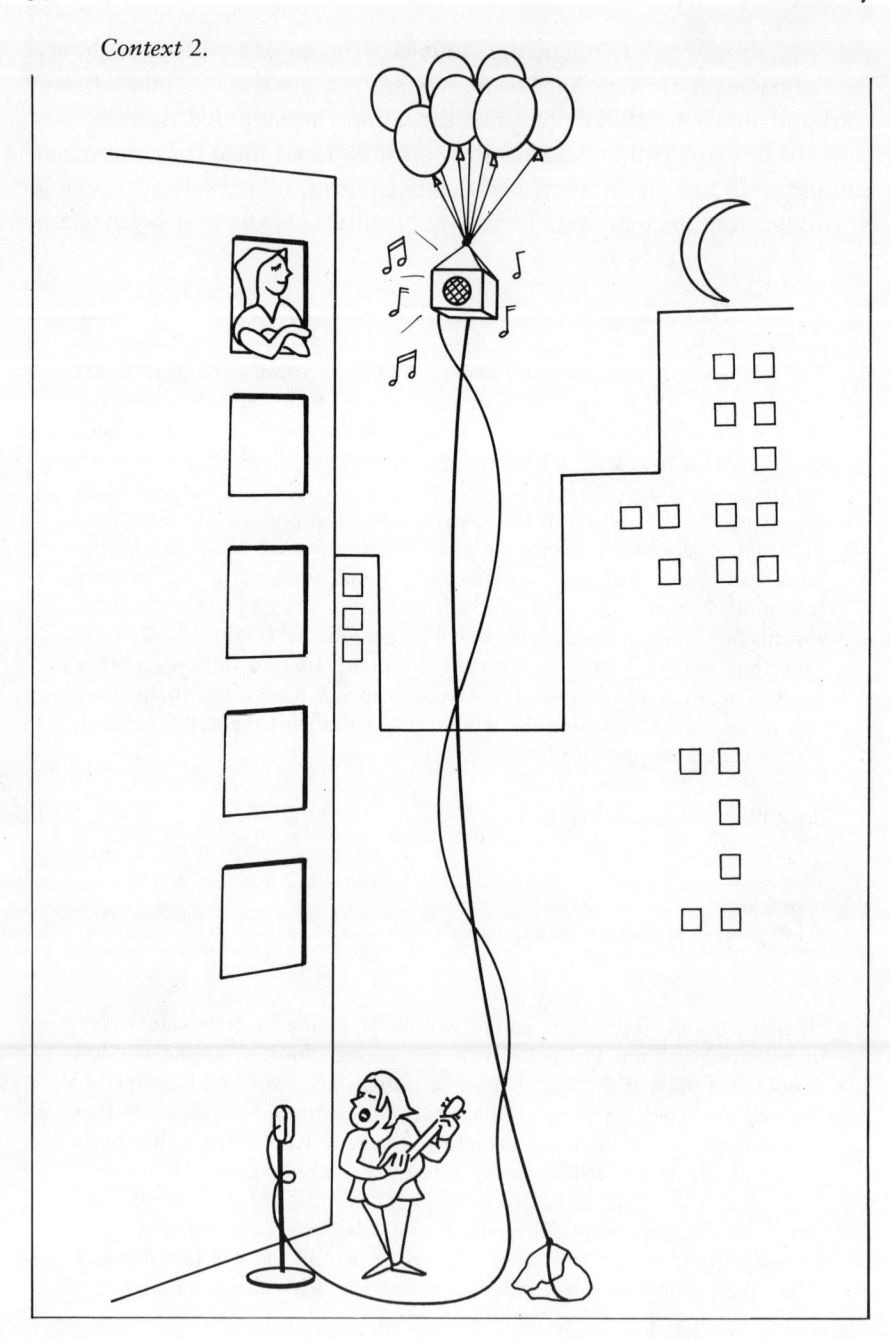

Adapted from Bransford & Johnson, 1972

text for the passages before they heard the passage, and other experimental subjects were given the context for the passage after they heard it.

The control subjects rated the passages low in comprehensibility and didn't recall much of the material. The subjects who were given the context after the passage performed at just about the same levels as the control subjects. The subjects who were given the context before they heard the passage, on the other hand, were helped greatly by it. They rated the passage as being much more comprehensible than did the control subjects, and they recalled about twice as much from the passage. Similar results were reported by Dooling and Mullet (1973).

Based on the script notion, the explanation of these findings is relatively straightforward. In the washing clothes passage, the hearer has a script available, but the passage is written so that there are no cues as to what script might be relevant. There are no concrete nouns or verbs in the passage, so the topic is effectively hidden. In the ballons passage, things are more concrete, but in this case the person does not have a script available, since the event is novel. So in both cases the person is left without a script, and confusion and lack of recall follows. When one reads the two passages without context, one gets a particularly clear example of how scripts are important in comprehension. Without a script, everything gets lumped together, and one is quickly ready to throw up one's hands in frustration. A more graphic example of the importance of knowledge in comprehension could hardly be given.

3.5 Recall and reconstruction: summary

From the results reviewed in the last few sections, one could conclude that what is stored when verbal material is processed is something like the meaning of the material, and that individual sentences are totally lost in all this. This conclusion is made especially attractive by three findings. The first is that subjects can't distinguish inferences from sentences that were actually presented (Johnson, Bransford, & Solomon, 1973). The second is that the four-idea sentences were recognized most often in the Bransford and Franks (1971) experiment, even though such sentences had never been presented. These findings are comparable to what has been found concerning the encodings stored for individual words, discussed in the last chapter. Finally, we have seen that comprehension of prose passages depends on matching the material with a script in order to make sense out of it. These sections could be summarized by saying that recall of sentences and prose passages may be a reconstruction based on the script which was activated in comprehending the material. From this point of view, "encoding" material would entail matching it with a script.

Based on the results discussed so far, it is undeniably true that one's knowledge plays an important role in comprehension and recall of verbal material. However, recent evidence also shows that one can sometimes still recall the specific verbal material that was presented. Thus, if scripts are used to comprehend verbal inputs, the verbal input itself also plays a role in recall.

3.6. Interpretation and nothing else?

Before one completely accepts the idea that nothing about the actual sentences or words is remembered, some other data must be considered. In an interesting series of studies, Kolers (e.g., 1975) has investigated the retention of sentences that were read by subjects. In one study, half of a list of sentences was printed normally, while the others were printed in inverted form—that is, they were printed upside down and backwards (Kolers & Ostry, 1974). Recognition for the sentences was tested by presenting some old sentences in the same orientation as they were in the original list, while other old sentences were presented in the opposite orientation. Speed to read the sentences was the measure of recognition.

Perhaps surprisingly, Kolers and Ostry (1974) found that recognition was best when an old sentence was re-presented in its original orientation even after 32 days. That is, inverted test sentences were read faster if they had been inverted in the original list 32 days earlier. These results indicate that subjects had some memory for the exact form of the sentences. A number of other studies have also found that memory for sentences contains information about the surface form as well as the meaning (e.g., Anderson, 1974a). Thus, one cannot conclude that the act of studying verbal material entails storing information about the meaning of the material and nothing else.

Meaning and wording. Much of the support for a reconstructive view of memory comes from studies such as that of Sachs (1967), in which subjects have difficulty recognizing changes in the wording of sentences, so long as these changes don't affect meaning. This is taken as evidence that the meaning of the sentence is what is encoded and is what determines recognition. However, there is one problem with such studies that raises some questions about whether meaning alone is the crucial determinant of recognition. In most, if not all, of the studies discussed so far, the restructured test sentences contain the same words as the original sentence. (This can be seen in the example sentences in section 3.2.) therefore, the recognition sentence which has the same underlying meaning also contains the same major content words as the original sentence. Thus, the reason that the subject is confused might be at least in part because the same words were involved.

If the meaning alone were the crucial determinant of recognition, then subjects ought to be confused by a sentence that contained different words but was equivalent in meaning to the original sentence. That is, they should think that the new sentence was in the passage. However, a recent study by Hayes-Roth and Hayes-Roth (1977) demonstrated that subjects in a memory experiment will still be able to say that the new sentence (same meaning but new words) is different from an old one. Therefore, the words are part of what is stored, which supports the results from Kolers's research discussed in the last section.

Finally, two important recent studies have graphically demonstrated that specific information can be recalled after a passage has been comprehended (Anderson & Pichert, 1978; Hasher & Griffin, 1978). In the Anderson and Pichert study, subjects heard a description of a house as part of a longer story about two boys playing hooky from school. The subjects were told to read the story from one of two points of view: half read the story from the point of view of a perspective buyer of the house in question, and the other subjects took the perspective of a potential burglar. After reading the story, all the subjects were asked to recall as much of the story as they could; recall differences were found, depending on the point of view taken by the subject. For example, prospective homebuyers recalled that the roof leaked, while prospective burglars recalled that the family had a valuable coin collection. So far, these results support the notion that recall depends on the activated schemas and the interpretation given the story. Anderson and Pichert then asked the subjects to recall the story again, but this time the subjects were told to use the other perspective. If it were true that recall of details depended solely on schemas activated at input, then switching the subject's perspective should make little or no difference in recall, because the switch comes after the story has been listened to. However, Anderson and Pichert found that switching perspectives resulted in subjects recalling details from the story that they had been unable to recall the first time, indicating once again that details are stored, independent of the interpretation given the story. Hasher and Griffin got similar results, using a slightly different situation.

Summary. As we saw earlier, a number of studies have indicated that the surface forms of sentences are not retained for very long, and that all memory for sentences is based on their meanings or interpretations. Further research indicated that subjects often could go beyond the meaning of each specific sentence, sometimes combining the meanings of related sentences, and sometimes bringing in other information based on the presented sentences. From these sorts of studies, some investigators argued that comprehending a verbal message entailed working through a script and retaining nothing about the specific form of the message and that all recall of verbal information was based on reconstruction from stored meanings. This seems to be too strong a conclusion. There is evidence that there is also some storage of the surface form of specific messages and that this information can also contribute to recall.

3.7 Knowledge and reconstruction in recall

From the discussion in the last few sections, it seems that two sorts of information are encoded when an individual goes through some experience: specific information from the event itself, and additional information concerning things that the person thought about when the event occurred, as the result of the match between the input and the person's scripts. These two sorts of information must somehow be sorted out and used to produce some specific response on a recall test. This is the reconstruction process that has been mentioned several times already and was discussed by Bartlett (1932). It also corresponds closely to the point of view outlined in chapters 1 and 2.

Let us now consider in detail how all this information can be used to guide later recall, by moving away from experiments concerning recall of verbal materials and examining some research concerning the ability of a chess master to recall the positions of the pieces in a chess game. This is a concrete example of reconstruction based on knowledge, as Bartlett discussed, that yields some additional insight as to what might be occurring with the recall of verbal materials.

Chess masters' recall. Chess masters have an extraordinary ability to recall the pieces on a chess board. In the basic task, the master is shown a board with pieces on it for five seconds. This board is then removed, and the master is given an empty board and a set of pieces. The task is to put the pieces in the positions they occupied on the just-seen board. Even a very brief glance at a board with twenty-five or thirty pieces on it is suf-

Reconstruction and recall

ficient to produce near-perfect recall by a master, so long as the position of the pieces is taken from a game played by other chess masters (DeGroot, 1966; Chase & Simon, 1973; Simon & Gilmartin, 1973). The game in question does not have to be familiar to the master doing the recall, but it must have been played by masters; if the pattern of chess pieces comes from a game played by weak players, the master's recall will be much poorer than with the position from a master game. In addition, if the same pieces are simply randomly placed on the board, then the master's recall is no better than that of the nonplayer. In summary, the chess master doesn't simply have a great memory; the master has a great memory for master-level chess positions. This would indicate that the master's knowledge about chess must play a large role in producing the great recall. This point has been elaborated by Simon and his colleagues (e.g., Chase & Simon, 1973; Simon & Gilmartin, 1973).

Chess masters' knowledge. Simon and his colleagues argue that the master's memory ability is due to the master's knowledge of patterns of chess pieces. Through years of play and study, the master has acquired a voluminous knowledge about the patterns of pieces that appear in master-level chess games. Therefore, the test board is initially examined on the basis of this knowledge, and recall then depends on the use of this same knowledge. In other words, the master possesses many scripts for master-level games.

The model of Simon and his colleagues can be outlined as follows. The master scans the test board, and in so doing finds familiar patterns. Whenever such a pattern is found, it is assumed that the name of that pattern is stored in "working memory," a store with a capacity of only five to seven names. The master keeps scanning the board until all the familiar patterns have been found, or until no more pattern-names can fit in working memory, or until time runs out. At recall, the process is reversed. The master retrieves the name of one pattern from working memory and uses the name to place the pieces on the board. Another pattern-name would then be retrieved, and those pieces replaced, and so on. This would continue until no more pattern names were left in working memory. In this formulation, the model would correspond closely to the views of other theorists concerning the recall of categorized word lists (see section 1.5). In this case also it is assumed that the person stores category names, which come to mind when the list is presented. So long as the set of category names is relatively small (as in the chess situation), the person can recall the category names, and recall the specific words from the category names. Thus, models of recall in two very different areas—chess playing and organized lists of words—postulate very similar processes. This point of view is also similar to the concept of scripts just discussed.

The model of Simon and his colleagues is simple and straightforward, and it provides a concrete example of how one's knowledge can be applied to a recall situation. However, there is one critical assumption which plays an important role in this model, and which must be considered further. Simon is one of the foremost researchers in the area of computer simulation of human behavior. The model of the chess master's recall has been developed as a computer program (Simon & Gilmartin, 1973). In such a model, it is very convenient to use a label to designate each pattern of pieces, because it enables one to store and retrieve the relevant information easily. However, a problem arises here, because chess masters do not have labels for every pattern that they can recognize. If there are no names for patterns, then the Simon and Gilmartin model loses much of its appeal. (It is sometimes stated that "nonverbal labels" could be used to refer to patterns, but it is not clear what a "nonverbal label" might be. The notion is unambiguous in a computer program, but not in a model of human memory.)

Second, the notion that a pattern of pieces is represented by a label is very similar to the notion that a word is represented by a node in memory. We saw some problems with this idea in the last chapter, and further problems will be raised in chapter 8. It is also important to emphasize that recall of verbal material does not always depend on recall of category names. For example, in section 1.6 we examined "subjective organization" of random lists of words. In this case, the person has no ready-made labels available, but knowledge and organization still play a role in recall. In addition, it is probably true that many of the scripts that we possess are not coded verbally. Therefore, by considering recall without specific labels, we shall be able to make conclusions with wider relevance. The specific situation in which verbal category labels are available would then be a specific case of the more general use of knowledge in recall. Therefore, let us consider further what might happen if there were no labels to refer to patterns of chess pieces.

Scanning chess boards and "scanning" memory. If there are no pattern names, it would mean that after scanning the board, there would be no simple summary available to the chess master to serve as the basis for reconstruction of what was seen. In order to outline a plausible model of how recall might occur without a verbal or nonverbal summary, imag-

Reconstruction and recall

ine the initial scanning of the board by the chess master. Since the chess board is too large to be seen in detail with one glance, the master must use a series of eye movements to examine it. Simon and Barenfeld (1969) have argued that the master's chess knowledge is used to direct the scanning of the board in the first place. The master uses knowledge about the importance of the various pieces, and about attack and defense, in order to examine the board. That is, the master looks for the important pieces and the relationships between them.

We could also assume that the master uses exactly the same information to recall the board. That is, since the master examined the board initially with a series of visual fixations, then recall of the position might depend on the master's ability to regenerate this sequence of fixations. Thus, what we need is a method whereby the sequence of fixations might be retrieved from memory. (One interesting point to note here is that people who do things like play chess or bridge well can usually recount a recent game in great detail, even though they have made no conscious attempt to remember it. This would indicate that something in the way they play the game itself results in their ability to recall it later. This makes it plausible to tie together the master's chess-playing knowledge and recall performance.)

Assume for simplicity that at some point during the initial scanning of the board, the chess master noted that the position came from the middle of a game. At recall, this information initiates the recall attempt. If the board position came from the middle of a game, then the master now has expectations about what pieces might have been where. These expectations are a set of cues which can be used to retrieve specific fixations from memory. Let us assume further that the master remembers that the black king was in such and such a position. There are now several other potential cues available, which would come from the master's expectations as to what other pieces ought to be on the board and where they ought to be in relation to the black king. Each of these possibilities would point to only a small number of possible fixations, and so if one of those fixations had indeed occurred when the master looked at the board, it would now be retrievable. In this way, the master would work through the possible patterns that might have occurred. At each step, knowledge about what might have occurred would be combined with information in memory, so that recall would go beyond simply guessing. Thus there is a combination of two different sorts of information, the general knowledge from past experience (the script), as well as the specific information from the just-seen board. Both of these are necessary to generate accurate recall. The difference between the master and the novice is twofold, based on this analysis. First, the novice would probably not efficiently scan the board intitally, due to lack of experience. However, even if the novice did look at all the pieces on the board, there would not be a specific enough set of cues available to retrieve any specific piece or pieces. The situation is comparable to that which occurs when a person reads a long list of words without generating a set of summary cues. Without summary cues, there is not enough specific information available to retrieve any specific words, if we discount recency. With summary cues, small groups of words can be retrieved separately, just as the master retrieves small groups of pieces.

To summarize, we can explain how the chess master can reconstruct the series of fixations from memory if we assume that the specific cue for each specific fixation comes from the master's knowledge of what to look for next. This knowledge is used to determine what to try to remember next.

Recall and knowledge: perception "turned inward." Although a chess master's ability to recall chess positions is related to knowledge about chess, we all go through exactly the same sort of activity whenever we recall anything. For example, consider again the importance of category organization and grouping in recall, as discussed in chapter 1. One's knowledge about categories works in exactly the same way when one is recalling a list of words as the chess master's knowledge works when he or she is recalling a chess position. Given that one can remember the category names that one thought about while the list was presented, then these categories can serve to retrieve the specific words, exactly as the chess master retrieves the specific pieces.

These sorts of examples could probably be multiplied many times by considering the way that we remember things in our ordinary lives. For example, if I go to the park with our son, I can probably recall what we did in the park better if I know the park well. This would be because my knowledge (my script for "going to the park") would give me a set of retrieval cues to help remember just what we did today. As another example, someone who knows a lot of psychology would be better at remembering the content of an article in a psychological journal than someone who didn't know as much psychology. As a still further example, a knowledgeable mechanic would probably remember the sequence of events involved in fixing a car better than a novice, even if the mechanic only observed someone else fix the car. This general point of view will also be

Reconstruction and recall

important in the discussion of the role of imagery in recall, to be discussed in chapter 7.

In all these cases, it is important to reemphasize that the person is not simply guessing. Knowledge plays a role, as has been noted, but not by itself: that would simply be educated guessing. Presumably, in the cases which we have discussed, knowledge is being used to cue the specific information in the person's memory. The distinction which we have made here between specific experiences and general knowledge is an important one in recent cognitive theorizing. In the literature, general knowledge is sometimes called "semantic memory," while specific experiences are called "episodic memory" (Tulving, 1972). In the next chapter we shall consider in some detail the relation between general knowledge and specific experiences.

One point that bears reemphasis here is that exactly the same knowledge is involved in both perception and recall in these various situations. To return again to the chess master, the same information that is used to scan the board in the first place is used to recall what was seen. If the scanning of the board and identification of familiar configurations is an example of perception, then the recall process could be looked upon as "perception turned inward." This point of view will be elaborated further in chapters 5, 6, and 7.

3.8 On the function of retrieval cues

Chapter 2 began with a consideration of the dual-process, or the generate and test, model of recognition and recall. In the course of the discussion, it was argued that such a model was not adequate, because it does not seem that marked nodes are retrieved and tested at recall. The notion of retrieval of an encoding was brought forth as an alternative. The discussion in the present chapter has been concerned with how one's knowledge is used in order to retrieve encodings. However, there is still one point that ought to be discussed concerning how cues work to bring about the retrieval of an encoding. In the discussion of the chess player's recall, it was argued that the master has knowledge available about likely patterns on a chess board, and this knowledge can be used to retrieve the specific fixations that were seen on the just-displayed board. This knowledge could serve to retrieve specific fixations in at least two ways. On the one hand, the knowledge could serve to provide a set of alternatives, which could each be examined and tested for recency. However, this is simply a restatement of the dual-process model rejected in the last chapter.

Retrieval cues could also work in another way, which does not entail the assumption that alternatives are tested one at a time. An analogy can make this possibility clear. Assume that you are trying to attract a paper clip with a magnet, but you cannot bring the magnet close enough to the clip to attract it. One way to get the clip might be to bring a second magnet to bear, thus increasing the field and attracting the clip. Retrieval cues could work in this way. Let's say that the recency and context of the memory problem just presented to the chess master is enough to separate out those fixations from all those that the master saw earlier. However, since all of these fixations are relatively recent, and from the same context, no specific fixation can be pulled out of the mass, even though the entire group of recent fixations is "primed" and ready to be recalled. When the master begins to work through the knowledge of chess positions, this adds an additional source of "pull" on the fixations in memory. In this way, those fixations which meet the criteria of (a) having recently occurred in this situation, and (b) being likely in the middle of a game, would be "pulled out" of the pack and "recalled." In this way, one doesn't have to talk about generation and test as two separate steps. Rather, one can assume that relevant fixations will usually be recalled because only relevant fixations are being "pulled" by both sorts of cues—recency and context information, and chess knowledge.

In summary, the cues can be conceived of as working in one step, with the "testing" occurring through the action of the contextual-recency information. Estes (1975) presents an interesting discussion of this issue.

3.9 Summary and conclusions

If recall depends on encodings or interpretations of events, then recall is a two-step operation. First, the encoding must be retrieved, and second, the original event must be decoded from this encoding. This chapter has examined some recent research concerned with how a specific event is recalled. At one extreme is the reconstruction view, which is often attributed to Barlett (1932), and which has recently come into favor again. This view argues that all we have available at recall are the things that the event made us think about or do, and the original event must be reconstructed from this. (It should be noted again that the view that everything is reconstructed from an encoding is not strictly Bartlett's view, although recent

Reconstruction and recall

theorists often attribute such a view to him. In his own writings, Bartlett seemed to say that parts of the original event were also available to help guide the reconstruction [pp.89, 209]. This is the position we have arrived at in this chapter.)

Some evidence to support the extreme reconstructivist position comes from recent studies of sentence memory that show that subjects often incorrectly "recognize" sentences, if these new sentences fit the meaning of an original sentence, without being physically identical to an original sentence. However, there is evidence that the specific form of the original event is important also. It seems that in many cases the critical sentences were so designed that both meaning and wording were contributing to recall. When the two are carefully controlled, the specific form of the original sentence does seem to play a role in recognition of a sentence. Thus, as in the last chapter, we are led to the conclusion that dealing with a given environmental event, such as the presentation of a word or a sentence in an experiment, is a complex and multifaceted activity.

There are two further points. The discussion in this chapter indicates that any given experience can serve to initiate many different activities on the part of a subject. All these various activities can play a role in what the subject remembers later, but in order to do so, the various sorts of information must each be recallable when needed. That is, one possible reason that verbatim recall does not always occur with sentences is because the specific words are more difficult to recall than an image that the sentence might make the person think of. The next chapter considers further the idea that certain aspects of an event might be more recallable than others.

Finally, psychologists interested in memory sometimes say that they are interested in such questions as: "What is stored when a word is presented?" In a related mode, one comes across discussions of whether words or images are stored in memory. Based on the discussion in the last two chapters, it might be better to rephrase such questions slightly. It isn't really a question of whether one "stores" the words in a sentence, so much as it is one of whether or not you can remember what words you just read. Although this isn't a great change in emphasis, the perspective is shifted slightly, and may lead to different sorts of explanations. When one asks if one can remember the specific words that were read, this leads to questions about what the act of reading might entail, and why one might not be able to recall the specifics of one act of reading. In the same way, rather than asking "Are images stored?" one could ask if a subject can remember a specific event that had been imagined. This again leads to further questions about what imagining something entails, and how an imagined event might be remembered or forgotten. This point will be considered further in chapter 7.

In conclusion, words aren't things that are taken in and stored. Indeed, no external event is taken in and stored. Rather, external events can be examined, and they can make us do various things, including making us think. The question of interest becomes how we are able to remember what we did at a given time.

4
Time and some related issues

4.0 Introduction

The temporal order of events is an important component of our psychological experience, as is the perception of intervals of time. The concept of time has also played an important background role in theorizing. The most well-known use of temporal concepts in theorizing is the use of contiguity, or closeness in time, as an explanation for associations between ideas. It could be argued that before contiguity in time could have an effect, the organism would have to be able to keep track of the temporal sequence of events. Thus, associations would be based on our ability to group events in time.

We have had occasion to invoke "time" in explanations at several points in the earlier chapters. The most important of these points concerned the role of recency in memory.

However, although temporal concepts may be indirectly important in psychological theorizing, there has only been sporadic direct interest in this area among psychologists. One purpose of the present chapter is to consider how it is that we can order events in time, and how this is related to our perception of the duration of a temporal interval. The conclusions from this discussion will then serve to illuminate some of the concepts discussed in earlier chapters, as well as providing background for the discussion in part 2.

Memory for temporal order. We can begin with a study by Yntema and Trask (1963), which was concerned with memory for temporal order. They presented subjects with a deck of 220 cards, with two words on each card. Half the cards were test cards, which contained two test words. The subject attempted to identify which of the test words had occurred more recently in the list. Some of the words were new items, which the subject had not seen on the training list. For the other test words, the number of words since their original presentation (the "lag") was systematically varied. The results showed that subjects could judge the relative recencies of the test words with reasonable accuracy. Let us arbitrarily designate the two words on a test card as A and B. If the lag since the original presentation of A was 32 items, then B with a lag of 8 items was judged more recent than A 75 percent of the time. By the same token, if B had a lag of 136 items, A with a lag of 32 was chosen more recent 75 percent of the time. If one item was new, then the old item was judged more recent 75 percent of the time even with a lag of 136 items. So while performance was not perfect, the temporal discrimination was reasonably good.

From a theoretical point of view, the interesting aspect of this experiment is that there seems to be no way to construct the temporal order logically from the stimuli. One can sometimes deduce temporal order because of some characteristic of the events in question (e.g., I know I mowed the front lawn last because I remember that it was almost dark as I finished it, and I remember that it was light when I finished mowing the front, and I know I mowed both the front and back). With the Yntema and Trask procedure, such inferences do not seem possible, because there are no external cues available from which order could be deduced. In conclusion, the study by Yntema and Trask was important because it indicated that temporal order could be discriminated by people in a memory experiment without any external temporal cues. These basic findings have been replicated several times.

4.1 Models of temporal order in memory

We can now briefly consider several possible explanations for the ability of people to order events in time, as demonstrated by Yntema and Trask. One possible explanation is that some sort of verbal cues are used to label the temporal order of events. If so, then comparing verbal labels would give one temporal order. A second possibility is that events are somehow automatically "tagged" nonverbally in memory concerning their order of occurrence. According to such a view, temporal order could also be determined directly from the memories themselves. Finally, we shall consider the view that temporal order can't be determined from the memories directly, but rather must be obtained by somehow comparing the memories to some standard, which allows one to deduce their relative order of occurrence.

Verbal cues to temporal order. Anderson and Bower (1972) seem to assume that temporal order can be remembered through the use of covert verbalizations. They were particularly concerned with the temporal order of words from a single free-recall list, and they theorized that such a list could be subdivided into *early words, middle words,* and *last words.* These verbal cues would be included as part of the encoding for each word. One could then determine which of the words was more recent by comparing the verbal time tags encoded with each of them.

This sort of a model may be plausible when considering acquisition of a single free-recall list, and it may be able to explain the results of Yntema and Trask, but it will not do if we wish to explain the ordering of events outside the laboratory. For example, we can remember some of what we did today, some of what we did yesterday, and some of what we did the day before, and we can do a reasonable job of determining what events occurred on what day. However, it is difficult to conceive of any sort of verbalization which could support this type of ordering. Extending the single list situation to a sequence of days, one might say that events are tagged as occurring "today," "yesterday," "day before yesterday," and so on. The crucial problem for this sort of an explanation is that events which occurred yesterday were tagged as occurring "today" when they occurred. Since everything is tagged as occurring "today," there is no ordering possible based on such tags.

Absolute time. An alternate point of view would argue that our experiences are somehow automatically stored in an ordered list, based on their order of arrival. Such a model would explain Yntema and Trask's results in the following way. When a test card is presented, the subject begins to search the encodings in order, starting from the present and going "backward" into the past. Therefore, the item that is "found" first is the most recent item. One problem for this model is that it predicts too high a level of performance. According to a model based on temporal ordering in memory, the very act of encoding an item adequately enough for recognition or recall insures that the memory trace is laid down in temporal order. Therefore, if an item is recalled or recognized at all, its temporal position is automatically known. If this is true, then a subject should not be able to correctly recognize an item without being able to designate its temporal position. However, an experiment by Winograd (1968) demonstrated that subjects could do just that.

In addition, this absolute time model may predict that items never seen before ought to be recognized as being very old, which is the opposite of what Yntema and Trask found. This prediction would come from the assumption that the subject searches backwards in order through the encodings from the list until one of the items from the test card is found. Since a new item isn't encoded in memory, the other item on the test card will always be found before the new item is. Therefore, the new item should be judged as being very old, which is not what occurs.

A still further difficulty for this temporal memory model is that discrimination in the Yntema and Trask study got worse as the recency of the two items decreased. If the lag since the more recent item was zero (that is, if the more recent item had just been presented), then the most recent item was correctly chosen 100 percent of the time, even if the other item had a lag of four. However, if the lags were four and eight, then the more recent item was chosen correctly only about 70 percent of the time. Thus, a difference in lag of four items became more difficult to discriminate as the items became less recent. According to the temporal memory model, the discrimination between lags of four and eight should have been as good as the discrimination between lags of zero and four items. In sum, these various findings make it unlikely that a simple temporal memory model will be adequate.

Reconstructive time. Let us now consider the notion that memory for temporal order is derived *from* encodings, but is not directly represented *in* encodings. That is, temporal order is derived from information encoded when an item is presented, but there is no "time tag" per se. In order to reconstruct time from information in memory, one needs some sort of a scale on which to compare the encodings which are to be ordered. This implies that we need some sort of reference point to which the two memories can be compared. One reference point that seems worth considering would be time present. That is, perhaps memories are scaled for recency by comparing them in some way with how things are now. The memory which is most similar to the way things are now, in some yet-to-be-specified way, is the most recent memory. By ordering a group of memories on the basis of their similarity to the present, one gets a time scale. Obviously, this brief outline raises further questions. First of all, what is this "present" that is being used to scale other memories? Secondly, if memories can be more or less similar to the present, there must be some aspect that is changing, and so can serve to make memories more or less similar. What is this change that is involved? Let us now consider these questions.

4.2 The psychological present: the psychological state

In order to see what sort of information might be involved in temporal judgment, consider a subject who is studying a list of words. In this case, we shall assume that for each word, the subject produced a referential encoding, as discussed in chapter 2. The first thing to note about these encodings is that they do not contain the sort of information needed for recency judgment. Each encoding is different from the others, and there is no way of telling which came first. Thus, we must assume that although the subject is conscious only of making the encoding, other information must automatically be included in the encoding. This information might be of the following sort. At any given time, there are a host of events, both internal and external, which are occurring, and which are represented in the nervous system. (A related idea has been proposed by Anderson & Bower, 1972, and Bower, 1972.) For example, one feels a certain degree of hunger, and/or a certain degree of fatigue. One may be tense or relaxed, and so on. All these events could be combined together to form the "psychological state" of the person, or the psychological present. In addition, there may be other bodily changes, such as cyclical or rhythmical changes, that are represented in the nervous system, but of which we are not conscious. These too may be incorporated into the encoding given an item. If so, then it might be possible that the entire "state of the brain" at any given time is made part of any conscious encoding. In any case, the item is encoded against the "background" of the psychological state of the organism at any given time.

It is also possible to assume that information from recently occurring events are also part of the background for a given encoding (e.g., Estes, 1975). This notion will be considered later. For the present, we shall assume that only one "item," plus background information, is present in a given encoding.

Changes in the psychological state: from present to past. The important thing about this background, or contextual, information is that it is constantly changing. For example, one gets more or less fatigued as the list of words goes on, one may get hungrier, and so on. Therefore, as two encodings get farther apart in time, their backgrounds will be less and less similar, and as a given encoding gets less and less recent, its background will become less similar to the present background. In this way, one can order encodings along a dimension of similarity to the present, and this could serve as the basis for our sense of time (Bower, 1973; Estes, 1959). In addition, if two items come from the beginning of the list, they occurred long ago as far as the list is concerned, and they are both relatively different from the present. It would then be difficult to discriminate their recencies, because both are so different from the present. This means that there ought to be a whole group of items in the recent past which one would have difficulty discriminating from each other as far as recency is concerned. In addition, according to this model, if two items come near the end of the list, and therefore are very recent, then it is easier to tell them apart than two comparably-spaced items at the beginning of the list. These predictions fit the findings of a number of experiments on judgments of relative recency, most notably that of Yntema and Trask.

Background information, psychological states, time, and recall. Let us very briefly look at the sorts of evidence that are supportive of various aspects of this model of temporal ordering. The model assumes that bodily changes play a role in determining the temporal ordering of events. Therefore, if retrieval of an encoding depends on a match with what has been stored, then bodily states ought to play a role in recall. One study with human subjects investigated this (Rand & Wapner, 1967). Subjects studied a list of words either standing or lying down. A recall test was then given, and half the subjects recalled in the same posture as they had originally studied the words, while the other subjects recalled the words in the posture different from the original one. The results showed that better recall occurred if the subject's posture was the same for both study and recall. This supports the idea that "postural cues" serve as aids to retrieval because they are also part of the original encodings.

Other studies which might also be relevant here are those concerning "state-dependent" learning in humans and animals (see Hilgard & Bower, 1975, pp.514–516). In such studies, an organism learns something while under the influence of a drug. It has been found that recall of this material is most efficient if the organism is under the influence of the drug at recall. This indicates that some aspect of the subject's state under the influence of the drug was incorporated into the memories of the events. If the state at recall was similar to the state at learning, it might be expected to facilitate retrieval.

In summary, these sorts of results support the notion that the state of the organism enters into the encoding produced when an item is studied during an experiment.

4.3 Background information, retrieval, and associations

We can now take this idea concerning the role of background information in encodings, and use it to tie together some of the topics which were considered earlier.

Recency again. The importance of recency as a retrieval cue has been discussed in several places in these chapters on memory. It is obvious that if recency does indeed play an important role as a cue, then it must do so through the background information. Recency might be an effective retrieval cue because the last few words in a list have much background information in common with the state of the subject when recall is asked for. Rundus (1971) reported that the recency effect in free recall is made up of those words that were being rehearsed when recall was asked for. Therefore, all of these words would be essentially identical in background information, and thus would be very similar to the state when recall begins. Therefore, one important factor in the recall of these words would be that the background information is very similar to that of the state of the person at recall. That is, it is being argued that one reason the very recent events can be almost effortlessly recalled is because there is such a strong "pull" from the present.

Associations. The notion that ideas are linked to each other by means of the "gentle force" of association was an important one in the empiricist philosophy that strongly influenced American psychology. Associations are still with us today, although the association may now be between a stimulus and a response, or a response and reinforcement, or between two nodes in memory, rather than an association between ideas.

There is one problem which remains after one explains some given behavior on the basis of associations between items. If one demonstrates that, after A and B have been presented together many times, there results a situation in which presenting A makes a person say B, one hasn't said why this comes about. One has not produced a psychological mechanism that can explain the association itself. Why indeed do associations occur? Why is it that pairing items in experience results in a tendency for one item to be a cue for the other?

It is sometimes assumed that the associative connection between two items is literally a connection between the items. For example, Pavlov originally argued that salivary conditioning came about because when two brain centers were activated at the same time by external stimuli, a pathway was formed between them. Once such a pathway was formed, activation in one brain center could spread to the other, and the second brain center would then be activated without its original stimulus being present. In this sort of a view, the association is brought about by an actual neural link being formed between the centers of excitation representing the stimuli in question. An idea very similar to this exists in cognitive theorizing today, when theorists describe associations by drawing arrows between nodes in memory. We shall see examples of this in chapter 8. In any case, we can see here that the use of the term association is as a literal link between the "items" in question.

In these sorts of explanations there is at least an implicit assumption that, on a psychological level, one can go no deeper than simply talking about frequency of pairings in past experience. That is, a path is set up because neural circuits work that way, and there isn't much that psychologists can say. However, let us take some of the ideas discussed in the last few sections and try to apply them to the notion of an association, to see if we can go any deeper. First of all, let us go back to the discussion of interference in chapter 1. One very important point that came out of that discussion was that one could have interference between two memories without any interaction among the memories themselves. In the model developed in chapter 1, if a given cue is not specific enough, it may be relevant to more than one response. When that happens, and no differentiation can be made, interference occurs. However, the two memories do not interact; there is no path between the two memories, and one memory doesn't "write over" the other.

Let us now extend this sort of reasoning to the discussion of associations. That is, perhaps there is no link formed between items when they are paired in one's experience. Even though one item serves as a cue for the other, the items might be independent of each other. Thus, there might not be anything specific that actually *is* the association. Items can be associated, in the sense that one item can become a reliable cue for another. But on a deeper level, the association itself has no independent existence. There is no "path," literally or figuratively, between the items.

Let us consider this a bit further. We have assumed that background information can play a role in recall, because of the strong effect that recency can have on memory. If this argument is at all reasonable, then perhaps the same mechanism serves as the basis for association through contiguity. That is, if two events occur in close succession, especially a number of times in close succession, then there should be a large overlap in the background information in their encodings (Estes, 1959; Bower, 1972). The encoding for one item could then serve as the cue for the other item, through overlap of background information. The situation would be comparable to the influence of recency on recall of the most recent words in a list. In summary, we could have two words associated without their being an actual link of any sort between them. The association comes about because of the background information which they have in common.

This conclusion has some important implications. In the last chapter, it was argued that retrieval cues work because they provide an additional source of "pull" which can assist in the retrieval of specific encodings. This discussion of background elements points out one way in which this "pull" can come about. If two items have been strongly associated in the past, then the background information that they have in common could make it much more likely that one item would lead to the recall of the second. There are other ways in which cues could work, or course, but this might be one way. Based on this notion, then, one item "primes" the recall of another because, in some sense, the two items are partly the same item, due to their overlap in background information. In the same way, we shall argue in the next two chapters that perception of one item may make it easier to perceive certain other items. This "priming" by background elements could play a role here also, as we shall see in the later discussion.

4.4 Developing general knowledge from specific experiences: episodic versus semantic memory

Tulving (1972) has argued that there are two different sorts of memory systems. One type is concerned with specific personal experiences, each of which is recorded separately in a sort of autobiographical record, called "episodic memory." It consists of a chain of episodes. Some examples of the types of things available in episodic memory would be: last night we went to a party; the day before yesterday I played tennis with my father; I just heard the telephone ring.

The other type of storage is not based on specific personal experiences, but has to do with more general information about concepts and their interrelations. The specific time and place at which the information was acquired is not available. Tulving calls this type of storage "semantic memory," a term used by many investigators to refer to information stored about words and their meanings. Two examples of information from semantic memory would be: I know the words to "Mary Had a Little Lamb"; broad-leaved weeds grow in hot weather. As far as each of these examples is concerned, I can recall no specific time at which the information was acquired. The knowledge of the chess master concerning patterns of chess pieces is also information in semantic memory. The discussion in the last chapter concerning the way in which general knowledge is used to recall specific experiences is one example of the interaction between semantic and episodic memories.

Tulving also argued that these types of memories exist because there may be two types of memory stores, as mentioned. The memory store concerned with episodic memory is sensitive to the perceptual features of individual unique events, while the semantic memory store is concerned with the more general conceptual relations that are represented by an event. The specific characteristics of an event are usually ignored, and only its more general aspects are stored.

However, before we assume that general knowledge develops because the semantic memory system stores only general aspects of events, it might be interesting to consider the possibility that all events are stored in the same way. General knowledge, which is not tied down to any specific context, might then come about through the way in which memory works, rather than there being some specific difference between general and specific knowledge. It should be noted that Tulving did not place very strong emphasis on the distinction between two separate memory *stores*. He seemed to make the distinction as much for convenience as for anything else. In any case, this is an important issue, because the notion of general knowledge will be important in several later chapters, and it has already played a role in earlier chapters.

Interference and general knowledge. It has been argued that any experience is stored in memory as an encoding plus background information. Furthermore, in order to recall any one specific encoding, it is necessary that cues be available that will "spring" that encoding from among all those which have been stored. There are two sorts of information which can be used as cues with human subjects. On the one hand, one can use information about the encoding itself, such as "Do you remember the words from the experiment you were in today?" If you had only one experience of studying some words in an experiment today, then this cue could be sufficient. On the other hand, background information can also be used to bring about the retrieval of an experience. For example, if the experiment had taken place in a distinctive room, which you had never been in before or since, then returning to that room could serve to cue the experience of studying the list. Reproducing the specific bodily state that obtained at that time might also help to reinstate the whole experience of studying the list.

Let us now take the general notion of interference that was developed in chapter 1 and try to apply it to the development of general knowledge from specific experiences. As an example, let us assume that a person meets someone new and hears that person's name being used in several different situations. In each of these situations, there are three components which are of particular importance to the present discussion: (1) the appearance of the new person; (2) the sound of the new person's name; and (3) the background information from each separate encounter with the person and the name. In each encounter with the person, at least two of these things remain relatively constant: the appearance of the person, and the sound of the person's name. However, the background information changes each time as the person is seen in a variety of contexts. Thus one acquires several encoded episodes about this person with each episode uniquely specified by its background information. After several such encounters, one might be able to produce the person's name on seeing the person, or pick out the person's picture on hearing the person's name, without specifically being able to recall the situation in which the person's name was learned. The question that needs to be considered further is exactly how the knowledge about the name can be retained while the knowledge about the specific experience is lost.

One way to approach this question might be to extend the interference notions developed in chapter 1. It was argued that interference occurs because one cue is relevant to too many items. In the same way, if we consider the background information to be a more or less separable "item," then we could have interference occurring at the level of background elements. That is, each encoding that contains this person's face also contains the name, so that seeing the face would be a specific cue for recall of the name. However, each encoding that contains the name and the face also contains a unique set of background elements. Therefore, seeing the face, or hearing the name, or both, will still not be specific enough to pull one specific set of background information from memory. Therefore, the name will give the face and vice versa, without any very specific feeling of where the connection was learned. Thus, general knowledge has evolved out of specific experiences because of interference among sets of background information.

According to this point of view, whether or not a specific experience is reinstated at recall will depend upon the cues used to initiate recall. If the cues are specific enough to produce one specific experience, including background information, then the subject won't feel that the knowledge is context-free. For example, if one has heard someone else use the new person's name recently enough, then the background information from the present state could serve as an additional retrieval cue. In such a case, that recent experience with the name will be recalled in its temporal context. Thus, with the proper cues, one might even be able to recall when one had learned the definition of each of the words that one knows, which is the paradigmatic example of the allegedly context-free nature of semantic memory.

On the other hand, with no relevant background elements, a cue that is related to more than one experience will produce an answer that is in general terms, and this will be because the specific background elements unique to each encoding will not be produced. Wickelgren (1975) has presented a very similar argument.

It might be worthwhile here to briefly mention some recent theorizing by Estes (1975), which attempts to deal with temporal order in a different way. Estes argues that the memory of the occurrence of earlier events is incorporated as part of the encoding of later events. If the first three items on a list are a, b, and c, then the encoding of b will contain as part of it the trace of the encoding of a, and the encoding of c will contain both earlier encodings as parts. Therefore, when a is recalled, it can serve as a cue for b because a is part of the encoding of b, and so on. This point of view is an alternative to the background-elements notions discussed in this chapter. The basic difference between the present point of view and that of Estes is that the present position has not considered the possibility that traces from previous items are actually part of the encoding of a given item. If this addition is made, it may make it easier to deal with a broader range of memory phenomena. On the other hand, Estes does not seem to deal with the specifics of background information in his theorizing. However, the two points of view may not be incompatible in the long run.

In any case, there is at present little specific that can be said about these issues, and the important point is to make it clear that there may be several processes mediating the role of temporal factors in memory.

4.5 Summary

This chapter has considered how we can recall the order of events in time. It was argued that if the notion of an encoding could be broadened to include background elements, along with the conscious activity being carried out, one might be able to explain the ability of people to recall items in temporal order. These ideas were also related to questions concerning associations between mental events, and the development of context-free knowledge from specific time-bound experiences. Given that this chapter is correct in emphasis, if not in specifics, then this is an area that could be very important in our understanding of cognitive functioning.

4.6 Summary of part 1

There have been several important themes in these four chapters that will also be important in the discussions to follow. First, we saw that mental activities do not depend on mental objects. Recall of an item depends upon the activities that one carries out when dealing with the item. One doesn't physically take in an item; one examines the item and thinks about it. Having done this, one may or may not be able to remember what item caused one to carry out the various activities. This theme will be repeated a number of times in the chapters to follow, in the discussions of pattern recognition and attention, and of concepts.

A second major theme was that one's knowledge serves as the basis for directing one's activities. It was argued that recalling some given event might depend heavily on one's knowledge about that event. In the next several chapters, we shall consider in more detail how one's knowledge is used in directing various other activities which are carried out over time. Chapters 5 and 6 will be concerned with pattern recognition and attention. In both these areas, recent theorizing emphasizes the use of knowledge to process information over time. These ideas will also serve as the basis for the discussion of imagery in chapter 7. In part 4, we shall examine how knowledge is used in problem solving, and in part 5 we shall examine cognitive development from this point of view.

The overriding organizational principle in the discussion that follows is that we are dealing with situations in which people are using information available in memory in order to deal with the task at hand. What we need to know in order to understand what people do is the sort of information available and how it is being used.

TWO
Pattern recognition and attention

5
Pattern recognition

5.0 Introduction to part two

One of the central notions developed in part 1 was that the ability to remember some event depends upon "what one did" during that event. These "encoding operations" must be considered broadly, because they can entail overt actions, such as scanning a scene and talking about it, as well as covert "actions," such as imagining some situation related to the to-be-recalled item. Obviously, another way of describing these covert actions would be to say that one thinks about things when an item is presented, and what one thought about can influence what one will recall.

The main issue in part 3 will be, What does it mean to say that a person thinks about something? First, however, in part 2, we shall consider how people deal with external objects in the real world. This will then lead naturally to a consideration of how people deal with "internal objects" in the "world of thought."

Chapter 5 will deal with pattern recognition, or perception, beginning with a brief discussion of feature analysis models of pattern recognition. These sorts of models have been studied extensively in recent years, and some important positive conclusions concerning pattern recognition can be derived from this work. However, feature analysis models have some basic inadequacies, one of which is that they fail to explicitly deal with one important aspect of perception—the fact that perception is extended in time.

Therefore, we shall then go on to consider some recent theorizing which looks at perception as an activity carried out over time. One important aspect of this theorizing is that it assumes that one's knowledge plays an active role in perception. Thus there will be important similarities between the discussion in the present chapter and the point of view presented in part 1. This point of view will then be extended to the phenomenon of selective attention in chapter 6. This will give us a basic set of concepts which we can use in part 3 to analyze questions concerning the medium of thought. In addition, we shall see that the ideas developed in part 1 will occur again in the discussion in parts 2 and 3.

5.1 Introduction to recent theorizing

The basic question in the area of pattern recognition is how it is that external events, especially novel events, can be consistently responded to, or classified (Neisser, 1967). This does not imply that the person verbally classifies the pattern. For the present purposes, a consistent response will be taken as a form of classification.

Templates and features. Much recent theorizing concerning pattern recognition has centered on the relative merits of template models versus feature-analysis models. Template-matching models of pattern recognition argue that the basis for classification of patterns is a set of internal models, or templates. When a new pattern is presented, it is compared with all the templates stored in memory. The template that provides the best fit classifies the pattern. It is now generally agreed that any system of this sort, which works on an overall, global analysis of the new pattern, will not adequately account for human pattern recognition (Neisser, 1967; Lindsay & Norman, 1977).

One alternative to template matching is a system whereby only parts, or features, of the pattern are used to determine the classification. The basic design of such a feature-analysis model is hierarchical. At the lowest level, there are simply receptors that register the presence or absence of stimulation. At the next level, a set of feature analyzers determines which features are contained in the as-yet-unrecognized input. The feature analyzers receive input from the receptors. At the final level of analysis, there is a set of pattern recognizers, each of which stands for one pattern that the person can recognize. Each of these pattern recognizers receives input from the feature analyzers, so that the "firing" of the pattern recognizers depends upon firing of the feature analyzers. This organization of feature-analysis models will be made clearer in the next section.

Pattern recognition

"**Defining**" **features.** At least two different sorts of feature-analysis models are possible, depending upon how the features are used. On the one hand, each class of pattern could be defined by a small, closed set of features ("defining" features—Smith, Shoben, & Rips, 1974). One set of features, devised to deal with printed capital letters, is shown at the top of Table 5.1. As can be seen, there is a small set of features, and each letter contains only a few of these features. (It should be noted that some features are more complicated than others, in that they depend on the relation between parts.) In this model, each pattern or letter is defined by a small group of defining features—it is assumed that each type of letter is classified on the basis of a different small group of features, and all the members of each class all contain the defining features for the class, and no other pattern contains just these features.

However, there are two problems that can be pointed out for the notion of defining features. First, as can be seen in the bottom of Table 5.1, there are many additional patterns which fit the various sets of defining features, but which aren't classified as letters by human observers. That is, those features in Table 5.1 serve to classify letters only in a severely restricted set of circumstances—a set of circumstances in which only a small set of capital letters are presented as the possible stimuli. This problem may not be

Table 5.1. A set of features for recognition of capital letters.

	Letters of the alphabet (block)								
Features		A	E	F	H	L	T	K	M	D
Straight										
Horizontal		+	+	+	+	+	+	−	−	−
Vertical		−	+	+	+	+	+	+	+	+
Diagonal /		+	−	−	−	−	−	+	+	−
Diagonal \		+	−	−	−	−	−	+	+	−
Curve										
Closed		−	−	−	−	−	−	−	−	+
Open vertical		−	−	−	−	−	−	−	−	−
Open horizontal		−	−	−	−	−	−	−	−	−
Intersection		+	+	+	+	−	+	+	−	−
Redundancy										
Cyclic change		−	+	−	−	−	−	−	+	−
Symmetry		+	+	−	+	−	+	+	+	+
Discontinuity										
Vertical		+	−	+	+	+	+	+	+	−
Horizontal		−	+	+	−	+	+	+	−	−

simply overcome by changing the features and how they are combined, because there are other reasons to believe that most of the patterns which we can recognize are not defined by a small closed set of defining features. For example, consider the forms that are classified by adult readers as being printed capital A's; there is no small closed set of features common to all of them. Some capital A's are pointed at the top, but some are not; some have a horizontal line, but some do not; some are closed at the top, but some are not. An exclusive set of common features is not to be found. Many other categories are of the same sort; it seems impossible to specify a small set of features that defines only the members of the category. Consider the category *dogs*. Are there features that all dogs, but only dogs, have in common? Rosch, Mervis, Gray, Johnson, and Boyes-Braem (1976) asked people to list the features common to various dogs, and found that there were no features specific to all dogs and only to dogs. In short, it does not seem possible to specify defining features for many classes that we have no trouble recognizing.

Of course, it could be argued here that the problem is simply that we have not yet identified the relevant features in any set of patterns. The difficulty therefore is not that the features don't exist, it's just that we haven't gotten around to figuring out what they are yet. This objection may indeed be true, but unfortunately it doesn't help us to understand pattern recognition at this time, so we shall assume that there are no small sets of defining features to be found. Furthermore, if one does make this negative assumption, it makes things much more interesting as far as cognitive theory is concerned.

All features. Given these difficulties for models based on defining features, the second sort of feature-analysis model assumes that all features contribute to all classifications. One such model was Selfridge's Pandemonium model, which was a computer program for letter recognition (Selfridge & Neisser, 1960). As a first step, a set of feature analyzers, similar to those in Table 5.1, was built into the program. (Examples of features are the number of vertical lines and the number of horizontal lines). After the features were chosen, a sample of 330 hand-written letters was presented, with their names. Each letter was tested for all the features, and those features that were found were stored in the computer's memory with the name of the letter. This resulted in a record of how often each feature had been found in each type of letter. Consider the "vertical lines" feature. Seventy-two of the 330 letters in the sample contained three vertical lines. Of these 72 letters, 25 (35 percent) were Ns, 18 (25 percent) were Ms, 6 (9 percent) were As, and so on. Four vertical lines occurred only eight times in the sample, and 75 percent of the time the letter was an M. Summaries of this sort ("weighted" probabilities) were computed for all the features processed by the program.

These summary data were then used to identify unknown letters. Assume that an unknown letter is presented and feature analysis indicates that it contains three vertical lines. Based on the data just discussed, the probability is .35 that the letter is N, .18 that it is M, .09 that it is A, and so on. If more features were available from the unknown letter, one could get these probabilities for each feature, total them, and choose the classification with the highest total as the classification for the letter.

Conclusions. If we accept for the moment a model based on these weighted probabilities, there is at least one very important consequence: we must reject the intuitively appealing notion that there is some essence contained by all patterns of the same type. All we have, according to the weighted-features model, is a set of features more or less important for each letter, rather than one small set, all of which are present each time a specific letter is present. Thus, a letter could be classified as an E even if the most frequent feature in past E's was not present, so long as those features which were present specified an E better than they did anything else. Furthermore, the values stored for the various features depend upon the specific set of letters which have been seen to that point. So not only do all features contribute to identification of all patterns, but their relative contribution at any time depends upon the specific sample of patterns which has been experienced to that time.

This conclusion has broader ramifications, because, as mentioned, some theorists have recently argued that there are defining features for human concepts like *bird* (e.g., Smith, Shoben, & Rips, 1974). However, part of "having the concept of bird" is being able to identify birds. Therefore, if there are no defining features for the pattern *bird,* as the present discussion indicates, there may not be any defining features for the concept either. This has important consequences for some recent models of thinking and knowledge, which will be considered in chapter 8.

5.2 Sequential processing in pattern recognition

The discussion so far has been an oversimplification, because there is a fine structure to pattern recognition which has not been considered. A feature-analysis model such as that just discussed assumes that all the features in a pattern are processed at the same time—"in parallel." However, there is evidence that all the features from a given object are not taken in at once. If so, then the feature-analysis model is inadequate. We shall now consider the sequential aspects of perception and discuss a different way of explaining pattern recognition. However, the main results from the discussion in section 5.1 will also be important in the discussion to follow (see section 5.6.).

Eye movements in visual exploration. Most of the detailed analysis of a visual pattern is done with the fovea of the retina, which can process only 2 ° of the visual field at any time (Gaarder, 1973). When looking straight ahead, one can just barely see one's arms out of the corner of one's eye when the arms are straight out to the side. The angle of vision from one arm to the other is 180 °. However, the fovea sees clearly only the center 2 ° of this field: approximately 1/90 of the complete field of vision. Therefore, in order to analyze a relatively large visual object in any detail, the object must be examined with a series of eye movements, causing the various parts of the object to fall on the fovea. Thus, if two features are seen in different fixations, then they will be processed at different times. If we wish to consider how patterns are processed, we must consider what happens as patterns are scanned over time.

Scanpaths in visual recognition. Recent work by Noton and Stark (1971, 1972) has provided evidence that feature analysis in visual pattern recognition is a sequential process over time. Noton and Stark begin with the fact that any object except a very small one must be scanned by moving the fovea over it in a series of eye movements. They argue that this sequence of eye movements is what is stored in memory when a pattern is first encountered, and that recognition of the pattern at other times entails running off the same sequence of movements, or scanpath. That is, a pattern serves as a cue for the retrieval of a relevant scanpath. This will be elaborated further shortly.

In an experiment designed to test these ideas, subjects' eye movements were photographed when they studied a series of pictures and when the same pictures were presented for recognition. The crucial question was whether the same scanpath would be carried out during study and recognition of a given picture. Noton and Stark found that about 65 percent of their recognition records showed the same scanpaths during study and recognition. Given that subjects theoretically could have produced many scanpaths while looking at such pictures, these findings are impressive.

Based on these sorts of results, Noton and Stark proposed that the inter-

Pattern recognition

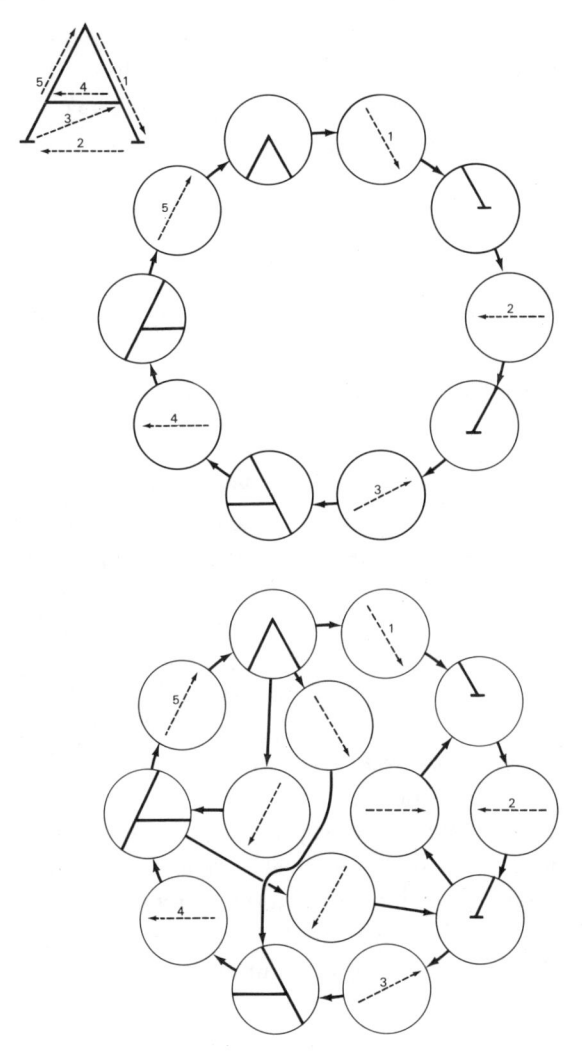

Figure 5.1. *Top:* Hypothetical feature map for a capital A. Numbered arrows represent eye movements used to scan letter. *Bottom:* Elaborated feature map, based on additional experience with pattern.

nal representation of a visual pattern is a "feature ring," as shown at the top of Figure 5.1 for one hypothetical subject for a capital A. The ring is a sequence of alternating fixations and eye movements. Each fixation contains some information from the pattern, and the eye movement command tells the subject what will be seen if the eyes are moved in a certain direction. A hypothetical command for a letter A would be: "If you are looking at the point at the top, then if you move obliquely down to the right, you will see a horizontal line coming in from the left to intersect the line you are moving along."

It is important to note that the feature ring for any given pattern will be different for different subjects. The crucial point is that for a pattern to be recognized, any given subject must have stored some feature ring for that pattern, and the ring must match the pattern that is presented. This point of view is very similar to that discussed in chapter 3 concerning the chess master's ability to recall chess positions. It was argued at that time that the master's ability was based on knowledge of the organization of pieces, in a way very similar to the knowledge postulated by Noton and Stark. Similar ideas were also expressed by Hebb (1949) a number of years ago. Obviously, though, several questions remain. First, what about those pictures that are recognized without the same scanpath being run off? Noton and Stark try to deal with these responses by assuming that fixations that were not originally part of the scanpath can also become part of the feature ring. These additional fixations are incorporated in the center of of the feature ring at the bottom of Figure 5.1. This results in a bit more flexibility in the scanpaths that the subject has available. It might be helpful here to use the term *pattern map* instead of Noton and Stark's feature ring. The way we acquire information about a new neighborhood over time may provide a useful analogy to the way we acquire information about a new pattern. (Neisser, 1976, makes a similar argument.) With experience in a neighborhood, one learns interconnections among the various landmarks, and one is able to produce new routes as needed. Analogously, with some experience exploring a pattern, one can acquire alternate scanpaths, and one can develop a general knowledge of the locations of the features relative to each other. Such a "map" could result in recognition occurring on the basis of a new scanpath that was not produced before.

A more difficult problem for Noton and Stark's model, however, is the fact that objects can sometimes be recognized from a single brief fixation. Noton and Stark (1972) attempt to deal with this by arguing that the subject would then run off an *internalized* sequence of eye movements by *switching attention* to the various parts of the figure in a way corresponding to the feature ring. Exactly how this occurs is not made totally clear, but it is an idea worth pursuing. An alternative that Noton and Stark do not consider is that in some cases there may be enough informa-

Pattern recognition

tion available in a single fixation to unambiguously specify one scanpath, so that the whole path would not have to be run off either overtly or internally. In order for this to be more clear, Figure 5.1 has to be modified a bit. It is assumed that all that is represented in each fixation is the area that falls on the fovea. However, this is too drastic a limitation; although the best vision is at the fovea, there is still some information extracted extra-foveally. Therefore, the pattern map in Figure 5.1 ought to look like that at the top of Figure 5.2, in which each fixation is assumed to include less precise information from the areas of the retina outside the fovea. When the information is laid out in this way, one can see that if a given fixation is only present in one class of feature maps, then the person wouldn't need additional information. Two hypothetical maps are shown at the bottom of Figure 5.2, and it can be seen that some fixations unambiguously specify one of the maps, while other fixations do not distinguish between them. Based on this, some individual fixations would differentiate the two hypothetical patterns. That is, some fixations would retrieve only one of the two maps.

To summarize, the research of Noton and Stark supports the idea that recognition involves a sequential series of steps, linked together by motor movements, which we have called a *pattern map*. This is generalized information developed through experience in examining various sorts of patterns. This sort of a notion will be important in chapter 7 when we consider visual imagery as a basis for thinking. Based on Noton and Stark's work, a "feature" of a pattern is the information that is extracted from a single foveal fixation. Pattern recognition would then entail two processes: extraction of information from single fixations, and going from one fixation to the next.

5.3 Parallel processing within fixations

We have seen that it seems reasonable to argue that visual pattern recognition is an act extended over time, in which an object is examined with a series of foveal fixations. The next important question concerns what happens at each fixation, and there is evidence that the information within a given fixation can be taken in "in parallel," which means that the various parts of a fixation can be taken in more or less at once.

Hochberg's research on depth cues. Consider the two forms shown in Figure 5.3a. They are perceived as being three-dimensional objects with depth. Hochberg (1968) was interested in ascertaining what features,

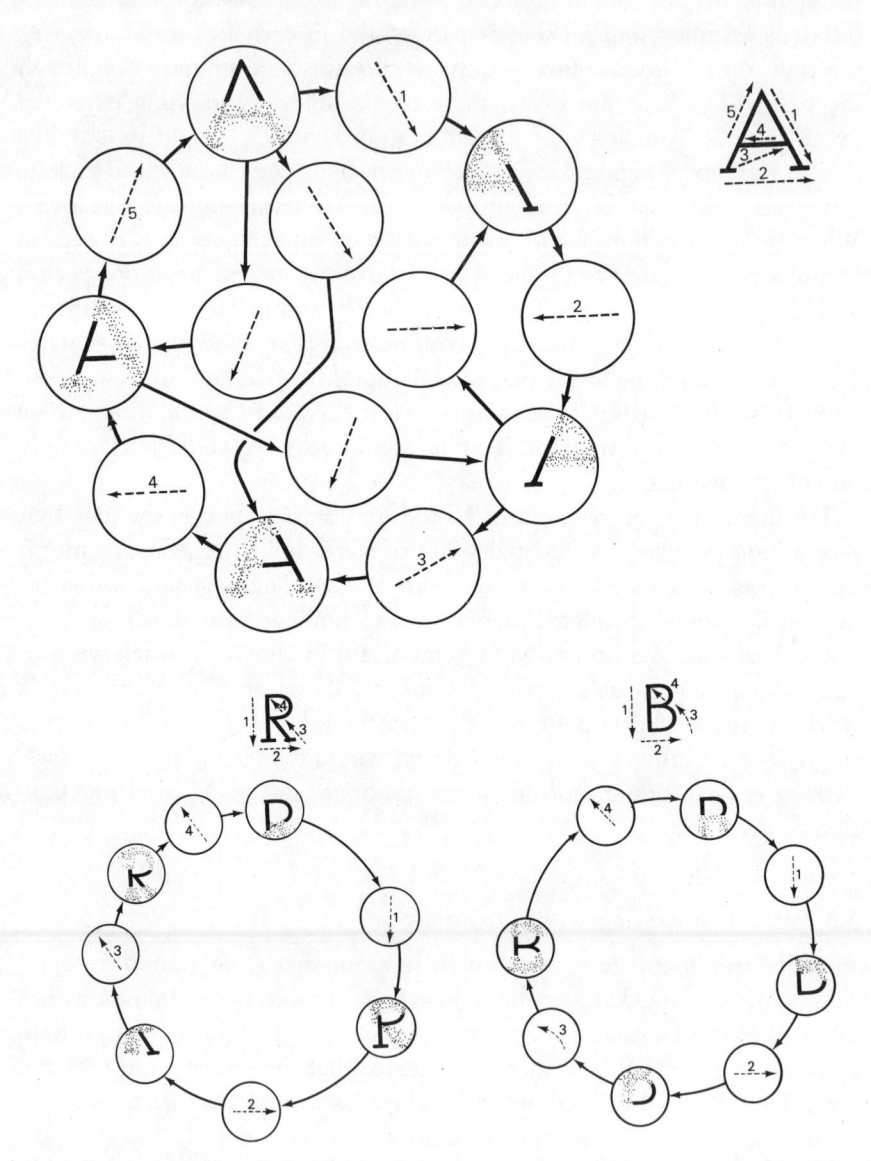

Figure 5.2. *Top:* More elaborate pattern map, showing more information in each fixation. *Bottom:* Two different maps, showing how different patterns produce some fixations that are similar and some that are different.

Pattern recognition

which he called *cues*, were responsible for the impression of depth in these forms. In order to examine the perception of depth more closely, the forms were cut into a series of slices, as shown in Figure 5.3b. For each of the forms, two methods of cutting were used. In one case, the cuts were arranged so that all the vertices were cut. This method was used on the upper form in each pair. In the other case, the slices were arranged so that the vertices were left complete, as seen in the two lower forms. The forms were presented to subjects by presenting the slices one at a time, in left-to-right order, so the subject never saw the complete forms all at once.

Figure 5.3. Hochberg's study of depth cues. The two patterns at the top are seen as three-dimensional. When each is presented in slices as in b, depth is lost. When sliced as in c, depth is preserved.

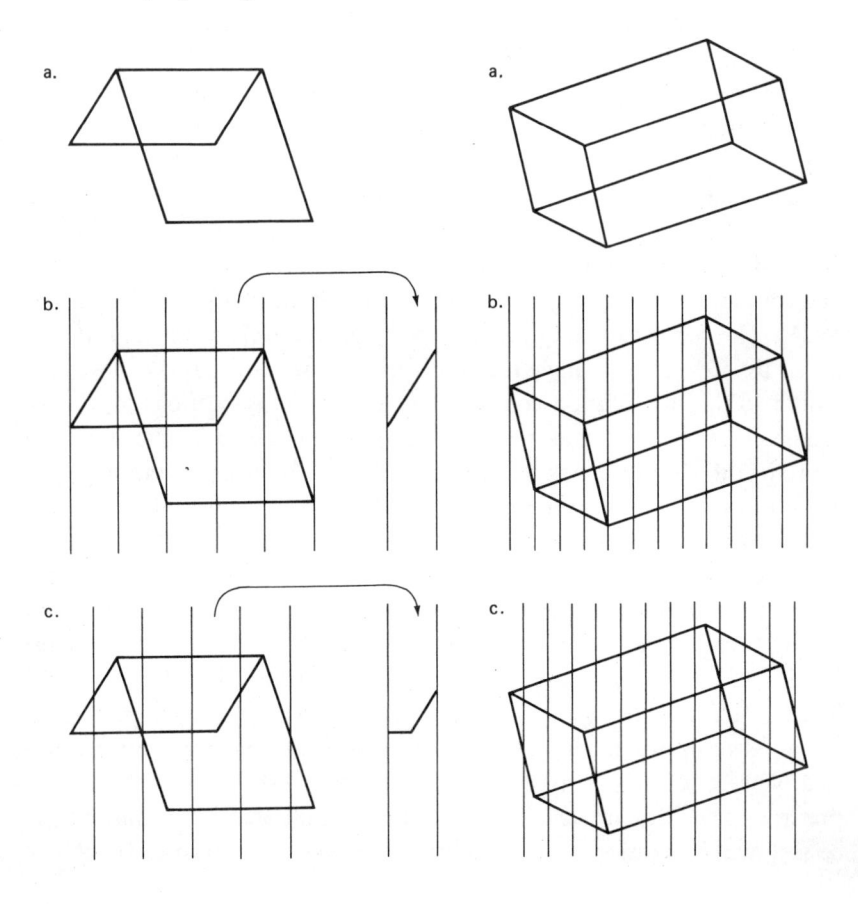

When the slices were presented at about a one-half second rate, so that presenting all the slices took about five seconds, subjects reported that the two lower forms in Figure 5.3b still looked like three-dimensional objects. However, the two upper forms were seen as being *flat* when the slices were presented at the same half-second per slice rate. Hochberg argued that the perception of depth results from the presence of certain cues or features in a pattern, and each of these cues must be analyzed as a whole in order for it to be effective. That is, all the parts of each cue must be processed in parallel. With the two upper forms in Figure 5.3b, the crucial features are cut and presented on separate slices. Therefore, each half of each feature is analyzed separately, and no cues to depth are found. This doesn't happen with the other figures. Thus, we have evidence here that visual pattern recognition depends upon information extracted from foveal fixations.

Hochberg argues that the information from foveal fixations is integrated in a "schematic map," which is "a matrix of spacetime expectancies (or assumptions)" (1968, p.324). This is similar to Noton and Stark's feature ring. Neisser (1967, 1976) has advocated a similar notion.

Other studies of parallel processing within fixations. Shiffrin and his colleagues have carried out many studies which indicate that essentially all the information with a single foveal fixation can be taken in at once, to the degree to which the acuity of vision allows it. For example, in one study an array of 49 dots (7 rows by 7 columns) was briefly presented, and half the time one dot was missing out of the array (Shiffrin, McKay, & Shaffer, 1976). The subject's ability to pick up the position of the missing dot was tested by presenting a single test dot after the array. The test dot was presented so that its location coincided with one of the locations in the just-presented array, and the subject was asked if there had been a dot in the array in the test dot's position. Even with very brief presentations of the array of dots, subjects were accurate in detecting the positions of missing dots. Thus, they could take in the entire array in one fixation, and could do so with enough accuracy to correctly place missing dots. These results support the notion that parallel processing of the whole visual array occurs during each fixation. Further evidence for parallel visual processing comes from studies by Egeth (e.g., 1966), and Schneider and Shiffrin (1977; Shiffrin & Schneider, 1977), among others. However, since in many cases visual patterns are much bigger than the area of visual field which can be clearly seen, we must scan them with a sequence of fixations. This means that two processes are usually involved in visual pattern recognition: processing within fixations, and switching from one fixation to the next.

5.4 Orientation and recognition of patterns

If it is true that recognition of a pattern like a letter is based on a set of simple features, such as parallel lines and right angles, then it ought not to matter what orientation the pattern is presented in, so long as the relevant features are present. On the other hand, if recognizing a pattern depends upon an organized map of features, with the location of the features relative to each other being important, then changing the orientation of the pattern ought to disrupt recognition.

Rotation studies. Cooper and Shepard (1973) examined the amount of time subjects needed to recognize letters presented at various orientations, and found that the time it took to categorize letters depended upon how far away from normal the test letter was rotated. In terms of the present discussion, it might be argued that scanning the various features is disrupted if the features of the test letter are not in their expected locations. The farther the test letter is rotated from the normal, then the harder it might be to match the features to one's knowledge, because more extrapolation has to be carried out.

A number of studies have shown that similar organization of features occurs in recognition of faces. Turning pictures of familiar faces upside down interferes with the ability of adults to identify them (Hochberg & Galper, 1967).

In summary, these results are still more evidence that it is necessary to take into account the locations of the various features relative to each other and not simply the presence or absence of features. In this way, these results are supportive of those of Noton and Stark.

Multiple paths and ambiguous figures. Consider the three pictures in Figure 5.4 The one on the left is a young woman, the one on the right is an old woman, and the one in the middle is ambiguous—it can be seen as either the young women or the old one. According to the view of pattern recognition which we have been considering, the middle picture must be ambiguous because there are two pattern maps which could be used to process it. If so, different parts of the ambiguous figure might be differentially important to one or the other of these pattern maps. That is, certain parts of the ambiguous figure could "retrieve" the pattern map for a young woman, and other parts of it could retrieve the pattern map for an old woman. Chastain and Burnham (1975) tested this notion by presenting an ambiguous figure, similar to the one in the center of Figure 5.4, in segments. Two different orders of presentation were used, with each order

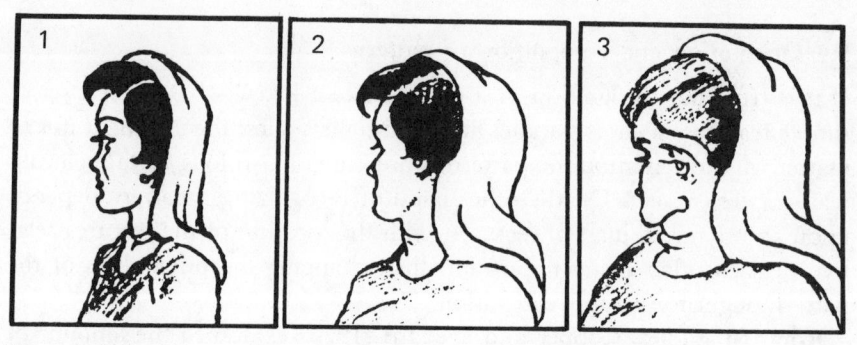

Figure 5.4. Ambiguous figure: Young woman–old woman, with an ambiguous figure in the middle.

beginning with a segment that was more characteristic of one interpretation of the figure. The *same* segments were shown to all subjects, but their order of presentation differed. The results indicated that the different presentation orders influenced the perception of the ambiguous figure. Furthermore, if only the initial segments were presented, subjects were not able to guess what the figure was supposed to be from just that single segment. This would be expected if a figure is ambiguous, because, by definition, an ambiguous figure should contain no parts that specify only one pattern map. Since the subjects could not use only the initial segment in making their interpretation, it could be argued from this that the initial segment only served to initiate the processing sequence, but that more information had to be obtained from the figure before any interpretation could be made.

Summary. The research in the last few sections indicates that there seem to be two components involved in processing patterns—the sequence of visual fixations, and the extraction of information within each fixation. The former is a serial process, and the latter may be parallel. Thus, pattern recognition is extended in time and seems to be based on knowledge concerning the "layout" of patterns in space and time. The use of this knowledge is fourfold. First, it serves as the basis whereby a pattern is processed, as we have seen. Second, one's knowledge actively facilitates the processing of patterns. Evidence for this will be considered in the next section. Third, this knowledge may serve as the basis for recall of a pattern, as discussed in chapter 3. Finally, this knowledge may be the basis for selective attention. This will be considered in the next chapter.

5.5 Expectations and perception

A number of studies in various areas have shown that perception is made easier to the degree that one's knowledge can be used to help process the information.

Expectations in reading. If we are reading lines of print containing ten to fifteen words, only four or five fixations might be made per line, which means that we won't look directly at most of the words. One difficulty that a model of reading must face is how it is that we can read words that our eye has not directly fixated. Furthermore, as mentioned earlier, our eyes are not able to pick up material clearly except when looking straight at it. In order to explain how we can "take in" groups of words at once without being able to see all of them clearly, Hochberg (1970a, b) argues that any time we fixate a word, we are generating hypotheses about what the next few words will be. We take in as much information as we can from the words that can be partially seen, mainly such things as general shape, length, and perhaps some letters. We then attempt to confirm our expectations by moving our eyes as far down the line as we have predicted. The new word we fixate, as well as other peripheral information taken in, serves to confirm or disconfirm our hypothesis. If the hypothesis is confirmed, then we "see" the words that intervened between our fixations, even though we never actually looked directly at them. To the extent that our hypothesis was not confirmed, we have to take in some more information. One informal bit of evidence that supports this notion is that we often overlook errors in printing when we are reading for meaning. If we don't fully examine every word, but simply take in some limited information from the words in the periphery, then we don't see them clearly enough to note that a letter is missing or changed.

One way to experimentally test Hochberg's model would be as follows. Let us say a person is in the the midst of reading a sentence. This means that she or he has fixated one or two words at the beginning of the sentence and is ready to move the eyes further along. Before the eye movement occurs, the reader must formulate a set of expectations as to what words will be seen. Even though the next few words can't be clearly seen, some of their general characteristics can be made out, and these will be incorporated into the prediction. Now, let us assume that *as the reader's eye is moving, the sentence is changed,* so that it is not the same as what it was before the eye movement occurred. Since the change occurs while the eye movement is being carried out, the change will not be seen. However, depending upon the degree of change, the reader's predictions will be more or less disconfirmed. Therefore, it ought to take longer to process the changed sentence, and processing time ought to increase as the amount of change increases. This sort of method was employed by Rayner (1975), using a very sophisticated experimental apparatus, and the results supported the predictions, indicating that one's expectations play a part in reading. Processing is made easier because one can take some information about what one just saw in the periphery and use it to predict what one will see when one makes the next fixation.

Expectations in listening to sentences. Rayner's study did not examine the question of the subject's making predictions on the basis of the context provided by the earlier words in the sentence. A number of other studies have shown that subjects use such information in order to process the later words in a sentence.

In one study, subjects tried to identify words that were presented in noise (Miller, Heise, & Lichten, 1951). In one condition, simple grammatical sentences were used as stimuli. An example would be: He has the wrong socks. In another condition, the same sentences were presented in reverse order: Socks wrong the has he. In each case, the subjects tried to recognize each individual word. In the case of the sentences, however, the subjects should have been able to use their knowledge of grammar to predict the kind of word that ought to come next in the sentence, even though they might not be able to predict much about its meaning. From this, it would be predicted that words in sentences ought to be recognized better than the same words in reverse order, and that was what was found.

Thus, these results indicate that one's expectations, based on earlier information, influence the ease with which stimuli can be recognized.

The word frequency effect. A closely related phenomenon concerns the fact that frequent words are recognized much more easily than are infrequent words (Broadbent, 1967; Morton, 1970) under conditions of high-speed visual presentation. The same sorts of phenomena occur in tests of recognition of words presented auditorily with a noisy background. It is much easier to hear frequent words over a noisy background than it is to hear infrequent words. The infrequent words must be made much louder relative to the noisy background before they will be perceived.

It is possible to greatly reduce the effect of word frequency by giving the subject a set of alternatives beforehand, one of which will be the word that is presented. In this case, low frequency words are recognized almost as well as high frequency words.

Pattern recognition

Broadbent (1967) and Morton (1970) developed a model to explain the word frequency effect which assumes that the effect occurs because of the role of one's knowledge in perception. They assume that in order to perceive a word, one must have some information from the environment and match this information from the environment with what one knows about the various words in the language. The word-frequency effect is assumed to occur because the high frequency of certain words in our past experience has biased us to require less information as proof that a given word has occurred.

Thus the information presented to the senses is not the only determinant of what will be perceived in a given situation. The person's knowledge concerning the sorts of events which can appear in that situation also plays an important role and to the degree that an event matches one's knowledge, perception of that event will be facilitated. This point is discussed further in section 5.12.

The "resonance" analogy. The role of one's knowledge in pattern recognition is illustrated by this analogy. If one has a set of tuning forks, and if another tuning fork is struck, the new tone will cause one of the original set to vibrate, or to resonate, if the frequency of the new tone is matched by the frequency of any of the original tuning forks. Thus, the new tone is "recognized" through the resonance of one of the old tuning forks. In the same way, one could argue that humans recognize patterns, not by "taking them in" and "processing" them, but by resonating to them. This could be what one means when one says that we use our knowledge in order to recognize patterns. In order to recognize a pattern, we must be able to match this pattern with one of our own, in order to "resonate" to this pattern. It is also interesting to note that the notion of resonance has been used by a number of theorists in speculating about how retrieval from memory takes place (e.g., Flexser & Tulving, 1978; Hunt 1973; Lockhart, Craik, & Jacoby, 1975). If this notion turns out to be fruitful in these two areas, it will point to further similarities between memory and perception.

5.6 Pattern maps and novel patterns

If one's knowledge consists of pattern maps, then recognizing a pattern involves running off a series of fixations that corresponds to some pattern map in memory. However, if a pattern is novel, then there is no map in memory to correspond to the pattern. Therefore, in order to recognize a novel pattern, the person would have to *construct* a map to match it. The first fixation that the person gets of the novel pattern would serve as the entry point into the set of maps which are in memory. Since this fixation wouldn't match any fixation in memory, due to the pattern's novelty, the match would have to be on a more general basis. This could occur in the same way as the "best match" procedure in Pandemonium, as discussed in section 5.1. That is, it could be argued that the features from the first fixation would be matched with fixations in memory, and the best match would serve as the basis for retrieval of a map to direct further processing.

Once a pattern map has been retrieved, the person could then combine this specific information with the information in the first fixation, in order to determine how the rest of the pattern ought to look. In this way, the person could predict how the rest of the pattern ought to look, and various parts of the pattern could then be examined. If they also looked as they ought, then the pattern could be recognized, even though it had never been seen before.

Pattern maps, frames, and scripts. Minsky (1975) has recently presented a more detailed discussion of how knowledge might be used in perception, similar to the point of view presented here. He argues that in order to perceive something, we must match that input to a "frame," one's knowledge about a stereotyped situation, such as the layout of a typical kitchen. According to Minsky, we have many frames available, and perception entails choosing the appropriate frame and matching it with the input. Furthermore, Minsky argues that if no frame is available, one must be constructed, based on what information is available.

Minsky uses the notion of frame very broadly: there are frames for pencils, for rooms, and for complex events like birthday parties. In the present discussion, we have used several different terms for these different sorts of events. For example, in the present chapter, we have used the term *pattern map* to refer to the knowledge used in perceiving a relatively simple pattern. Also, in chapter 3 we used Schank's (1975) term *script* to refer to the knowledge used in understanding complex events like birthday parties. On the one hand, it might simplify things to adopt Minsky's broad use of the term frame to cover all these situations. On the other hand, however, it may result in an oversimplification if we are led to believe that exactly the same processes are involved in perceiving an A and in attending a birthday party. Therefore, at present, it might be better to use several terms and relate them as follows: pattern maps are used to perceive objects in frames, and frames form the scenes that make up scripts. Once again, it may be true that the same processes are involved at all these levels, but for the

Pattern recognition

present we shall be somewhat cautious. Palmer (1975) discusses these issues further.

Also, if it is true, as was argued earlier, that there are no set of defining features for any given class of patterns, then there might not be a single frame that can summarize all kitchens or birthday parties. That is, there must be a whole set of frames that would represent the various possibilities in kitchens. This point is relevant to the script notion also. It is probably true that we do not possess a single script for an event like eating in a restaurant because there are many possible variations on eating in restaurants and no single script could deal with all of them. This point will be elaborated further in chapter 8.

However, even if these elaborations are necessary, it is important to emphasize the basic similarity between Minsky's and Schank's points of view and the present one.

5.7 Pattern maps within pattern maps: recognition of more complex patterns

Many patterns that we can recognize are more complicated than capital letters. A face, for example, is a pattern made up of eyes, a nose, a mouth, and other parts. An eye, however, is also a pattern made up of parts. This then implies that the map for a face is made up of several other maps, in a hierarchical structure. If this were so, it would mean that one would first have to recognize each part of the face before one could recognize the face itself.

On the other hand, it might be possible to recognize a face without recognizing all the parts in great detail. The first glimpse that one had of a face might result in an entry into a pattern map for a face. In this case, something like an eye or the nose would be contained in only one fixation, and the face could be recognized without analyzing all the parts in detail. It would only be necessary that each fixation contain detailed enough information to carry things forward. The important point is that when an entire eye is seen at a distance in one fixation, as part of a face, there is not the same amount of resolution as when the eye can be examined close up with a series of fixations. Therefore, it may be true that the eye that is "recognized" as part of a face is different from the eye that would be recognized if one were asked if the person had large eyes. Thus, one could have a map for a face that was at least in part independent of the maps for its parts.

Letters versus words. Words are also patterns which are analyzable into parts: the letters that make them up. Based on the hierarchical or pattern-within-pattern model, it would be expected that the letters would have to be identified before the word itself could be recognized. On the other hand, if there are pattern maps for words, then recognizing words would not necessarily take longer than recognizing letters.

These ideas have been tested in a study by Reicher (1969). Letter stimuli were flashed very briefly to subjects, so that it was difficult to identify them. The unknown stimulus was then "masked," or wiped out, by presenting an array of lines where the stimulus had just been presented. The subject then saw a pair of test letters, and the subject indicated which of the two test letters had been in the briefly seen stimulus. The most important finding was that the same letter was recognized better when it was presented in a word than when it was alone. As a concrete example, the individual to-be-recognized letter might be K, and the two choices might be K and D. In the word condition the stimulus would be WORK, and the choices would again be K and D. It is important to note that both K and D are the last letters of English words which begin with WOR. Therefore, subjects cannot simply guess a letter correctly because the letter ends a word. The most important finding of the study was that, in comparison with the condition in which K is presented alone, presenting WORK improved the identification of K when D was the alternative choice. This result has been replicated several times (e.g., Wheeler, 1970; Thompson & Massaro, 1973).

The fact that a letter is recognized more accurately in a word than alone supports the notion that there are feature maps for words which do not depend upon the feature maps for the individual letters.

Another way of putting it is to say that the results of Reicher's study indicate that identifying a word is not a hierarchical process in which letters are first individually identified. The information in a given fixation can be used in the identification of a letter *or* a word.

5.8 Hierarchical structure of knowledge

There has recently been some importance attributed to the fact that many human concepts or patterns are hierarchically organized. For example, robin and wren are members of the category *birds;* and men and women are *people.* It has been argued that if human categories are hierarchically structured, then there must be fewer features involved in the definitions of the upperlevel or more abstract categories. For example, the concept *per-*

son supposedly would be defined only by those features that are common to both men and women.

> The number of defining features contained in an item's meaning decreases as the item becomes increasingly abstract; for example, *robin* contains more defining features than *bird*. This assumption seems unavoidable when one views meaning in terms of defining features. (Smith, Shoben, & Rips, 1974, p. 217)

This argument would presumably also hold true for pattern recognition—classifying an object as a bird would presumably be based on fewer defining features than classifying it as a robin.

If one accepts the assumption that there are defining features for classes of patterns, then all of this seems reasonable. However, it was argued earlier in this chapter that such sets of features do not exist. There is no closed set of features that defines all people or all men or all women. In addition to the indirect conclusions from the earlier discussuon, there is some more direct evidence that more abstract categories are not defined by fewer features than less abstract categories.

Classifying physical objects. If it were true that more abstract categories depended upon fewer features than less abstract categories, and if information is extracted from a pattern over time (Massaro, 1975, chap. 3), then it ought to take less time to extract those fewer features to make the more abstract categorization.

Let's say a subject is presented with a picture of a rocking chair and is asked: "Is this a piece of furniture?" versus "Is this a chair?" versus "Is this a rocking chair?" According to a strict interpretation of a hierarchical model based on defining features, it should take longest to answer yes to the rocking chair question; the furniture question ought to be answered most quickly. However, this has not been found. The crucial variable seems to be the frequency with which a specific word has been used to label a given object. For example, for dogs with infrequent names, such as "Alsatian," the more abstract question ("Is this a dog?") is answered more quickly than the more concrete question ("Is this an Alsatian?"), even though the answer is yes in both cases. However, for more familiar dogs, the name question is answered faster (Conrad, 1972; Hutcheon, 1970, reported in Bartram, 1974). Thus the hierarchical model based on defining features is not supported.

5.9 Ease of recognition

The evidence in the last few sections indicates that human knowledge is not structured in a strict hierarchy. However, we have all had the experience of briefly seeing some object out of the corner of our eye and being able to tell the object is a person, without being able to tell if it is a man or a woman. Based on such examples, it seems that there must be some difference between the abstract category *person* and the more concrete *man* and *woman*. Otherwise, so the argument goes, how could you know it was a person without being able to tell that it was a man or a woman?

In order to see one problem with this argument, let us consider a slightly abnormal situation in which it might be possible to identify something as a man or woman without being able to identify it as a person. You are riding in a car down the center of a wide street. You glance to the side and you see a man leaning against a lamppost. However, you later learn that you were driving by the studio of a sculptor who produces lifelike statues. So the object that you saw had the appearance of a human male, rather than a female, but it was not a person. Thus one can sometimes identify specific characteristics of an object without being able to identify its general characteristics, which are supposedly based on only a subset of the features used to identify the specific characteristics.

Although this example is a little bizarre, it serves to make an important point. The ease and accuracy with which a given object is classified *depends upon the objects that it must be differentiated from*. It is usually easy to classify objects as people because the other alternatives are very different. On a street in the city, an object is either a car, a person, a fire hydrant, a lamppost, a mailbox, or a building. At this level of analysis, it is easy to tell if an object is a person or not. This is not because *person* is defined by only a few features, but because *it only takes a few features (that is, a gross analysis is all that is needed) to differentiate a person from those other sorts of objects*. The amount of analysis that is necessary in order to classify a given pattern depends in a large part on the types of patterns that the pattern in question must be differentiated from. Usually when a man can be present, a woman can be present also. If so, then one would have to make a relatively careful analysis of the person, in order to determine if one has seen a man or a woman. Thus, the features that define a person are relative to the other objects that might possibly be present. The features that define a person in one situation may not be defining in another.

Based on all this, the notion that human knowledge is strictly hierarchical is once again brought into question. It is true that many of our categories are hierarchically organized, in that men and women are people, and people are animals, and animals are living things, and so forth up the

Pattern recognition

hierarchy. In the sense that our categories are ordered in this way, then human knowledge is hierarchical. However, this does not mean that the categories are literally built on one another. The definition of an abstract category is not pulled out of the features that define the lower level categories. The reason that *person* is a more abstract category than either *man* or *woman* is that anything that is a man *or* a woman can be called a person.

5.10 A related question: abstract pattern maps?

There are many additional issues in this area which are important, and one or two can be briefly mentioned here. The first concerns the abstractness that pattern maps can take. For example, if someone is told, "Look for a fruit," does this mean that there is a "fruit" map which then becomes relevant? Is this fruit map different from the maps for apples, pears, and other fruits? The discussion in the last few sections does not support the idea that there is some abstract representation constructed by the subject during learning, and that can serve to stand for a whole class of objects. Some further evidence regarding abstract feature maps comes from two studies by Potter. In the first study (Potter, 1975), subjects were shown a series of briefly exposed pictures. The subjects' task was to attempt to recognize one brief picture in the series. Recognition of the target picture was facilitated if a verbal description (e.g., boats on a beach) was presented before the series was shown. Potter also found that the verbal description facilitated recognition just as much as earlier presentation of the picture itself. This could be taken as evidence that there is a generalized map for boats on a beach which somehow contains information that applies to all pictures of boats on beaches. One question that arises here is, What information could possibly be common to all pictures of boats or beaches, and so could facilitate recognition? Potter doesn't address the question, but the result of the second study made the question less important. The later study by Potter (1976) found that actually seeing the target picture was a better cue than the label, which raises difficulties for the notion of a boats-on-beaches pattern map. These results therefore are in accord with the point of view outlined in the last few sections.

Locke versus Berkeley on abstract ideas. The question whether there are feature maps which correspond to whole classes of objects, such as all fruits, is one which has a long history. For over two thousand years philosophers have argued about whether or not humans are able to formulate "abstract" ideas, which could stand for, or symbolize, a whole class of objects. One discussion of interest here was between Locke (1690, rpt. 1964) and Berkeley (1710, rpt. 1963), two well-known philosophers of the British Empiricist Movement. The British Empiricists argued that all human ideas came from experience, rather than being innate, as some other philosophers had argued. However, the British Empiricists differed among themselves as to the existence of abstract ideas. Locke argued that humans could form "abstract ideas," which can stand for whole classes of objects. For example, Locke argued that from all our experiences with white objects, we could pull out some notion of "whiteness," which was common to all these experiences. This whiteness could then be contemplated by itself, according to Locke, and would be an abstract idea, because it would no longer be tied down to any particular white object. In the same way, it would be argued that there is an abstract idea of "fruit," or "person," or any class of objects with which we can deal.

Locke's argument was criticized by Berkeley, who argued that Locke was incorrect because he, Berkeley, could not find these abstract ideas which Locke argued played an important role in thought. Berkeley found that whenever he formulated some supposedly abstract idea, such as *person,* his idea always took the form of some specific person. He could not think about *person* in the abstract; he could only think about specific examples of people. These examples didn't have to be familiar people, but they always had specific characteristics, such as a specific size. Thus, Berkeley attempted to refute Locke's argument through introspection.

Studies of recognition of visual prototypes. There has been some recent experimental work in psychology that is taken as support for Locke's notion of abstract ideas. Much of this work has been carried out by Posner and his colleagues (summarized in Posner, 1973, chap. 3). Posner argues that we can classify new faces because our past experience with faces has left a *trace system* in our memories. This trace system summarizes our experiences with faces, because all the elements that appear again and again in faces would be strongly represented in this trace system. This provides a "central tendency," or "prototype," which is a single instance of a face, somehow distilled out of all the faces which we have seen. As an analogy, if we took many pictures of faces, superimposing one face over the next on the same piece of film, some features would get darker and darker, because they occurred again and again. After a while, there would be a "new" face formed on the film corresponding to none of the faces which were actually photographed. This composite face corresponds to the prototype that

Pattern recognition

Posner believes is pulled out of our experience with a class of visual patterns. This prototype can then serve to represent the class *face* in our thought.

In order to provide support for these ideas, Posner and his colleagues (e.g., Posner 1969; Posner & Keele, 1968, 1970) have conducted a series of studies concerned with the development of new categories. In the basic design, a small number of random dot patterns are used, such as those at the top of Figure 5.5. Each pattern, called a prototype, serves as the basis for a new category to be learned by the subject. Additional category members are generated from each of the prototypes by moving some of the dots around randomly. This results in several sets of patterns, each of which has been generated from one prototype. Some examples of these generated patterns are shown below one prototype in Figure 5.5. Subjects are then given the four sets of patterns, *without the prototypes,* in a learning task. They have to learn to respond to each pattern with a number from one to four. The experiment continues until all the patterns generated from the same prototype are put into the same class by the subject. Once this occurs, one could argue that these subjects have learned four new visual categories which are of the same sort as the more typical visual categories we know, such as *pencil, car, house, person,* and so on.

Posner has argued that since each of the classes is generated from a prototype, then the prototype will be "abstracted" by the subject as he or she gets experience with all the patterns because the prototype is central to each class, as we saw earlier. Thus, subjects will have a representation of each prototype in memory *even though the prototype has never been pre-*

Figure 5.5. *Top row:* Three examples of prototypes used by Posner and Keele (1968). *Bottom row:* Four patterns generated from the prototype on the right.

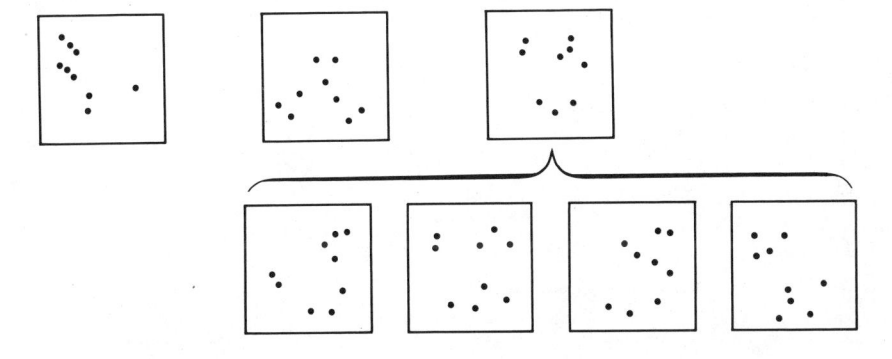

sented. "Thus a prototype serves as an internal representation of a whole set of individual patterns (Posner, 1973, p. 54)." Posner refers to the prototype by the term "abstract idea," and he suggests that the prototype is the same thing that Locke referred to in his theory and that Berkeley couldn't imagine.

In order to examine what the subject has stored about each of the classes, a transfer task is presented after the learning task has been completed. Another set of patterns is presented to the subject, and each of the new patterns is to be put into one of the four classes which were just learned. The patterns in the transfer task are of four kinds: (1) Old patterns—patterns which were classified in the learning task. (2) Prototype—the prototype from each class, which had not been seen before. (3) New distortion—other patterns generated from the same four prototypes, but which had not been seen during learning. (4) Control patterns—generated from other prototypes, but not included in the learning task. There are two important measures of performance on the transfer task. First, how well does the subject classify these various sorts of patterns, and second, how quickly does the subject respond to each pattern? The results from several experiments are presented in Table 5.2, and the support for the notion that the subject extracts the prototypes while learning the categories is only mixed. First, the prototypes are classified correctly more often than are new distortions, which supports Posner's theorizing, but the prototypes are not classified as well as the old patterns. This indicates that the subjects don't simply pull out the prototype as they are learning the classifications.

Table 5.2. Results on classification transfer studies with visual patterns

	Old pattern	Type of Transfer Pattern Prototype	New distortion	Control
Posner & Keele (1968)—Experiment III				
% Error	13.0	14.9	38.3	—
Reaction Time (sec.)	2.01	2.28	2.87	2.91
Posner & Keele (1970)—Experiment I				
% Error	20	32	56	—
Reaction Time (sec.)	2.88	2.93	3.75	—
Posner & Keele (1970)—Experiment II				
% Error	18	35	49	—
Reaction Time (sec.)	2.39	3.05	3.20	—
Strange, Keeney, Kessel, & Jenkins (1970)				
% Error	12	26	47	—

The second bit of negative evidence comes from the reaction-time measure, also shown in the table: the old patterns are classified more quickly than the prototypes. Once again, if the prototype was serving as the representation of a whole class, then the prototype ought to be classified fastest. There are other studies which also show the same pattern (e.g., Homa, Cross, Cornell, Goldman, & Schwartz, 1973).

It should also be noted that Medin and Schaffer (1978) have recently argued that it is possible to explain the results from the studies in Table 5.2 without assuming that the subject has abstracted the prototype. Medin and Schaffer propose that one doesn't have a single representative of a class at all. Rather, one remembers the various specific patterns that one has seen and classifies new patterns by comparing a new pattern to the old patterns that one remembers. This point of view supports the present discussion. At present a reasonable conclusion from the results of prototype studies is that the results are not definitive in supporting the notion that visual prototypes are extracted when a person learns to classify new sets of visual patterns.

Abstract attributes. A related question concerns the type of information extracted from a pattern when the pattern is being examined to determine if it contains some abstract attribute. Let's say you meet a person for the first time, take one look at the person's face, and decide that the person is cruel. Soon after doing this, you can remember that the person was cruel without remembering what the person looked like. This could be explained in either of two ways. First, it might be that the pattern map for a cruel face is of an abstract nature, since it is more general than any specific face. Therefore, if cruelty was perceived using such a map, then one wouldn't remember anything else about the face, assuming that the pattern map is central in determining what is recalled. On the other hand, it could be argued here, as was argued in section 5.6, that you must use a relatively concrete description of the face in question in order to recognize it as being cruel. If so, then it would be argued that the reason that the face couldn't be recalled is because the specific set of fixations couldn't be recalled, while the description of cruelty could.

One way to differentiate between these two views concerning the abstractness of the pattern map would be through the possibility of interfering with processing through changes in nonrelevant attributes of the to-be-analyzed pattern. If a subject is asked to determine if a geometric form is a square, then according to the notion of abstract maps, the subject would simply look for four right angles and four sides of equal length connected in the appropriate way, without analyzing any of the more concrete attributes of the pattern. That is, the color or texture of the outline of the square would be irrelevant; all that would matter would be the presence of generalized right angles and sides. Therefore, if it could be shown that processing a square is slower if the four corners are each a different color, or something of that sort, it would indicate that concrete features were being used as the basis for the pattern map.

In summary, recent research does not support the idea that we have abstract representations in memory which are used as the basis for pattern recognition and for thinking about classes. This conclusion is supported by the analysis in chapter 2 and 3 concerning recall of verbal material, and also by the analysis earlier in this chapter. The same conclusion will arise several times in part 3.

5.11 Pattern recognition, concepts, and internal representations

The conclusions from this chapter have important implications for theories of thinking, one of which deserves brief mention here. We have concluded that there are no closed sets of features defining any classes, and that more abstract classes are not built on more concrete ones. Therefore, classifying an object, or recognizing a pattern, is not based on activation of some internal representation, or some internal object in the world of thought. Recognizing an object is more fruitfully considered to be one way of examining that object over time. To the degree that specific knowledge plays a role in directing this examination, we could say that the object has been recognized. Thus, there may not be any internal objects which serve as the objects of thought.

Also, if one examines objects by scanning them, one may imagine these objects by carrying out an "internalized" act of scanning. However, as we shall see in chapter 7, this does not mean that there must be an internal object to be scanned.

5.12 "Top down" versus "bottom up"

If one considers the feature analysis model discussed in section 5.1, one can see that processing goes from the bottom up, in the sense that the sensory receptors are at the "bottom" of the model, and the pattern recognizers are at the "top." In this sort of a scheme, the information from the outside world works its way up until it is recognized. The person's knowledge has little or no effect on what occurs, in this extreme view. However, the discussion in this chapter leads to the conclusion that pattern recognition also works from the top down, in the sense that one's knowledge plays an important role in perception. (This view has recently been advocated by several theorists, including Hochberg, 1978; Minsky, 1975; Neisser, 1976; Palmer 1975; and Norman & Bobrow, 1975). Examples of the use of knowledge in pattern recognition were discussed in section 5.5. We saw that perception depends greatly upon one's expectations concerning the types of patterns which might occur. Recognition of a given pattern is made much easier when that pattern is expected by the perceiver. In this way, pattern recognition works from the top down, in the sense that one's knowledge about patterns would be at the top. This distinction between top down and bottom up processing is an important one, and it will serve to organize the discussion in the next chapter.

5.13 Summary and conclusions

In this chapter we have considered recent research in pattern recognition, and some related questions. Two major conclusions were drawn. First, there are no defining features for the various patterns that we deal with, and second, pattern recognition is a sequential process that takes time. The chapter began with a consideration of feature-analysis models of pattern recognition. There are two general forms of such models, depending upon whether one assumes that each class of pattern is defined by a small closed set of defining features. It was concluded that it might be better to assume that there are no defining features, and that all features contribute more or less to all categories.

In addition, it was argued that feature analysis models were in need of elaboration in that they usually assumed that all the features in a pattern were analyzed in parallel. However, there is evidence that visual patterns are processed sequentially, as a series of fixations. Evidence to support this claim was discussed. It was concluded that recognizing a pattern depends upon matching that pattern with information in memory, and that the ease with which one can do this varies from pattern to pattern. Finally, some questions concerning abstract versus concrete categories were considered, such as whether patterns are hierarchically structured, with abstract classes defined by fewer features than concrete classes.

6
Selective attention

6.0 Introduction

We have seen that matching a new pattern to past experience is an act which extends over time. When we examine a face, we scan the face in a series of fixations. One could say that we selectively fixate the various parts of the face over time. Thus, pattern recognition has implicit in it a selective aspect. This selective aspect of human functioning has been studied under the topic of attention. One of the major advances in recent years has been the hypothesis that perception and attention might be two aspects of the same process, rather than two separate processes, one concerned with analysis of stimuli (perception), and the other concerned with selection from the analyzed stimuli (attention). The present chapter will briefly review research and theorizing on attention in order to follow the development of this point of view.

We shall begin with a discussion of Broadbent's (1958) filter model of attention, one of the earliest information-processing models. The filter model was basically a bottom-up processing model, which did not greatly emphasize the use of knowledge in perception. The filter model had difficulty dealing with certain experimental results, so Treisman (1960) proposed a modified filter model, which placed more emphasis on the role of one's knowledge in attention. However, Treisman's model is insufficient from our point of view, because it did not go into detail concerning the

Selective attention

fine grain of the processes involved. Therefore, the main thrust of the discussion will concern recent theorizing which attempts to tie together attention and top-down models of perception. In addition, recent work concerning limitations in processing capacity will be important in the discussion.

6.1 Shadowing: the basic data

Cherry's (1953) experiments on shadowing were the most influential early studies of attention. In the basic task, the subject hears two messages at the same time, one presented to each ear, via headphones. The subject repeats aloud, or shadows, the words in one of these messages as soon as they are heard. The subject is not to repeat any of the words from the second message—the rejected or ignored message. Thus, the subject must actively attend to and process the shadowed message. The question of interest was what happened to the material in the rejected message.

Cherry tried to determine what sort of analysis was made of the material in the rejected message by changing that message as the subject was shadowing the other message. The experiment started with two male voices reading prose passages. One message was presented to each ear, and the subject shadowed one of them. After a time, and unannounced, the rejected message was changed in any of a number of ways. After a while, the original male voice would be reintroduced, so that the rejected message would end the same way as it began. After the session, the subjects were asked about the materials in the rejected message, and they could report almost nothing about it. A change from English to German and back again was not noticed, indicating that the subjects were not identifying the words in the rejected message. However, a change from the male voice to a tone and back again was always noticed by the subjects, and a change from male to female was almost always noticed. Thus, it seemed that not much more than the gross physical features were extracted from the rejected message.

These findings were supported by the results of a similar experiment by Moray (1959, Experiment I). The shadowed material was a prose passage, and the to-be-ignored material consisted of a list of seven words, which was repeated for a total of 35 times in the to-be-ignored ear, although the subject obviously wasn't told this. After the shadowing task, the subjects were given a recognition test, and the seven words from the repeated list were not recognized any better than new words. The to-be-ignored material seemed to have made no impression whatever on the subjects.

In summary, the basic data from shadowing experiments indicate that when subjects shadow one message, they get almost nothing out of the to-be-rejected message. The basic question is then how people are able to deal with one message, so that they can shadow it, while getting almost no information out of another. We shall consider two general orientations to this question, one based on Broadbent's theorizing, and the other evolving out of pattern recognition models.

6.2 Broadbent's filter model

Boradbent's (1958, 1971) filter model assumed that information could be taken in along any of a number of sensory channels, which are defined by some physical characteristic which can be used to separate relevant from irrelevant material. Examples of channels would be words heard in the left ear, or words spoken by a female voice, or words written in blue ink.

It is important to emphasize that channels were defined in terms of physical characteristics, rather than in terms of meaning or content. According to the filter model, before the more complicated processing of meaning can occur, the message on any given channel must reach the *central processing system*. This system may be considered to be quivalent to consciousness. Broadbent assumed that this system was a strictly serial processor: that is, it processed items in series, one at a time. Therefore, out of all the messages available on all the sensory channels at any time, only one can get processed in further detail, so that its meaning is extracted. This is where selective attention occurs: it is brought about by a filter between the sensory channels and the central processor. This filter can be set to pass only those messages with certain physical characteristics, those corresponding to the sensory channel being attended to. The message on this channel will then be analyzed further, so that its meaning will be extracted.

Thus, according to Broadbent's filter model, the sensory channels hold unanalyzed stimuli. Before an item gets through the filter, we don't know what it is. This model explained the results from shadowing experiments by assuming that the message on the rejected channel never gets to the central processor, and so is never processed for meaning. Since only the grossest physical characteristics of the rejected message serve as the basis for the rejection of that message, only they can be reported. In sum, very little emphasis is placed on the use of one's knowledge here. The processing is basically bottom-up. (Broadbent, 1958, briefly mentions more complicated, top-down possibilities, but they were not elaborated in the filter model.)

6.3 Processing the meaning of the rejected message: problems for the filter.

Broadbent's filter model argued that the shadowed message is attended to only because it contains certain physical attributes, such as that it is coming in the left ear. This means that *words* aren't getting through the filter, *meaningless sounds* are. If this is so, then attention should never switch to the rejected message because of the meaning of the words in the message. However, it was soon demonstrated that the meaning of the words in the rejected message could influence attention, which indicated that the rejected message was being processed as more than a string of sounds.

Some examples of processing the rejected message. Moray (1959, Experiment II) varied a typical shadowing experiment by presenting instructions on the *rejected* channel that told the subject to switch the shadowing to that channel. These instructions were noticed by the subjects only about 10 percent of the time. However, if the instructions were preceded by the subject's own *name* on the rejected channel, the instructions were noticed about one-third of the time, a significant proportion, even though it didn't have the physical characteristics of the to-be-shadowed channel. Neisser (1969) reported a comparable finding in a visual shadowing task. The fact that one's name can be noticed significantly more frequently than other words indicates that there is additional processing of the material in the rejected channel.

Several studies by Treisman (e.g., 1960, 1964) provide further evidence that the rejected message is processed as speech. In one study, subjects shadowed a prose passage in one ear and ignored another passage in the other ear. At a point unknown to the subject, the two messages changed ears. For example, if the shadowed message was "now is the time for . . ." the sudden switch would put "all" into the rejected ear, and some random word from the other passage would now appear in the to-be-shadowed passage. Treisman found that subjects would often follow the message to the rejected channel for a few words before getting back to the correct channel. Therefore, the information on the rejected channel must be analyzed as words also. The content of the shadowed message couldn't result in the subjects' inadvertently switching to the rejected channel if the information on this channel was a string of meaningless sounds.

To summarize, these several results are taken to indicate that some detailed processing is carried out on the material in the to-be-ignored channel. If not, then it is hard to see how one could explain the frequent switch of attention to one's name on that channel, or the following of a meaningful message to that channel.

Treisman's reformulation of the filter model. Based on these results and others like them, Treisman (1960) attempted to reformulate the filter model. The first major change was that the all-or-none characteristics of the filter were altered. The basic decision as to what message to attend to is still made on the basis of physical characteristics, such as locations or voice. However, the rejected message is not completely blocked. Rather, it is *attenuated*, or lowered in strength. It gets through, but less strongly than the attended message.

The second change was the addition of the assumption that all messages are analyzed for meaning. Treisman assumed that our memories contained a set of "dictionary units," each of which corresponds to a word. If one of these units is fired by the appropriate input from the environment, then one will perceive that particular word. Since the words on the rejected channel are attenuated by the filter, then there is much less of a chance that any of them will be strong enough to fire its respective unit. Therefore, the words in the rejected message will usually not be perceived. In order to account for the fact that one's name can often break into attention, Treisman assumed that the dictionary unit for one's own name had a very low threshold. The low threshold means that it can be fired even if an attenuated signal activates it, so one's name will be heard even on the rejected channel. Finally, there is the question of why a highly probable word on the rejected channel will be shadowed, as when "Now is the time . . ." switches to the rejected channel and is followed by the subject. Treisman argued that when a word is perceived, the thresholds of the dictionary units for words that were more or less probable in that context would be briefly lowered. Therefore, a very probable word will be heard even on the rejected channel. This aspect of Treisman's model is particularly important to the present discussion, because it emphasizes the role of one's knowledge in attention. The assumption that perception of one word lowers the thresholds for related words is an example of top-down processing, which is very similar to the conclusions drawn in chapter 5.

However, one difficulty with Treisman's model concerns the notion of dictionary units. First of all, these units are taken to be the representations of words in memory, and it was argued in chapters 2 and 3 that there are

Selective attention

no isolated units in memory, each corresponding to a word. Secondly, it was argued in the last chapter that perception entails a sequential analysis of stimuli over time, and it seems that these monolithic dictionary units do not function in this way. In an elaborated version of this basic model, Morton (1970) mentioned that information can be summed over time to activate a dictionary unit, but this still doesn't get at the temporal aspects of processing that were discussed in the last chapter. These aspects of processing will be elaborated further in section 6.5. However, given this difficulty, Treisman's theorizing is important because her point of view requires that we take into account the perceiver's knowledge in order to understand perception and attention.

6.4 Kahneman's limited-capacity model

In an interesting addition to the models of attention, Kahneman (1973) has argued that paying attention could be looked upon as doing work. At any given time, there are many activities that could be carried out: those that have been activated by receiving an input from the external world. However, external input alone is not enough to actually have the activity carried out. When a person attends to some activity, this provides the additional energy needed to carry it out.

Since there is only a limited capacity available for attending to activities, or, to put it another way, only a limited amount of energy available, then one cannot deal with all the activities that could be carried out at any time. Kahneman (1973, chap. 1) argues that a number of factors determine how the limited attention capacity will be allocated among the activities that have received inputs at any given time. Two of these factors are especially relevant here. First, there are enduring dispositions, both learned and innate. For example, capacity is automatically allocated to any conversation containing one's name, which is a learned disposition. Capacity also seems to be automatically allocated to novel events, which may be an innate disposition. Second, the momentary intentions of the person influence allocation. As an example, in a shadowing experiment the subject attempts to repeat what is being said in the left earphone. This intention would result in capacity being allocated to messages that come in the left earphone.

Kahneman's model seems to be fundamentally different from Broadbent's, which assumes that there is a bottleneck somewhere in the processing system which allows only one activity to be carried out at once. In opposition to this, Kahneman argues that if the main task being carried out were easy enough, then there ought to be extra capacity available to carry out other tasks.

Kahneman's view of attention as a limited capacity to carry out activities is interesting, and may help to explain many phenomena, as we shall see in several sections that follow. However, there are questions that can be raised concerning the notion that attending to some activity results in that activity being given an additional boost of energy. Consider a parent feeding a young child. The presentation of the spoon results in the child's taking the food. Now a food that the child dislikes is placed on the spoon. The child takes one mouthful and thenceforth refuses to eat when the spoon is presented. One effective method to get the child to eat in such a situation is to *distract* the child with a toy or some silliness on the parent's part. When the child is sufficiently distracted, the touch of the spoon to the child's lips results in an automatic opening of the child's mouth, and the child will now take in the food.

The important point about this example is that the activity of eating was carried out when the child's attention was taken up by something else. Therefore, the additional energy from attention was not forthcoming, but the activity was capable of being initiated by the spoon. This indicates that the input from the environment alone is enough to initiate at least some activities. If so, then attention may not entail adding energy to some activities so much as turning off others. At least in the case of eating, it will run off automatically unless stopped. Therefore, if one attends to one's own eating, one would not seem to be adding more energy so that the act can be carried out.

At the very least, the above example, if valid, indicates that things are more complicated then the simple allocation of energy in Kahneman's model. However, the notion of limited capacity—without energy—will be important in later sections. The notion of cognitive capacity (attention or conscious capacity), has also been recently examined experimentally by Posner and his colleagues (see Posner & Snyder, 1975, for a summary).

6.5 Neisser's synthesis model

Several theorists (e.g., Hochberg, 1970a, b; Neisser, 1967, 1976) have recently argued that pattern recognition and attention are two aspects of the same phenomenon. As mentioned earlier, this is an important insight, because it points the way to an integration of much research.

Neisser (1967) argued that perception is not simply the activation of

Selective attention

something inside us by an input from the outside. Perception could be looked upon as a synthesizing process. One perceives something by synthesizing that thing; that is, by making it. (The reader may recall the discussion of resonance in section 5.5.) The notion of perception as a synthesizing process was originally proposed as a model of speech perception (e.g., Liberman, 1970). It was argued that one perceives a sentence by using one's own speech-production mechanisms to produce a sentence to match the input. Neisser proposed this model as a general model of perception: Perception of any event is the result of the synthesis of that event by the perceiver.

Neisser argued that conscious attention is the activity of synthesizing a percept. Therefore, a subject can report only the grossest characteristics of a rejected message because the rejected message does not receive detailed synthesis. In order to determine which input would receive detailed synthesis, Neisser argued that there were preattentive mechanisms, which worked before attention took place. These mechanisms serve to segregate the total input into groups, so that one group can be selected for detailed synthesis. In addition, these preattentive mechanisms were set to detect certain important inputs, such as one's name. One problem with Neisser's model is that it does not really say how one's name bursts into consciousness when the preattentive mechanisms pick it up. It is just said that the preattentive mechanisms are set to respond to certain important inputs, and when they do, these inputs are attended to. Also, there is a problem with Neisser's assumption that active synthesis is equivalent to conscious awareness. A task like driving or avoiding obstacles when walking is often carried out with a minimum of attention and awareness. According to Neisser's model, such tasks must not receive active synthesis, and so must be carried out using the preattentive mechanisms alone. As Kahneman (1973, chap 7) comments, it is difficult to see how these relatively precise tasks could be carried out using the relatively global and undifferentiated preattentive mechanisms.

6.6 Top-down models of pattern recognition as models of attention

As mentioned earlier, a number of theorists have recently argued that pattern recognition and attention are not two separate phenomena, involving two separate processes, but rather two sides of the same coin. From this point of view, perceiving an object and attending an object are one and the same process: when one perceives something, one attends to it; and when one attends to an object, one perceives it. Given this orientation, much of the discussion from chapter 5 becomes relevant to attention.

We shall now consider this point of view in some detail, because of its potential importance. The discussion that follows is based mainly on the work of Hochberg (1970a, b, 1978) and Neisser (1976). However, the present discussion is a modification of their views, so that probably neither Hochberg nor Neisser would agree with the present formulation.

Knowledge and perception. It was argued in the last chapter that perception depends upon knowledge, because one's expectancies play a role in perception. The perception of a given object entails matching that object to a pattern map—the analogy of resonance was mentioned in the last chapter. The ease with which an object will be matched depends in part on how probable the object is in the present context. This view was called a top-down view in the last chapter. If you go past someone's office, then only a glimpse of the person is needed for you to see them. However, the same glimpse won't suffice if you are in a restaurant that you have never been to before. Under these circumstances, the brief glance won't serve to identify the person. Perception is as much top-down as it is bottom-up.

Cyclical aspects of perception. It was also argued in the last chapter that perception is a sequential or cyclical activity. For example, it was argued that visual perception begins with a visual fixation that is matched against the pattern maps we know. Based on this match, we will then make another fixation, and then another, until there has been a sufficient match to specify one pattern. Thus, the process involves fixation → match (resonance) → new fixation → further match (resonance) → etc. This is the sequential or cyclical aspect of perception. At each point at which a fixation must be matched with knowledge, we are talking about resonance, and top-down processing becomes important.

The same sort of reasoning would hold for perception of an auditory message. For example, if one is listening to someone else talk, one listens by matching one's knowledge to the message as the speaker goes on talking. When the speaker begins, one may have little expectation as to what will be said, so little top-down processing can occur. One must then make a match through detailed analysis of the message. However, once one has analyzed the beginning of the message, one's knowledge and expectations can come into play, making further processing much easier. The early part of a verbal message cuts down the possibilities for the rest of the message, which facilitates processing. The scripts discussed in chapter 3 may play an important role here, since they represent one's knowledge about various types of events, and they can therefore serve to facilitate processing of messages about those events.

Now if a given word in a sentence is very unlikely, one will have difficulty processing it. Basically, the matching processing will be relatively slow because the word is unlikely. Therefore, one may not have time to hear the word, especially if other words follow right after it and serve to "mask" it. One will say "Come again?" On the other hand, one may find oneself stopping to try to figure out what the word was, thereby missing words that follow it in the message. Thus in order to perceive some input, one must have adequate time to match one's knowledge to that input. The amount of time that one needs depends upon how likely the stimulus is, among other things. Another important factor in whether or not one will perceive some event is the amount of practice that one has had. For example, adults riding in a car are much more able to read messages on billboards than children are, because adults have had more practice in reading. Perception is a skill that improves with practice (Neisser, 1976).

Selective attention. Returning now to the main discussion, Hochberg (1970a) explains selective attention in the shadowing task by assuming that processing the attended channel interferes with processing the other channels. Assume that a subject is instructed to shadow a message in the left ear. Two messages are then presented, one to each ear. Based on the instructions, the subject can usually do nothing more than listen carefully to the voice in the left ear, since the subject has no prior knowledge concerning the content of the message.

However, once the subject has heard the first few words in the shadowed message, there are a number of factors which will help to keep attention to that message. First, the sound of the voice will stay the same and so will its location. These are two sources of information which will make it easier for the subject to resonate to the shadowed message. Also, any expectations based on sequential probabilities and the like will also favor words in the shadowed message. If one hears "He went to the refrigerator and opened . . ." then "the door" would be strongly expected, along with a few other phrases. These expectations also make it more likely that further words in the shadowed message will be recognized.

In summary, it is being argued that attention entails matching an input to one's knowledge. That is, attention entails resonance, just as perception does. Furthermore, the likelihood that one will attend to a given input at any time depends on the ease with which one will resonate to that input at a given time, relative to any other inputs presented at the same time. Since there are several factors working to make the resonance to the words in shadowed message more probable, then it is likely that the person will stay with that message. However, if these various factors are also relevant to the to-be-ignored message, then the subject may sometimes mistakenly shadow a word in that message. For example, if a word in the to-be-ignored message fits into the shadowed message, it may be shadowed even though it is in the wrong message. Also, if the same voice was reading both messages, that ought to make shadowing more difficult, and so on.

We have seen that selective attention comes about because the to-be-shadowed message can be matched more easily than the other message. This also results in an inability to get much out of the rejected message. As soon as the first sounds from the to-be-shadowed channel are heard, the subject attempts to match them, and this match sets up expectations as to what will come next in that channel. This match is assumed to take time, and all the while the first sounds from the to-be-ignored channel are coming in. By the time the subject has matched the initial words from the shadowed channel and repeated those words, the initial sounds from the to-be-ignored channel will be long gone. Therefore, no response could be made to that information. Thus it can be argued that while the subject is actively dealing with the primary task, he or she cannot break away to deal with the other channels. However, if it is easy to process the to-be-shadowed message, because, for example, of its familiarity, then the subject could "switch off" from that message and get material from the other channel. Even under the best circumstances, though, there would not be much time to get detailed information from the rejected channel, because the subject would have to keep checking things on the primary channel. This is one reason why one's name can sometimes be heard on the rejected channel when other words are not. One's name is such an overlearned stimulus that simply hearing the first sound(s) results in our being able to recognize and attend to it. In summary, in order to get information from the other channels, one must switch back and forth in the "dead time" when the main task is more or less under control.

Expectations. There is some ambiguity surrounding the term *expectation* that ought to be briefly discussed before going further. Saying that one's expectations are important in the perception of a message gives the impression of a person actively imagining what will be heard next. As Neisser (1976, chap. 5) mentions, this use may raise some problems, because it is usually not possible to predict the exact word or words that will be heard next. If this is so, then the subject ought to have a great deal of difficulty following any message that was not known by heart, because there would have to be a constant revision of expectations, due to the lack of perfect predictability.

However, there is a second way in which one can talk about using knowlege and expectations that may not encounter these difficulties. We have argued that listening to a message is a cyclical activity, involving sampling from the input and matching something from memory to this sample. Thus, when a word has been heard at time t, a sample of the input is then taken at time $t+1$. This input sample may not be complete enough to specify a single word unambiguously, which means that what the subject hears will depend on the word from memory that can be matched to this sample. If we then assume that the word that will be matched at time $t+1$ depends, at least in part, on the words that have been matched through time t, then one could say that the subject expects certain words at time $t+1$. That is, if the words heard through time t serve to differentially cue certain words at time $t+1$, then expectations are operating. Sequential order of words, among other things, would be important here. Expectation in this context means that there is an influence from one time to the next on what will be heard. In this way, one can say that expectations influence perception and attention without assuming that the subject must have a complete description of the stimulus available before anything can be perceived. Rumelhart (1977, chaps. 2 and 3) makes a similar point.

It should also be pointed out here that there may be a basic connection between this notion of the influence of earlier events on later events and the discussion of the temporal ordering of events in chapter 4. At that time it was argued that background information could serve to "link" two events in memory, in that overlap of background information could make it possible for one event to cue another. These factors could also be working here. In other words, the fact that a given word can produce an expectation for another word could be explained in part by the overlap in background information in memory. Such a conclusion would bring about a basic connection between the notions concerning perception and attention developed in part 2 and the ideas concerning memory developed in part 1. In sum, to produce an expectation for some event is to be a retrieval cue for that event.

Perception and memory. We have seen that perceiving a message entails resonating to that message. Remembering that message, however, may involve something more. We saw in chapters 1, 2, and 3 that the ability to recall some event may depend on a detailed set of retrieval cues, which must be developed as the person studies the material. Therefore, if one is working hard to keep up with some verbal message, as when one is shadowing it, one may not have time to carry out any elaboration "in the cracks" of the message. Therefore, one might not be able to remember much more than the grossest aspects of the shadowed message.

In this context it is important to point out that there is evidence that subjects in a shadowing experiment usually cannot report much about the shadowed message after they have finished (Norman, 1976, p. 16). Theorists have usually emphasized the inability to recall anything but the grossest features of the rejected message, and that has also been emphasized in this chapter. However, not much detail can be reported about the shadowed message, either, especially if the shadowing task is difficult (although it is more than can be reported about the nonshadowed message). This would be expected if the subject would have to do some further elaboration before detailed recall could be expected. With a difficult shadowing task, the subject would have no time to think about what was being shadowed, so later recall should be difficult.

Perception and awareness. The point of view in this section is similar to that of Neisser, discussed in section 6.5, but there are some important differences, one of which bears emphasis here. It has just been argued that perception and attention can be independent of memory, in that it is possible to perceive and attend to something without being able to remember it later. If so, then one might be able to carry out a relatively complicated perceptual task without being aware of it, in the sense of not being able to report afterward how one did it. Hochberg (1970a) argues that awareness is always after-the-fact, in that *as we carry out some activity* we cannot report on what we are doing. The reporting must depend upon the memory for what was done. (It is true that one can sometimes produce a running verbalization as one carries out some task, but this is not strictly a report on the task. This point is discussed further in chapter 9.) If verbal report is equated with awareness, then one can carry out detailed analysis in order to do something like driving without being able to recall any of it later. In this way, this model can be differentiated from that of Neisser (1967).

6.7 On hearing and attending to one's name

There is one difficulty with the analysis so far concerning why we are so sensitive to our names. We have presented Hochberg's (1969) viewpoint that the efficiency with which one can recognize one's own name can make up for the lack of expectations for it in the situation. One usually attends to the words in the shadowed message because they are easiest to match, all other things being equal; one usually does not attend to the words in the to-be-ignored message because they are too difficult to match. That is, since the words in the rejected message do not match expectations, the subject will not be able to recognize most of them in the small gaps that occur when the shadowing task gets easy. One's name, though, is easily recognized, so it can be heard even if only a very short time is available. One could summarize this by saying that there are two factors contributing to whether or not a given word is heard in some situation: (1) How strongly it is expected, and (2) how easy it is to recognize. These factors combine to determine what is heard at any given time.

The problem that this analysis may not deal with is that when one's name is heard, it usually brings with it a disruption of shadowing performance. According to Hochberg's model, the name should be heard, but the subject should be able to keep on shadowing. However, the subject's name often takes the subject's attention away from the main task, which doesn't seem to be explainable on the basis of Hochberg's model. One might say that if one's name is heard, one automatically switches attention to it, because hearing one's name is a signal for something important to follow. There is a second possible explanation as to why hearing one's name can interrupt shadowing, and it is worth considering in a bit more detail.

Maintaining versus switching attention. According to Hochberg, attention is maintained so long as expectations about the shadowed message can facilitate processing of that message. However, if this were the only aspect of attention, then one never ought to switch attention from what one is currently doing to something else. For example, assume that you are listening to a familiar song. Since the song is familiar, you have detailed expectations as to how it is going to sound at the next point in time. Therefore, you should stay "locked in" on the song, and you should not be able to switch attention to something else until the song is over. However, this obviously is not true. If someone called your name loudly enough, or tapped you on the shoulder, you would break away from that song.

Therefore, it seems that we now have a reasonable explanation of how attention is maintained, but we now need to elaborate this model to explain how it is that one's attention can be interrupted under certain circumstances. In order to do this, we must first digress briefly.

Habituation of the orienting reflex. In Pavlov's classic work on conditioned reflexes in dogs, he noted an interesting change in their behavior before any conditioning occurred. Assume that a dog was being conditioned to salivate to a tone. The very first time the dog heard the tone, the dog's ears would stand up, it would get very quiet, and it would turn toward the source of the sound, as if to listen to it clearly. This set of responses was called the orienting reflex, or the "what is it" reflex, by Pavlov (cited by Razran, 1961). After a few presentations of the tone, the orienting reflex dropped out, or habituated. The dog simply stood quietly while the tone was presented, and conditioning could then occur.

This orienting reflex is not restricted to sounds; it will be made to any stimulus, so long as the stimulus is a novel one. As the novel stimulus is presented several times, the orienting reflex drops out. At that point, the subject ignores the now familiar stimulus. One reason that the habituation of the orienting reflex is important is because it is not due to simple fatigue of the receptor organs. In order to demonstrate this, one simply has to present a stimulus regularly, say once every 30 seconds. The first few stimuli will produce orienting reflexes, but they soon will habituate. As long as the stimulus is regularly occurring, there is no further orienting reflex. However, if one of the stimuli is now omitted, the subject will produce an orienting reflex at the time at which the tone should have occurred. Obviously, if leaving out a stimulus can produce an orienting reflex, then it was not that the subject could not hear the regular tones, but that the subject simply was not attending to them.

In order to explain the habituation of the orienting reflex, Sokolov (1963) argued that the subject is constantly building a model of the external world. So long as the events in the world match this model, then there will be no response made to them. However, when an event occurs that does not match the subject's model, an orienting reflex will occur. The reason that the orienting reflex habituates is because ultimately the subject adds the new stimulus to the model, at which point no responses will occur.

Expectations, scripts, and switching attention. Let us now try to expand the earlier discussion of expectations to incorporate Sokolov's model of the world. We could translate this into terms already used here if we say that the shadowing task is set into the script of an experiment. That is, subjects use their prior knowledge, as well as what they can pick up while in the experiment, to develop a script for the experiment. We are now saying that at any point in time, the input at that point serves to produce not only specific expectations about the to-be-shadowed message, but also produces some expectations about the rest of the situation as well. This makes these expectations equivalent to Sokolov's notion of a model of the environment. If we can now assume that the subject checks these broader expectations (checks the script) against the environmental input as frequently as possible, then we may be able to explain why one's name on the rejected channel can sometimes catch one's attention.

It was argued earlier that people are very efficient at recognizing their own names. However, subjects would not come into a shadowing experiment *expecting* to hear their names on the rejected channel. One's script for an experiment wouldn't include that. Therefore, recognizing the name should result in an orienting reflex as the subjects try to produce a new description of the whole situation, or match a new script to it. Later the subject will be able to remember the name, if only because of the surprise it produced. This explanation predicts that if the subject's name is repeated several times, the amount of disruption that it causes should decrease greatly.

According to this argument, one's name disrupts shadowing because of two factors: first, it is an easily recognized word, and second, once it has been recognized, it produces a conflict with the subject's script of the situation. This conflict produces an orienting reflex that disrupts the shadowing. If this general point of view is on the right track, there is an important similarity between this model of attention and some notions discussed earlier concerning encoding, in addition to the obvious connection based on the script notion. We have concluded here that maintaining versus switching attention depends in part on the subject's script of the entire situation, including both the main task and as much of the other elements in the situation as can be attended to while dealing with the main task. The reader may recall the discussion of the role of background information in memory encodings in section 4.3. At that time, it was argued that encodings contain information in addition to that provided by the word itself. The present discussion has reached a similar conclusion: While carrying out a task, one is dealing with more than just that task. Thus, encoding and selective attention may be two sides of the same coin.

To return to shadowing, these notions can also explain why subjects can report that a voice on the rejected channel changed into a tone. It seems reasonable that a subject could pick up enough information about the rejected channel during easy parts of the shadowing to tell that a voice was present, even though no words could be identified. If the voice switched to a tone, the tone could probably be identified while shadowing, and the subject could then note the change. However, this sort of change might produce a much smaller disruption in shadowing than hearing one's name, because the subject's script would not need the major overhaul that seems to be required when one's name is heard on the rejected channel. There might be a continuum of more or less disruption in the ongoing task, depending upon the degree of reorganization required in one's expectations at any time. The full-fledged orienting reflex might only occur when a major reorganization of one's script is required.

To summarize, it has been argued that one attends to one's name on the rejected channel for three reasons. First, there are times when the shadowing task is easy enough so that the subject can try to listen to the rejected message. Second, since the time that the subject can break away from shadowing will be very brief, only very familiar words will be recognized. One especially familiar word is one's own name. Third, when the name is heard, it will produce an orienting reflex because it is such a strong violation of the subject's expectations. There are probably other words in the language, like "is," "an," and "the," which are so frequent that they can be recognized relatively easily "in the cracks" in the shadowing task. However, since these are words that are to be expected if the rejected message is like the shadowed message, there should be no conflict with the subject's script for the situation, and the words would then be quickly forgotten, as Hochberg (1970a) argues. A similar viewpoint has recently been proposed by Shiffrin (1976).

6.8 Conclusions from recent models of selective attention

Based on this survey of models of attention, there are several general ideas which have been proposed by a number of different theorists. First, whatever is being attended to at any given time influences what will be attended to in the immediate future. Secondly, information is sometimes obtained from the rejected channel because some items, such as one's name, are processed more easily than others. Finally, Kahneman and Hochberg have made explicit the idea that capacity limitations are important in attention. With a difficult message as the main task, the subject will not be able to switch to the rejected channel often enough to get much information out of it.

6.9 On "analyzing the meaning" of a message

In Broadbent's (1958) original filter model of selective attention, it was argued that the central processor took unanalyzed stimuli and turned them

Selective attention

into meaningful objects. This was assumed to be a separate step in processing a stimulus, in addition to processing the sensory features of the stimulus. This general idea, that processing the meaning of an input is a distinct stage in stimulus processing, is one that is very prevalent in various areas of modern cognitive psychology. For example, in chapter 8 we will consider several variations on the theme that behavior depends upon the activation of concepts by stimuli, which corresponds to the extraction of meaning in the attention models.

It has been emphasized in this chapter that attention is closely tied to expectations, as was argued by Hochberg and Neisser (1967, 1976). If a word occurs in a sentence, then the earlier words in the sentence will influence the processing of that word. There are several aspects of the sentence context that play a role here. On the one hand, the grammatical structure of the sentence is important. It is more probable that a common noun will follow "The very large . . . ," than will a verb. Also, the content, or meaning, or subject matter also plays a role. If one is talking about psychology, then one expects certain words to come up; if one is talking about hockey, one expects other words.

The question of interest is how the subject matter plays a role in the generation of expectations. Is it helpful to assume that part of the processing of the sentence entails extracting the meaning as the sentence goes along? It is important to note that this question is not really limited to linguistic stimuli at all. Since expectations play a role in the processing of all types of stimuli, then it is worthwhile to ask whether the "meaning" of all stimuli is processed in order to formulate expectations as to what will come next. Based on a model like that of Hochberg, it is not necessary to assume that processing the meaning of a stimulus is a separate stage of processing. It is true that when one attends to a word in a verbal message, it is because one has made predictions and the word matches these predictions. However, these predictions themselves are made in terms of the *words* that might be heard next. Nothing in them pertains to "meaning" per se. If one assumes that from any given string of words people can generate candidate words that might appear next, then one might be able to deal with expectations and attention without dealing explicity with meanings.

Rather than explicitly talking about extracting meanings, one might say that two words have similar meanings because they can be used similarly in the language. Therefore, one would not make a hard and fast distinction between similarity of grammatical use and similarity of meaning. There is a continuum involved—some words can be used in very similar ways, and some words are almost completely different in use. At one level, we say that words are unrelated; at a second level, we say that words are members of the same grammatical class; and at still another level we say that words are similar in meaning. Based on this analysis, when one says that certain words are expected because of their meanings, one is saying that those words can fit best into the present context. There is still not a separate operation concerned with processing the meaning. (This point is elaborated further in chapters 8 and 9.)

Thus we could tentatively conclude that there is not a separate aspect of a sentence or word called its meaning, which is extracted in a separate cognitive act. This is a conclusion that will be reached a number of times in the chapters to follow, and it is consistent with the discussions of recall and pattern recognition in earlier chapters.

6.10 Consciousness and attention

The topic of consciousness has become important once again in psychology. However, on the surface at least, we have come a long way from the interests of the first psychologists, who tried to study consciousness through the technique of introspection. When present-day psychologists introduce the term, it is usually in the context of discussions of information-processing models, so consciousness becomes one aspect of the particular model in question. We have discussed consciousness indirectly at several points in the last few chapters, but it might be worthwhile to take some time to consider the way in which the term is currently being used. Since cognitive processes seem to be closely related to consciousness, and since consciousness is such a complicated concept, a careful consideration of how the term is used might enable us to clear up some potential confusion. Obviously, given such an important and complicated area, we can do little more than scratch the surface here. Even with this in mind, however, some specific discussion of the concept of consciousness is necessary.

Consciousness in processing models. As we have seen in these last two chapters, many present-day models argue that information is processed through a series of stages as it works its way into the organism. Consciousness is sometimes identified with one of these stages. For example, in Broadbent's (1958) filter model, consciousness occurs when an item reaches the limited-capacity serial processor. More recent theorists have also argued that consciousness is a mechanism. For example, Posner and Snyder (1975) argue that consciousness is a specific mechanism with a limited capacity, which may carry out processing of many different sorts. Hence, we can be conscious of, or consciously attend to, only a very limited number of activities at any given time. This view is somewhat different than Broadbent's, in that Posner and Snyder feel that consciousness can carry out several different sorts of processing. In Broadbent's model, the central processor analyzed items for meaning, but the lower-level analyses were carried "outside" of consciousness.

LaBerge and Samuels (1974) present a similar view. Conscious attention is conceived of as a center in the nervous system, which can activate other centers, and which can be activated by other centers in the nervous system. According to Posner and Snyder, LaBerge and Samuels, and several other theorists, processing of a given input can be facilitated when conscious attention is directed toward that item. This occurs because the activity from the attention center helps to activate the representation in memory corresponding to the item, which makes it easier to process the item.

In summary, it is common in present-day cognitive theorizing to have consciousness equated with a mechanism of the nervous system. The limited capacity of consciousness is due to the limited capacity of this mechanism.

On consciousness as a mechanism. Let us consider how this attention center works. The following representative excerpts can give the flavor of the theorizing involved.

If a subject is asked to determine whether a digit is present in a field of letters, he need simply to check to see whether there is activation in that area of memory that represents digits. (Posner and Snyder, 1975, p.70)

In the second stage of perceptual learning, the subject must construct a letter code from the relevant features, a process which requires attention. By rapid scanning of the individual feature detectors . . . a higher order unit is formed. (LaBerge and Samuels, 1974, p.299)

When a stimulus occurs and activates a code, a signal is sent to the attention center, which can "attract" attention to that code unit in the form of additional activation. (LaBerge and Samuels, 1974, p.298)

It is possible for the cognitive system to call for the testing of specific outcomes while temporarily blocking output from the system as a whole, to compare the consequences of different outcomes and to choose outcomes that produce one or another desired alternative. (Mandler, 1975, p.53)

These excerpts make clear a basic problem that arises from viewing conscious attention as a limited-capacity mechanism: There is a tendency to attribute to this mechanism the very phenomena the mechanism is brought forth to explain. For example, Posner and Snyder allude to checking for activation in an area of memory in order to determine if a given type of object is present in the environment. Supposedly, this answers the question of how we can tell if such an object is present in the environment. However, consider this phenomenon further: in order to understand how we can check an environmental array to determine if it contains a digit, we have postulated exactly the same sort of process, but this time it is carried out on "objects" in memory. Thus, we have not really gone any further. In addition, this point of view seems to require that there are "mental objects" in memory, which can be "scanned" as needed. The last three chapters, as well as several earlier ones, have raised problems for this viewpoint.

LaBerge and Samuels propose the same sort of explanation, concerning how a letter code can be formed in memory. While the reader scans the letter, there is some internal entity, an attention center, that is "scanning feature analyzers." Once again, the phenomenon to be explained seems to have reappeared in the mechanism being used to explain it.

The same is true for the next passage, in which LaBerge and Samuels talk about an input sending a signal which "attracts" attention in the form of additional activation from the activation center. The basic reason for postulating this attention center was supposedly to explain human attention. However, in order to explain the switching of the reader's attention, it is argued that a signal from an input can attract the attention of the attention center. Once again the phenomenon of interest has appeared in the explanatory mechanism.

Finally, Mandler talks about the role of consciousness in decision making, and he argues that the cognitive system compares consequences and chooses outcomes. In this case we are trying to explain how a person chooses among outcomes, and once again the explanation involves the same phenomenon that was to be explained in the first place.

To summarize this, one problem with equating conscious attention with a mechanism is that this mechanism comes to possess all the specific phenomena that it was designed to explain. Thus, these explanations of consciousness have not added much to our understanding. At this point, it might be objected that the human terms used in these sorts of models are not to be taken seriously. We frequently use human terms to describe actions carried out by machines, especially actions carried out by computers. Since the above quotes were taken from information-processing theories, the theorists meant them only as convenient labels for operations that a computer could carry out. Therefore, so it would be argued, the above criticisms of these models were based on a lack of understanding of how those human terms are being used, because the human terms are not to be taken literally.

This response is not unreasonable, but as yet none of the theorists in question has gone further than use the humanlike terms. No actual computer programs have been developed, and there have been no discussions concerning how these various activities could be programmed. And even so, we do not know that the computer's program would be a good theory of how a human would do the same thing. Therefore, at present, it is reasonable to conclude that consciousness is not based on the activity of a limited capacity mechanism in the nervous system. In addition, there is at least one other reason for raising questions about the notion that consciousness is to be equated with a part of a processing model.

Consciousness and being conscious. Equating consciousness with one stage of information processing leaves out an essential aspect of the concept of consciousness—its complexity (Neisser, 1976, chap. 5). The concept *consciousness* is related to the concept *conscious*—one definition of consciousness is that it is the state of being conscious—and the concept of being conscious is a very complex one. Among other things, when we say that a person is conscious, we mean the person is awake (i.e., not unconscious), and that the person will usually respond to events in the environment. In this case, then, consciousness means "awake-ness," or responsiveness. In this sense, consciousness may be the same as awareness. A closely related use of the term conscious is related to a "mental act," as when one is conscious of a tree, or of a throb in one's stomach, or of a thought. In this sense, consciousness is equivalent to attention or perception, which, we have argued, are equivalent to each other. Neisser (1976, chap. 5) makes this point, as have other theorists. A third use of the term conscious is related to planned action, as when we say that such and such is a conscious action. In this case, it means that we thought about the act before we did it, and that we could probably tell others what we would do before we did it. From these various examples, one can see that consciousness is not a simple concept at all, and if we simply equate consciousness with a single stage of processing, or a processing center, we exclude most of the complexities of the concept. Natsoulas (1978) makes a similar point.

In sum, if we consider the relationship between being conscious and having consciousness, we see that several different, though interrelated, notions are involved. Furthermore, in none of these cases do we need to equate consciousness with a stage of processing, or a processing system. Consciousness is a term that can be used to describe various aspects of the behavior of people; it is not a mechanism.

Limited capacity of consciousness. One important aspect of recent discussions of conscious attention is that our capacity to attend to things is strictly limited, as we saw earlier in this chapter. This view stems directly from the theorizing of William James (1890), who argued that we could only be conscious of a very few things, perhaps only one thing, at one time. Given this basic assumption, it is a small step to postulate a mechanism which has a limited capacity as one of its characteristics. However, Neisser (1976) recently raised a very important problem for this point of view. As one example, he asks if we are attending to a single thing when we are listening to an orchestra playing a symphony. If we begin rather with the notion that people can sometimes attend to multiple inputs, or to a single complex input, then we might not be tempted to build an unchanging capacity limitation into our model. Some evidence discussed in section 6.3 supports this position.

To summarize, consciousness is not a mechanism, and it is not the result of the functioning of some specific mechanism. Consciousness is the state of being conscious, and it has several different aspects. It sometimes refers to attention and perception, sometimes to responsiveness, and sometimes to intentionality and planning. When one examines these various aspects of the term, it is obvious that a single mechanism or stage of processing is not involved. Also, it seems that the postulation of a mechanism with some specific capacity may be an oversimplification, because that capacity varies greatly, depending upon the person in question and what that person is doing. We shall consider the various aspects of consciousness in later sections: conscious perception and attention will be considered further in part 3, and planning will be considered further in parts 4 and 5.

6.11 Summary

This chapter has traced the development of models of selective attention from Broadbent's (1958) filter model to recent models based on expectations. The filter model explained selective attention by assuming that sensory channels were defined by physical features of stimuli. However, subsequent research demonstrated that the to-be-ignored message would sometimes be mistakenly shadowed if it fit the meaning of the shadowed message. Findings like these resulted in a reformulation of the filter model that did away with the all-or-none filter and that assumed that attending to a given word was influenced by prior words.

More recent models of pattern recognition and attention have extended these ideas further. For example, Hochberg argues that attending to some message entails setting up expectations and testing them by sampling information from the environment. While one is dealing with one message, one has only limited time available to sample other messages. This results in only a limited knowledge of the other messages, except in the case of easily recognized words, such as one's name.

With some elaborations, this sort of model could deal reasonably well with most of the major phenomena from the attention literature, as well as providing a point of integration for research on attention and pattern recognition. In addition, this sort of a model will be important in understanding language development.

6.12 Summary of part 2

The discussion in the last two chapters builds on the concepts developed in part 1 and leads to a discussion of the medium of thought in part 3. First, we have seen that it is possible to deal with perception of objects without assuming that there is something like a simple representation of an object in our heads. Rather, perceiving an object entails matching that object to a pattern map. This notion parallels the idea from part 1 that words weren't simply stored as objects in memory. The matching of an object to a pattern map is one part of the complex of events referred to as "encoding an object" in part 1. Second, the notion of expectations developed in part 2 fits well with the relationship between general and specific knowledge outlined in part 1. For example, the knowledge that the chess master uses in recalling a chess position can also be called the master's expectations about how a chessboard will look. It seems that the same concepts are important in discussions of memory and of pattern recognition and attention.

As far as the future is concerned, we shall see that the ideas developed in parts 1 and 2 will be increasingly important in later sections. First, our analysis of imagery and concepts will be a direct extension of the discussions in part 2. The discussion of problem solving will be based on parts 1 and 2, as will the discussion of cognitive development. We have now laid the groundwork for the rest of the book.

THREE
The medium of thought

7
Mental imagery as the medium of thought

7.0 Introduction to part three

We have now considered various aspects of how information is stored in memory and how this information is used over time, concluding with an analysis of pattern recognition and attention. This analysis leads us to a question that has been of interest since humans have contemplated their own capacity to think: the question of the medium of thought, or the form of our knowledge. We have already had occasion to address this issue in passing in the earlier chapters, but now we shall give it full attention. This is an area that has recently reemerged in cognitive psychology. There is much interest presently in the question of how we "carry out" our cognitive activities. Since it seems that the issues to be discussed here will be at the forefront of cognitive psychology in years to come, it is important to examine the various points of view very carefully (chaps. 7–9).

There are several alternate proposals as to the format of the information used in cognition, or the medium of thought. This chapter deals with a proposal with a long history, recently become popular again, that thought is carried out in images. Chapter 9 considers variants of a second possibility, that thought is carried out in words.

Symbols and thought. These points of view are variations on a common theme, that thought is an internal act carried out through the use of *symbols*. This symbolist conception of thought is probably the point of view implicitly held by most people, including most psychologists. The need for symbols for thought comes from the obvious fact that human thinking is concerned with things "out in the world." Therefore, in order to think about some object, one must be able to bring that object "inside." Something must serve as the object of thought, to be contemplated and "manipulated" in the same way as real objects are contemplated and manipulated. The symbol is the mental object that takes the place of the real object in our thought. Thus, it is reasonable to say that one scans one's images, assuming an imagery theory of thought, since images are substitutes for visual perceptions. Or, one gives oneself verbal self-direction, assuming a theory of verbal thought. These two positions, while very different on the surface, have in common the idea that one's thoughts serve as substitutes for events and objects in the world. One of the questions to be considered in the next few chapters is whether such a point of view is adequate as a description of what happens when one thinks.

Other possible views on thinking. We have mentioned only two theories concerning thinking: that thinking entails the production and contemplation of images, or that it entails the production of words. As just noted, these two ideas are variations of a more basic theme, as shown in the leftmost branch in Figure 7.1. Both images and words are symbols, so either idea depends upon the more basic notion that thinking is an activity that uses symbols. According to this view, all our thinking must take place in some medium (Price, 1959, p.298), and the most likely candidates for such a medium are images and words. It has also been argued that thinking is an activity that has its own special sorts of objects, sometimes called *universals* or *concepts* (Price, 1959, chap. X). This view has recently become important in cognitive theorizing and will be considered in detail in chapter 8.

It has also been argued that there can be "pure thought" independent of any symbols whatever. This view, which Descartes advocated (see Humphrey, 1963, pp.31–32; Vendler, 1972), argues that one is aware of, or conscious of, a thought directly, without having the thought "clothed" in any symbols. For example, I might walk outside one morning and think that it is a beautiful day without being aware of any imagery of any sort whatever, verbal or otherwise. I would still have had that thought, though, and would have been conscious of it, but it would not have been expressed through the use of any symbols.

According to a pure thought theory, thoughts are not experienced through symbols, they are simply experienced directly. Just as I am aware

Mental imagery as the medium of thought

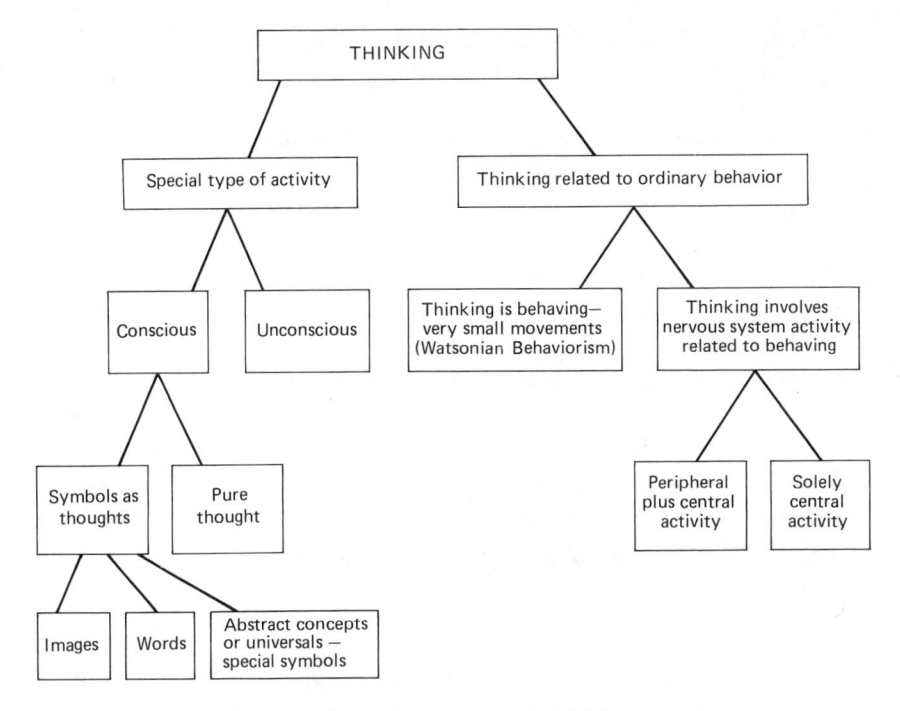

```
                            THINKING
                    ┌──────────┴──────────┐
          Special type                Thinking related
          of activity                 to ordinary behavior
         ┌─────┴─────┐              ┌────────┴────────┐
    Conscious    Unconscious   Thinking is      Thinking involves
                               behaving—        nervous system activity
                               very small       related to behaving
                               movements
                               (Watsonian
                               Behaviorism)
                                              ┌──────┴──────┐
    ┌────┴────┐                          Peripheral      Solely
 Symbols as   Pure                       plus central    central
 thoughts     thought                    activity        activity
  ┌──┬──┐
Images Words  Abstract concepts
              or universals—
              special symbols
```

Figure 7.1. A classification scheme for theories of thinking.

of a toothache directly, I am aware of my thought directly. I must express them to you through some symbolic medium, but I don't need symbols to be aware of them myself (Vendler, 1972, chap. 7). This is a view which we shall not consider further, however, because it may be untestable using psychological methods.

All these various ideas have one thing in common, that thinking entails the conscious awareness of something. This something can be called "a thought." Images and internal verbalizations are things that we are conscious of, as are thoughts like "It's a beautiful day," whether verbalized or not. There are several other alternative theories of thinking possible, as shown in Figure 7.1. One might argue that thinking is not a conscious activity, for example. It might be that the important thinking activities take place out of consciousness, and anything we happen to be conscious of at the time is either irrelevant to thought or an accompaniment of thought. This view is important in some theories of abnormal behavior, and we shall consider a variant of it when we examine problem solving in part 4.

Finally, one might argue that thinking isn't a special sort of activity at all. Rather, thinking is related to our more ordinary behavioral actions. Several variants of this view are shown in the right-hand portion of Figure 7.1. First, it has been argued that what we call thinking is nothing but behaving, but behavior of a very small magnitude. This view, which is the behavioristic view of John Watson, makes no distinction between thinking and behaving. On the other hand, it could be argued that thinking doesn't involve any responses at all—it involves only activity in the nervous system. There are two variants of this theory. The first view argues that activity in both the central and peripheral nervous systems is involved in thinking, while the other view argues that thinking involves only the central nervous system. We shall consider these "behavioral" views in chapter 9.

In order to prepare the reader for the following consideration of theories of thinking, the conclusion to be drawn from part 3 is that thinking is not a special activity involving symbols. Rather, thinking is closely related to behaving, but involves only central processes. A model of thinking will be outlined in part 5, to make this view explicit.

7.1 The imagist theory of thinking in philosophy

The theory that all thinking is based on images has a long history. Over 2000 years ago, Aristotle wrote: "The reasoning mind thinks its ideas in the form of images . . ." (in Mandler & Mandler, 1964, p.9). The imagist theory of thinking is based on two assumptions. (This account is based on Price, 1959, chaps. 7 & 9.) First, as in section 7.0, it is assumed that all thinking entails manipulation of internal or mental objects. The second assumption is that the basic mental objects are images. Here are two examples of the role assumed to be played by images in human thought. One comes from a philosopher, the other from a psychologist.

> We use visual images rather as we use maps or sketch-plans to find our way about a piece of hilly and wooded country; and when someone else asks us the way to Little Puddlecombe, we refer to this mental map and read off the answer. (Price, 1959, pp.235–36)

> If I am asked about the number of windows in my house, I find that I must *picture* the house, as viewed from different sides or from within different rooms, and then count the windows presented in these various mental images. No amount of purely verbal machinations would seem to suffice. (Shepard, 1966, p.203)

One important reason for emphasizing the role of images in thought has to do with the resemblance of images to the actual objects being thought about. The word *dog* has absolutely no resemblance to the object it sym-

Mental imagery as the medium of thought 147

bolizes; any sound or letter combination could have been used. However, images are similar to the object which they stand for. According to Price, it does not seem at all silly to say that one's image of a collie resembles a collie. If one could not produce an image that looked like a collie, in some sense, then one couldn't imagine a collie at all. Empirical evidence for this has been recently produced by Shepard and Chipman (1970). They asked subjects in one condition to group pictures of states on the basis of their physical similarity. They then gave the subjects only the names of the states, and asked them to group the states on the basis of physical similarity. In this latter case, the grouping must be based on the information that subjects can remember about the shapes of the states, because only the names were given. The results indicated great similarities in the groupings in the two conditions. For example, pictures of Illinois and Florida might be grouped together, because of their vertically elongated shape. In the same way, the names of Illinois and Florida would be grouped together, presumably because subjects could remember the similarity of shape. These results indicate that the "internal representations" of states share similarities and differences that are analogous to the similarities existing among the pictures of the states. This supports the notion that the image of an object "contains" the same characteristics as the object, in a sense.

Given that images are "similar" to objects, then it is argued that images can do things that simple words cannot do. For example, an image can have the same effect as the object, although to a weaker degree. Thus, because the image of a collie really is like a collie, it can influence the train of thought in the same way as seeing a collie would. Again, the image is a quasi-object, which takes the place of the real one. Evidence to support this contention comes from work in behavior therapy, in which imagining a situation can be used in relieving anxiety about the situation, because many of the same responses are aroused by the imagined situation (Mischel, 1976, chap. 11).

One could argue that the only reason words can influence the thought processes is because words can become capable of arousing images. This would be the only method whereby a word could become capable of substituting for the presence of an object during thinking. It does so because it arouses an image similar enough to the object to substitute for the object in thinking.

7.2 Images and abstract ideas

One problem for theories of thinking based on imagery has to do with the relationship between images and abstract ideas. For example, the idea *per-*

son refers to a whole class of individuals, no two of which are identical. Presumably, our ability to use the word *person* depends on our possessing the idea of person. According to the imagist theory of thinking, the meaning of a word is based on a visual image. Therefore, our ability to use words to refer to whole classes of things must depend on an appropriate sort of image, which could represent the class in question. Let us now examine one argument that something like an image could serve as the basis for our general knowledge.

Locke's imagist theory of knowledge. As mentioned in chapter 5, John Locke, an important British empiricist philosopher, argued that general knowledge comes about through the mental operation of abstraction. Any experience is analyzed into simple ideas, which were considered to be images by Locke (rpt. in Mandler & Mandler, 1964). As our experience grows, it happens that common aspects are found among various sets of simple ideas. For instance, it might be noted that the color of snow and the color of a piece of paper are the same. From the various specific ideas we have experienced, we are able to abstract the underlying essences, according to Locke. These essences are *abstract* ideas in that they do not correspond to any specific experience.

Two important aspects of Locke's theory must be emphasized. First, we are able to form these abstract ideas in consciousness. Thus, if the circumstances are right, one could imagine some abstract "redness," independent of anything else. Second, general knowledge, as exemplified by our ability to use general terms, is based on our having some information (a general image, or abstract idea) that stands for each general term.

Locke's theory has been criticized on a number of grounds. First, it has been argued that there is no universal "redness" that is the essence underlying our ability to use the term red. This point was discussed in some detail in chapter 5, from the point of view of pattern-recognition models. There does not seem to be any single feature or set of features which is the basis for recognizing any particular pattern. Depending upon the circumstances, very different features can serve to identify the same pattern. If so, then so single essence is involved. A second point of criticism of Locke's theory is that generalized images, of the sort postulated by the theory, simply don't exist.

Can images be general? Many theorists have argued that people cannot form generalized images. Rather, it has been argued that images are by their very nature specific, and that images cannot serve as the general symbols on which human thought depends. Berkeley (1710, rpt. 1963), criti-

Mental imagery as the medium of thought

cized Locke's theory of abstraction on these grounds. The essential point of the argument was that Berkeley himself could only think of specific objects and could not imagine generalized objects. If one can only imagine specific persons, or cars, or trees, or anything else, then how can these various specific images be *general symbols?* How can some image stand for the thought: "Every animal has a body," when one cannot imagine the generalized animal or the generalized body that such a thought needs?

Berkeley's modified imagery theory. Given that generalized images cannot be formed, then one either has to modify a strong imagery theory, or abandon it altogether. Some theorists have chosen to abandon imagery theories and instead have argued that thought must be based on other symbols. These other symbols are usually taken to be words. (Various aspects of this notion will be considered in the next two chapters.) However, Berkeley tried to develop a modified imagery theory which could overcome the problem posed by the lack of general images. He started from the premise that our images can only be specific images. Even so, he argued that images and diagrams can be *used* by us to stand for a whole class, such as the class of triangles.

But here it will be demanded, how can we know any proposition to be true of all particular triangles, except we have first seen it demonstrated of the abstract idea of a triangle which equally agrees to all? . . . To which I answer, that, though the idea I have in view whilst I make the demonstration be, for instance, that of an isosceles rectangular triangle whose sides are of a determinate length, I may nevertheless be certain it extends to all other rectilinear triangles, of what sort or bigness soever. And that because neither the right angle, nor the equality, nor determine length of the sides are at all concerned in the demonstration. It is true that the diagram I have in view includes all these particulars, but then there is not the least mention of them in the proof of the proposition. (Berkeley, 1963, pp.55–56)

In essence, Berkeley says that we can attend to only the relevant aspects of either the diagram in front of us, or of the image "in our heads." In this way, we can make some particular thing serve as a general symbol. The particular triangle, say, becomes a symbol for the class of triangles when we consider only aspects of it which are common to all triangles.

Generic images. There has also been another suggestion concerning how a specific image could serve as a general symbol (Price, 1953, chap. IX). Assume that you are discussing the high price of car repairs with a friend, and that the discussion is understood through the use of imagery. At some point in the discussion, your friend summarizes things by saying: "Any car needs lots of repairs these days." According to the imagery theory, you must have constructed an image to correspond to the sentence in order to understand it.

Price has argued that one could perhaps form a specific image of a car, but not an image of some familiar car, such as a Ford or Chevrolet. For example, a recent bank advertisement for car loans had a picture of a "car" made out of pieces of other cars, in order to get the point across that the bank would loan money for any sort of automobile. This car was not any specific sort of car, it simply was "a car."

In the same way, one might be able to imagine a car that was not any particular sort of car and so might be simply "a car." One might also be capable of imagining a person without being able to make out any of the specific facial or bodily features. Such an image might serve as the symbol for "a person." Price calls these sorts of images *generic* images, because he thinks they could refer to a whole class, or genus, of objects.

This theory may be compatible with the discussion in chapter 5 of the use of pattern maps in pattern recognition. It was argued that the information needed to identify something as a car or a person is different than the information needed to identify it as a Rolls Royce or a woman. The information needed depends upon the discrimination to be made. Therefore, one might use the same sort of "impoverished" information to form the image of a car or of a person, so that the specific object couldn't be identified any more precisely. This notion is also relevant to Berkeley's theory that one uses images in different ways. Different pattern maps might correspond to different uses.

However, even if one grants that people have the capacity to produce generic images, there still seem to be at least two problems for theories of thought based on them. First, this "generic" car is not an abstraction distilled out of all the cars one has seen. Rather, it is simply one specific sort of car which can't be identified any more precisely. This means that the image itself is not serving as the symbol. Rather, it is the image plus the fact that it cannot be named specifically which is important. Therefore, one must have the image share the stage with the word *car* here. This not only changes this aspect of the theory, but it also raises some questions about whether images can serve as the basis for the understanding of words, since it seems that one needs words to understand images, at least in some cases. Berkeley's "use" theory also reduces the importance of images in just this way.

A second problem for generic images is that there are some words for which even generic images won't do. Generic images for *car* and perhaps *person* aren't too implausible, but what about *truth* and *artifact* and *loyalty* and *malpractice?* Even a true believer in imagery would have problems just thinking of a useful image for such words, let alone producing one under pressure when the word was used in ordinary speech. Thus, even if generic images do occur to some of us at some time or another, it looks as if generalized thoughts can occur without them.

Summary. At present, there is not much support in philosophy for the notion that a pure imagery theory can explain all of human thinking. The basic problem is that humans can think abstract and general thoughts, such as "All children are nice people." It does not seem to be possible for an image, in and of itself, to represent such a thought. Therefore, at the very least, the imagist theory must be added to.

7.3 Imagery in early psychology

Given the philosophical background of psychology, much early work in the psychology of thinking was concerned with imagery.

Titchener's imagery theory. E. B. Titchener, an Englishman educated in Germany, directed the first psychological laboratory in the United States. Titchener and his students were interested in analyzing the structure of mental events, using the method of introspection, which entails trying to analyze one's own mental events into their basic elements. When Titchener and his students examined their own conscious experiences, imagery was almost invariably found to be present (Boring, 1950, chap. 18; Humphrey, 1963, chap. IV). This was not only visual imagery, but also kinesthetic imagery. Titchener argued that these sorts of imagery were the basis for thought, especially comprehension of meaning, which was for him a central aspect of thinking. He also felt that specific images could serve as vehicles for carrying the meaning of abstract or general terms. The following brief passages should make Titchener's ideas clear.

When I read or hear that somebody has done something modestly, or gravely, or proudly, or humbly, or courteously, I see a visual hint of the modesty, or gravity or pride or humility or courtesy. . . . Meaning in general is represented in my consciousness by another of these impressionist pictures. I see meaning as the blue-gray tip of a kind of scoop, which has a bit of yellow above it (probably a part of the handle), and which is just digging into a dark mass of what appears to be plastic material. I was educated on classical lines; and it is conceivable that this picture is an echo of the oft-repeated admonition to "dig out the meaning" of some passage of Greek or Latin. I do not know; but I am sure of the image. And I am sure that others have similar images. . . .

... The various visual images, which I have referred to as possible vehicles of logical meaning, oftentimes share their task with kinesthesis. Not only do I see gravity and modesty and pride and courtesy and stateliness, but I feel them or act them in the mind's muscles. (Titchener, 1909, rpt. in Mandler & Mandler, 1964, pp.167, 170, 172)

However, there soon developed a problem for Titchener's theory: evidence that thinking could occur without any imagery at all.

The Würzburgers—imageless thought. Külpe and his students and colleagues at Würzburg carried out much research on thought that contradicted the ideas of Titchener. In the first of the Würzburg studies, Mayer and Orth (1901, in Mandler & Mandler, 1964, pp.135–142) investigated the events occurring during the associative process. They presented stimulus words to subjects, and the subjects produced associations to them. Immediately after producing the response word, the subject attempted to report everything that had occurred in consciousness between the presentation of the stimulus and the production of the response. It was found that for a small proportion of responses, no conscious events intervened between presentation of the stimulus and production of the response. This result contradicted Titchener's theory of meaning. If producing an associated word is based on understanding the meaning of the stimulus, then according to the theory, an associated word could only be produced after an image had been formed in response to the stimulus. Mayer and Orth found that this did not have to happen.

Mayer and Orth's paper was soon followed by that of Marbe (Humphrey, 1963, chap. 2; Mandler & Mandler, 1964, pp.142–46), who investigated the psychological processes involved in acts of judgment. This particular act of thought was chosen because it was felt that judgment was one of the basic acts of thought. As an example, one task had the subjects judge whether or not a sentence read to them was understood. After so judging, the subjects reported any conscious events that had occurred. Once again, the results raised problems for the fashionable theories of thought. The subjects carried out many acts of judgment, but they could not report any specific conscious event that made the act a judgment. It seemed that the subjects were able to make judgments, and knew that they were making judgments, without having any particular event available in consciousness which identified the act as one of judgment. Not only were the acts not accompanied by any specific images, they were not characterized by any particular conscious events whatever. In summary, the work of the Würzburg psychologists indicated that theories of thinking based solely on images, or any other conscious events, could not be correct. This was one important reason for the downfall of such theories. A second important reason was the rise of behaviorism in America.

Behaviorist criticisms of imagery. A sweeping objection to the usefulness of imagery in psychology came from Watson (1919, 1930), who essentially dismissed imagery, as well as any other mental phenomena, as being irrelevant to the concerns of an objective psychology. They couldn't be studied objectively, by definition, since they were subjective mental phenomena, so they were outside the realm of scientific inquiry. In order to pave the way for an objective psychology of "thought," Watson argued that the basic component of thinking was talking to oneself. "Thinking" was not any mysterious "inner" or "mental" process, but was simply normal speech of a very low amplitude. Tiny speech movements were actually being made, and these resulted in "inner speech." The reason that we mistakenly think that such speech is "inner" (or mental and unobservable) is because these movements are so minute that we are not aware of them. This meant that there was no such thing as a mental process or mental event. Such events were really actual overt behaviors, but of a low amplitude. This propsal of Watson's played an important role in putting imagery outside the mainstream of psychological inquiry for about forty years.

7.4 Imagery in memory

In the last twenty years, imagery has made a strong comeback in psychology. Much of the recent interest in imagery stems from research concerning the role of imagery in memory (e.g., Paivio, 1971). As this interest grew and expanded, theorists began to debate broader questions concerning the role of imagery in thinking (e.g., Kosslyn & Pomerantz, 1977; Pylyshyn, 1973). In the next sections, we shall consider the role of imagery in memory and in thought.

Imagery versus meaningfulness in memory. About twenty years ago, Paivio began doing research on some of the factors involved in recall of words (Lambert & Paivio, 1956). This research led to the conclusion that the "concreteness" of a word was the most important factor in its recall, with concrete words (words which refer to concrete physical objects, such as *table* and *car*) being easiest to recall. From there it was but a small step to the additional conclusion that concrete words derived their concreteness from their ability to produce images when they were heard. Paivio then carried out an extensive series of studies to demonstrate the validity of this conclusion and to convince others that imagery was truly the crucial factor (much of this research is summarized by Paivio, 1971).

There were at least two reasons why other psychologists were skeptical concerning the usefulness of imagery as an explanation for the recall results. First, the behavioristic influence was widespread and the skepticism toward mentalistic concepts still strong. Second, much research had shown that verbal factors were important in determining recall (e.g., Underwood & Schulz, 1960), and Paivio was arguing against these established data. The verbal factor that had been shown to be important was the "meaningfulness" of an item, defined as the ease with which the item produced other words as associations.

Paivio showed that the supposed influence of verbal meaningfulness may have in reality been brought about by imagery. Subjects were asked to rate words on verbal meaningfulness and on how easily the words evoked images. These two measures are highly correlated, but it is possible to vary imagery while holding meaningfulness values constant, or vice versa. A number of studies (summarized in Paivio, 1971, chaps. 7 & 8) have shown that imagery has a stronger effect on recall than meaningfulness, and that the effect of meaningfulness may only be weak at best when imagery is held constant. This demonstration paved the way for a surge of interest in the role of imagery in recall. Much of the interest centered on mnemonic methods (methods of memorizing) using imagery that had been known for many years.

7.5 Interactive imagery and recall

Over 2000 years ago, the Greeks had developed methods of memorizing which were based on imagery (Yates, 1966). One of these, the method of loci (places), has recently received experimental study (Bower, 1970). The method of loci is used to enable one to memorize a list of items in a specific order. One first needs a list of places known to the subject and that can be recalled in order. The items that are to be remembered are "placed" one by one in the various loci as you "stroll" through them. In order to place an item in a location, one imagines the location and imagines the item in that location. At recall, one simply walks through the loci in one's imagination, and at each location the item placed there will be "seen" and can be reported.

The specific instructions on the use of this method contained the follow-

Mental imagery as the medium of thought

ing points (Yates, 1966, pp. 6–10). Once a set of loci had been memorized, it could be used again and again, because after a time the old images became obscure and new images could be learned. The loci should not be too much like each other, because similarity of loci produces confusion. They should also be moderate in size. If the locus is too large, the image that is placed on it will be vague; if the locus is too small then the images will be overcrowded. The loci should not be too brightly or dimly lit. If they are too bright, then the images will dazzle; if they are too dark, the shadows will obscure the images. These instructions are particularly interesting because of their realistic aspect. The loci are referred to as being brightly lit or large in size, just as if they were real places. It is almost as if one were dealing with real objects placed in real loci. This point is important and will be returned to later.

A more modern memorizing method uses a previously learned rhyme scheme instead of the loci (e.g., Miller, Galanter, & Pribram, 1960). The rhyme scheme uses phrases like: one is a bun, two is a shoe, and so on. In order to use this method, one first learns the rhyme scheme. One then takes the list of to-be-recalled items, one by one. An image is formed which combines the to-be-recalled item and the rhyming word. For example, if the first word is *car,* then one would form an image of a car with a bun. At recall, each number is used as a cue to retrieve the rhyming word that goes with it. The rhyming word in turn serves as a cue to retrieve the image, and the to-be-recalled word can then be recalled from the image. This technique has been called the "peg-word" method.

In a series of studies using either the method of loci or peg-word, high levels of recall were reported. Subjects who are taught to use the peg-word technique recall from two to seven times more after a single exposure to a list than subjects who are simply told to learn some number-word pairs. Furthermore, it seems that the crucial determinant of later recall is the formation of an interaction between the images of the to-be-recalled words. If the pair is boy-car, then a boy jumping on a car, or driving a car, will produce good recall. If the subject is instructed to imagine the car in the garage and the boy sitting on the porch, then recall will be poor. By instructing subjects on the types of images to form, it has been demonstrated that interactive imagery produces higher recall than various other methods. These other methods have included noninteractive, or static, imagery; rote verbal repetition of the pairs; and simply asking the subject to learn the pairs (Paivio, 1971; Bower, 1970b, 1972b).

7.6 How does imagining assist memorizing?

There seems to be little doubt that asking subjects to produce interactive images facilitates learning. However, there is a bit of a paradox involved here. An interacting image contains a lot of information in it, since it is based on at least two objects interacting. And yet, even though an interacting image adds to the memory load, it results in increased levels of recall. What is the "cognitive glue" that holds images together?

What might imagining do to remembering? There are several obvious possibilities as to why interactive imagery facilitates recall. First of all, in order to imagine an interaction between two objects, you must put them into some sort of meaningful relationship. It seems obvious that making something more meaningful makes it easier to recall. A second idea, related to this, is that in order to produce a meaningful interaction, one must use one's own knowledge, which could make the items more memorable. Third, an interactive image serves to make the pair of objects into one unit. It provides a coherence, a unity, a wholeness, that keeps the two objects together in memory. This supposedly can come about because there are "structures" in one's knowledge that can incorporate the two items into a unit. As an example, Simon (1972) has argued that if a subject generates an image of a whale smoking a cigar, then what is stored is a representation of the cigar, the whale, and the *relation* "smoking" that obtains between them. Simon further assumes that items must be related before they can be stored. It should also be noted that Simon does not say that these structures and relations are stored in visual terms. That is, according to Simon, the information could be encoded in any format. The important thing is that the relation is encoded, but it could be encoded verbally or in terms of concepts. Indeed, Simon explicitly argues that the relations aren't encoded visually, but are encoded in terms of abstract concepts. This point of view will be discussed in detail in the next chapter. For now the important point is that things must be related in order to be recallable. A fourth possibility is that the image serves to make each pair distinctive and unique, and so facilitates recall. These are the main sorts of explanations put forth by theorists who have considered the problem of imagery and recall (e.g., Bower, 1972b; Paivio, 1971, pp.385–389).

Criticisms of these explanations. The first two explanations just mentioned are based on the idea that using one's knowledge to develop a meaningful interaction somehow makes the pairs more memorable. However, these explanations don't say anything about how a meaningful in-

Mental imagery as the medium of thought 157

teraction makes a pair memorable, so these explanations don't explain very much. Furthermore, there is some question about whether "meaningful" interactions are involved at all. Consider the pictures shown in Figure 7.2. These pictures have been found to facilitate paired-association learning (Wollen, 1968; Epstein, Rock, & Zuckerman, 1960). The interesting thing is that some of the "interactions" are not meaningful, in the usual sense of the term. In what sense is a whale smoking a cigar a "meaningful" interaction? And yet recall is facilitated if subjects produce these sorts of images, or see pictures of this sort. Therefore, meaningfulness, in the sense of being related to the things that we know well, doesn't seem to be crucial.

The second two explanations just outlined assume that an interaction or relation (whale smoking a cigar) somehow makes a given pair a cohesive unit. However, this simply leaves us with the question of how the interaction or relation produces unity. In addition, in some cases an imagined relation between two items can facilitate recall, while other cases of seemingly similar relation does not facilitate recall. For example, using the

Figure 7.2. Pictures which facilitate paired associate learning.

method of loci, placing an object *in* a corner, or *on* a landing, or *next to* a statue results in the object's being recalled when the person walks past the locus in imagination. However, we can also ask a subject to imagine the to-be-recalled objects in pictures, and to imagine these pictures *next to* each other on a wall. In this case, recall is not facilitated nearly as much as with the loci. So what is it about *next to* in this situation which results in its being less effective? Nothing at all is said.

Based on the discussion in the last several chapters, one can develop a different sort of model of the relation between imagery and memory. Let us first consider what "imagining something" entails.

7.7 Imagination and knowledge

At least since Aristotle, it has been assumed that sensations are the basic elements out of which mental life is built. Theorists have assumed that images are faint replicas of sensations which have been experienced earlier. Thus, according to this view, the image that accompanies a word is simply a reinstatement of the sensory processes that were active when the word was used. This view is still prevalent in cognitive psychology.

However, there is at least one important reason for questioning the idea that images are simply reexperienced sensations, and it is the fact that one can imagine things that one has never seen. For example, I can imagine my wife riding on an elephant, although I have never seen her do it. Since we imagine things like this all the time, it seems that we do not simply recall past scenes and examine them when we imagine things. That is, one must begin to deal with how we can imagine something which we have never seen before.

In one sense, this discussion of imagery parallels the discussion of recognizing new patterns in chapter 5. If we have never seen the situation which we are now imagining, then we must be using our knowledge of the world in order to create a situation which corresponds to what it would be like if we were actually seeing the situation in question. Imagery isn't so much like internal seeing as it is pretending to see (Ryle, 1949). It is as if one says: "If the world were thus and so, then it would look like this . . ."

This parallels exactly the argument in chapter 5 concerning recognition of new objects. At that time it was argued that in order to recognize a novel object, one had to use one's knowledge in order to create a pattern map which would "accept" the object. In the same way, in order to imagine some novel situation, one creates the pattern map without the situation being present. (Neisser, 1976, makes a similar argument.) Therefore, before we can attempt to understand why imagery might facilitate recall, we must first briefly consider imagining itself from this point of view.

7.8 Imagining and perceiving

It has just been argued that the ability to visually imagine something depends upon knowledge about how the thing would look. This implies that pattern maps are used in creating visual images. There is also evidence that the visual system itself is involved in visual imagery. This evidence comes from several studies which have domonstrated that carrying out visual tasks interferes with visual imagery, and vice versa.

Interference studies. One study of this sort was carried out by Atwood (1971). Subjects heard a series of phrases designating imaginary scenes, such as "pistol hanging from a chain," which they were instructed to visualize. Immediately following each phrase, one group of subjects saw either a 1 or a 2. Their task was to verbally respond "2" if they saw a 1, and vice versa. A second group *heard* "one" or "two," and verbally responded with the other number. A third group had no interfering task between phrases. The results indicated that, relative to the group with no interfering task, presenting the numbers visually interfered more with later recall than did verbal presentation. Atwood argued that when the numbers were presented visually, the subjects couldn't deal with them and visualize the scenes at the same time. Therefore, later recall was interfered with. When the numbers were verbally presented, there was no interference with visual imagery, so later recall was not interfered with very much.

Atwood also demonstrated that a verbal interfering task was more disruptive than a visual task when the phrases involved abstract ideas which could not be directly visualized, such as "the theory of Freud is nonsense." Listening to the numbers is more disruptive with abstract phrases supposedly because listening interferes with the verbal processing of such phrases.

From results of this sort, it has been concluded that there are at least two relatively independent "processing systems," a visual system and a verbal system. Visual imagination requires the use of the visual processing system, and verbal imagination (as in subvocal speech) requires use of the verbal system. This accounts for the selective interference by visual versus verbal tasks found by Atwood and others (e.g., Brooks, 1968; Bower, 1970b; Kosslyn, 1975). We shall have more to say about verbal processing in chapters 8 and 9. For the present, the important finding is that visual processing interferes with visual imagery, which supports the idea that visual imagery entails use of visual information.

Additional support for this conclusion comes from a study by Segal and Fusella (1970) concerning imagery and signal detection. Subjects were required to detect low-intensity visual or auditory signals. At the same time, some of the subjects were instructed to either visually or auditorally imagine various things. It was found that visual imagination interfered more with visual signal detection than did auditory imagination, with the reverse effect holding for auditory detection. These results can be explained if we assume that subjects couldn't maximally process stimuli in a given modality when they were using that modality in order to carry out the imagination task.

Rotation studies. A set of striking results concerning the close relationship between imagery and perception comes from studies carried out by Shepard and Cooper and their colleagues (e.g., Cooper & Shepard, 1973). In these studies, subjects were asked to determine if two different visual forms were actually two views of the same form, or if they were really two different forms. An example of two such forms is shown in Figure 7.3. In this case, the answer is that both forms are two views of the same form, because if the form on the left is rotated, it will correspond exactly to the form on the right. The variable of interest in these studies is how far the one form has to be rotated in order to make the two forms correspond. In some cases, the angle of rotation is very small, and in other cases the angle is large. One very important finding is that the time it takes to report

Figure 7.3. Example of item used by Cooper and Shepard (1973). Are both items two views of the same item, or are they different? Answer is "same."

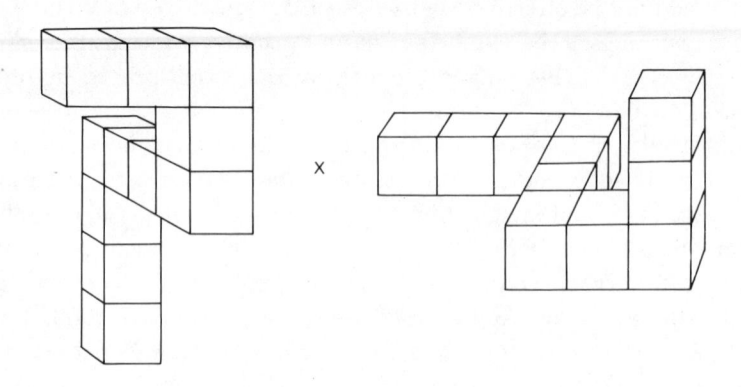

that two figures are the same is a direct function of the angle of rotation. That is, if the two figures differ by a small angle, then the "same" response is much faster than if they are separated by a large angle. Shepard argues from this that something like an "internal rotation" is occurring, and this rotation occurs at some more or less constant rate of speed (from these studies, the rate seems to be 60 ° of rotation per second). This part of the process seems to be almost directly comparable to actually observing the actual patterns being rotated for you.

In addition, several of these studies have found that this rotational process occurs in the same way if the subject only imagines one of the forms, and then must determine if the imagined form is the same as a form presented by the experimenter. This procedure is carried out by first instructing the subject to image the stimulus form in a specified orientation. The second form can then be presented in any orientation, and it is found that the quickest responses occur when the orientation of the presented form corresponds to that of the imagined form, and the respose time lengthens as the angle of rotation between them increases. This finding is obviously of importance for the present discussion, because it points to a strong correspondence between imagery and perception.

Based on these studies, Shepard (1978) argues that when the person "rotates" a figure in imagination, or imagines the figure rotating, there is a set of states set up in the visual centers which corresponds to the states that would correspond to actually seeing the object rotate. One final study provides additional evidence to support this claim. Consider again the two figures in Figure 7.3. If these two figures are alternately presented for brief durations, people will report seeing one single form rotating back and forth in space between the two locations. (The viewer is not told that two separate pictures are being presented in alternation. The pictures are presented and the subject is asked to describe what is seen. Most people describe a single stimulus moving back and forth.) However, in Figure 7.3, it is obvious that there is "empty space" between the two forms. What happens to this empty space when the single figure is seen as rotating? Very simply, Shepard (1978) argues that in some sense, the seen figure moves *through* this empty space, just as a real figure actually would move through it. Robins and Shepard (1977) demonstrated this in the following way. They flashed a small spot of light at various times at the point marked x in Figure 7.3 and asked subjects to determine if the spot was flashed before or after the moving figure passed through that point. Subjects had no trouble doing this—if the flash occurred very soon after the left-hand figure went off, they reported that the figure hadn't gotten to that point yet. If the flash occurred just before the right-hand form went on, they reported that the flash occurred after the figure moved through that point. Thus, even though the actual display consisted of two stationary flashing pictures, people "saw" one single moving form, and they could report the "position" of this form at any given time.

These studies provide strong support for the claim that perception and imagination are basically similar activities, and that they use the same mechanisms.

7.9 Patterns maps and sequential processes in visual imagery

We have now considered some evidence that imagining something entails much of the same information and mechanisms which are used in actually perceiving that thing. We can now go back to the question of why imagining two objects in an interaction facilities their recall. A possible answer to this question will come from a consideration of what is involved in looking at something like a whale smoking a cigar.

It was argued in chapter 5 that patterns aren't "taken in" all at once in a single glance. Visual acuity is not precise enough outside the fovea. Therefore, patterns are taken in with a series of directed glances, so that various parts of the pattern are foveally fixated over time. If we can only see an object by moving our eyes over it in a series of fixations, and if imagining is like seeing, then perhaps our ability to imagine an object depends upon an imagined sequence of foveal fixations. Perhaps the basis for our seeing someone's face in our mind's eye is a sequence of imaginary fixations, corresponding to a sequence of fixations that would actually occur if one was examining the object in question. (Neisser, 1976, has recently made a similar proposal.)

Sequential processes in recall of a visual image. If visual imagining is constructing a sequence of fixations, then it might follow that in order to recall a real or imagined scene, one would have to run through the same sequence of fixations that one went through on seeing or imagining the scene originally. (A similar argument was made in section 3.7 concerning chess master's recall.) If so, then we must explain how a sequence of fixations is reconstructed at recall. What information is used to lead from one fixation in memory to the next? If each of these fixations is conceived of as a separate entity, then putting the sequence back together becomes the crucial operation for the present discussion.

Mental imagery as the medium of thought

Fixation$_x$ to fixation$_y$. If one is looking at a face, one may start with the mouth, go up to the nose, then out to one ear, back to an eye, and so on. When one is fixating any one of these points, the others will be in the periphery of the picture. The fovea of the eye produces the clearest vision, but the other parts of the retina can also register some detail. So if one is fixating the nose, the eyes and mouth are grossly registered. Each fixation therefore has a center of focus and other objects in the periphery.

These peripheral objects, in conjunction with one's knowledge, could serve to lead from one fixation to another during the subject's attempt to reconstruct a sequence of fixations. Fixation$_x$ could serve as a cue for fixation$_y$, if fixation$_y$ centers on one of the objects that is in the periphery of fixation$_x$. In addition, the point that is the center of fixation$_x$ should be in periphery in fixation$_y$. Finally, some objects in the periphery of fixation$_x$ should also be in the periphery of fixation$_y$. In this way, one can use what one is looking at now, plus one's knowledge of how things look, to predict what the next fixation will look like. This could serve to cue the next fixation. This can be repeated until enough fixations have been retrieved to enable one to reconstruct the interaction and produce the word that is to be recalled.

The specific processes involved here would be assumed to parallel rather directly those involved in visual recognition, which were discussed in section 5.6. The information in a given fixation "gets one into" one's collection of pattern maps. The information in the fixation is then combined with the knowledge represented in memory to predict what a related fixation would look like, and so on.

As an oversimplified example of how this reconstruction might occur, let's say that a subject has been presented with the two pairs of objects in Figure 7.4. The subject examines them, and the fixations which are produced are shown under the pairs. From any one of the fixations, it is clear what other fixations will occur, given the above hypothesis.

To summarize, a sequence of fixations could be "held together" by the information overlap from one to the next. When one is in the midst of any given fixation, real or imagined, then this fixation contains in it some information which could serve to retrieve other fixations from the same scene. In this way enough information could be gathered to enable one to recall the whole scene. Thus, if sequential processes are important in the recall of real or imagined visual information, then each fixation may itself serve in part as a cue for the next. In addition to the overlap of objects just discussed, it might be that one fixation could lead to another because of

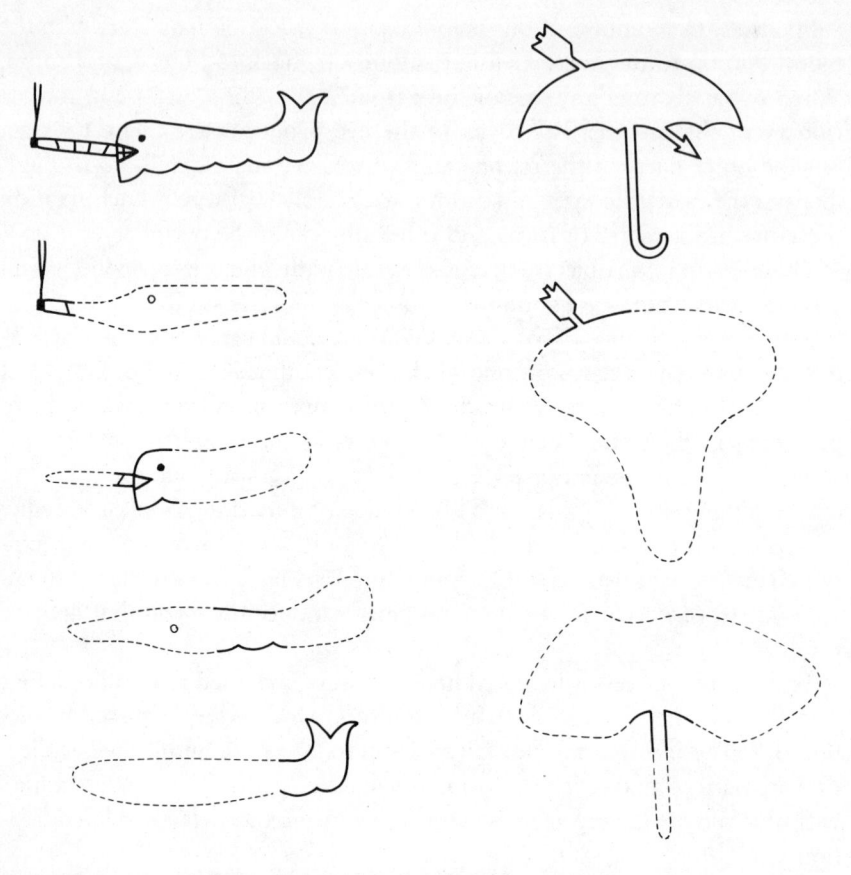

Figure 7.4. Hypothetical patterns of fixations derived from scanning compound pictures.

more specific similarity between them. I recently attended a lecture on imagery in recall, in which the speaker asked the audience to try to remember a series of words by forming interactive images of each consecutive pair of words. One pair was car-book, and I imagined the wheel of a car rolling over an opened book. Besides the factors which have already been discussed, one aspect of this pair bears further mention. In my imagining, I clearly saw the tread of the tire. I then saw it roll over something flat, and then I saw the opened book with the tread mark across it. Therefore, the two objects in question were linked by a similar element, the tread mark, which could facilitate recall. A knowledge of how objects look when tires roll over them would be important here.

Finally, in addition to the sequence of visual fixations involved in scan-

Mental imagery as the medium of thought 165

ning a picture of constructing an image, other information might also be available. For example, let's say I am examining the picture of the whale smoking the cigar in Figure 7.4. The look of the whale's mouth with the cigar in it reminds me of the hero in a gangster movie I just saw, who always had a cigar in his mouth. At a later time, I might be given the whale or the cigar as a cue to recall. In addition to initiating retrieval of the visual fixations involved, either of these objects could cue my recent memory of the gangster from the motion picture. This could then serve as an additional cue. So any extraneous information which the subject thinks of while examining a picture or producing an image must also be considered as a potential source of cues. Anderson and Bower (1973) have claimed that all facilitation allegedly due to imagery is really due to "semantic enrichment" of this sort, and that visual processes per se are not directly involved. They wish to argue that all information is stored and manipulated in the form of abstract propositions, which are not equivalent to the sorts of low-level visual information being discussed here. We shall discuss this view further in a later section and in chapter 8.

To summarize, this discussion of imagery has emphasized the similarities between imagining and seeing. It was speculated that the facilitative effect of interactive imagery and pictures on recall was based on some very specific effects, having to do with visual fixations and eye movements, both real and imagined. Thus, it is argued here that the visual aspect of this process is crucial. In order to encode an interaction between items in such a way that it will facilitate recall, the encoding would have to be in visual terms. According to the present discussion, it is only the visual aspect of the encoding that gives the subject information about both objects at once. As Neisser (1976) also mentions, the requirement that the subject encode the imagined interaction between two objects literally changes the way in which the objects are imagined, and thereby changes the encoding. Neisser gives the example of the pair shark-crib. If one imagines a shark in a crib, one would also imagine parts of the shark occluded by the bars of the crib. This is obviously very similar to the point of view presented here, which argues that the change in the way in which each item is encoded results in one being able to cue the other. Given this background, we can now turn to the broader question of the role that imagery plays in thought in general.

7.10 Scanning rooms versus "scanning" images

When one recalls a visual experience, one gets a strong impression that one is "looking" at one's image in much the same way as one would look at the actual scene. Consider the passage from Shepard (1966) given at the beginning of the chapter.

If I am asked about the number of windows in my house, I find that I must *picture* the house, as viewed from different sides or from within different rooms, and then count the windows presented in these various mental images. No amount of purely verbal machinations would seem to suffice. (p.203)

The important aspect of this is that Shepard argued that he *counts* the windows *presented* in the image. The image is looked upon as something that can be presented and processed, just like pictures can be presented and processed. The image is the mental equivalent to a picture in the world, or the actual scene in the world. One aspect of Shepard's description is undeniably true: If one is asked to count the windows in one's house, one gets the definite feeling that one is counting the windows in one's image. The subjective impression is unmistakable. The same is true if one tries one of the mental rotation exercises as discussed earlier in this chapter. One gets the feeling that one is indeed rotating some thing. However, this does not mean that the subjective impression is accurate as an explanation of what is occurring (Pylyshyn, 1973). This is an important distinction because it has relevance to the more general question of the role of consciousness in thinking.

Kosslyn (1975) has recently advocated a position very similar to that of Shepard, and it is specific enough to serve as the basis for specific criticism. According to Kosslyn, the construction and interpretation of images can be understood through analogy to the graphics displays that can be produced by computers. The pictorial display on the cathode-ray tube depends upon a program that generates it. This program uses abstract structural information in order to produce a display that can be seen by an observer.

In the same way, according to Kosslyn, images are constructed on the basis of abstract information that is not directly conscious, but that has been obtained from earlier visual experience. This information is then "displayed" in a way analogous to the display on a cathode-ray tube, and can then be "processed" by a "mind's eye," which is comparable to the human eye which processes the display on the tube. The mind's eye is assumed to be a set of processes which search for various aspects of the image, such as lines or angles of various sorts. In this way, the image can be "processed" and new information obtained from it. So, for example, one can examine an image to see if it contains a window, or a rectangular object. The following makes Kosslyn's view clear:

Mental imagery as the medium of thought

> If images are sensory patterns that have been partially processed and stored, the question of how knowledge can be derived from images is quite similar to the question of how knowledge is derived from ongoing sensory activity. (Kosslyn & Pomerantz, 1977, p.60)

> Many of the same operators . . . that are used in analyzing percepts are also applied to images. (Kosslyn & Pomerantz, 1977, p.66)

Thus images are seen as being somewhat comparable to perceptual experiences, in that there can be information contained in an image of which one is not yet aware, in the same way as the visual scene can contain information that has not been processed at any given time.

The mind's eye analogy. In order to see some problems with the idea that one scans images in the same way that one scans rooms or pictures, let us analyze one such "use" of an image in some detail. Assume that one is looking at a display on a cathode-ray tube and one is asked if the overall shape is square or rectangular. Based on the discussion in chapter 5, one would make such a judgment in something like the following way. The initial fixation would serve as an entry into one's visual knowledge, or pattern maps. One would then use the available knowledge about squares versus rectangles in order to examine various aspects of the display, until one or the other alternative could be decided upon.

Consider what happens when one *recalls* whether or not a display was a square or a rectangle, assuming for the sake of discussion that the person examined the object in the display, but made no conscious judgment concerning its shape. As an example, one might ask a young child how many windows are in her room. A little later the child learns to use the terms square and rectangle. We then go back and ask her to recall if her windows are square or rectangular. According to Kosslyn's analogy, the recall process would go something like this. The information stored when the room was examined would be activated and used as the basis for creation of an image. This image would then be scanned, and the child would judge the shape of the windows. According to Kosslyn, the procedure would parallel the perceiving of the actual room.

However, when looked at carefully, there seems to be one difference between the series of fixations used to scan the actual room and those used to "scan" the image. When one "scans" something in one's imagination, all one has is the information obtained earlier from the object itself. One cannot reexamine the object in one's imagination in the same way as one can reexamine the real object, because there is no independent source of information available with an imagined object. One's memory for the object is all that one has. Therefore, if one is able to determine that the display contained a square, it must be because one's earlier examination of the display served to store information which makes such a judgment possible. This leads to the conclusion that "scanning" the image in order to make a judgment is either irrelevant or impossible. All that has to be done is for the person to use the available information, and for the "verbal system" to respond. If the series of fixations doesn't contain the relevant information, then no further machinations can produce it. In either case, all one has is what one got from the display in the first place. This view could be contrasted with the "mind's eye" view, discussed in the last section, in the following way: Kosslyn and Pomerantz (1977) argue that new *perceptual* information can be gleaned from an image. The present view, on the other hand, argues that another linguistic response is being made to the *same* perceptual information.

Seeing something new in an image. As an example of the sorts of distinctions that must be made here, consider the following. When one first comes into a newly-painted room, one is often impressed by the quality of the paint job, only to realize later that there are streaks and missed spots on the wall that one did not see earlier. One needs some exposure to the painted wall before one sees the flaws in it; based on a short exposure, the flaws will not be seen. According to the point of view being argued here, one would not be able to scan one's image of the newly-painted wall after a short exposure and "realize" that there were flaws in it. If the short exposure does not enable one to *see* the flaws, then it won't enable one to imagine them, either.

There is experimental evidence available which supports the claim that one cannot get more out of an image than one stored in the first place. Reed and Johnsen (1975) gave subjects a hidden figures test, such as that shown in Figure 7.5. In one condition, the complete figure and the test figure were presented together. In another condition, the complete figure was presented and was then removed before the test figure was presented, which means that the subject had to remember the complete figure, or imagine it, in order to determine if the test figure was contained in it. The important finding was that performance was much worse when the complete figure was not physically present—there were over 70 percent errors in the memory condition, compared with only 14 percent errors in the condition in which both objects were present. Furthermore, these errors did not simply result from poor memory of the complete figure. Reed and Johnsen showed that their subjects remembered the complete figures well

Mental imagery as the medium of thought 169

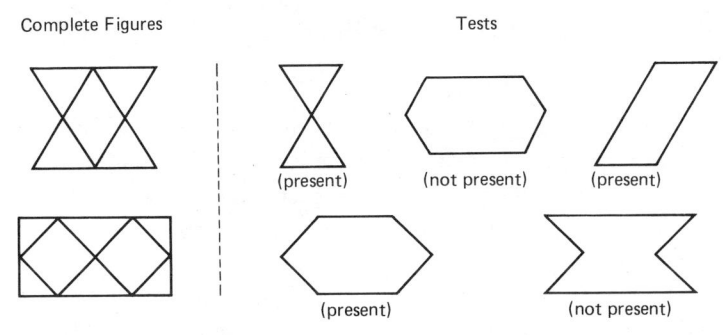

Figure 7.5. Hidden-figure test. The task is to determine if the various test figures are contained in the complete figures.

enough to draw them accurately, even though they couldn't identify figures hidden in them. One possible explanation for the difficulty in identifying hidden figures in an image is that the pattern map used to imagine the complete figure may not be able to serve as match for the hidden figure. That is, the way in which the complete figure is constructed may mean that the sort of information needed to identify the hidden figure is simply not available. For example, if the first figure in Figure 7.5 is scanned on the basis of two overlapping triangles, then the series of fixations wouldn't be the sort that could be matched with a parallelogram. Also, if one can't "view" an image as a "whole," then one ought not to be able to try out alternate scan paths, because the memory load would be too great. In short, on both logical and empirical grounds, it is reasonable to conclude that one can't get new information from images.

Counting windows in images. To return to Shepard's quote, then, the reason that one can "realize" that there are three windows in one's living room, although one never counted before, is because being able to imagine the room accurately and being able to report the number of windows both depend on the same basic information. One doesn't scan the image to get new information—one uses the same information to support a new verbalization. It seems much more straightforward to assume that the verbal judgment and the visuial image are both based on the same visual information, with neither being logically prior to the other. One experiences the image and reports that one saw a square as part of one and the same act, irrespective of what one's subjective impressions may be. The reason that one can make new judgments about visual information from memory is because the information obtained from an earlier visual inspection can serve as the basis for multiple verbal responses, as was argued in sections 5.7—5.9.

There has been a controversy recently between those who argue that images are pictorial or perceptual in nature (e.g., Kosslyn, 1975) and those who argue that images are based on more abstract information (e.g., Pylyshyn, 1973). The present position falls between these extremes. It does seem that visual imagery is based on perceptual information, and that the visual system is involved. On the other hand, it also seems to be true that images aren't scanned like pictures or "rotated" like pictures or objects can be. The present position is that visual imagery is based on relatively low-level perceptual information, but that the perceptual information, not the image-as-an-object, is the important factor in behavior.

Images, abstract propositions, and mimicry. It should be pointed out here that some theorists have argued that the evidence cited in this chapter does not necessarily mean that visual imagery involves low-level perceptual information, as we have concluded. For example, Anderson (1978) advocates a theory of thinking based on abstract propositions. This point of view will be discussed in detail in the next chapter, but should be briefly mentioned here. Basically, Anderson argues that thought is carried out in a medium not directly related to consciousness. That is, we are conscious of visual and verbal imagery, so we tend to think that our thought takes place in these media. Anderson argues that the medium of thought is more abstract than these various perceptual modalities and their related imagery. This abstract medium is called *propositional* after Frege (1892, rpt. 1965), who argued that the meaning of a sentence was a proposition, which was something different from the actual sentence. Anderson argues that all "meanings," of sentences and of any other environmental events, are represented in terms of these propositions. Furthermore, and most important for the present discussion, Anderson argues that one can always develop a theory of thinking based on propositions that will "mimic" any theory based on imagery or perceptual information. That is, both theories will make the same predictions, so it will be impossible to determine which theory is correct. Thus, according to Anderson's point of view, the discussion in the present chapter hasn't demonstrated what we have alleged it to demonstrate, that perceptual information is directly involved in thinking.

Anderson's point of view is a very influential one and will be discussed extensively in the next chapter. For the present, the only point to make is that Anderson's "mimicry" notion depends on one further assumption: that abstract propositional models of thinking are worth constructing. If this assumption is granted, then such a theorist will be able to mimic any theory based on imagery. However, one point of the next chapter is that propositional models are incorrect as descriptions of human knowledge. If this is true, then this eliminates the mimicry issue.

7.11 Consciousness, symbolization, and imagery

There are two further questions to be explored before the discussion is brought to a close. First, why do we produce images? Second, and related to the first, why are they conscious experiences?

Why do we produce images? It seems that we produce images because the information involved in thinking is often perceptual in nature. That is, our knowledge is of how things sounded or looked or felt, and so on. When we use this information in thinking, either by recalling it or using it as the basis for creation of something new, it still retains this perceptual form. Our thinking may not be any different than our experiences, in that both involve the concrete world. So if one has information available about how an object looked, then one will use this information as the need arises.

Images as symbols. This conclusion is related to the symbolist conception of thinking discussed earlier in the chapter. It has been argued by some theorists that we think in images because we need symbols to think in. From the present point of view, this statement misses the point. The visual information that we are thinking in is not a symbol of anything. It is simply our knowledge; and our knowledge is perceptual at its base, at least in many cases. It's not that an image serves to "clothe" our naked thought in a symbol. An image is simply the result of the fact that the information we use is of how things are.

In addition, the symbolist conception of thinking is based on the assumption that thinking is an activity that entails contemplation of symbols by the thinker. However, we saw in the last section that one doesn't contemplate images when one thinks. The image isn't an object to be contemplated. Rather, the conscious image is the result of the use of visual information to answer a question. A symbol is an object used to stand for some other object. Images, on the other hand, aren't objects. They are not things that are manipulated in thought. Images are created as part of the act of thinking. They don't stand for objects in the external world, they are one facet of what we know about objects in the external world. Therefore, we can't use images and contemplate them the way we use symbols.

Merely because our conscious experiences are similar when we look around a room and when we imagine ourselves looking around the room, that doesn't mean that our imaginary room has an existence in thought comparable to the existence of the real room.

It might be helpful if we got away from the notion that thinking is some sort of specific act that is carried out with symbolic objects. Rather, thought is simply behaving without external supports or external consequences. This is an idea that has been around for a long time (e.g., Sechenov, 1863, rpt. 1952) and seems to be a valuable one. The one addition that modern theorizing has added is that behaving entails the active use of one's knowledge. If our notions about behavior are expanded in this way, then we can see more clearly how thinking could be internalized behaving. If one must use one's own knowledge constantly in order to deal with the external world, then one can use this knowledge to think about that world as well. If one knows what will happen when various acts are carried out in various circumstances, then one can use this knowledge to think about carrying out those acts and ones like them.

Why conscious imagery? Even though an image comes about in part because we recall how something looked, or we predict how something novel would look if we saw it, why does the product of this have to be *conscious?* Why do we have to consciously imagine the room in order to count the windows? Why can't we answer the question by using our knowledge without it becoming conscious?

One answer to why images are conscious experiences immediately presents itself. If consciousness is intimately related to expectations and pattern maps, and imagery is related to them also, then imagery will be conscious. We have argued that generating an image entails using one's knowledge of how things were when they were experienced, and this is exactly the same mechanism as that involved in conscious attention. So this is one possible explanation for the conscious experience of imagery.

The reason that it is important to ask why we are conscious of our images seems to be because images are different than the things that we are usually conscious of. We are usually conscious of events in the physical world. Images aren't events in the physical world, and so it seems that our being conscious of them needs explaining. However, perhaps we aren't directly conscious of events. Rather, perhaps we are conscious of external events because of our processing of them (Neisser, 1967, chaps. 4–8), and perhaps the processing involved in imagery is of the same sort. If so, then we ought to be conscious of images, because they are based on the mecha-

Mental imagery as the medium of thought

nisms that result in consciousness of other things. To put it crudely, perhaps being conscious of the table in front of us depends on the running off of a pattern map. If so, then since imagining the table entails running off the same pattern map, it too should be a conscious experience.

Here is one anecdotal bit of evidence to support this conjecture. A colleague of mine who is very interested in books recently misread an advertisement. He mistakenly thought that it said "Sale on Books," when it really said "Sale on Tools." We discussed the incident later, and he said that when he saw the ad the first time, he was conscious of the word "Books," even though it wasn't present. If we assume that this misperception was due to processes such as those discussed in chapter 5, then consciousness of objects is at least based on the interaction of perceptual processes and the objects in the world and not solely on the objects present in the world.

7.12 Summary and conclusions

The notion that producing and contemplating nonverbal images are central to thinking has a long history in philosophy and psychology. In its pure form it alleges that all human thinking depends upon the capacity to experience images. These images serve as the symbols on which all thought supposedly depends. On the basis of the material reviewed in this chapter, it is highly unlikely that the strong form of the imagist theory is true.

Locke's theory of knowledge was examined as an example of an imagist theory of cognition in philosophy. Locke argued that abstract images serve as the basis for our use of general terms, and that the human mind can contemplate such an abstract image in isolation. This theory was criticized by Berkeley who argued that he could not frame any abstract images, and that the only way in which a specific image could serve as a generalized symbol is through the use to which it is put by the thinker. These sorts of arguments have decreased the importance of the imagist point of view.

In psychology, imagery was also very important in early theorizing, since at that time psychology was strongly influenced by imagist theories in philosophy. The importance of imagery in psychological theorizing subsequently decreased greatly, partially because of new experimental data (the Würzburg findings on imageless thought), and partly because of changes in the theoretical orientation of the mainstream of psychology (the advent of behaviorism). However, imagery has recently become important again, especially in the area of memory.

Concerning the role of imagery in recall, asking subjects to learn pairs of words by imagining the objects that the words refer to in some sort of interaction produces much higher recall than asking the subject to simply concentrate on repeating the words continuously, or asking the subject to imagine the objects separately. Various possible explanations for this facilitation by interactive imagery were discussed. It was speculated that imagery might be an effective method of storing information because the series of imagined fixations comprising the experience of imagining something might be held together through the overlap of information from one fixation to the next. Finally, it was argued that images aren't symbols which are used in thinking. Rather, thinking entails the use of information, and when such information is concerned with the visual aspects of the environment, then visual imagery may be experienced. The relationship of these processes to consciousness was briefly discussed.

8
Concepts, internal objects, and thinking

8.0 Introduction

Many situations which involve thinking also involve talking: We often talk to ourselves while working on problems. The frequency of speech during many activities must have been one of the reasons why scholars began speculating on the possible role of such speech in the thought processes themselves. However, the role that one assigns to such speech depends upon the theory of language which one accepts. The present chapter will consider a theory that is very popular in present-day cognitive psychology, and that argues that nonverbal concepts underlie production and comprehension of sentences. If one accepts this point of view, then speech is not the basis for thought, because all thinking is carried out in the conceptual base. These concepts serve as the representation for sentence meanings, as well as for all other knowledge. Given the potential importance of this conclusion, this work is worth examining in detail. In the last chapter we briefly considered this point of view when we discussed Anderson's (1978), Pylyshyn's (1973), and Simon's (1972) theorizing concerning imagery. The present chapter will be a more detailed discussion of the position. The next chapter will consider the opposite point of view, which argues that speech itself is the basis for thought.

The discussion in this chapter will be in four parts. First, a look at recent models of sentence comprehension that argue that comprehending sentences entails construction of conceptual networks, and second, the abstract concepts out of which these representations are constructed. We shall conclude that conceptually based comprehension models are incorrect because abstract nonverbal concepts are not able to function as required by these models. Third, an alternative way of looking at sentence comprehension, and the chapter ends with a brief discussion of what the conclusions mean for theories of thinking.

8.1 Constructing semantic representations: concepts and sentences

In recent years, a number of psychologists, computer scientists, and linguists have tried to produce explicit models of what occurs when people extract the meaning from a sentence (e.g., Lindsay & Norman, 1972; Norman & Rumelhart, 1975; Schank, 1972, 1973; Anderson & Bower 1973; Anderson, 1976). The central idea behind this model building is that comprehending a sentence, or witnessing any event, adds to our knowledge. All our knowledge is represented by nonverbal concepts, and the acquisition of knowledge is based on our ability to take the basic concepts which we possess and to combine them as needed in order to represent any information which needs to be stored.

Concepts, events, and episodes. According to Lindsay and Norman (chap. 10), any concept is defined by its relations to other concepts. Three sorts of relations predominate in our conceptual knowledge. First, a concept can be defined by specifying the main class into which it falls: "A dog is an animal. . . ." Secondly, the definition of a concept often refers to properties possessed by the members of the class specified by the concept: "A dog is an animal *with four legs and a tail*. . . ." Finally, defining a concept often entails pointing out an example of the concept: "A dog is an animal with four legs and a tail, like Fido." In this way, concepts are defined by making explicit their relations to other concepts. This results in knowledge being represented as a complex interlocking network of concepts. Figure 8.1 makes the complexity and the interrelatedness among concepts clear in a hypothetical example of someone's conceptual base. The concept with which the search through knowledge began was *tavern*.

These concepts can now serve as the building blocks with which to represent *events* and *episodes*. In this system, the representation of an event is built around the action that takes place; the other aspects of the event are defined in relation to the action. The basic structure of an event is shown

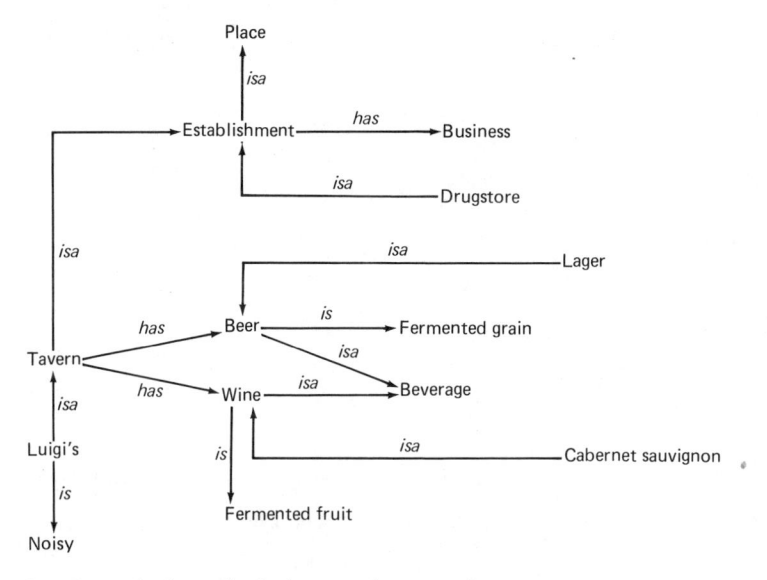

Concepts, internal objects, and thinking

Figure 8.1. Part of a hypothetical semantic network.

in Figure 8.2 and the parts of an event are outlined in Box 8.1. These various parts of an event are new relations which are added to the model, which means that concepts can be related to other concepts in all the ways outlined in Box 8.1. A more concrete example is diagrammed in Figure 8.3. The two sets of empty brackets mean that the concepts that fit there are complex, and their definitions are given by the multiple arrows leading away from the brackets.

Episodes consist of the structures built out of a group of related events. Concepts in common serve to hold the separate events together in one episode. We can take the information about the *tavern* in Figure 8.1, and add the following to it to produce the episode in Figure 8.4.

Figure 8.2. Schematic structure of an event.

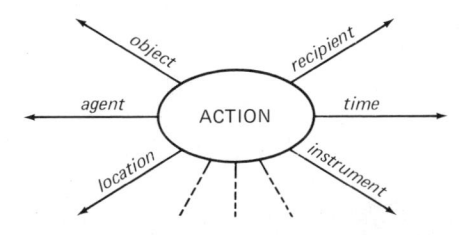

Box 8.1. The Parts of an Event

Action	The event itself. In a sentence, the action is usually described by a **verb:**
	The man was **bitten** by the dog.
Agent	The actor who has caused the action to take place:
	The man was bitten by the **dog.**
Conditional	A logical condition that exists between two events:
	A shark is dangerous **only if** it is hungry.
	John flunked the test **because** he always sleeps in lectures.
Instrument	The thing or device that caused or implemented the event:
	The **wind** demolished the house.
Location	The place where the event takes place. Often two different locations are involved, one at the start of the event and one at the conclusion. These are identified as **from** and **to** locations:
	They hitchhiked **from La Jolla to Del Mar.**
	From the University, they hitchhiked **to the beach.**
Object	The thing that is affected by the action:
	The wind demolished the **house.**
Purpose	Identifies the purpose of the event:
	Jack took Henry to the bar **to get him drunk.**
Quality	A descriptor, one that modifies a concept:
	The surf was **heavy.**
	There were **93** people in class.
Recipient	The person who is the receiver of the effect of the action:
	The crazy professor threw the blackboard at **Peter.**
Time	When an event takes place:
	The surf was up **yesterday.**
Truth	Used primarily for false statements:
	I do **not** like you, Hubert.

Concepts, internal objects, and thinking 179

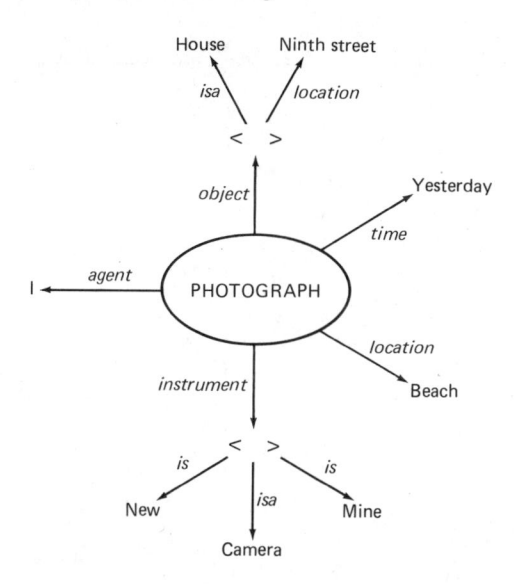

Figure 8.3. Representation of complicated event.

Bob drinks beer.
Mary hit Louise hard yesterday at Luigi's.
Al own's Luigi's.
Bob likes Louise.
Al's dog, Henry, bit Sam because he yelled at Mary.
Louise drinks wine.
Mary likes Bob.

The complex episode is built out of three separate events, each of which is built around a different action. Some additional information has been added to help fill things in. From this diagram the interrelatedness of the events is apparent, with the same concepts being pointed to from different directions.

In summary, this model is an attempt to specify the way in which information is stored in our memories. It is assumed that our knowledge is constructed out of concepts related to each other in various specified ways, and that all of our experiences form an interrelated network of concepts and relations.

Schank's analysis of conceptualizations underlying comprehension. In the Lindsay and Norman (1972, chap. 10) model, everything is organized around actions. Schank (1972, 1973) has attempted to carry out a still

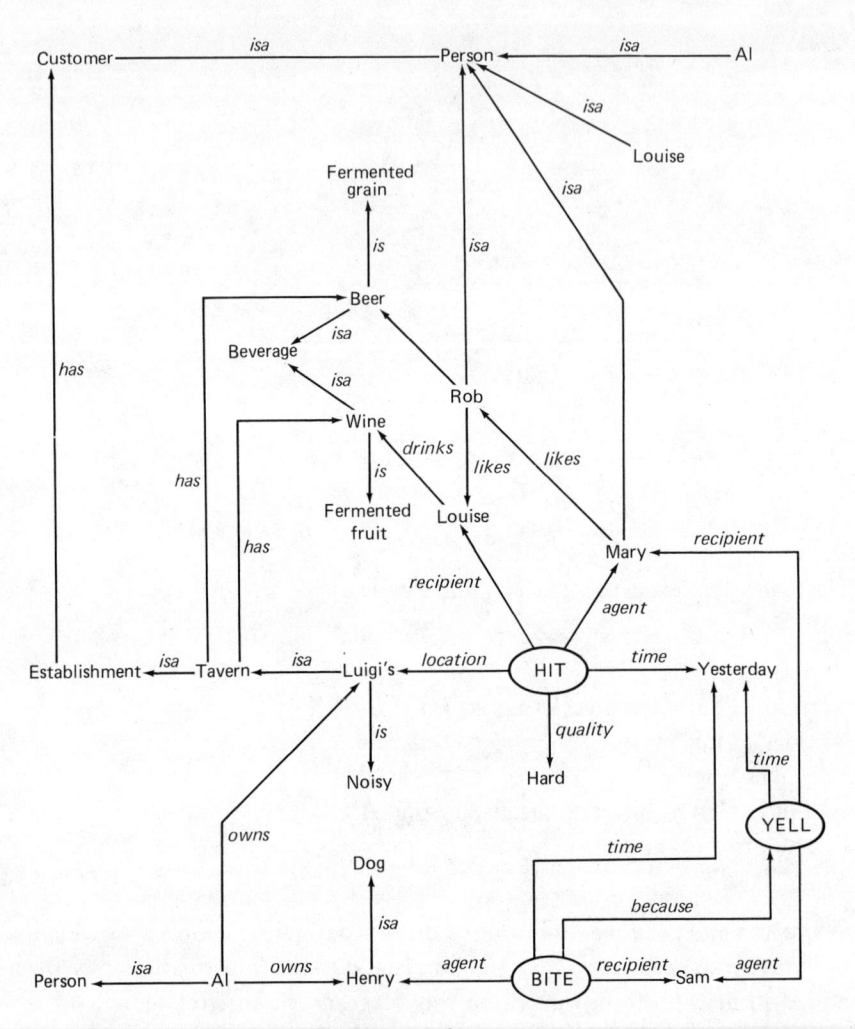

Figure 8.4. Network representing an episode.

deeper analysis of actions, into the conceptual "primitives" involved in thinking about actions and in understanding sentences. These primitives are assumed to be most basic concepts, out of which more complex concepts are constructed. More recent formulations of Lindsay and Norman's model (e.g., Norman & Rumelhart, 1975) have also been influenced by Schank's point of view.

As an example, consider the sentence "Peter put the package on the

Concepts, internal objects, and thinking 181

table." This is diagrammed in the top of Figure 8.5 in the manner of Lindsay and Norman's model. Schank's (1973) analysis begins with a consideration of what is involved in Peter's putting the package on the table. The package initially was not on the table, then Peter did something, and this resulted in the package's being on the table. To restate this in a slightly different way, Peter did something that caused the package to change its location from some unknown place to the table. Thus, *put* is analyzed as involving a change of location of an object, among other things, and the

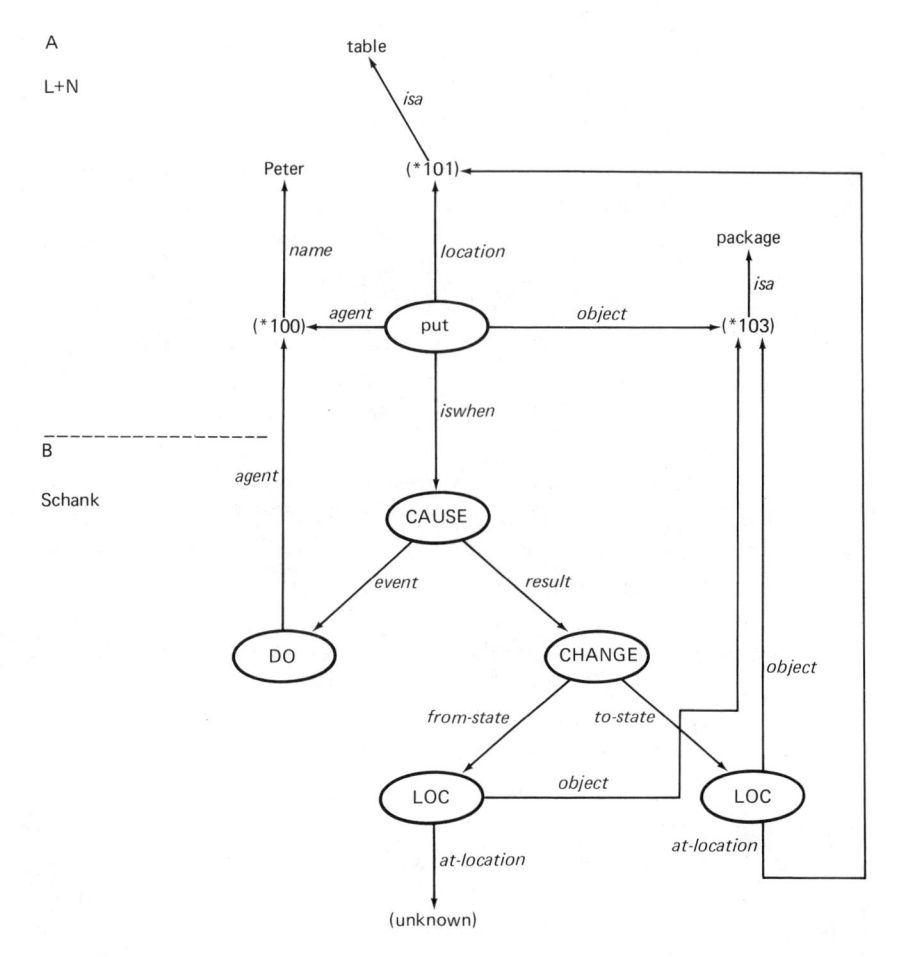

Figure 8.5. Representation of sentence "Peter put the package on the table." According to Lindsay & Norman (*top*–A), and expanded into Schank's format (*bottom*–B).

actor is the one who brought this change about. The bottom of Figure 8.5 shows how this sentence would be analyzed by Schank.

This sort of analysis makes explicit some similarities among various sentences which fit the way people understand the sentences. The two sets of sentences below can make this clearer.

Set A	Set B
I was holding a book	I was holding a book.
I offered it to John.	I offered it to John.
He accepted it.	He accepted it.
He took the book from me.	I gave the book to him.

The two episodes are identical, except for the last sentences, which are made up of different words. However, the two little stories mean just about the same thing, as do the last sentences of each set. If those last sentences were simply diagrammed according to Lindsay and Norman's format, then they would look very different. If we analyze the action involved from Schank's point of view, though, we can see why they are very similar if not identical in meaning. In both cases, the book started in my possession, the book changed possession, and the book wound up in John's possession. The difference between the two sentences is that in one, John performs the action that results in the book's transfer. In the other, I perform the action. These actions could be looked upon as being of the same sort, because they result in the transfer of possession of the book from me to John. Schank (1973) calls this sort of action TRANS, and it is one of the basic actions which form part of our conceptual base. More complex actions are represented in memory by combinations of basic elements such as TRANS.

To summarize, Schank argues that one can analyze the meanings of sentences into basic conceptual elements. These elements involve things like change of location from one time to another, and change of state (such as emotional state). This is the level of analysis which is assumed to occur when people understand sentences. Schank argues that there are several reasons why such an analysis probably occurs when people comprehend sentences. First, since there are many ways to express the same meaning (that is, since a given sentence can be paraphrased in many ways), it seems to be most efficient to keep the meaning separate from the various ways in which it can be expressed. This conceptual analysis separates the meaning from the words and therefore makes paraphrasing simpler, at least according to Schank. Secondly, people are able to make inferences from the things they hear, and Schank argues that analysis into conceptual elements simplifies inference making. Other theorists have proposed similar reason for postulating these concepts (see section 8.5).

Anderson and Bower's propositional model. Another recent model that deals in a similar way with concepts and knowledge is that of Anderson and Bower (1973; Anderson, 1974b). They assume that our memory of any sort of experience is in the form of abstract *propositions,* rather than some replica of the event itself. A proposition is made up of concepts related to each other in various ways. So, for example, the meaning of a sentence like "The big man over there is my brother" would be represented by several propositions: the man is big; the man is over there; the man is my brother. Anderson (1974b) makes it especially clear that these propositions are different from the words that they can be expressed in.

> A proposition is defined as an abstract memory representation which is structured according to certain rules of formation and which has a truth value. Although propositions are asserted by English sentences, propositions are not sentences, nor are they made out of words. Rather, a proposition is a more abstract entity composed out of concepts referenced by words. This distinction between propositions and concepts on the one hand and sentences and words on the other is at the heart of all propositional models of long-term memory.
>
> Subjects in these experiments learned simple sentences like *A hippie is in the park.* It is assumed that subjects store the sentences as propositions and as strings of semantically unrelated words. There is no hard evidence to support this assumption, but all subjects claimed to treat the sentences as meaning-bearing entities. There were frequent reports of imagery and semantic elaborations of the propositions. (p.452)

According to this position, no matter how information is acquired, it is all stored in the same format, independent of the various sense modalities. If this is so, it would mean that there is no such thing as visual imagery, if visual imagery is assumed to mean some sort of visual storage of information. There would only be propositions, which are not specifically visual. In the same way, there would be no verbal imagery. According to this point of view, the only way in which one could tell that some bit of information had been acquired visually, say, is because the proposition representing that information would contain a notation that this information had been acquired through vision. Information acquired verbally would have a *verbal* tag in the proposition. However, except for these tags, there would be no differences in the representation of visual and verbal information.

Bower and his associates (Bower, Munoz, & Arnold, 1972; Bower &

Winzenz, 1970) have carried out several experiments in order to show that verbal and visual information is stored in a common format, presumably these abstract propositions. Subjects were given pairs of words to learn, such as dog-bicycle. For some of the pairs, the subjects were told to form an image linking the two words. For other pairs the subjects were told to make up a sentence linking the two words, but nothing was said about forming an image. The subjects were then given a recall test, in which one member of each pair was presented and the subjects attempted to recall the other member of the pair. Two results are important. First, the sentences linking the two words facilitated recall about as well as did the images, relative to a control group. It could be argued that the reason sentences and images work equally well is because they result in the same information being stored in memory; that is, abstract propositions. The second important result is that the subjects had difficulty remembering which linking method was used for which pair. If, as Anderson and Bower argue, all information is stored in a common format, then this result can be explained. One simply must assume that the *visual* versus *verbal* tags can be forgotten independently of the rest of the propositions. One then could not recall how a given bit of information had been acquired.

Conceptual models: summary. These models are but a sample of a large amount of research of this sort that has been carried out recently. There are differences among the models, but for the present discussion the similarities are more important. The basic assumption underlying this research is that knowledge is made up of concepts related to each other in various ways. These concepts are assumed to be abstract, in the sense that they are not related to any sensory modality. Thus, according to these models, comprehending a sentence or perceiving an event entails carrying out a "cognitive act"—constructing the representation of that event out of concepts.

8.2 Concepts: philosophical background

In the last section, the term *concept* was mentioned several times, but nothing specific was said about the concepts themselves. Since they are the most important elements in these models, they are in need of examination.

Anderson and Bower's analysis of concepts. Anderson and Bower (1973, chap. 2) make reasonably clear what they believe concepts to be. Each concept is represented by one node in the memory network, and at this node is all the information defining the concept in question. This in-

Concepts, internal objects, and thinking

formation is assumed to be a set of abstract features which define the concept and is above and beyond any particular instance of the concept. Thus the concept of dog consists of just that information common to all dogs and therefore serves to define the class. It is assumed that a single element in memory can represent this information.

> It is . . . economical to grant the mind the power to introduce a new element, the idea of the universal concept which is an abstraction from the instances. (Anderson & Bower, 1973, p.20)

It is important to emphasize that Anderson and Bower argue that these concepts are new *elements;* that is, they are mental objects that are assumed to have some sort of existence. Thus the mind couldn't "introduce a new element" if this element wasn't some sort of "thing." Obviously, there are problems with the existence of these things, because we are not talking about physical objects here. However, the quotation seems to require that we assume that these concepts have some sort of existence, as do the models outlined in section 8.1. Perhaps the point could be made clearer if we try to restate it on the neural level. One might say that "the mind introduces a new element" means that there is some specific center or circuit in the nervous system that serves to represent the abstract concept in question. This center or circuit would then be assumed to be active when the concept is being used. In this way, one can take a step toward clarifying the "existence" of these mental objects called concepts (see Konorski, 1967). For the present we shall assume that these concepts must have some sort of mental existence, analogous in some way to the physical existence of real objects. These concepts represent the meanings of words, as well as representing any class of objects that can be "thought about," whether the class has a name or not. From this point of view, thinking about something is a mental act that entails an object—a concept—in the same way as any physical act entails an object—a physical object. This is an important point, and will be important in the critical analysis of this point of view.

There is a direct parallel between the analysis of concepts proposed by Anderson and Bower (1973) and that proposed by philosophers over the years. In philosophy, the question of the nature of concepts has usually been examined in the context of our ability to use general terms, such as the word *person*. Concern about concepts thus becomes focussed on how humans can use certain words. Three sorts of answers to this question have been important in philosophy. *Realists* have argued that each of the external events which we call "person" contains some essential characteristic, and this is the basis for our using the word to refer to it. This theory assumes that this essential characteristic is real, that it has an existence in the external world. It is *in* the object. *Conceptualists* have also argued that there is some essential characteristic which is common to all the things we call persons. However, they disagree with the realists, because they argue that this essential characteristic comes about from the way in which the objects are analyzed. That is, we humans create the essential characteristic because of the way in which we process stimuli. This is Anderson and Bower's point of view. Finally, *nominalists* have argued that all the various things that we call persons do not have to have any specific thing in common, except the name that we give them. Thus, there usually is not any essence that is in all objects of a given class. From this point of view, thinking does not entail manipulation of concepts, because concepts are not mental things that can be manipulated. Nominalistic concepts are not things which can be said to exist. Anderson and Bower (1973, chap. 2) explicitly critize a nominalistic argument before adopting their conceptualist position, and we shall consider their argument at a later time. First, let us consider these three positions in a bit more detail.

Realism: Plato's forms. The strongest form of this sort of a theory was advocated by Plato. The basic problem with which he was concerned was how people come to understand words such as *virtue*. The reason that this raised problems was that any specific act which is called virtuous is only an instance of virtue, rather than virtue in a general sense. If we have only seen specific instances of virtue, then how does the generalized knowledge, which enables one to use *virtue* correctly, arise?

Plato tried to deal with the problem of general knowledge by assuming that such knowledge did not have to be acquired. Since all we ever experience are specific instances, it did not seem possible to ever develop truly general knowledge. Therefore, Plato assumed that the knowledge that makes it possible to use general terms, or universals, was present in our souls before birth. This knowledge consists of a set of ideas or *forms*. Each of these forms stands for one unchanging universal, and we use the forms to interpret particular experiences as instances of universals. Experience therefore does not serve to produce new knowledge within us. At most, it can serve to activate the forms already available to us. In this way the universal becomes conscious.

Plato's argument went as follows: First, universals became conscious; second, the doctrine of forms was based on the assumption that every time a word such as *virtue* was used, there had to be some repeated characteristic that was always present; third, universals are innate in humans. It should be noted that Bregman (1977), Weimer (1973), and Palermo (1978) have recently argued for a point of view very similar if not identical to Plato's. We shall not discuss this theory explicitly in this chapter; however, the criticisms to be raised later, if correct, argue against a Platonic point of view.

Locke's theory of abstraction. Other theorists have argued that one does not have to postulate an innate basis for human concepts. For example, Locke argued that concepts are the result of operations carried out on information acquired through experience, as we saw several times in earlier chapters.

In Locke's theory of knowledge, the elements of thought are ideas, which are initially derived from external objects through sensation. The basic building blocks of knowledge are the simple ideas, which are taken directly from external objects, and which occur in consciousness automatically when an object is experienced. This is the first way that knowledge in the form of ideas is derived from experience. Other simple ideas were assumed by Locke to be derived from reflection, which is the mind's contemplation of its own internal activities.

Several aspects of these simple ideas bear emphasizing. Locke assumes that simple ideas are the only sources of our knowledge, and we cannot have any ideas that are not ultimately made up of simple ideas derived from one of these two sources of experience. Furthermore, these simple ideas are unalterable in form. They are derived from experience and cannot be added to by imagination. Finally, note the emphasis that Locke places on consciousness in the acquisition of knowledge: we are conscious of all the simple ideas, whether they derive from perception or reflection.

This theory must be carried a bit further if it is to be able to deal with the fact that our knowledge consists of more than simple ideas. Locke attempts to do this by considering the ways in which specific ideas can be used to produce general knowledge. When we see an apple, its redness and its roundness are experienced together. However, Locke argued that the mind can abstract one simple idea from all the others and contemplate it independently from other ideas. So, for example, although the redness of an apple is never perceived independently of other aspects of the apple, one can still form the idea of redness independently of all the other characteristics. In addition, Locke also argued that there is some common nucleus to all the experiences categorized as red (produce simple ideas of redness), and that we are capable of consciously dealing with this essence in and of itself. In this way, one has produced an abstract idea, or abstract image, of red, that can be used as the basis for extending the word *red* to new objects.

Abstraction. The use of words begin to stand as an outward mark of our internal ideas, and those being taken from particular things, if every particular idea that we take in should have a distinct name, names must be endless. To prevent this; the mind makes the particular idea, received from particular objects, to become general; which is done by considering them as they are in the mind such appearances, separate from all other existences or other concommitant ideas. This is called abstraction, whereby ideas taken from particular beings become general representatives of all the same kind; and their names general names, applicable to whatever exists conformable to such abstract ideas. Such precise, naked appearances in the mind, without considering how, whence, or with what others they came there, the understanding lays up (with names commonly annexed to them) as the standards to rank real existences into sorts, as they agree with these patterns, and to denominate them accordingly. Thus, the same colour being observed to-day in chalk or snow, which the mind yesterday received from milk, it considers that appearance alone, makes it a representative of all that kind; and having given it the name whiteness, it by that sound signifies that same quality wheresoever to be imagined or met with; and thus universals, whether ideas or terms, are made. (Locke, 1690, rpt. in Mandler & Mandler, 1964, pp.38–39)

Locke's theory is an example of conceptualism, because he argued that the concepts which we use arise out of the functioning of the human conceptual apparatus. Secondly, note that he assumed that there was some common element or elements present in all objects which were referred to by the same word. Thus, Locke and Plato agree that underlying every term which we use, either a simple term or a general term, there is one corresponding conceptual "essence." Plato thought the essence was outside us, while Locke thought we produced it when we analyzed experiences. Finally, Locke argued that this analysis of experiences into ideas took place consciously. This also was not too different from what Plato had said regarding the role of consciousness in concept formation.

Concepts and family resemblances: nominalism. Locke's theory was criticized on several grounds by Berkeley (1710, rpt. 1963). The first criticism, already considered in chapters 5 and 7, concerned Locke's contention that humans can consciously formulate abstract ideas, or abstract images. Berkeley argued that any image that he could form to represent some generalized term, such as "body," would be some specific body. He could not find generalized images in his conscious experience. This is one argument against both Locke and Plato, both of whom said that our concepts are based on elements that are available to conscious inspection.

Concepts, internal objects, and thinking

Berkeley also raised a second, and perhaps more interesting, problem for theories such as Locke's and Plato's. Both these theories assumed that behind each general term was one single essence, which was present in all the members of the class referred to by the term. Thus "bodiness" is in all bodies, "human-ness" in all humans, and so on. Berkeley argued that this assumption was based on a mistaken idea concerning general terms. Simply because we use the same word in many different situations, it does not mean that all the situations have one single thing in common. Berkeley argued that because we say "the person's body, "the body of the dog," "the body of the report," and so on, we can be seduced into mistakenly thinking that all the situations in which those utterances are used contain something in common, the essence "bodiness."

Let us examine wherein Words have contributed to the origin of that mistake. —First then, it is thought that every name has, or ought to have, one only precise and settled signification; which inclines man to think there are certain abstract, determinate ideas that constitute the true and only immediate signification of each general name, and that it is by the mediation of these abstract ideas that a general name comes to signify any particular thing. Whereas, in truth, there is no such thing as one precise and definite signification annexed to any general name, they all signifying indifferently a great number of particular ideas. (1963, p.58)

This is an argument that has been reemphasized several times by more modern philosophers interested in conceptual thinking. For example, Austin (1939) says this about general terms:

Clearly [the notion that since we use the same word in each case, there must be some single identical thing present in each case] depends on a suppressed premise which there is no reason whatever to accept, namely, that words are essentially "proper names." But why, if one identical word is used, *must* there be one identical object present which it denotes? Why should it not be the whole function of a word to denote many things? (p.38)

The similarity of this quote to the earlier one from Berkeley is easily seen. This same point of view has been argued in great detail by Wittgenstein (1958), whose influential *Philosophical Investigations* contains examples of general terms which are not used in one single way. This is a further elaboration of Berkeley's objection to the notion of abstract ideas. Here is a well-known quote from Wittgenstein.

66. Consider for example the proceedings that we call "games." I mean board games, card-games, ball-games, Olympic games, and so on. What is common to them all? . . .—For if you look at them you will not see something that is common to *all*, but similarities, relationships, and a whole series of them at that. To repeat:

don't think, but look! —Look for example at board-games, with their multifarious relationships. Now pass to card-games; here you find many correspondences with the first group, but many common features drop out, and others appear. When we pass next to ball-games, much that is common is retained, but much is lost. —Are they all "amusing?" Compare chess with noughts and crosses [tic-tac-toe]. Or is there always winning and losing, or competition between players? Think of patience. In ball-games there is winning and losing; but when a child throws his ball at the wall and catches it again, this feature has disappeared. Look at the parts played by skill and luck; and at the difference between skill in chess and skill in tennis. Think now of games like ring-a-ring-a-roses; here is the element of amusement, but how many other characteristic features have disappeared! And we can go through the many, many other groups of games in the same way; can see how similarities crop up and disappear.

And the result of this examination is: we see a complicated network of similarities overlapping and crisscrossing: sometimes overall similarities, sometimes similarities of detail.

67. I can think of no better expression to characterize these similarities than "family resemblances"; for the various resemblances between members of a family: build, features, color of eyes, gait, temperament, etc. etc. overlap and criss-cross in the same way.—And I shall say: "games" form a family. (1958, pp.31e–32e).

The notion of family resemblance means that two members of the same class (say, two games) do not have to have exactly the same features in common. Indeed, it might be the case that two members of the "same" family do not have *any* features in common, even though they are given the same name. They would be linked only through intermediate members of the family. This conclusion is very similar to that drawn in chapter 5 concerning the lack of "defining features" in pattern recognition models.

8.25 Philosophical analysis: summary. To summarize, most present-day philosophers seem to accept some version of nominalism in explaining concepts. (See the articles "Concepts" by Heath and "Universals" by Woozley, both in the *Encyclopedia of Philosophy* (Edwards, 1967). See Price (1953), for a statement of a nonnominalist point of view.) As far as the present discussion is concerned, if the nominalistic position is accepted, it raises problems for conceptual network models, because there are no concepts out of which to construct them. According to nominalism, concepts are not "things" that can be mentally manipulated—according to nominalism, concepts are not things at all. However, the analysis considered in these sections was carried out by philosophers and has not had a terribly strong effect on psychological theorizing. Accordingly, psychologists in a number of areas (e.g., Konorski, 1967; Posner, 1973; Sutton-Smith, 1973) explicitly assume that thinking entails the manipulation of internal representations of environmental events, as do the conceptual network theorists whom we have already considered. Therefore, let us consider some experimental results which support the notion of concepts as family resemblances.

8.3 Studies of family resemblances

In an impressive series of studies, Rosch (e.g., 1975a,b; Rosch & Mervis, 1975) has argued that many human categories are based on family resemblances of the type discussed by Wittgenstein. Rosch's analysis goes further than that of Wittgenstein, however, because she argues that all of the members of a given category are not "equally good members" of the category.

Rosch argues that there is no small closed set of features or attributes that is possessed by every member of any category, as was also argued in chapter 5. Rather, there are many features that contribute toward membership in a given category, such as "dog." Furthermore, no feature is possessed by all dogs and only dogs, and no dog contains all the features common to all dogs. Some features, such as four legs, are possessed by almost all the members of the category, but are also possessed by members of many other categories. Other features, like the particular shape of a Pekingese's face, are possessed by only a few members of the category. Therefore, some features are more "typical" of dogs than other features, and some dogs are more "typical" because they contain more of these typical features. Rosch argues that most of our categories have structure, in that their members can be ordered in terms of how typical they are of the category as a whole. Furthermore, according to Rosch, the more typical members may serve to represent or stand for the whole category during perception or conception. (Conception is thinking about the category in question. The most typical member would be thought about, and would substitute for the category as a whole.)

Several different sorts of evidence have been brought forth to support this analysis. In one experiment, subjects were given a group of items that were all members of the same class, such as dogs (Rosch, 1975a). The subjects were asked to rate how well each item fit their image or idea of the meaning of the category name. They had no trouble doing this, and there was consistency in ratings from subject to subject. This meant that the categories were structured, in Rosch's terms. In another study (Rosch & Mervis, 1975), subjects were given the names of items from various categories and asked to list the attributes possessed by each item. It was found that all the members of a given category did not have one small set of attributes in common. Rather, there was a distribution of attributes, with some attributes present in more members and other attributes present in fewer members. Furthermore, those items that possessed more of the typical attributes were the same items that had been rated highly by the subjects in the other study as fitting their idea or image of the meaning of the category name. Thus there was a high correlation between ratings of typicalness, and typicalness as defined by possession of typical attributes. One potential difficulty with Rosch's method is that subjects were asked to list the attributes possessed by the various items. It might be argued that attributes are not consciously recallable, so the results don't indicate that there are no attributes in common, they merely indicate that people can't tell you what the attributes are. However, the fact that there is a high correlation between listed attributes and typicalness ratings indicates that the recalled attributes may indeed be those used in dealing with the concepts.

One other more complicated study (Rosch, 1975b) deserves mention for several reasons. The purpose was to examine the possible structure in human color categories. Rosch argues that color categories are based on family resemblances in the same way that object categories are. There are better and worse reds, just as there are better and worse dogs. Some reds are "redder" than others, even though they are all called red by naive subjects. If so, then the best red ought to be used by people when they have to mentally deal with red. This was tested in the following way. Subjects were shown pairs of colors, and they were to respond "same" if the colors were identical, and "different" if they were not. The important variable was the time it took to respond.

Assume that we have two pairs of stimuli, each of which contains identical colors. However, one pair contains two good reds, the other pair two off-reds. In both cases the subject's response is "same," and in both cases the time to respond is approximately the same. Assume now that we warn the subject in advance that the next two stimuli will be red. According to Rosch's model, the warning should make the subject think of red, which means that the subject should think of a good red. This will occur before the stimuli appear. Since the subject should already be thinking of the good red before the pairs appear, this should help the processing of the good reds, as discussed in chapter 5. In terms of this experiment, it means that time to respond "same" should decrease for the good reds when there is a warning, and should increase for the off-reds. This is what was found, and the results therefore support the idea that some relatively concrete information about the category, such as the appearance of a typical member, was what was being activated by the warning. Rosch concluded that there is no general representation of the entire category that subjects can mentally manipulate. Rather, one typical member of the category is used to stand for the entire category.

This research is very important as far as conceptual models of thinking are concerned. Rosch has presented empirical evidence that there is no closed class of features that defines any given concept (at least the concepts that she and her colleagues have analyzed). This means that theories arguing that concepts have some sort of existence, as bundles of features or as nodes, are called into question on empirical grounds.

A potential problem: best examples as representatives of a class. One important aspect of Rosch's model is the idea that when we think about a category, we use one specific item, the most typical item, in order to represent the whole category. That is, the *meaning* of the category name is represented by this one item. This is a very important claim because of its potential importance to theories of thinking. Assume for the sake of discussion that you work as a dogcatcher, and your best example of a dog is a golden retriever. One day you are ordered to pick up any and all stray dogs that you see from now on. If Rosch's model is correct, then this sentence would be represented by something like an image of you catching a golden retriever. However, this raises a problem, because the sentence does not mean that you are to pick any stray golden retrievers; it means that you are to pick up stray dogs. When examined closely, Rosch's point of view is a sophisticated imagery model, and it runs into many of the problems discussed in chapter 7.

Thus, according to Rosch's model, it seems that you would respond in exactly the same way to an order to pick up all dogs as you would to an order to pick up all golden retrievers. However, it is obvious than an order concerning dogs would not be confused with an order concerning golden retrievers, even for someone who thought that golden retrievers were the most typical dog. Therefore, the assumption that a typical item serves to stand for a whole category does not seem to be correct. This takes nothing away from Rosch's valuable contributions concerning the family resemblances basis for human categories, but it does raise problems for the notion that a typical item stands for the entire category. The basic problem with this notion seems to be that if concepts are based on family resemblances, then *no* item can stand for the whole category, even the most typical item.

Given the difficulties in finding a suitable abstract or concrete symbol to stand for a concept when it is thought about, perhaps it would be simpler to drop the idea that we need things to stand for concepts when we think about them. Perhaps we understand a sentence about dogs simply because we understand the sentence, and for no other reason. Perhaps nothing *stands for* a category when we think. This idea has already been discussed in the context of imagery in the last chapter, and will be discussed further later in this chapter and in chapter 9.

To summarize this important work, Rosch has produced empirical evidence that human categories are not based on a simple set of features that are present in all the objects in the category. There are many features that contribute to membership in any category, and some members of the category contain more of these features than other members do. The crucial determinant of category membership may be either that a given object contains more of the features related to one category than it does for any other category, or that it contains more of the important features for one category. Thus, this work presents additional evidence that the search for mental objects is misdirected.

Other negative evidence for concepts as nodes in memory. We have already considered several results in other contexts that also argue against the notion that concepts can be considered to be single nodes in a network. These results are worth considering briefly here. First, the generate-test, or dual-process, model of memory discussed in chapter 2 is based on the assumption that each word is represented in memory by a single node, which is marked when a word is presented. However, recent memory research indicates that this sort of model cannot adequately deal with the data. Second, in the discussion of pattern recognition in chapter 5, we saw that pattern recognition theorists do not believe that patterns are represented by closed sets of features in memory, which supports the present conclusion. Third, if pattern recognition and attention are sequential processes extending over time, then single nodes are not adequate to deal with the fine grain of these activities. In summary, there are several empirical reasons for questioning the notion that there are basic conceptual elements out of which all our knowledge comes. Let us now consider the logic of concepts a bit further, especially the logic of "having a concept."

8.4 What does one have when one has a concept?

We have argued that to have a concept is not to be in possession of something that can be acted upon and used in thinking. The concept *dog* is not some sort of internal picture or statue that takes the place of real dogs when we are thinking; a concept isn't a symbol. One reason that concepts seem to be "things" is that we say that we "have" them, and usually we talk of having things. However, we sometimes use "have" in a slightly different way, as in: "He has a top-spin backhand that's unreturnable." This sentence refers to the effectiveness of a tennis player's backhand drive. Obviously, the player doesn't possess any material thing; no physical object is involved here. To have a top-spin backhand means that one can do things, such as: hit the ball accurately; hit the ball hard; hit the ball accurately and hard from almost anyplace on the court; and do these things a good percentage of the time. This is what the player "has," and the use of "has" in this context is an extension of its literal use.

In the same way, one could argue that to have a concept entails being able to do things (Ryle, 1949, chap. IX), and there seems to be a family of activities involved in having a concept. Consider the concept dog. First of all, in order to possess this concept, one would have to be able to recognize dogs, especially new dogs. However, in addition to knowing what dogs looked like, one would have to know other things about dogs. For example, someone to whom "bow-wow" was a meaningless noise could hardly be said to possess the concept dog. The relationship of dogs to cats would have to be known, also, as well as the differences in behavior and temperament among the various breeds of dogs, and so on. Possessing a concept entails a number of different activities, and the more of them one can do, the more detailed is one's concept.

In summary, these last several sections have argued that concepts do not entail specific mental objects that are used in thinking. Several sorts of evidence support this conclusion. First, the assumption that general terms always refer to one single sort of situation does not seem to be correct. Second, studies have indicated that many human categories are based on family resemblances, which means that no single mental object could stand for the category. Finally, an analysis of the term *concept* indicated that a search for mental objects was misdirected. To acquire a concept does not mean that one's mental possessions have increased. Rather, it means that one has become able to do some new things.

8.5 A critical examination of arguments in support of abstract conceptual models

We have now considered several different sorts of evidence which argue against conceptual network models. This evidence, while raising problems for these models, is obviously not conclusive, because there is much more involved in these models than the few points considered so far. Specifically, there are a number of additional reasons that investigators have brought forth to support the adoption of models based on abstract concepts, and the points raised so far in this chapter are not directed at these other reasons. Therefore, it would be particularly important if it could be shown that these reasons, which allegedly support abstract conceptual models, do not in fact do so. Let us briefly consider some of the reasons brought forth by various theorists to support the adoption of abstract conceptual models. Hayes-Roth and Hayes-Roth (1977) and Kosslyn and Pomerantz (1977) present more detailed discussions of these issues.

Semantic elaboration of sentences. In section 8.1, there is a passage from Anderson (1974b) in which he defined the term proposition and presented some evidence to support the claim that sentences were stored as abstract propositions. Anderson mentioned that there was no hard evidence to support the claim, but all his subjects claimed to treat the sentences as "meaning-bearing entities" and frequently reported "imagery and semantic elaborations of the propositions." But are these two activities evidence that sentences are analyzed into propositions made up of abstract concepts related to each other in various ways? In learning to speak, one learns, among other things, how to describe various sorts of situations. If so, it is easy to see how one could produce an image on hearing a sentence—one would use this knowledge in the other direction. In the same way, just because people produce semantic elaborations when they hear sentences doesn't mean that sentences are analyzed into abstract propositions. For example, the elaboration could be based on the subject's imagining the situation described by the sentence. This would not necessarily involve abstract concepts, as just mentioned. Furthermore, even if the subject responds directly to the sentence with other sentences, this does not require that we assume that the subjects possess abstract concepts. It could just as easily, and perhaps more simply, be argued that one of the things that we learn when we learn to speak is how to produce utterances in response to other utterances. This point is elaborated further in section 8.9 and in the next chapter.

Mediational confusions. Several studies by Bower and his associates (Bower, Munoz, & Arnold, 1972; Bower & Winzenz, 1970) were cited in section 8.1 as providing evidence to support abstract conceptual models. In these studies, subjects were given pairs of words to learn, some by using a sentence to link the words, the rest by using visual images to link the words. The important findings were that sentences and images facilitated recall equally, and that at recall, subjects couldn't correctly report the method by which they learned individual pairs. These results were taken as evidence that all pairs were encoded in the same way, as abstract propositions. However, there is an equally plausible explanation possible for these results: When you tell the subject to produce images for half of the pairs and sentences for the rest, you make it very likely that both images and sentences will be produced for all the pairs. Given a pair like dog-bicycle, it is difficult to say "The dog is riding the bicycle" without having some sort of an image, and the same is true for verbalizing while visually imagining. Therefore, it is not surprising that subjects had difficulty in reporting how they tried to learn each pair—they may very well have used both methods. In sum, these results are by no means compelling evidence that sentences and images are stored in the same abstract format.

Efficiency of retrieval. Both Anderson and Bower (1973) and Schank (1975) argue that models based on abstract concepts are much more efficient than models that do not postulate such entities. Specifically, these theorists assume that the alternative to an abstract conceptual model would be a model in which every instance of every event would have to be stored. Such models would be too complicated to be of interest, according to these theorists. A quote from Anderson and Bower (chap. 2) in section 8.2 made their view clear, and Schank says almost the same thing:

> The first thing to consider is that a proposition cannot be stored in memory simply in the form of a natural-language sentence. Since it is possible to say the same thing in a number of different ways, it is unreasonable to suppose that people are constantly checking to see whether another proposition which they have stored in one way in memory is the same as another proposition they have stored somewhere else in an alternate form. (p.171)

Schank concludes from this that all sentences are translated into a common form, that of interrelated abstract concepts.

Once again, these arguments are not very compelling when looked at carefully. First of all, since very little is known about the way in which information is retrieved from memory during conversation, it is not necessarily true that storage of natural-language sentences is indeed inefficient. Furthermore, when sentences are translated into networks of concepts, each concept becomes associated with many different sentences, thereby adding a source of confusion in network models. Also, if people have to translate various sentences into a common format, then a translation operation has to be carried out for each sentence. However, if people can match new sentences to sentences already stored, then only one sentence must be transformed. That is, to match two strings of words (two sentences), if you have rules for transforming one string into another, you only have to transform one string to see if you can produce the other. Thus, storing sentences may be more efficient than network models in at least one respect.

Summary. We can thus see that not only are there negative findings concerning abstract conceptual models, but that some of the alleged positive aspects of these models are not strongly supported. The remaining reason for considering abstract conceptual models to be plausible cognitive models is that computer theorists use these sorts of models in computer programs that can exhibit some characteristics associated with understanding and producing language. However, simply because a computer can carry out some task, it doesn't mean that the way in which the computer does it is in any way similar to the way in which humans carry out the same task. Based on the discussion in this chapter, language comprehension may be one example of a task which humans and computers carry out very differently.

8.6 What do network models describe?

Let us assume that humans do not possess the sorts of concepts postulated by network models of memory. This leads us to two further questions. First, do the network models in Figures 8.1–8.5 describe anything at all? Second, if we do not build conceptual networks when we comprehend sentences, then what does happen when we comprehend a sentence? The rest of this chapter will be concerned with the answers to these questions.

Conceptual networks without concepts. As far as the networks are concerned, it seems that they might describe our knowledge. Let us examine again the network in Figure 8.4. That network describes three events, a hitting, a biting, and a yelling. These three events, since they have been witnessed by the "owner" of the network, would be stored as sets of visual fixations, corresponding to the fixations involved in actually witnessing the events originally. Therefore, the events would not be analyzed in the same format as in Figure 8.4, because the various aspects of these events would be included in the visual information itself. For example, the fact that everything took place at Luigi's would be evident from the visual information itself, as would be the fact that Mary hit Louise hard. In addition, the fact that Henry the dog bit Sam *because* Sam yelled at Mary, and that the yelling got Henry excited, could also be obtained relatively directly from

Concepts, internal objects, and thinking 199

the temporal aspects of the nonverbal "record" of these events, which the person presumably stored when witnessing them.

There is other information also available in Figure 8.4, the various other concepts. For example, the network contains the fact that Luigi's is a tavern, which is an establishment with customers, and that wine and beer are served at a tavern. This sort of information is not like the record of the events that took place recently at Luigi's. Rather, this information is a record of a bit of the person's knowledge about language. If the person's knowledge about the various people involved is the result of storing some visual information, then the rest of Figure 8.4 shows what the person knows about translating this visual information into words.

The way these two sorts of knowledge are related is shown at the bottom of Figure 8.6. The various cases such as *agent* and *recipient* are no longer needed, because the visual information makes that explicit. In addition, in our reformulation *agent* is simply a word possibly related to one person in each of the events described. There are at least two ways in which the linguistic network shown in Figure 8.6 could have developed. First, all the connections shown could have been explicitly pointed out to the person by other speakers. Thus, perhaps the owner of the network was told that the persons who frequent a tavern are called customers. On the other hand, the person could have made an inference at one time or another that these people must be customers. Finally, there might be certain words that have not yet been applied to the events in question, although they could be. For example, the owner of the network knows the sorts of things that can be called persons. The owner also has a clear record of what the thing was that Henry bit. Therefore, the owner could say that Henry bit a person, if asked. However, the occasion to do this might not yet have arisen, so the description has not been applied.

To summarize, it seems that networks of the sort shown in Figures 8.1–8.5 are an amalgamation of three separate sorts of information. First, there is nonverbal information, acquired through witnessing an event. Second, there are verbal descriptions, applied to these events both by the person and by others. Third, there is the person's knowledge of language itself, leaving open the possibility of saying other things about the events.

The basic question that motivated the construction of conceptual network models is what happens when a sentence is comprehended. We have just concluded that conceptual networks are not constructed during sentence comprehension. Therefore, we must now turn to the question of what people do when they comprehend a sentence.

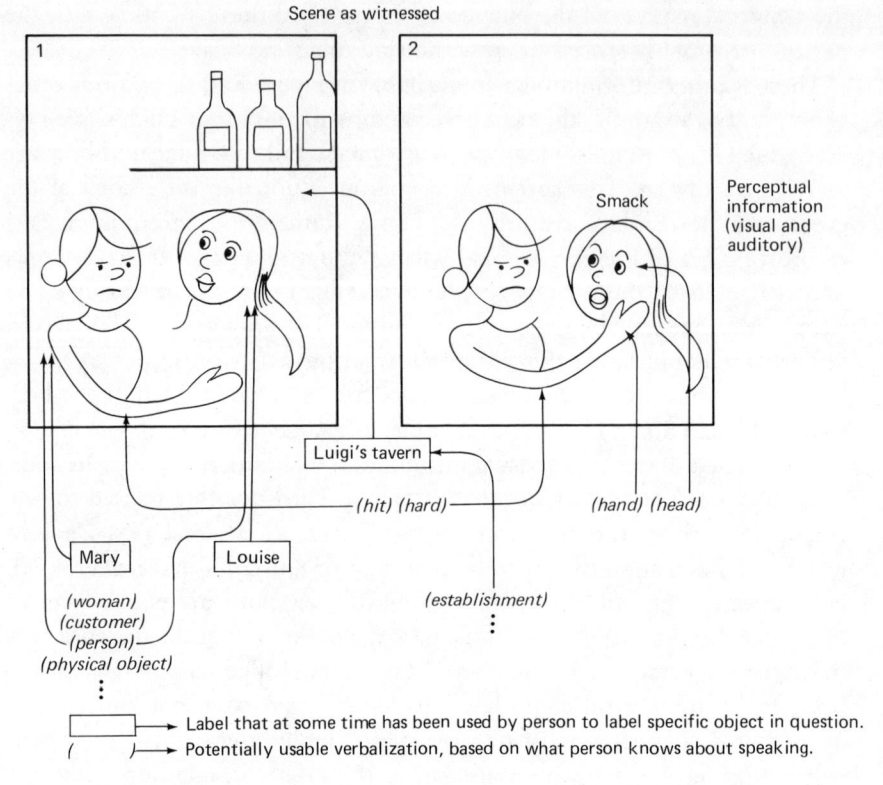

Figure 8.6. Alternative formulation concerning knowledge about an event.

8.7 Recognizing sentences

As a first step, since sentences are collections of words, perhaps comprehending a sentence is simply the result of recognizing the words in the sentence. After we have recognized the words, we can then go "deeper" and imagine a situation that would fit the sentence, although this imagined situation is not necessary for understanding the sentence. Thus, sentence comprehension would be a case of auditory pattern recognition. However, recognizing a sentence is more than simply recognizing the words, for two reasons. First, if only the words were important, then *Dog bites man* would be the same sentence as *Man bites dog*. Second, one can sometimes recognize all the words in a string of words without recognizing the string as a sentence, as in *My hand foot hurts*. The difference between mere word

Concepts, internal objects, and thinking 201

lists and sentences may lie in the way each word in the string of words is recognized versus how each word in a sentence is recognized.

Transition networks as models of sentence recognition. According to the discussion in chapter 5, recognizing a familiar face is the result of carrying out a specific series of visual fixations which matches the knowledge that one has concerning how that familiar person looks. We now need to consider a comparable sort of knowledge concerning the "layout," or structure, of sentences. One model of sentence structure which has recently been incorporated in psychological models of sentence processing is called a transition network (Woods, 1970; Kaplan, 1975). Such a network is essentially a summary of the ways in which words can be strung together in order to produce acceptable sentences in English. A simple network is shown in Figure 8.7. It is made up of states (the circles) connected by arcs (the arrows). In order to generate a sentence using this network, one begins at the start state and follows a complete path to the end on the far right. If one takes the words that one encounters on such a path, one gets a grammatical sentence of English.

This sort of a network can also be used to process sentences. As one hears the words, one begins at the start state and uses the words to direct one through the network. If a series of words can lead one from the start

Figure 8.7. A network for recognizing sentences.

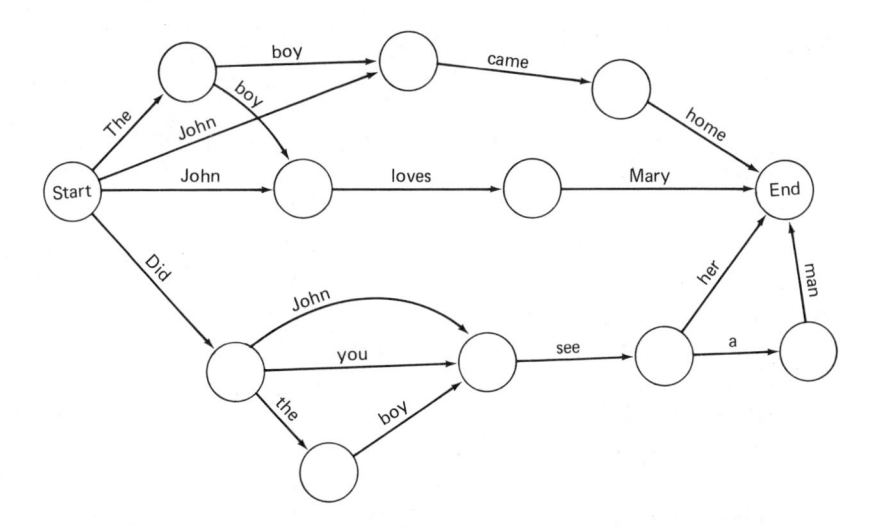

state to the end state, then one can say that the network recognizes the sentence.

One can see in Figure 8.7 that the same sorts of words and phrases appear in more than one sentence. For example, *the boy* appears in three sentences, as does *John*. We can, therefore, simplify matters if we eliminate these words from the network and substitute the term NP (noun phrase) for them. We can then add a separate smaller network to analyze NPs. If we do this, we get the networks in Figure 8.8 In addition, it is possible to simplify things still further, since one could add categories like *verb, adjective, adverb,* and so on, to the network. This would permit more and more consolidation.

To summarize, the networks in Figure 8.8 give the flavor of how transition networks function in sentence recognition. Such a network is the summary of a great many sentences, each of which is made up of one sequence of grammatical classes out of the various possible sequences in the network. These networks, therefore, are a summary of the layouts of sentences, in a way comparable to the pattern maps discussed in chapter 5. A transition network such as that in Figure 8.8 can deal with a great many new sentences, so long as the new sentence is made up of one of the sequences of grammatical classes in the model. In addition, transition networks are interesting in that they seem to be based on the same sorts of expectancies that were discussed in chapter 5 and elsewhere. As such, these networks may be compatible with models of pattern recognition and attention based on expectations. A similar point of view is expressed by Kintsch (1977, chap. 6) and Rumelhart (1977, chap. 3).

In addition, these transition networks can be organized to deal with semantic factors in sentence recognition. As mentioned in chapter 5, recognition of words in sentences is influenced by the earlier words in the sentence. Based on this, one would have to organize the transition networks in Figure 8.8 so that the relative probabilities of each of the various paths are taken into account as the words of a sentence are heard. In this way, semantic constraints within sentences can be dealt with. There are also semantic constraints across sentences, however, and the networks in Figure 8.8 cannot deal with these. That is, if one is listening to a conversation about baseball, then one's expectations concerning later sentences will be influenced by the earlier sentences which one has heard. Therefore, it seems that in addition to possible word-to-word networks, as in Figure 8.8, one must deal with possible sentence-to-sentence networks, which deal with relations within conversations. Obviously, this sort of a notion is

Concepts, internal objects, and thinking 203

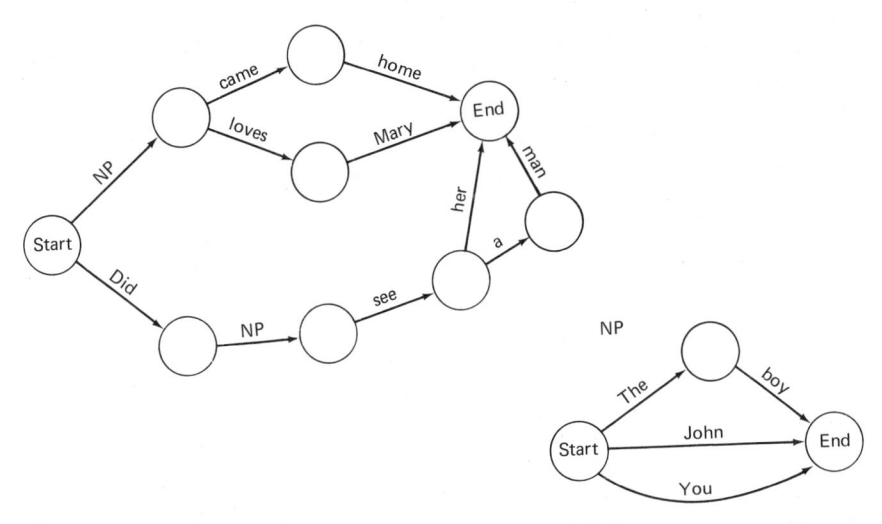

Figure 8.8. A simplification of the network in Figure 8.7.

essentially the same as the script idea discussed earlier (see section 3.4), and this was one of the reasons that scripts were developed.

8.8 Abstract grammatical classes

This very sketchy introduction has shown how one could try to deal with sentence recognition in a way that has some psychological plausibility. However, in doing this, we have raised a potential problem.

In the discussion in the last section, it was argued that networks could be analyzed in terms of grammatical classes. What is the basis for these grammatical classes? For example, what characteristics define the members of the noun class? One reason that this is a potential problem is that we do not want these features to be abstract features. Since it has been argued in several places that humans do not possess abstract concepts, then we would not want to posit such knowledge now. We need a way of characterizing the strings in a transition network without relying on abstract knowledge.

One way in which listeners might be able to use information about grammatical classes is through a distributional analysis, which is based on the positions that a word can fill in the sentences of a language. As an example, *boy* and *girl* are heard in very many similar sentences, and they occur in the same positions in these sentences. From this information, these words could be classed together. (Braine, 1963, made a similar proposal.) Furthermore, since *dog* also appears in many of these sentences, it could be grouped with *boy* and *girl*, although *boy* and *girl* are more closely related to each other distributionally than either is to *dog*. *Car* and *house* also appear in some of the same sentences as *boy*, *girl*, and *dog* do (e.g., The house is dirty; The car is ugly.) So one could have a grouping here, based on the overlap of positions in utterances. It follows from this that one cannot think of the grammatical class *noun* as some all-or-none class with an explicit definition. Rather, the *noun* class is really a family of classes. When they are looked at in this way, a transition network model may be able to deal with grammatical classes.

8.9 Meaning and use: sentence-to-sentence moves in language games

A further potential difficulty faced by a model without concepts concerns the information used in producing a sentence. When someone is describing some event witnessed previously, then the sentences that are produced are based on the nonverbal information that the speaker remembers. However, assume that someone says the following to you: "I refuse to watch detective shows, and that's all there is on TV tonight." You listen to the person and say: "I guess you won't be watching TV tonight."

Let us consider the basis for your reply. What you said does not seem to be based on perceptual information of the sort used in describing a sunset. Rather, it seems to be based relatively directly on what the other person said and on the inferences that can be drawn from it. These inferences are of the following sort. If someone says something like: "I hate doing X," then that person will usually not do X of his or her own free will. Therefore, if someone says "I hate X," and "I have the opportunity to do X," then one can conclude that the person will not take advantage of that opportunity.

In essence, we are saying that the meaning of an utterance is what you can do with it—the inferences that can be drawn from it, the requests you can make with it, the praise and the warnings you can give, and so on (Austin, 1965). Wittgenstein (1958) argued that the meaning of an utterance is the use to which we put that utterance. He also argued that learning a language could be looked upon as learning a game—a "language game." Actually, learning a language entails learning a number of different language games. One game would entail learning how to produce verbal descriptions for events in the world. Other games might involve learning how to respond to verbal commands; learning how to reason verbally; learning how to talk about one's own inner states, feelings, beliefs, thoughts. From this point of view, learning to speak means learning to make "moves" in these various language games. The inference that was described in the last paragraph is an example of making a move in a "reasoning language game." You have learned that, from sentences of one sort, you can produce another sentence. And you have learned this by listening to the way in which people use the word *hate* in sentences, and what they do and say before and after using it.

This could be described by saying that one learns "sentence-to-sentence moves" in a language game (Sellars, 1963, chap. 5). The utterance you produce is based on moves that you make from the utterances that you hear. Another more common example of a language game involving sentence-to-sentence moves is learning to answer questions concerning something that one has just said. If you are telling someone else about something, and a third person asks what you are talking about, you can answer the question with something like: "I was just saying that . . ." This utterance, your reply to the question, is based on what you were saying and the question that the person asked. So, once again, your answer is a move in a language game based on what has been said. When one learns to give verbal descriptions for physical events, one could say that one has learned moves "into" a language game. In the same way, responding to a verbal command with a nonverbal response is a move "out of" a language game. In each case, there may be several different sorts of language games involved, as when a verbal message can cause one to look for something, imagine something, or do any of a number of things.

It is important to emphasize how these sentence-to-sentence moves would be learned. Verbal descriptions depend upon the characteristics of the external event. Sentence-to-sentence moves depend upon the characteristics of the *sentences* that one has been listening to. Thus, the pattern of sentences is the basis for sentence-to-sentence moves, just as an external event is the basis for a verbal description. The pattern of sentences is an event in the world, no different from a car going by. In each case, a speaker may produce an utterance, and in each case the utterance is related to other events. However, in one case the event is a series of sentences.

Imagery and "perceiving games." There is an important parallel between the discussion of imagery in the last chapter and this discussion of verbal reasoning. Based on the earlier discussion of pattern recognition, we concluded in the last chapter that imagery depends upon one's knowledge of how the world would look under various conditions. We could rephrase this conclusion in terms of the present discussion and say that imagery consists of moves in a "perceiving game." That is, from a given description of the perceptual world, one can use one's knowledge to describe how the world could be changed. This may be equivalent to a move in a language game.

Thinking and language games. If verbal reasoning consists of a certain set of moves in a language game, it has important implications for theories of the relationship between language and thought. These implications will be considered in detail in the next chapter, but a brief discussion would be helpful here. Let us go back again to the discussion of the dogcatcher who is ordered to bring in all stray dogs. Assume that the dogcatcher efficiently picks up all the strays that are seen, and only stray dogs. Given that the category *dog* is based on a family resemblance of the sort discussed earlier, then there is no simple set of perceptual features on which to base this activity. In the same way, there could be no simple conceptual element that would underlie the whole category. Therefore, the reason for the dogcatcher's efficient action might simply be that he or she knows how to use the word *dog,* and the dogcatcher remembers what he or she was ordered to do: pick up dogs. Thus, any object that can be called a *dog* will be picked up. Based on the discussion in this chapter, the verbal label might be the first step in deciding to pick up an animal. (This is an idea which has been around for a long time in psychology, as "verbal mediation." It will be considered in detail in the next chapter.)

In summary, there may be some situations in which thinking consists of moving in a language game, in the sense that (a) how something is dealt with depends on how it fits into the language, and (b) in order to carry out some actions you must remember specific words.

8.10 Summary

This chapter has considered a model of thinking that has had a long history and is currently very influential in cognitive psychology, the idea that thinking is an activity that entails the manipulation of concepts. The discussion was concerned with one specific manifestation of this point of view, that comprehension of sentences entails construction of conceptual networks, which serve as the internal representations of all our knowledge.

The chapter began with a brief discussion of several of these conceptual network models. Questions were then raised concerning whether human concepts are the sorts of things which can serve as building blocks in conceptual networks. Several sorts of evidence were considered: philosophical analyses of concepts and psychological studies of family resemblances. It was concluded that concepts are not internal things that stand for or represent external objects when we think. Rather, concepts are multifaceted capacities which we acquire.

The chapter concluded with a brief discussion of Wittgenstein's (1958) notion of language games as an alternative conception of sentence meaning. We now turn to the theory that sentences themselves serve as the medium of thought.

9

Language as the medium of thought

9.0 Introduction

Based on the discussions of imagery and concepts in the last two chapters, it seems that in some situations thinking is carried out in words, in the sense of moves in a language game. However, this conclusion does not specify exactly the way in which this verbal thought is carried out. Over the years, psychologists have concentrated on a number of different possible roles of language in thinking. This chapter will critically review this work.

Directive function. Many psychologists have argued that language is important because we use our own speech to direct our other activities. According to this view, producing words and/or sentences plays a vital role in controlling motoric acts. This point of view parallels the notion discussed in chapter 7 that we "scan" images when we think. According to the imagery-scanning model, an image is a quasi-objective thing, in the sense that we can acquire new information from it. In the same way, the directive function of speech model argues that the sentences we produce are quasi-objective entities also, in that they can direct our other activities just as sentences from other people can direct our activities.

Furthermore, some psychologists (e.g., Sokolov, 1972) have argued that *all* thinking is verbal thinking in adult humans. Research in a number of areas has attempted to show that even nonverbal tasks come under verbal

Language as the medium of thought

self-control in humans. This will be one of the focal points of the later discussion: If human thinking can sometimes be moving in a language game, must it always be moving in a language game? We shall see that much thinking can occur independently of language. We shall also argue that the speech that does occur during some thinking tasks does not serve to direct other activities. It is immediately obvious that language doesn't serve to direct all activities, because we all do things that we cannot describe very well, like riding a bicycle or hitting a tennis ball. Ryle (1949, chap. 2) makes a distinction between knowing how to do something, which may not entail verbal knowledge at all, and knowing that something is the case, which does entail verbal knowledge. The point to be made in this chapter is that even when we can describe some other motoric act in detail, the verbalization still does not serve to direct that other act.

Role of feedback from speech muscles. A second idea, closely related to the directive function hypothesis, is that the speech muscles are important in thinking and actually participate in all verbal thinking activities. According to this view, the reason that a string of verbal thoughts stays together is because covert speech muscle activity helps to keep them together. Thus, a second question to be considered is whether moves in language games involve the speech muscles. Much early evidence supported the view that msucles are important in thinking, but more recent work indicates that thinking can occur without feedback from the muscles. The most important of these studies showed that a human could still think after his muscles had been paralyzed by curare.

Language as the source of concepts. The final aspect of language-thought theorizing is that the things that we think about change as we acquire language. It is argued that learning the semantics of a language provides a human being with a conceptual system which is not available to those who have not learned the language; it is not simply a vehicle for expressing the concepts that we know before learning the language. Rather, according to this view, the language itself provides a whole new way of organizing the world that could not have occurred without it. We shall see that this conclusion too can be questioned.

To summarize, there are three potentially different uses for language in thinking. (1) Language could be important because it enables the thinker to produce a series of self-instructions which serve to direct other activities. (2) The speech muscles could be important in stringing thoughts together. In such a case, verbal thought would involve real articulation. (3) Learning a language could provide the units, the verbal concepts, with which we think. We can now turn to a review of the major theories in this area. In each case, we shall first present evidence supportive of the position, and then evidence that goes against it.

9.1 Russian theorizing

There has been a strong emphasis on the role of speech in the higher mental processes for more than one hundred years in Russian psychophysiology. Many of the ideas which are being advocated today can be seen in the exact same form in the writings of Sechenov (1863, rpt. 1952), perhaps the dominant figure in the history of Russian psychology.

Sechenov and Pavlov. Sechenov's first major contribution to the study of the higher mental processes was his theory of the reflex nature of thought. He was a physiologist, and he assumed that the basic mechanism for producing involuntary muscle movements was the reflex. In applying this analysis to thinking and voluntary movements, Sechenov claimed that thinking was the first two-thirds of a reflex: sensory input and excitation of a cortical center. However, the overt response was inhibited. The development of the human capacity to think is based on this inhibition of overt movements. According to this point of view, there is no difference between the basic mechanisms of overt responding and those of thinking. The only difference is at the output stage. This basic idea will be central in a model of thinking to be outlined in chapter 16.

Sechenov's second contribution to the study of the higher mental processes was to emphasize the role of speech in the development of these inhibitory processes. Initially, stimuli in the environment elicit whole complexes of responses, involving various muscles, including the speech muscles. However, gradually the complex of reflexes becomes restricted to the speech system alone, with the other muscles being inhibited. Thus, children develop some voluntary control over their movements: they now speak aloud without acting. Finally, the overt speech is itself inhibited, resulting in silent speech-for-self, or thinking (Sechenov, 1863, rpt. 1952).

The third important aspect of Sechenov's theorizing concerned the basis for the linkage between successive "thoughts." Sechenov advocated a chaining theory, in which the series of reflexes is chained together into one stream because the feedback from the first reflex serves to initiate the second reflex, and so on. When verbal control over overt movement occurs, a series of speech reflexes is produced. Therefore, there must be some mechanism to link this string of verbal thoughts to one another. Sechenov argued that feedback from the speech muscles served this role. Even when the actual speech disappears and becomes covert, the speech musculature is still active. This is necessary to produce the feedback to initiate the next sentence.

Pavlov's views concerning the role of language in human functioning were similar to those of Sechenov. In addition, one further function of speech in thinking was emphasized by Pavlov (Razran, 1961). Pavlov is best known for his investigations of conditioned salivary reflexes in dogs. However, he felt that the knowledge gained from studying conditioning in animals had very limited applicability to humans, and this was because of the development of speech in humans. Pavlov felt that once humans learned to speak, the ways in which they could be conditioned changed greatly. As an example, consider a person who has been conditioned to salivate when a metronome is heard, much like Pavlov conditioned his dogs. The metronome becomes a signal for food. However, the word *metronome* could substitute for presentation of the metronome. Thus, with a verbal human, conditioning could be brought under the control of a signal for a signal. The system of words and their related concepts is thus a second signal system, because words can become signals for the signals in the physical world. Furthermore, Pavlov argued that the words stood for whole concepts, or classes of objects, rather than specific objects. Therefore, as a result of the language system, a much wider type of generalization could occur with humans than was found with animals.

To summarize the views of Sechenov and Pavlov, language and speech were seen as playing important roles in the human mental processes. First, speech served as the mechanism whereby thinking could be carried out without overt movements being necessary. This occurred because inhibition of all gross peripheral movements, including those in the speech musculature, took place. Second, the feedback from the speech muscles served to link successive verbal thoughts together, or served to initiate the motor response that was under the control of the verbal thought. Third, internal speech could be used for self-direction by the subject, through emphasis being placed on specific aspects of the environment. Finally, learning linguistic concepts resulted in a new way of organizing the environment.

Directive speech: Vygotsky and Luria. The basic ideas brought forth by Sechenov and Pavlov can be seen in the theorizing of Vygotsky (1962) and Luria (1961). Vygotsky noted that animals could exhibit behavior that seemed to be based on thinking, and also that the earliest verbalizations of children had nothing to do with directing their activities. Therefore, thought and speech have separate origins. However, at a point early in every human's life, speech and thought come together, and from then on speech is crucial to thinking. Vygotsky theorized that the child's use of speech to direct his own activities arises first from the child's previous interaction with others. "The child starts conversing with himself as he has been doing with others. When circumstances force him to stop and think, he is likely to think aloud (p.19)."

This overt directive speech decreases greatly with age, and by about five years of age is almost totally gone. In addition, the speech changes from relatively complete sentences to single words and phrases. According to Vygotsky, the fragmentation and disappearance of spontaneous speech results from the child's increasing differentiation of speech for himself (which serves to direct activity) from speech for others (which serves to communicate). Ultimately, the directive speech becomes internalized completely as inner speech or verbal thought. Vygotsky also felt that learning words changes the content of thought as well. Two processes culminate in the use of words. First, analysis of the environment must occur. Objects must be analyzed into their attributes, so that different objects can be seen to have attributes in common. But at the same time, *synthesis* of physically different objects into classes also takes place. Thus, the world is organized in a particular way after words are learned, and this has a great influence on the elements that are the content of thought.

Luria, a student and colleague of Vygotsky, carried this line of theorizing still further. Luria has analyzed the developing ability of children to control their own overt responses through their own speech. He assumes that the child's control of the speech system develops faster than control of other overt responses. Therefore, the child can formulate the verbal description of an action before actually carrying out the action. However, once the action is formulated verbally, its meaning directs the child's performances and can help in the production of responses that could not be produced without internal speech. The development of this verbal influence or control of thought stems from the socialization of the child, especially the child's relationship with the caretaker, usually the mother. The child learns to organize the world according to the words the mother teaches, and the memory of her verbal instructions serves to stimulate the child's self-instruction when the need arises. In addition, language enables the child to organize the word in a new way.

Present relevance of these ideas. The most recent and extensive statement of the theory of the directive function of a speech is that of Sokolov (1972).

> In psychology the term "inner speech" usually signifies soundless mental speech, arising at the instant we think about something, plan or solve problems in our mind. . . . In all such cases, we think and remember with the aid of words which we articulate to ourselves. . . . (p.1)

Sokolov follows Sechenov's theorizing concerning inhibition in thinking. This inhibition of the motor components of psychic reflexes develops gradually with age and is crucial in the development of the higher mental processes. The direct connection between the ideas of Sokolov and those of Sechenov discussed earlier is obvious.

Summary. In summarizing the Russian theory of the directive function of speech, it should be emphasized that the development of language is assumed to serve several purposes. First, speech allows overt movements of other sorts to be inhibited, for which speech is a substitute. Second, kinesthetic impulses from the speech musculature direct or select the ideas that are aroused while a problem is thought about. This is the basis of volition in humans. Third, the learning of words results in a new organization of the external environment.

There are several differences between the Russian directive speech notion and the conclusion from the last two chapters that in some cases thinking is moving in a language game. First of all, it was argued in section 8.8 that language games become important when the subject matter is abstract enough so that simple perceptual information will not do. The Russians have argued that language becomes important in all activities, abstract and concrete. Thus, it is important to note that one could believe that language is important in thinking without accepting the Russian view totally. We shall criticize various aspects of the Russian view in later sections.

9.2 Brief history of the study of speech and thought in the United States

In the United States, there have been two discernible streams of research concerned with the relationship of speech and other complex processes. However, as time has gone on, the differences between these streams have gotten much smaller. For the sake of simplicity, the present discussion will keep the two separate.

Watson's peripheralism. When Watson (1913, 1930) attempted to make psychology a strictly objective science, one of the first orders of business was to eliminate anything "mental" from consideration. According to Watson, thinking really consisted of behavior, just like any other behavior, but this behavior was greatly reduced in magnitude. Since we were not able to detect our own subtle movements when we were thinking, we attributed thought to some mysterious entity called the mind. But thinking is really just behavior, mainly subvocal talking. The creative aspects of thought are assumed to come about through the manipulation of words until a new pattern is accidently hit upon. Watson also noted that any responses could serve to stand for an object in the environment, just as words did, but that for humans, words were probably crucial.

In its simplest form, this theory states that by measuring the peripheral activity, one has measured thinking. This version of the theory assumes that one peripheral response triggers off the next, so that the central nervous system plays a very small role, if any, in determining what responses are produced. A less extreme version of the theory states that while central processes may be involved in thinking, these central processes are strongly influenced by what happens in the periphery. Sechenov's (1863, rpt. 1952) theory, which has already been discussed, is of this sort. It is assumed by Sechenov that the speech centers in the cerebral cortex, or central nervous system, play a dominant role in selecting responses, and these centers are influenced by feedback from the speech musculature.

More recent developments. By far the most productive present-day psychologist who would align himself with Watson's position is McGuigan (e.g., 1966, 1970, 1973). However, McGuigan has taken the extreme peripheral theory proposed by Watson and softened it a bit. For example, it is now assumed that central processes play a part in thinking (which McGuigan considers to be simply covert speaking). However, the following excerpt makes it clear that McGuigan still places emphasis on peripheral feedback from actual responding. The quotation is directly concerned with reading, but according to McGuigan similar things occur in problem solving and any other situation is which covert speech is produced.

During the visual reception of language stimuli (reading), one orally responds to those linguistic components (the words that constitute the prose being read). In first learning to read, the child makes large (and inefficient) articulatory movements when he attempts to pronounce the written word. As with any skill, when proficiency increases, the gross amount of muscular activity becomes reduced and efficiency increases—as one learns to read, swim or ride a bicycle, intial large-scale and erratic movements become woven into smooth, highly coordinated response chains. And, these response chains may most efficiently be run off at the covert level. Hence, the covert oral behavior that persists in the adult continues to function during the performance of linguistic activities. However, those who are relatively less proficient in performing a linguistic task must exaggerate their oral behavior in order to bring their comprehension "up to par." . . . Similarly, under demanding conditions, normal people enhance their reading proficiency by exaggerating the amplitude of covert oral behavior; sometimes we read aloud for this purpose. (McGuigan, 1973, p.365)

Thus, the covert activity from the peripheral organs is needed to activate information and integrate activity in the central nervous system, which is necessary for complex higher activities. The subject who increases the amplitude of these covert peripheral responses thereby sends more information into the nervous system, which increases the chances of activation of additional relevant information, among other things. This idea has had a long history in the psychology of thinking, under the name *reinforcement theory* (see Humphrey, 1963, chap. 7). In this context, the term reinforcement means that the peripheral activity is necessary to reinforce the central activity that is going on. Supposedly, with a more difficult task, the central processes require a stronger push, so more peripheral activity occurs with difficult problems.

Thus, although American peripheralism was originally very different from the Russian view, over the years the peripheralist position has been softened so that the two are almost identical.

Mediational theory. The second theoretical position which has developed in the United States also places speech in an important position as far as thinking is concerned, but in a slightly different way. The basic impetus came from the theorizing of Hull (1930, 1931), who made extensive use of internal responses as important theoretical mechanisms. These internal responses served to chain groups of simple responses together, so that they could be reproduced in their entirety as needed once the first member of the chain had been stimulated by the appropriate conditions. (This is similar to Sechenov's chaining notions.) Hull's followers used this notion of a central mediating response when they analyzed human behavior, and it was assumed that internal speech responses served as complicated links between stimuli and responses. These responses were initially assumed to be completely in the central nervous system, with no peripheral consequences.

The reason that such internal responses were hypothesized was because when humans and animals were compared on the same sorts of tasks, humans exhibited behaviors which could not be explained by the simple stimulus-response mechanisms assumed to be the basis for animals responding.

The simple association concepts that accounted quite adequately for much of the behavior of lower animals were inadequate to account for man's ability to solve complex problems without trial and error, his ability to respond in an equivalent manner to stimuli with widely discrepant perceptual features and his superiority in making delayed responses. . . . To account for these behaviors, Miller and Dollard (1941) utilized the concept of "cue-producing responses." These are responses, usually verbal labels, that serve to mediate or transfer behavior from one stimulus to another. (Jeffrey, 1970, p.224)

These ideas are obviously very similar to the Russian notions, although they arose relatively independently.

There seems to be some disagreement among mediational theorists as to whether learning to speak results in new ways of organizing the world. On the one hand, it has been argued that any responses can serve as mediators under appropriate circumstances, as we have just seen. However, as we shall see later, some mediational theorists have argued that the language system enables the subject to organize things in new ways. This assumption makes mediational theory equivalent to Russian theorizing.

Summary of theories and outline of the remaining discussion. As has been mentioned several times, these three theoretical positions (Russian, peripheralism, and mediational), while beginning from different sources, are now nearly identical. Three general assumptions are found in the work of most of the theorists mentioned. First, any overt response is assumed to be based upon prior formulation of a verbalization, usually a description of what will be done. Second, feedback from production of this sentence is assumed to be the crucial stimulus in initiating the motor response. Third, the things we can think about are assumed to be changed when we learn a language.

We now have a relatively clear picture of the components of the speech-as-thought, or linguistic-mediation-of-thought, theory of thinking. There are three aspects of the theory to be considered: the idea that learning to speak results in new ways of organizing one's world; the notion that feedback from the speech muscles is important in keeping the stream of thought together; the claim that speech is important in all sorts of thinking tasks, not only verbal tasks. Once again, one could still argue that speech is important for thinking without accepting any of these claims.

9.3 Language learning as the source of concepts

The first part of the theory to be considered is the idea that learning to speak is the basis for the learning of true concepts, through the learning of word meanings. It is assumed that once humans acquire these concepts, they organize and structure their worlds differently than nonverbal organisms do. Several different lines of evidence have been used to support this view. The general finding is that verbal humans behave differently than nonverbal organisms, human or otherwise, in a number of simple learning situations. It is then argued that a new conceptual organization, brought about by language, is the basis for the differences in behaving. We shall criticize this position by showing that verbal responses do not serve as the basis for complex responding, and by showing that verbal responses do not serve to organize the world in a new way, because verbal responses must be learned like any other responses.

Semantic conditioning. Many studies have shown that the human verbal system has a great influence on the types of conditioned responses which are produced in conditioning studies (Razran, 1961). For example, in one Russian study using conditioned salivation, the positive stimulus was the word *good* and the negative stimulus *bad*. After conditioning was established, sentences were presented as generalization stimuli. Sentences with positive feeling tone (the Soviet people love their motherland) produced strong salivation, even though they were very dissimilar physically to the original positive stimulus. In the same way, sentences of a negative connotation produced little or no salivation, irrespective of whether or not *bad* was used in them. This is a clear example of how far away from the simple physical characteristics of the stimulus one can go and still find generalization. The explanation is that the generalization is produced by the connections set up by the meaning of the stimuli.

These results can be taken as supporting the claim that learning to speak results in a new way of organizing the world. If the generalization of the salivation response from one stimulus to another is taken as an indication that two stimuli are equivalent, then the basis for equivalence is greatly altered when one acquires a language.

Luria's research on the influence of speech on perception. Another set of studies carried out by Luria and his students (Luria, 1961) demonstrates how the relative "strengths" of physical stimuli can be changed by verbal instructions. For example, children aged three to five are taught to squeeze a rubber bulb when pictures are presented. A red airplane on a gray background is the signal for a left-hand response, and a green airplane on a yellow background signals a right-hand response. After the responses are learned, it can be shown that the child has attended to only the color of the airplane and not to that of the background. Presentation of a red airplane (originally part of the cue for a left-hand response) on a yellow background (originally part of the cue for a right-hand response) produces a response with the left hand. A green airplane (right-hand originally) on a gray background (left-hand originally) produces a response with the right hand. In both of these cases, the compound stimulus is responded to only on the basis of the airplane. Thus, in the original situation, the airplane was the stronger element in the compound.

However, the relative strengths of the various components can be changed with verbal instructions. If the child is told to squeeze the bulb with the right hand when the green airplane on the yellow background is presented because "the plane can fly when the sun is shining and the sky is yellow," then the response is controlled by the background. Language can, therefore, change the perception of the environment by altering the relative "strengths" of stimuli, and thereby influencing what is attended to.

Transposition and verbal responses. One of the earliest and most well-known studies that examined verbal mediation of learning was that of Kuenne (1946) concerning transposition. The results are often cited as evidence that concepts based on language change the way in which humans organize the world. Transposition involves a two-stage discrimination-learning experiment. In the first stage, the subject is given a simple discrimination problem to solve. The stimuli differ in one dimension, e.g., size. An example would be two squares of different sizes, 2 cm on a side versus 3 cm on a side, with the 3 cm square arbitrarily chosen as correct. In the second stage, a new pair of stimuli is presented and the subject is tested for generalization. A "near" test would have 3 cm and 4 cm squares. A "far" test might have squares of 15 cm and 20 cm on a side. A transposition response entails choosing the same relative member of the test pair as was correct in training. In the near test, this means picking the 4 cm square and ignoring the previously correct 3 cm square. For the far test, the 20 cm square would be chosen by a transposing subject.

Kuenne (1946) argued that the ability to transpose on a far test was related to the subject's linguistic response to the situation. "In the case of an organism possessing verbal responses . . . behavior in a discrimination situation presumably becomes cued to some extent to such words as 'bigger,' 'larger,' 'brighter,' etc." (Kuenne, 1946, p.316). According to Kuenne, the relevant rule is something like: "The bigger one is always correct." She found that children who could describe the situation correctly when questioned, or who spontaneously verbalized the general rule, transposed on both near and far tests. Children who could not verbalize the relevant rule transposed only on the near test, much as do test rats. However, evidence from a number of other sources indicates that language, per se, may *not* be crucial in these tasks. First, there is evidence that verbalization and transposition do not invariably go hand in hand (see Zeiler, 1967), for a review). Some children verbalize the solution rule and yet do not give far transposition, while other children verbalize nothing and yet transpose on the far test. Even more impressive is recent research concerning the performance of deaf persons on these sorts of tasks.

Conceptual thinking in the deaf. If language is crucial for conceptual thinking, then people who are greatly deficient in their ability to speak ought to show a comparable deficit in their concepts. One group with a demonstrated speech deficit is the deaf, who are often many years behind their hearing counterparts. However, a large number of experiments by Furth and his colleagues (e.g., Furth, 1966; Furth & Youniss, 1965) have shown that this speech deficit is not matched by a "thinking deficit." As an example, the ability of deaf subjects to use symbols for concepts such as "and," "or," and "not" was assessed using nonverbal methods (Furth & Youniss, 1965). It was found that they did as well as hearing subjects from middle-class urban environments. Furth and Youniss argued that any performance deficit shown by the deaf was due to the restricted environments in which they are often raised, rather than an inability to think because of a specific language deficit. Furth (1966) presents much data that support this view, raising problems for the theory that conceptual thinking is dependent upon having learned a language and/or the ability to put things into words.

From this brief review, it seems that there are reasons for questioning the claim that learning to speak results in learning new ways of organizing the world. This is an important conclusion, worth pursuing further. If we look at word-learning in some detail, we will be able to see that there are still other reasons for rejecting the idea that learning words produces anything really new as far as concepts are concerned.

9.4 Language as the basis for "nonapparent" concepts

If one argues that learning a language involves learning new concepts, it obviously means that any such concept would not have evolved "spontaneously" out of the subject's nonverbal experience. Thus, one is saying that the concept in question is not "apparent" to the subject simply on the basis of the subject's examination of the environment. An example of this might be the group of activities which we call games (Wittgenstein, 1958). It was argued earlier that there was no one feature or group of features that was common to all games. In such a situation, having learned the word *game* might result in one's grouping together activities that one would not otherwise have considered similar without the label.

However, consider the following point. How did the concept of *games* (or any other concept) develop in the first place? Such concepts must have a nonlinguistic basis, because the language itself developed gradually, without being taught. That is, the first person to speak was not taught to speak by any other speaker. Thus, if some concept is not "apparent" to the child independent of the language, then the concept was not apparent to those who developed the language either, assuming that their perceptual apparatus worked like ours do. But if the concept was not apparent, then the people who developed the language could not have used the concept, because they had no speakers to teach it to them. Therefore, in order for any concept to be included in a language, it must be an "apparent" concept. Thus, any child would evolve the same concepts as those in the language, even if the child never learned to speak, simply through nonverbal experience. (There is one important limitation to be made here. We are dealing with concrete concepts here, not ones like virtue and truth. These latter concepts probably would never have developed without language, although this does not mean that they are qualitatively different from more concrete concepts, such as dog. This point will be discussed further in a later section.)

In order to make this analysis of the "apparentness" of concepts more clear, let us reconsider the hypothetical dogcatcher of the last chapter. It was argued that the only way in which this public servant could efficiently follow an order to pick up all stray dogs would be if he or she could remember the specific words in the order. Based on the view that language creates new concepts, it would be argued that if the linguistic concept dog had not been available, the dogcatcher would not have been able to do anything like what was done following the verbal order.

However, let us consider the following situation. Assume that we are in a community in which no one can talk. One member of this community, who is familiar with dogs, witnesses a dog carrying out some terrible act and sets out to capture these dangerous creatures. Based on the specific dog seen first, the person would go after other animals, and the physical appearance of these latter dogs would lead to the capture of a wider and wider range of animals. However, based on the family resemblance among dogs and what our dogcatcher knows of them, there would ultimately be an end to the animals that are captured. Thus, the nonverbal dogcatcher might do a reasonable job of capturing dogs, even without the verbal concept.

However, there would be two important differences between a dogcatcher with the verbal concept and one without it. First, possession of the verbal concept means that one could be instructed to capture dogs, which would result in an immediate understanding of the range of the order. A dogcatcher without the verbal concept might be able to only gradually widen the range of "capturable" animals, depending on those already captured. However, ultimately the nonverbal dogcatcher would catch all dogs. Second, given the family-resemblance basis for concepts, there will not be a hard and fast distinction made by our nonverbal dogcatcher concerning those creatures that should be captured and those that should not be—such as a sheep that looks like a poodle. However, it is also important to note that a *verbal dogcatcher would have made exactly the same sorts of confusions in learning to use the word* dog *itself,* and for exactly the same reasons—the family-resemblance basis for human categories. Thus language may serve as a summary for a great amount of nonverbal experience, so a person does not have to personally experience everything. However, language may not produce any qualitative changes in the concrete concepts that one will evolve and use.

Transfer of verbal responses versus transfer of other responses. The conclusion that language does not really bring anything new with it is strengthened if we briefly consider the notion of verbal mediation, that production of the verbal response serves as the basis for transfer of other responses. However, we must now consider the production of the verbal response—on what is it based? It is based on having learned the language, and according to the analysis so far, this means that it is based on learning the family resemblance among the things to be called dogs, which features are more important, and so on. But it is also obvious that in this way the verbal response is not different than any other response—all are based on prior learning of the same sort. Once again we see that language is not a qualitatively different sort of response.

9.5 Language and concepts: conclusions

Our analysis indicates that language serves to summarize past experience, but it does not serve to produce organizations of experience that could not have come about without it. It may be true that if each one of us had to start from scratch, without the summary of experience that language provides for us, then civilization would not have evolved very far. However, if one of us lived for a very long time, then that person might be able to get pretty far, as far as conceptual evolution is concerned. Thus, according to the present point of view, the basic limitation is time, not lack of language.

In summary, our first conclusion is that learning words serves as a great shortcut, in that we can pick up things without having to go through the experiences ourselves. Words may also help us deal efficiently with certain sorts of problems, those which involve abstract classes. However, we do not really learn anything new when we learn words.

We can now turn to the second aspect of the language-thought theory, the idea that feedback from the speech muscles is important in thinking. Even though language does not produce new concepts, we might still need to actually *say words* in order to move in language games.

9.6 Use of speech muscles in thinking

There have been several ways in which investigators have tried to produce evidence demonstrating the role of muscular feedback in thinking. First, attempts have been made to measure such activity during tasks which require thinking. Second, attempts have been made to eliminate or interfere with thinking by eliminating or interfering with the activity of the speech musculature. Early work in this area indicated that there is much activity during "thinking" tasks, which supports the view that feedback from the periphery is important in thinking. However, some other work has demonstrated that people can still think without muscle feedback, which means that muscle activity is not necessary for thinking, although it is often present when we think.

Activity in speech musculature during thinking: early research. There were many early investigations that provided evidence that activity in peripheral organs, especially the speech organs, was present during tasks involving thinking. Two of the most famous studies are those of Jacobson (1931a, rpt. in McGuigan, 1966) and Max (1935, rpt. in McGuigan, 1966; 1937). Jacobson's most important finding was that instructing the subject to imagine that he was going to count produced electrical activity in the lips or tongue, even though no movements could be seen. Jacobson also found (1930, 1931b), that imagining other types of motor activities also produced activity in the appropriate muscles.

Max found that when deaf mutes were given thought problems to solve, there was an increase in electrical activity in the muscles of the fingers, used by the subjects in sign language. Max also found activity of this sort during dreams.

Sokolov's Research. Sokolov (1972, chap. 4) has also performed extensive studies of electrical activity in the speech musculature. The general finding is that covert activation of the speech musculature is present in many different types of thinking tasks. Activity is seen first while the subject is listening to the presentation of a problem. During problem solving of many sorts, there is also activity in the tongue and lips. The intensity of responses in the speech apparatus is a function of the degree of difficulty of the problem and the degree of sophistication of the problem-solver. For example, with arithmetic problems, slower calculators showed larger and more frequent speech responses. Also, children show much more of this activity than do adults.

A final series of experiments was conducted concerning the role of inner speech in concrete reasoning tasks, such as Raven's Progressive Matrices. With all but the simplest problems, solution of these tasks was also accompanied by activity in the speech musculature.

Additional research. There have also been many studies carried out in the United States, especially by McGuigan (1970, 1973), which have had very similar results.

Hallucinations. In an early study of a schizophrenic subject who reported that he heard voices, it was found that breathing rate and activity in the chin muscles increased greatly during the reported hallucinatory experience. There was no change found in the activity of the patient's left arm. McGuigan (1966) concluded that covert speech and the resulting feedback from the muscles led to the patient's hearing voices.

Reading. McGuigan and his associates have carried out a number of studies concerning the relationship of muscle activity in the lips, chin, and tongue during reading (e.g., McGuigan, Keller, & Stanton, 1964; McGuigan & Rodier, 1968; McGuigan & Bailey, 1969). The basic findings are straightforward. Activity in the speech musculature increases during reading when compared to the activity when the subject is at rest. Furthermore, it increases more for poor readers than for good readers among adults, and increases more with children than with adults.

McGuigan and Rodier (1968) found that the amount of covert activity in the speech musculature during silent reading was related to the environment in which the subject was reading. Compared to activity in a silent background, the subject's covert speech activity increased if auditory prose was played. This also occurred if the passage that the subject was reading was played backwards in the background. However, simply introducing noise resulted in no increase in covert verbalization while the subjects were reading silently.

Handwriting. McGuigan (1970) found that activity in the tongue and chin increased more when college students wrote words than during non-linguistic control tasks.

Dreams. McGuigan and Tanner (1971) measured activity in the speech musculature and several neutral areas during dreams of various sorts. It was found that when the subject reported afterward that the dream had contained conversations, there had been an increase in activity in the speech musculature during the dream. The increases in the speech activity did not occur during dreams which were reported as being mainly visual.

In summarizing all these results, it seems that there is no doubt that covert activity is present during mental activity of the sort which would be called thinking, and much of this activity is in the speech muscles. Furthermore, the activity seems to be restricted to the muscles involved in the task, and is not just due to a general arousal of the whole body. However, as we shall now see, it is premature to conclude that this peripheral activity is necessary for thinking to occur.

Occupying speech muscles and interference with thinking. The results reviewed so far, while impressive, are only correlational. One way to show that this speech-muscle activity is necessary for thinking is to show that if speech-muscle activity is eliminated, then the capacity to think about a task also disappears.

In two early studies, Pintner (1913, cited by Humphrey, 1963) was able to perform silent reading while constantly repeating the syllable *la* overtly, and Rizzolo (1931, cited by Humphrey, 1963) was able to solve problems while producing a constant e sound. Thus, these two studies indicated that feedback from the speech musculature was not necessary for thinking to occur.

Sokolov (1972) has performed many experiments on the interference with thinking caused by a concurrent verbal task, and his results are very similar to those of Pintner and Rizzolo. One set of experiments examined the influence of recitation of verbal material on the perception and comprehension of other verbal material. The subjects either recited verses of greater or lesser familiarity, or counted aloud while trying to understand and remember texts of various levels of difficulty. The first few attempts at

Language as the medium of thought

comprehension while reciting verse were almost totally disrupted. However, with more experience in the situation, the subject's performance improved, even though the verses were still unfamiliar. Individual words could now be continuously understood, but there was still no memory for the words or for the general meaning of the text.

When the recitation of verses was replaced by counting, a completely automatized activity, the task became so easy that the subjects were not only able to listen to the words and understand them, but they were also able to think about what they heard. This last finding is of particular importance. Most subjects, after some practice in the situation, reported some sort of inner speech, and yet the organs of speech were involved in recitation of something else. This seems to indicate that inner speech is not based simply on small movements of the speech muscles, and that thinking can occur without the participation of the speech muscles. These conclusions are reinforced by studies which have attempted to eliminate thinking by eliminating peripheral feedback.

Elimination of peripheral feedback. In an early study, Dodge (1896, reported by Humphrey, 1963) anesthetized his own lips and tongue. In this way he removed all feeling of motion of the lips and the feeling of position of the tongue. If one can assume that the anesthesia was essentially total, then there was no feedback from the speech musculature. However, Dodge found that he could still talk, and he also experienced inner speech. A more elaborate experiment along the same lines was carried out by Smith, Brown, Toman, and Goodman (1947), which entailed administering a heavy dosage of curare into the bloodstream of a subject (one of the experimenters served as the subject). Curare paralyzes the skeletal musculature, so the subject was unable to breathe and had to be given artificial respiration. Furthermore, he could move no muscles—his eyelids even had to be lifted for him. However, even with this seemingly total elimination of peripheral muscle feedback, including that from the speech muscles, the subject reported afterwards that his consciousness had been completely normal throughout this period. In addition, he remembered verbal statements that had been read to him, in the correct order, and his electroencephalogram was normal throughout. This seems to be very strong evidence that the speech muscles are not needed for verbal thinking.

Summary of research on peripheral feedback in thinking. It seems that there is not a great amount of support for the notion that feedback from the speech musculature is necessary for thinking. There is no doubt that activity in the speech musculature occurs in many tasks concerning thinking; the results on this point are conclusive. However, it seems to be possible to interfere with or eliminate this feedback without greatly reducing the capacity to think, and, perhaps surprisingly, without even eliminating inner speech. Thus, it seems reasonable to conclude that if some thinking is indeed inner speech, then this speech is a central phenomenon that seems to be relatively independent of the peripheral musculature.

9.7 The role of speech in problem solving

The last important assumption of the speech-as-thought theory is that speech serves to direct problem solving. We concluded at the very beginning of the chapter that speech probably played a role in solving abstract problems that could only be formulated verbally. The question of interest in the present section is whether the speech that occurs during other sorts of problem solving also plays a role in thinking about those problems. We shall conclude that this speech does not serve to direct one's own activities, as the speech from someone else might.

Vygotsky's research on directive speech. As mentioned earlier, Vygotsky carried out a number of investigations of the directive function of speech, which, unfortunately, are reported in only very general terms in his book (Vygotsky, 1962). The basic purpose of Vygotsky's research was to show that the production of speech was an important part of solving problems. The speech of children was recorded during various types of activities and the speech was classified as either speech for the purpose of communication or speech-for-self, which seemed not to have any communicative purposes. It was found that speech-for-self, which Vygotsky took to be self-directive in function, increased greatly when the child was faced with a problem situation. The more difficult the problem, the more self-directive speech was produced. Furthermore, the amount of this external self-directive speech increased from age two to four, which was taken as an indication of increasing cognitive development.

The amount and comprehensibility of the speech that was overtly produced was also decreased greatly from age three to seven. This indicated that speech-for-self was becoming more and more differentiated from speech for others. Speech for others, or true communicative speech, becomes more frequent and comprehensible in this age range. Therefore, Vygotsky concluded that one cannot understand the overt problem-solving speech of the seven-year-old (or the adult, for the matter) because the speech is not produced in order to communicate. The speech that children produce during problem solving is for themselves.

At least one recent study has provided additional support for Vygotsky's theorizing. Kohlberg, Yaeger, and Hjertholm (1968) analyzed the overt speech produced by children who were working on various tasks. They found that the amount of speech-for-self increased from age three to four, and then decreased from then on, as Vygotsky reported. It was also found that highly intelligent children started to produce speech-for-self at an earlier age than average children, and that the decline and disappearance of this speech occurred earlier for the intelligent children. Kohlberg et al. also felt that this finding supported Vygotsky, because Vygotsky's position is that speech-for-self serves an intellectual function. It would be expected that more intelligent children should produce this type of speech earlier in life. The cycle of decline and disappearance should also be advanced for them. It was also found that there was a tendency for more speech-for-self to be produced on more difficult problems.

There were two other interesting findings, which are not directly relevant to the present discussion, but which will be important later. First, the amount of speech-for-self produced by the child was postively correlated with the amount of communicative speech produced by the child: The children who produced more speech-for-self also talked more in general. Second, the children who produced more speech-for-self were more active socially: they tended to interact more with other children. In summary, this study provided strong support for Vygotsky's theory.

A study by Gever and Weisberg (1969) also examined speech-for-self as a function of age in various problem situations. The children were kindergartners, first-graders, and third-graders. The basic task used was a card-sorting task, in which the basis for sorting the cards varied over three levels of difficulty. In the simplest task, four cards had pictures of trees on them, four cards had pictures of cars, four cards had pictures of people, and four cards had pictures of animals. One card from each of these classes was placed on the table and the children were asked to put each of the other cards on the appropriate pile. For the hardest task, the classes were things like means of communication and containers.

Several of the results supported Vygotsky's theory. (1) The amount of speech-for-self decreased with age. (2) The harder tasks produced more speech-for-self. (3) There was a tendency for the younger children to produce more speech-for-self on the easier tasks, while the older children produced more speech-for-self on the harder tasks. This follows if one assumes that younger children find the easiest task (as defined by the adult experimenters) hard enough to cause them difficulty, which results in speech-for-self. The other two tasks are based on concepts that the youngest children did not even know, and so could result in little or no speech-for-self. For the older children, on the other hand, the easiest task is so simple that no speech-for-self is needed, while the harder tasks result in its being produced.

As indicated, these results concerning directive speech supported Vygotsky, but there was one important result that did not. A significant proportion of the children solved the hardest problem without being able to tell the experimenter the basis for their sorting. This would indicate that they probably had not produced the labels when they were sorting the cards originally, either covertly or overtly.

Thus, the most reasonable conclusions based on these studies seem to be that (a) speech-for-self in children first increases and then decreases as the age of the child goes from about two or three to seven; and (b) difficult problems result in more speech-for-self being produced. However, this speech may not be necessary for solution of problems.

As mentioned earlier, other studies have also found that subjects can carry out thinking tasks seemingly independently of language. Furth's (1965) work with deaf subjects indicates that they can solve conceptual problems even when their ability to speak is severely limited. Their ability to solve problems is usually much less deficient than is their ability to speak. Also, studies of transposition and related phenomena have shown that "advanced" performance is not always linked to verbalization in such situations. Children who perform at an advanced level cannot always verbalize the solution rule, and children who seem to be able to verbalize the solution rule do not always perform at an advanced level.

Luria's research on directive speech. Luria and his students have carried out many studies of the development of children's ability to direct their behavior through their own speech (Luria, 1961). The basic situation is to present varying instructions and then examine the child's proficiency in responding. It is found that at the earliest ages studied (2½ years), the child can start an activity on command, but speech cannot inhibit an already begun activity. For example, if the child is told to take a ring off a peg and then in the middle is told to put the ring on again, this will simply speed up the removal of the ring. At this stage, the only way an ongoing activity can be stopped by another person's command is by giving the

Language as the medium of thought

command loudly enough to slightly startle the child. Another person's command works here not because of its semantic content, but rather because it is an intense stimulus. Also, at this stage the child cannot respond motorically at all while producing a verbal self-instruction.

Later (age 3½), children can respond correctly to an instruction from someone else, and their own speech begins to influence their own behavior. However, the influence of speech is through its motoric characteristics, not its meaning. Thus, if the child says "go, go" while performing an action, the action will be performed twice. This would seem to be an example of the child's self-direction through the meaning of the speech, but it turns out that the meaning of what the child is saying has no effect on what is done. If the child says "stop, stop" while pressing a lever, it is still pressed twice. If the child says "I'll press twice," one long press is given that lasts as long as the verbalization. The simple motoric aspects of the speech produced by the child are what influences other motoric response at this stage.

Finally, after several intervening stages, the children can follow their own instructions according to their semantic content. They now make two discrete presses when saying "I'll press twice." This is an extremely important point in development, because the children can now instruct themselves as others have instructed them. This enables them to carry out the complicated planning which characterizes human intention, according to Luria.

There have been a number of attempts to replicate the sequence of development postulated by Luria for the development of verbal control over behavior, but the results have been mixed. Miller, Shelton and Flavell (1970) tried to replicate Luria's procedure as exactly as they could, but found no evidence to support the stages postulated by Luria. The verbalizations seem to be an additional task required of the child, in that speaking made it harder for the child to do the other task at the same time. Miller et al. found that even though the children were instructed to verbalize *before* squeezing the bulb, they could not consistently do this. Sometimes verbalization accompanied the motor response, and sometimes followed it. If the verbal response comes simultaneously with or after the motor response, how can the verbal response direct the nonverbal response? A similar finding has been reported by Grice (1965) for both verbal and nonverbal mediators. Lack of support for Luria's findings is also evident in studies by Wilder (1969) and Jarvis (1968).

Summary of research on directive speech. To summarize, there is not strong support for the notion that speech serves a generalized directive function. First, the work of Vygotsky is very general and does not go much farther than showing that young children do speak while working on problems. It says nothing about the directive aspect of this speech. Luria's work is also inconclusive. It shows that the ability to follow verbal instructions develops with age, but it does not demonstrate that the child's own verbalizations are causally related to solution of the problems. Finally, recent research that has attempted to replicate and extend the work of Vygotsky and Luria has had mixed results. Thus people do talk when they are solving all sorts of concrete problems, but this speech may not serve a cognitive function. In sum, there is little support for any of the three components of the speech-as-thought hypothesis.

9.8 On "self-direction"

It was mentioned at the beginning of this chapter that there was a parallel between the directive-function-of-speech point of view and the "image-scanning" point of view critically analyzed in chapter 7. According to the symbolist notion of imagery, an image is a quasi-object, in the sense that an image can be "scanned" in order to obtain more perceptual information from it. In the same way, it does not seem unreasonable to argue that one's speech during problem solving serves to direct one's other activities in the same way that someone else's speech can direct one's activities. However, in chapter 7 it was concluded that the symbolist conception of imagery is incorrect, in that one cannot obtain new perceptual information from images. On closer inspection, it may be that the symbolist conception of speech-for-self is also incorrect, in that one's speech may not direct one's own activities the way someone else's speech can. This is an important issue and deserves to be examined further.

Direction from others. In order to make the issues clear, let us begin with a brief and highly simplified version of what might be occurring when someone else's speech plays a part in directing one's activities. An outline of a plausible sequence of events is presented in the top of Box 9.1. The interaction begins with the readiness of person A to speak. Based on the discussion earlier in this chapter, and for the sake of simplicity, we can assume that this readiness is the state of the central nervous system that, if allowed to run off, would result in some verbal message being produced. The next step is the production of this message by A. In the next step, person B, the to-be-directed person, hears the message, and in the next step

Language as the medium of thought

this message is processed by B's using knowledge to recognize the message, as discussed in section 8.8. Actually, steps 3 and 4 may be intertwined into one step, but it does not materially change the discussion if they are kept separate. The verbal message, once recognized, can "get B to thinking" in any of three ways, as discussed in section 8.9. First, B can produce additional verbalizations in response to the message from A. In this case, A has stimulated B into verbal thought. On the other hand, A's message could result in B's imagining some event, in which case A has stimulated B's nonverbal thought. Finally, both these things could occur, as when B imagines something and talks about it, in response to the message from A. Also, the verbal message can result in other behavior on the part of the hearer, as when we ask someone to pass the salt, or when we order someone to do something (assuming that the conditions are right).

"**Self-direction?**" We can now take this outline and apply it to the situation in which one says something aloud when one is alone. This verbalization is then followed either by further verbalization, nonverbal imagery, or both. Although this situation seems comparable on the surface to the situation outlined at the top of Box 9.1, it may not be.

Box 9.1. Direction through Speech

Direction from someone else's speech

Time

1. Readiness to speak by A.
2. Sentence spoken by A.
3. Sentence heard by B.
4. Sentence matched by B.
5. Sentence serves as basis for further verbalization, perceptual elaboration, or production of some other response.

"Self-direction"

Time

1. Readiness to speak by A.
2. Sentence spoken by A.
3. Sentence heard by A.
4. Sentence matched by A.
5. Sentence used as a basis for further verbalization, perceptual elaboration, or production of some other response.

The situation in which one talks to oneself is outlined at the bottom of Box 9.1. The first step entails a readiness to speak on A's part, as before. The message is then produced and A hears what has been said. The input is then matched with a sentence and processed. The processed sentence serves as the basis for further elaboration by A, as discussed in the last section. Thus, it seems that we have a reasonable sequence here, and it is therefore reasonable to talk about self-direction. However, there is one crucial difference between the sequence at the top of Box 9.1 and that at the bottom, which concerns step 4. At the top, step 4 entails recognizing an input sentence, but at the bottom, *the result of step 4 is the same as step 1*. That is, the "matching" of one's own input sentence puts one right back in the same state that one was in before in before the sentence was produced. To put this a slightly different way, the "brain state" at step 1 is the same as that in step 4. Thus, one gains nothing by assuming that one listens to and interprets one's own sentence. It can be seen from the bottom of Box 9.1 that if *thinking* of a sentence is followed by other "thoughts," verbal or nonverbal, then these same thoughts would follow from the state in step 1. The same is true for other behaviors. In short, we come to the conclusion that it is mistaken to say that one's verbalizations direct oneself. It is true that one's verbalizations may be followed by other behaviors, but one is not directing these activities by the earlier verbalizations. The outline at the bottom of Box 9.1 is just another way of saying that one can't communicate with oneself—how could one tell oneself something one didn't already know?

9.9 Moving in language games, verbalization, and consciousness

It would now be helpful to consider briefly what "verbal thought" entails, based on the discussion so far in part 3. There are some difficult issues involved here, but some discussion may help to make things a bit clearer.

Once again, it seems reasonable to suppose that some thinking can take place only in language, specifically, thinking of an abstract nature, such as certain sorts of reasoning. For example, it is highly doubtful that something like a legal system or a scientific theory could develop without language. Furthermore, learning to speak enables one to acquire information from others, which means that concrete information can sometimes be transmitted linguistically. This serves to shortcut the need for experiencing every situation in order to learn about it. Thus, even in situations in which thinking may occur in nonverbal terms, language can serve to provide information used in thinking. These two uses of languge, as a reasoning tool and as a method for transmitting information about the world, were considered in section 8.9, when the notion of "language games" was introduced. Verbal reasoning involves sentence-to-sentence moves in a language game, while acquiring information about the world through a linguistic message is an example of a move out of the language into the world. That is, you take a verbal message and use it to construct a perceptual description of some event—you have moved out of the language game. In order to understand verbal thinking more clearly, we must analyze further what a sentence-to-sentence move in a language game would entail.

Symbolization and sentences. Based on the discussion in the last chapter, we do not construct a meaning from each sentence that we hear. Therefore, if we respond to someone else's sentence with another sentence, either overtly or covertly, it is because we are responding to the pattern of words produced by the person in some particular context. Thus, we respond because we have learned that, in a given situation, utterances of a certain sort are to be responded to with utterances of other sorts. Furthermore, based on this point of view, when we reason verbally we are dealing with sentences as complicated patterns of words, but perhaps as nothing more.

This point has important implications for a symbolist view of verbal thought. When we construct a perceptual description from someone else's sentence, then the sentence is serving a symbolic function, in the sense that the sentence tells us something about something else. However, when we reason verbally, the sentences we use serve as perceptual patterns, not as symbols. As an analogy, consider the following. When a flag is used in various ceremonies, it serves a symbolic function. However, as that flag is being made, it is empty of symbolism, and at any time its appearance simply serves to direct the flag-maker's activity. It may be that, as a flag acquires its symbolic function through its use in certain culturally-defined ways, so a verbal utterance acquires its symbolic function through certain aspects of its use, and production of a sentence "for oneself" may not be one of the ways in which a sentence is used symbolically.

Although this analogy may make the present argument a bit clearer, this still seems to be a not very acceptable notion to most people; it is hard to conceive of sentences as being empty strings of elements. However, based on the analysis to this point, it may not be totally implausible, since we have seen several reasons for rejecting the idea that sentences are vehicles carrying meaning and that our task as listeners is to unload this meaning.

Some relevant evidence. There is evidence from a study by Moeser and Bregman (1972) that supports the notion that people can learn sentence-to-sentence moves in language games. Moeser and Bregman (1972) examined the learning of an artifical language; they gave new words to college students who learned to use these words to "talk" about some novel geometric forms the experimenters provided. In order for the subjects to acquire the rudiments of this "language," Moeser and Bregman found that the first words had to be introduced in conjunction with the geometric forms. That is, each new word had to have some concrete referent in the world. However, once the subjects had acquired some words, new words could then simply be introduced in sentences and the subjects could, from then on, use the words correctly in new sentences to communicate about the geometric forms. Thus, once the subjects had the basics, new words could be "made meaningful" by simply placing them in sentences, indicating that people can use a pattern of words as the basis for production of further utterances.

Subvocal verbalizations and consciousness. As a final point, let us briefly consider the relationship between the moves in language games and consciousness. The argument concerning consciousness and imagery in chapter 7 may be relevant here also. It was argued in sections 7.10 and 7.11 that it is not quite correct to say that we are conscious of our images, in the sense of the image being an object that is contemplated "in consciousness." Rather, it was argued that creation of the image itself was a conscious act. This was based on the notion that consciousness comes about "from the inside out," and not the other way around. That is, the reason that one is conscious is not because there is something to be contemplated, but because one is using one's knowledge to match that input. Since creating an image requires the use of one's knowledge in the same way, creating an image is a conscious act. In the same way, one is conscious of one's internal verbalizations, not because one listens to oneself, in the usual sense, but because internal verbalizations are verbal images. These verbal images are created in the same way as visual images are, and so we are conscious of them. Indeed, based on the present discussion, it might be impossible to carry out any verbal thinking (or any sort of thinking, for that matter) that was not conscious. Such a conclusion may indicate that the present position is too strong, because many people have placed great importance on nonconscious components in thinking. However, within the context of the discussion in these last few chapters, this

Language as the medium of thought

sort of conclusion is not totally unreasonable. Therefore, it might be worthwhile to carry it to its extreme, to determine just where it must be cut back.

Moving in language games: summary. Based on this discussion, we are not conscious of verbal thoughts because we listen to what we say. We do not have to listen to what we say, because we knew it all the time. The seeming parallel between talking to someone else and talking to oneself breaks down because all one gets out of a sentence is what one puts into it in the first place. One reason why it seems reasonable to say that we talk to ourselves is that, if we are talking, it must be to *someone,* and since there is no one else present, there must be a part of us which is listening. However, based on the present discussion, this parallel should not be carried very far.

9.10 Several possible functions for overt speech during problem solving

We are still left with one question: Why do people talk aloud when they are solving concrete problems? If such speech is not helpful in thinking, then why does it occur? After all these negative conclusions, there are still several possible uses for language in concrete thinking tasks, although these uses probably are not thinking itself.

Speech-for-self as a masking stimulus. One possible use for overt speech during problem solving can be made apparent if the reader will imagine an attempt to do some difficult calculations, such as trying to balance the checkbook, when a friend comes up and tries to get your attention by gesturing in your face. Since you are in the middle of a calculation and do not want to stop, you move your paper and turn your head so that your friend's gestures are out of your line of vision. The reason that we turn away under such circumstances seems to be that the primary task (doing the calculations) is so difficult that one cannot deal with the gestures from the other person.

Now assume that you are balancing the checkbook and your friend comes up and starts to talk to you. You can no longer turn away, because your ears will still pick up the sound. In such a case, one may very well start to recite one's calculations aloud. McGuigan and Rodier (1968) found that subjects who were reading silently produced more covert speech activity when other prose material was presented aloud in the background than when nonverbal noise was presented. Thus, by analogy to averting the eyes to avoid dealing with a distracting visual stimulus, producing overt or covert speech activity may block out a potentially distracting verbal stimulus. Covert speech, since it may use the speech apparatus, may be "loud enough" to mask potentially distracting speech in the environment, just as visual imagery can interfere with visual detection (see section 7.8).

However, it should be noted that this explanation is based on one further assumption, and that is that *one's own speech does not distract oneself*. If one's own speech had to be interpreted, one would be no better off than if another person was being listened to. But one's own speech does not have to be interpreted because one does not listen to oneself in the same way one listens to others, as was argued in the last section. Therefore, one's own speech activity serves simply to block external inputs in a "noncognitive" way.

Speech and memory. Speech could also be important because it helps one remember what one has been thinking about. There is evidence that memory is improved by verbalizing the to-be-recalled material (Crowder, 1976, pp.60–62), and this could be one function of talking while working on a problem.

Speech and attention? It is sometimes suggested that verbalizing something may help you attend to it, in the same way as verbalizing something helps you to remember it. However, this is another parallel that may not work out. The basic problem is that one could not produce the verbalization in the first place without having attended to it. Therefore, listening to what you said can't help you attend to it, because you attended to it in order to say it. Therefore, it seems reasonable to conclude that speech-for-self may serve a masking function, and may facilitate memory, but it does not facilitate attention.

Possible communicative aspects of speech-for-self in all sorts of problems. A further possible function for speech-for-self may derive from the primary use of speech, that of communication between people. Vygotsky (1962) and Luria (1961) placed great importance on social factors in the development of speech-for-self, as was mentioned several times earlier in the chapter. The mother's having directed the child verbally was seen as the basis for the child's later self-direction through verbal means. Furthermore, Vygotsky placed emphasis on the social beginnings of speech-for-self in some of the research he conducted. He wanted to show that even though the speech did not sound communicative to a listener, it still was socially based. Vygotsky showed that when young children are placed in situations in which the social aspect of the speech is totally eliminated,

Language as the medium of thought

then the amount of speech-for-self uttered decreases greatly. For example, if a child is alone when working on a problem, then much less overt speech-for-self was produced. Also, when a hearing child was placed among deaf children, who could not hear anything the hearing child said, the hearing child's overt speech-for-self decreased greatly. This supported Vygotsky's contention that speech-for-self was basically social speech, which began to be specialized to serve the directive function needed for planful activities.

We have already extensively criticized Vygotsky's view that this speech-for-self serves as the basis for thinking. However, it seems worthwhile to stay with Vygotsky's analysis of the social nature of speech-for-self. One could then say that when one is working on a problem, especially in a social situation, there will be a tendency to talk aloud. This tendency comes about from the social aspects of speech: other people are effective "releasers" of speech. Some additional evidence to support the social basis of speech-for-self comes from the study by Kohlberg et al. discussed earlier. They found that children who produced the most speech-for-self also tended to produce the most speech in general. These data would support the idea that speech-for-self arises from the tendency of people to talk in social situations.

In summary, speech-for-self might be the result of a combination of aspects of the problem-solving situation: The person is working on a difficult problem, which taxes capacity; there is another person present, which initiates a tendency to talk. This could serve to inform others that one was having difficulty, without actually being an overt request for help.

9.11 An overflow model for production of speech-for-self

It has been argued that speech during problem solving could serve to mask potentially distracting verbal inputs, help in recalling important parts of problems, and serve to notify others that one has a problem. However, nothing specific was said about why this sort of speech is initiated in the first place.

Speech as a symptom. All the theorizing that has been considered so far has been based on the assumption that speech during problem solving is part of the solution attempt itself. The passage in section 9.2 from McGuigan (1973) concerning reading makes this explicit. "Those who are relatively less proficient in performing a linguistic task must exaggerate their oral behavior in order to bring their comprehension 'up to par' . . ."

(p.365). This assumes that the reader produces the overt mouth movements and speech as part of the attempt to comprehend. It is supposedly produced as part of the attempt to solve the problem of comprehending the passage. However, consider the following analogy: spots on one's face serve to warn others that one has the measles, but the spots were not produced in order to do that. In the same way, speech during problem solving may simply be a symptom of what is going on and not an explicit part of the solution strategy. Another possible analogy would be sweating while working on a problem. People probably sweat more when they work on harder problems, but no one would take this sweat to be part of the solution attempt itself.

A number of years ago, Thorson (1925) very briefly proposed an "overflow" theory of speech during problem solving. She argued that thinking was a process that involved only the central nervous system. However, at times this nervous activity could overflow into motor pathways, which would result in measurable activity in muscles, and sometimes in overt movements. Some of these movements could be speech movements. According to this idea, the motor responses that occur during problem solving are symptomatic of a solution attempt, but are not part of it.

Speaking versus keeping silent. Adults do not talk overtly during a large majority of their activities. Young children produce much more overt speech while they are carrying out these same activities. Once a child learns how to talk, everything becomes worthy of comment, and the child comments enthusiastically. This may in part come about because parents strongly reinforce speaking in young children. In any case, by the time children have mastered speech, they are ready and able to talk about anything and everything, and usually do. This is relevant to problem solving situations that have verbalizable aspects. Based on this, if there is anything that the child is attending to that is verbalizable, then the child will verbalize it.

Now one question that immediately comes to mind is why children ultimately stop talking about everything, and talk mainly in order to communicate socially. There are two points that are important here. The first factor in the decrease of these monologues may be pressure on the child to quiet down except when communicating socially. The tendency to talk about everything is gradually overcome by the child's incorporation of the rule that one only talks to communicate with others. This rule is also gradually narrowed to the point where children are taught to talk only to peo-

Language as the medium of thought

ple whom they know, except in some special situations. Thus the initial tendency to talk about everything is narrowed to a tendency to communicate socially with familiar people. However, the important thing to keep in mind is that the earlier tendency is to talk incessantly, and that these social rules are superimposed on top of this. One could say that at any time, these earlier jabbering tendencies are trying to get out, but are being held in check by later learning.

The second important aspect in the overall decrease of speech-for-self is the decrease of speech-for-self when one is alone. We reviewed some evidence earlier which indicated that less speech-for-self is produced when one is alone than when one is in the presence of others. This decrease may be related to the socialization pressures just discussed, in that if one is taught to communicate with those one knows, this might generalize to situations in which one is alone—there is no one there, so one says nothing. Furthermore, since no one is there to reinforce the child in any way after speech when alone, this speech would be expected to gradually drop out. In addition to these direct learning experiences, there might be a more "automatic" effect working to reduce the tendency to talk aloud when alone. It was argued earlier that speech-for-self does not serve any "self-communicative" function in the sense that we can't tell ourselves something which we already know. This might be another reason why we don't talk aloud when alone: since we know in advance what it will sound like if we talk, we don't have to do it. Thus, the knowledge that serves as the basis for verbal imagery also serves to stop one from talking aloud except when the goal is to communicate with someone else. This view will be elaborated further in chapters 10 and 16.

In sum, it seems that keeping silent when working on a problem is the result of some process or processes superimposed upon the earlier tendency to talk about everything in sight. Therefore, keeping silent might be looked upon as an *active* task which a person is constantly carrying out in noncommunicative situations.

Release of noncommunicative speech. We now place a person in a problem-solving situation. Based on the person's almost life-long practice, there is a strong tendency to talk about everything. However, since this is a problem-solving situation, and since the person is alone, this tendency is inhibited. We assume that this inhibition of talking is an active process, which means that some part of the person's attention capacity, or processing capacity, must be used to keep the words from spilling out. We know from chapter 6 that when people have to carry out multiple tasks at once, they must "juggle" the tasks so that their limited processing capacities will not be overtaxed. The same is true in this problem-solving situation.

It is useful to compare the present analysis of a problem solving situation to the shadowing tasks discussed in chapter 6. Based on the way most problem-solving experiments are set up, the primary task is solution of the problem, which is comparable to the to-be-shadowed channel in an attention study. In addition, the subject must try to pay some attention to the "to-be-rejected channel" to make sure that the speech apparatus is shut off. This is like trying to keep track of occasional signals in the to-be-rejected material while shadowing the other channel. From the discussion in chapter 6, we know that it is very difficult to attend to signals in the irrelevant channel while shadowing other material. Many of the signals will be missed because the subject will be attending to the shadowing task while the signal is coming in on the other channel. This occurs even if the signal on the irrelevant channel is one's own name. In addition, the more difficult the shadowing task, the fewer the signals that will be picked up on the other channel.

Exactly the same reasoning can be applied to the problem-solving situation. The subject is trying to solve the problem while actively keeping silent. If the problem is the primary task, then the subject will try to break away from the problem as often as possible to check on the speech apparatus. However, if the problem gets hard enough, then the subject will not be able to check frequently enough, and words will be blurted out. Thus, the reason that speech occurs during difficult problems is because concentration on difficult problems interferes with the inhibition of the speech apparatus. Furthermore, if one can assume that there can be degrees of inhibition of the speech apparatus, then one can deal with covert activity in the speech musculature in the same way. If a problem is not too hard, then there will only be a slight breakdown of the inhibition, so there will simply be electrical activity, but no overt movements. As the problem gets more and more difficult, there should be more and more activity, until overt speech actually occurs.

This framework can also deal with the age differences in amount of speech produced during problem solving. The fact that children produce more of this speech than adults do would be explained by the assumption that the world is full of new situations for them. The younger a person is, the more new things are encountered. These new things will require complicated processing, which will tax the child's ability to monitor the speech apparatus, so talking will occur. In addition, the finding that children who produce more speech-for-self during problem solving also produce more social speech is relevant here. The present point of view would argue that the more social a person is, the harder it ought to be for that person to inhibit the speech apparatus. Therefore, such a person ought to talk more when solving problems also.

Finally, we have the fact that less speech is produced during problem solving when the person is alone. This would be accounted for by assuming that the presence of another person increases the tendency for one to talk, all other things being equal. This should result in less of an initial tendency to talk when the person is alone, so things should be easier as far as keeping silent is concerned.

In conclusion, the elaborated overflow model offered here does not assume that the overt verbal activity during problem solving is intentionally initiated by the problem solver. It is not part of the person's solution attempts. Rather, in a sense it is initiated or released by the problem and is a result of the difficulty of the problem interacting with the limited capacities of the problem solver.

9.12 Summary

The discussion of the role of language in thinking has centered on three different but related hypotheses: (1) Speech serves to direct other nonverbal activities in humans—speech has a directive function. (2) Feedback from the speech musculature is necessary for inner speech to occur. (3) Learning to speak results in the acquisition of a set of concepts which are not available to a nonspeaking organism. Variations of these ideas have been advanced both in Russia and in the United States.

A critical review of the research related to each of the above hypotheses, as well as a logical analysis of the hypotheses themselves, indicated essentially no support for any of them. First, there are both empirical and logical reasons for rejecting the idea that we must learn to organize the world in a new way when we learn how to speak. Language serves to summarize things for us, which makes certain sorts of thinking more efficient, and perhaps allows our thinking to reach a high level of abstraction. However, this does not occur because language has taught us anything new. Rather, learning language liberates us because knowledge can be summarized and transmitted to us, without our having to live each experience for ourselves. Secondly, it seems that language can serve as part of thinking without the peripheral musculature. Verbal thought is a central phenomenon that can occur when the speech musculature is involved with some other activity, or when the speech musculature is paralyzed. Finally, the speech that occurs during all sorts of nonverbal problems does not seem to serve a directive function. It was concluded that verbal thinking, when viewed as "moving in a language game," does not require the peripheral speech apparatus, and does not require the "interpretation" of one's own speech. Terms like "talking to oneself," "speech-for-self," and "self-direction" must not be taken literally.

However, there is no doubt that much overt speech occurs while humans of all ages try to solve problems of all sorts. Several possible functions of such speech were considered: a masking function, a memory function, an attention function, and a communicative function. Lastly, an "overflow" model was proposed as a mechanism whereby such speech might occur.

9.13 Summary of part 3: is there a medium of thought?

Based on the discussion in part 3, the question "Is there a medium of thought?" should be answered in the negative, for two reasons. First of all, consider "*a* medium of thought." We have seen that there is evidence that information from multiple modalities can be used in cognitive functioning. In chapter 7 we examined the use of visual imagery in cognition, and the evidence indicates that visual information is used in many situations. The same seems to be true for verbalizations, in a restricted sense, as discussed in chapters 8 and 9. Other modalities are probably also used, although we haven't discussed them. Thus there are multiple media involved, and not one single medium, as the conceptual network or propositional models would have one believe.

Secondly, there is the "medium of *thought*" aspect. This phrase implies that thinking is a separate activity which is carried out in some medium. Based on the discussion in part 3, there is no reason to assume that there is any special activity called thinking. For example, we saw in chapter 7 that "thinking in imagery" does not entail a special sort of act carried out on images. Rather, it entails the same activity as is involved in actually perceiving something. The act is not special, it is just carried out internally, somewhat independently of external events. In the same way, the discussion in the present chapter, coupled with that in chapter 8, indicated that verbal thought entails production of speech in the same manner as in com-

Language as the medium of thought

municative situations. However, the overt aspects of this speech are inhibited. Once again, no new act is involved here. Finally, the discussion of the status of concepts in chapter 8 gives further support to the contention that thinking is not a special activity involving special sorts of objects.

In conclusion, one could say that thought does not involve symbolization. Rather, thought involves behavioral activities which are inhibited at output. This point of view will be elaborated further in Part 4 and especially in Part 5.

FOUR
Problem solving

10
Problem solving as selective recall and imagination: outline of a model of solution of practical problems

10.0 Introduction to part four

We can now broaden our focus to examine several areas of complex cognitive functioning. We shall begin with problem solving, an area that has historically been considered to be separate from other aspects of cognitive functioning. The present section considers several sorts of problem solving from the point of view of knowledge and imagination. It will be argued first that one can understand problem solving if one knows what knowledge the subject brings to the problem. We shall see that this knowledge is of two sorts: problem-specific knowledge, and more general knowledge concerning the broader context. In both cases, this information is retrieved from memory by the problem situation. That is, in these chapters, a problem will be looked upon as a retrieval cue. Second, once the problem solver recalls some problem-specific information from memory, it must be determined whether or not this information will result in solution of the problem. Imagination becomes important at this point: the problem solver must try to imagine if a solution from some other situation will work in this new situation. In addition to its theoretical interest, the area of problem solving is important because of its obvious practical relevance. We are constantly solving problems of various sorts, from fixing a leaky faucet to trying to modify a psychological theory so that it is more in accord with the facts. The discussion in part 4 will point out what we know presently about how solutions to problems are created.

Practical problem solving and the psychological mainstream. At the present time, there are three general areas of research in problem solving which could be distinguished. First, there is the extensive body of research that has come out of the work of Newell and Simon (e.g., 1972) and their colleagues and students. This work was originally concerned with the computer simulation of behavior, and with the question of whether computer programs could serve as theories of human behavior. Much recent work carried out by investigators from this point of view has been concerned with "move" problems of various sorts. In move problems, there is a set of moves or operations that are possible at any time, and the problem usually entails finding the correct sequence of moves to change the problem into the goal. A simple example of a move problem would be tic-tac-toe, and more complicated examples would be chess and theorem proving in logic. We shall consider some recent research in chess and other move problems later in this chapter. The work in computer simulation has been very important in shaping cognitive psychology, and the present discussion of problem solving has been much influenced by this work.

The second area that could be distinguished in present-day problem solving research is that of concept formation. This is an area which has evolved out of experiments in discrimination learning in animals, but at the present humans are almost exclusively the subjects. This work will be discussed in chapter 11, where we shall see that the same factors are involved in these problems as in the others which shall be discussed.

Finally, we have the area of "practical" problem solving (Duncker, 1945, p.1), or "insight" problem solving, which shall be one of the main concerns of part 4. In these problems, the subject must usually carry out some action in order to bring about the goal, although in some cases these problems can be solved without extensive action. The reader will get an idea of the sorts of problems involved here as the discussion proceeds. One important point to note about research in practical problem solving is that it is not presently at the center of interest of most psychologists, probably because most investigations of practical problem solving seem to be dealing with a rather exotic form of behavior. Certain terms, such as "insight," "fixation," and "spontaneous restructuring" are terms which are found in discussions of practical problem solving and essentially nowhere else in cognitive psychology. As an example, Wallas (1926), in an early analysis of problem solving, argued that solving a problem involved: (1) preparation; (2) incubation; (3) illumination or insight; and (4) verification. Of these stages, the second means that after the problem has been discovered and thought about consciously for a while, it was necessary for the solver to let the problem incubate. That is, the person did not consciously work on the problem, but thought about other things and let unconscious processes go to work. When the solution came, at stage 3, it would come suddenly in a flash of illumination or insight. Other psychologists also postulated similar stages in problem solving.

These stages were often postulated on the basis of reports of various creative individuals, such as famous scientists. As such, they were not based on direct experimental study. Indeed, given the definition of some of the stages, it is hard to see how they could be subject to direct test. In addition, experimental investigations which attempted to examine these stages did not meet with great success (see Vinacke, 1974, pp.356–61, for a brief review). Thus, there seemed to be nowhere to go in terms of connecting laboratory research in psychology with what seemed to be happening when people solved problems, so research concerning insight problems has become almost nonexistent. The discussion in the next few chapters will attempt to demonstrate that one can understand the behavior of subjects working on insight problems using the same concepts as were discussed in parts 1–3, and which will be applied to the other problems discussed in this section. Basically, problem solving will be looked upon as a situation that depends on a person's use of knowledge. To put it another way, the presentation of a problem serves as a retrieval cue, resulting in the recall of relevant information. In the present chapter, we shall consider how problem-specific information is recalled and applied to a novel problem. We shall begin by analyzing one situation in some detail, then broadening the analysis to consider several other situations.

In the next chapter, we shall consider the role of a problem-solver's broader knowledge in the solution of problems. The chapter will examine some important research concerning concept-formation tasks, or as we shall refer to them, classification tasks. The thrust of this work will be to demonstrate that "scripts," in the sense used in chapter 3, play an important role in problem solving. It was argued in chapter 3 that verbal messages are usually lacking in much specific information, and this information must be "filled in" by using a script, which is the hearer's knowledge concerning the situation being discussed. In the same way, many events which occur in problem-solving experiments are also in need of interpretation, and problem solvers use scripts to interpret these events. It will be argued that much of what people do in certain experimental situations is a function of their interpretation of the situation; that is, of the script that they are using.

In chapter 12, a variety of "insight" problems from the literature will be analyzed using these two notions: we shall see that in some cases a subject's behavior depends upon the specific information that is brought to the problem, while in other situations behavior depends on the script involved. It will be argued that these notions provide a straightforward explanation of behavior on "insight" problems, and no recourse to other sorts of explanatory constructs is necessary.

10.1 Problem solving: some general considerations

In the broadest sense of the term, a person has a *problem* when the present situation (the *problem state*) is not the situation the person wants to be in (the *goal state*). The series of steps which gets the person from the problem to the goal, or changes the problem into the goal, is the solution of the problem. One small difficulty with this definition of a solution is that there is not always a simple series of steps involved, as we shall see. However, this definition will do for the present.

Some psychologists distinguish between a situation in which one already knows how to bring about the goal, and a situation in which one has to create a new solution in order to bring about the goal. However, the following discussion argues that "creative" problem solving, in which a person produces a solution that has never been used before, is still based on past experience. This notion is not a new one (e.g., Selz, 1927, rpt. 1964), but it will be one of the cornerstones of all that is to follow. The purpose of the present chapter is to outline how knowledge is used in problem solving. In this chapter, we shall first consider one simple practical problem in some detail, in order to examine the various sorts of problem-specific information that people bring to bear as they work on it. In the second part of the chapter, a very different sort of problem, picking a move in chess, is considered from this same point of view. Finally, the chapter ends with some recent working concerning simple "move" problems, to point out some differences that seem to exist among various sorts of problems investigated by psychologists.

Problem solving

10.2 The candle problem

The first problem to be discussed in this chapter is Duncker's (1945) "candle" or "box" problem, as shown in Figure 10.1. The problem is to get the candle up on the wall so that it burns properly, using any of the objects on the table, and assuming that a hammer is available.

The different types of solutions usually produced by subjects are as follows: *Nails:* The candle is nailed directly to the wall, or is modified in some way so that it can be nailed, such as by wedging the nails into the side of the candle, or making a shelf with nails and putting the candle on

Figure 10.1. Duncker's candle problem.

it. This is a frequent solution, and many subjects give it first. *Melting:* The bottom or side of the candle is melted, and the resulting wax is used to attach the candle to the wall. This is also a frequent and early solution. *Matchbook:* The matchbook is used as a platform for the candle by nailing it to the wall. This solution is infrequent and will usually be produced late if at all. *Box:* The nailbox is used as a holder for the candle. The nails are removed, the box is nailed to the wall, and the candle is placed in the box. This is also a relatively infrequent solution and is usually given late. It is the solution in which Duncker was most interested.

How is it that subjects produce these various solutions? Consider how the problem-as-presented is matched with the problem solver's knowledge, and how the problem solver uses any relevant information which is available.

10.3 Recognizing familiar problems

As indicated earlier, the present point of view argues that all solutions attempted by a problem solver, including novel or "creative" solutions, are firmly based on past experience. Therefore, we shall begin by considering how a problem is recognized as being familiar, so that an old solution is simply reproduced. We shall then consider the more complicated situation in which a problem is not completely familiar.

Recognition of a problem as familiar depends on two factors: the goal is recognized as something done before, and the objects which are available are those which were used in achieving the goal in the past. These two separate factors probably work together as the problem is presented. First of all, hearing the instructions would serve to cue any past situations in which the same goal was accomplished. That is, when one hears "attach the candle to the wall," that phrase would serve to cue past successes directly. In addition, the presence of the various objects would serve to cue previous experience with this problem. Thus the instructions and objects serve to cue relevant past experience relatively directly, as discussed in chapters 1 and 2.

When the person can recall having solved this problem in the past with the objects presently available, then the old solution method can simply be run through again. This situation is represented in steps 1 and 6 in Figure 10.2, which serves to summarize the discussion. Figure 10.2 is read as follows. One starts at the top and goes through the steps, following the directions at the end of each step. Based on the outcome at a given step, one

Problem solving

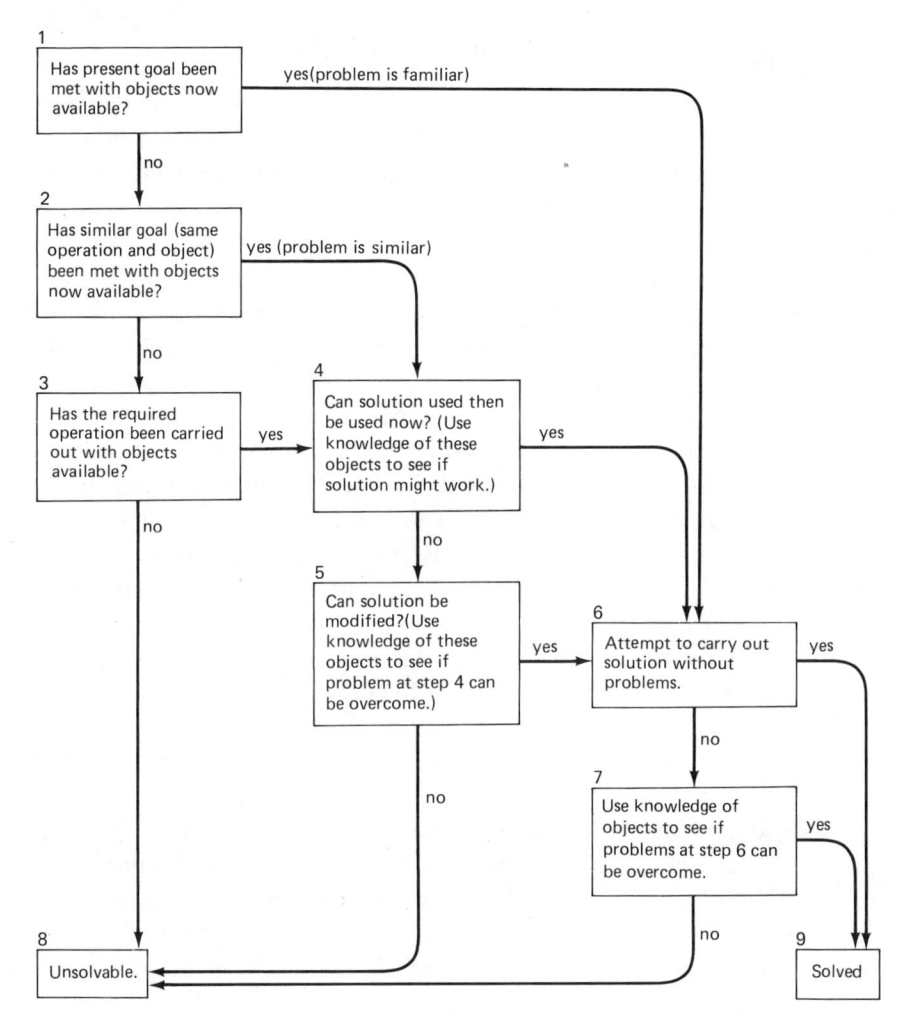

```
1. Has present goal been met with objects now available?
   - yes (problem is familiar) → 6
   - no → 2
2. Has similar goal (same operation and object) been met with objects now available?
   - yes (problem is similar) → 4
   - no → 3
3. Has the required operation been carried out with objects available?
   - yes → 4
   - no → 8
4. Can solution used then be used now? (Use knowledge of these objects to see if solution might work.)
   - yes → 6
   - no → 5
5. Can solution be modified? (Use knowledge of these objects to see if problem at step 4 can be overcome.)
   - yes → 6
   - no → 8
6. Attempt to carry out solution without problems.
   - yes → 9
   - no → 7
7. Use knowledge of objects to see if problems at step 6 can be overcome.
   - yes → 9
   - no → 8
8. Unsolvable.
9. Solved.
```

Figure 10.2. Framework for analysis of a problem.

may either skip several steps or work through all the steps in order. Based on the discussion so far, if a problem is recognized as familiar, the problem solver would skip steps 2–5.

To summarize, if a problem is recognized as familiar, then the subject can simply carry out the same solution as the first time. Essentially no further thought is involved.

10.4 Similar problems

Even though a problem might not be recognized as being totally familiar, the problem solver might recognize it as being similar to something done in the past. The person would therefore have some relevant knowledge. For example, let's say a person has used melted wax from a candle in the past to "glue" the base of the candle to a table, so that the lit candle stood solidly without falling over. This could be called an attach-a-candle-to-a-*horizontal*-surface problem. The candle problem is an attach-a-candle-to-a-*vertical*-surface problem. If vertical versus horizontal is ignored, the problems are identical, and perhaps the wax could be used in the candle problem. Therefore, we could say that two problems are similar if the same major object and basic operation are involved in both. The major object or objects in a problem could be defined as those that the basic operation is to be performed on. A person who glued a candle to a table solved a "candle-attaching" problem in the past, and the candle problem is also a "candle-attaching" problem. Based on this analysis, recall of a previous solution would come about because the new problem is a good enough match to the problem solver's knowledge so that a solution from some other problem would be recalled. In this hypothetical example, the instructions "Attach a candle to . . . ," plus the presence of the candle and matchbook, would make a match with past experience even though there would not be a complete correspondence.

This sort of a match is summarized as step 2 in Figure 10.2. When a problem is recognized as similar to an old problem, but not identical to it, the old solution method may not be directly applicable to the new problem. For example, gluing a candle with wax to a table is different than gluing a candle to the wall. Therefore some thought must be involved before a solution can be produced. This is noted as step 4 and will be discussed later.

To summarize the discussion to this point, the difference between a familiar and similar problem is that in the case of a similar problem there is only a partial match between the problem and the problem solver's experiences.

10.5 New problems: making past experience relevant

The most interesting and important situation occurs when the solution requirements of the present problem have not been met by a problem solver in the past, either specifically or more generally. This would mean

Problem solving 255

that steps 1 and 2 produce no match between the problem and the person's knowledge. In such a case, the match between the problem and the person's past experience would be even less exact than in the case of a similar problem. For example, many people decide to use the nails in the candle problem, not because they are things that have been used to attach *candles* in past experience, but as things that have been used to attach *objects*. Thus, the match is now based on previous "attaching" experience, which is less exact than the "candle attaching" experience which served as the basis for the "similar" match discussed in the last section. This match is based only on the "operation" involved in the problem and is summarized at step 3. This is the point at which many people begin to solve the candle problem. Since this match is not precise at all, the relevant knowledge cannot be directly applied to the problem, and thought must occur. In the next section we shall consider how a person formulates a solution to a nonfamiliar problem.

It should also be noted that the discussion so far has been simplified, because we have not considered a situation in which a person has carried out a similar operation in the past with different objects than those presently available. An example of this would be if a person had attached a candle to the wall using a candle holder, with no candle holder available in the problem. Such a situation would involve an attempt to locate another object in the problem that would serve the same purpose as the missing object. This situation will not be discussed further in order to keep things simple and because the factors involved seem to be similar to those being discussed in detail for the other situations.

As one last point, if there is no match at this highest level of generality (i.e., the "attacher" level), then the subject cannot solve the problem. Thus, one interesting aspect of this model is that it predicts that under certain conditions people ought not to produce any solutions at all to a problem. We shall consider some situations of this sort in chapter 12.

10.6 Producing a solution.

We have now come to the point at which the subject has decided on a method for attacking the problem. Assume that the subject has decided to try to use the nails to attach the candle to the wall. They have been chosen because they can be used to attach things to walls, but the subject has no guarantee that they will actually work. This is true for any solution method which is not simply an exact repetition of an old method.

Estimating adequacy of solutions. Let us consider some factors that might influence a naive subject's decision to use the nails to attach the candle to the wall, once this possibility has been thought of. Through past experience, most people have learned that in order to nail any Object$_1$ to any Object$_2$, some conditions similar to the following must be met. First, Object$_1$ must be made of a material which is softer than the nail and is not brittle. Object$_1$ must also be small enough so that the nail can go through it and into Object$_2$. Object$_2$ must also be softer than the nail and not brittle. This knowledge, which we all have available, serves as the basis for a person's determining if a potentially useful solution will actually work. Furthermore, it seems that one must distinguish between one's estimation of the adequacy of a solution "from afar" as it were, and what happens when one is actually carrying out the solution. This distinction is made in step 4, which entails a rough estimate as to whether the solution seems worth pursuing. No actual behavior has occurred as yet. In some cases, a potential solution could be so obviously inadequate that things never get past the formative stage. So, based on a specific problem solver's knowledge about the objects under consideration, a solution might or might not be estimated as being worth pursuing at step 6.

Estimation and imagination. Since the problem solver has never actually applied the solution in question to the present problem, there is no direct information available as to whether the solution will work. Therefore, if a problem solver is to determine the adequacy of a solution, an educated guess must be made as to whether the solution would work. Or, the person must *imagine* if the solution would work. Let us return again to a subject who has thought of using the nails to attach the candle to the wall. This person might imagine holding the candle to the wall and actually hammering a nail into it. However, at this point, the composition of the candle becomes important. Presumably, a person with reasonable experience with nails and candles would have come across some situation in which an object has been split by a nail and/or a situation in which a candle broke when a small amount of pressure was applied to it. These two sorts of experiences would lead the person to anticipate that the candle could not be directly nailed to the wall. Thus, it is being assumed that carrying out the solution in one's imagination can result in the retrieval of additional information which can influence one's decision as to whether or not a solution can be carried out.

As another example of how this assessment might work, consider a person who is considering using the wax as glue. Presumably, this person has had some experience using melted wax and glue in other situations. This would give the person some information concerning the strength of this wax-glue. In addition, we have all had some experience gluing things, which would also provide knowledge about when things can be expected to stay together and when not. As the person works through gluing the candle in imagination, this would result in retrieval of this earlier experience with candle wax as glue and with gluing objects to walls or vertical surfaces. This information would then influence one's decision as to the usefulness of the wax-glue.

In sum, it is being argued that carrying out an imaginary solution serves to retrieve information from similar situations, and this can be used to decide whether or not a proposed solution can be carried out. However, this does not mean that the person must contemplate the imaginary solution in order to determine if it will work. Arguments against the notion of contemplation of one's own images were made in chapter 7 and need not be repeated here.

Repairing inadequate solutions. If a solution which seemed plausible is found wanting, attempts are made to change those aspects of the solution which brought about the difficulties. If problems are noted at step 4, then the person essentially must start this mental problem solving all over again, at step 5. However, this time the problem to be solved is the specific problem that was discovered in the solution that was considered.

Assume that a subject has decided to try the nails, but then notes that all the nails are too thick to go through the candle without splitting it. Thus, a subproblem must be considered: How might the candle be made wider relative to the nails, or, alternatively, how might the nails be made thinner relative to the candle? There are at least two practical ways to do this: one could soften the candle by melting it a bit, then flattening it out so that it gets wider; or one could arrange the candle and nails so that the whole thickness of the nail is not used. This could be accomplished by putting nails along the sides of the candle, rather than directly through the candle. Presumably, these modifications would be thought of as the result of the retrieval of relevant information. For example, as regards softening the candle so that it would not be split by the nails, a person who has handled candles might have had occasion to notice that when a candle gets warm, it becomes soft and pliable, and can be manipulated without breaking.

If the person can devise a modification that seems adequate, an attempt can be made to use the solution, at step 6. Here again the person may find that in actuality the proposed solution will not work. If so, there must then be a further attempt to modify the solution.

10.7 Thinking out a solution: stopping and thinking

It has been suggested that one step in solving a practical problem is the assessment of adequacy of any solution which is retrieved from memory. This is usually referred to as "thinking out" the solution. It has been assumed that such a process occurs for similar problems and novel problems, as defined earlier, at step 4. However, such a process does not occur with familiar problems, since such problems result in these steps being bypassed. This seems reasonable, because we don't usually have to "stop and think" when a situation is familiar to us. Over the years, many theorists have commented on the fact that we have to "stop and think" when things are not familiar, or when things are not what we expect them to be, which may be another way of saying the same thing.

This then leads to a further question—Why is it that we must stop and think when a problem is not familiar? Why does one usually attempt to work out the solution mentally before taking action? No concrete answers to this question are available at present, but several comments could be made. First, it might be that action can be directly carried out in a familiar situation because such a situation makes a relatively precise match with the problem solver's knowledge. This might result in action without the need for prior thought. Another way of putting this is to say that a familiar situation may result in direct action because the person knows beforehand just how to achieve the goal. Direct action might occur in a familiar situation because there is a match possible between the desired goal and the person's knowledge, in that the person knows how that goal can be brought about. Thus, it might be that a match between the goal and the person's knowledge is necessary before any action can be carried out. Based on this, action comes about because relevant knowledge is available and because a desired goal serves to allow the relevant knowledge to be expressed overtly. This will be elaborated further in chapter 16.

From this point of view, the reason that similar and novel problems do not result in direct action is because any solution methods that are recalled will not bring about the exact solution to the problem, since the problem is not completely familiar. Therefore, the needed solution will not be matched by the person's knowledge, and there will be no action taken. Furthermore, "thinking out" a solution can enable one to actually carry out some act because one is able to produce the required goal, at least in one's imagination. When this occurs, there would be a more exact match between the goal required by the problem and the goal that one can bring

Problem solving 259

about, so action will occur. Success in imagining the goal will serve to provide a match to the problem and thus result in the "release" of the solution method which led to the imagined goal.

Once again, action occurs in a knowledgeable organism only when it serves to bring about some goal. If some action sequence does not bring about the goal in question, it will be modified "in thought" until a good enough match occurs so that the now-modified action can be carried out. This will be elaborated further in chapter 16.

One final point to be considered is why we can carry out a solution in imagination when we can't carry it out in actuality. One tentative answer to this might be that there is an additional requirement necessary before an action can occur: the match between the required goal and the person's knowledge. If there is no match, then action will not occur. However, the person could still imagine some solution, because the presentation of the problem could serve as a cue to retrieve the solution.

In summary, we can say the following about the relation between thought and action. Thought, in the sense of imagining some action before it is carried out, occurs because the action in question will not bring about the desired goal. Only when the action has been modified so that it will bring about the goal will the action be performed. Thus, the desired goal serves to block any action except one that will bring it about. This is discussed further in chapter 16.

10.8 Summary and conclusions concerning the candle problem

We have now considered one problem taken from the problem-solving literature, Duncker's candle problem. It was assumed that the subject first tries to determine if the problem as it is presented has ever been solved before. If so, the solution method used at that time is recalled and the subject carries it out. If the problem is not recognized as being a repetition of a previous one, the subject then determines if any problems have been solved with the same solution object(s) and general solution requirements. If such a problem has been solved before, with the objects available in the present situation, then the subject tries to carry out the solution again. If no similar problems have been solved before, the subject then determines if the most general aspect of the requirements, the required operation, has been carried out before, with objects that are available in the present situation. In any of these cases, if a potential solution method is recalled, the subject then estimates if the potential solution is worth trying. This is done by assessing if the potential solution can actually be carried out with the available objects. This entails the use of one's imagination, which serves to retrieve relevant information from memory. If the subject decides that the solution is worth trying, it is then attempted. It should also be noted that several studies have investigated predictions from this model concerning a subject's behavior on the candle problem, and there has been support for the model (e.g., Weisberg & Suls, 1973; Weisberg, 1979).

As mentioned earlier, Duncker (1945) was particularly interested in the use of the small box as a candle holder. Most subjects do not produce this sort of solution as one of their first solutions, if they produce it at all. From the present point of view, the reason that the box is used late is because the subject's experience with the objects in question results in other solutions being tried first. Those subjects with experience with candle wax will first consider gluing the candle to the wall, while others will consider nailing it. Only if these solutions are judged to be inadequate might the box come into play for most people. For example, if the wax-glue won't be strong enough, and a nail will split the candle, then the box might be useful as a shelf. Also, some subjects may decide that they need something to prevent the wax from dripping if the candle is glued or nailed to the wall. This could result in use of the box. Finally, some subjects may be familiar with sconces, and so may try to devise one, and thereby use the box. However, the typical urban undergraduate doesn't seem to solve the problem using this latter method (Weisberg & Suls, 1973). In conclusion, in order to understand why a given solution is produced early or late one must consider all the elements in the problem, both those given by the experimenter and those brought by the subject.

In summary, based on this analysis, novel or creative solutions to a problem can come about in several ways. First, the requirements for solution of a new problem may have enough overlap with those of an already known problem to enable the person to use an old solution method. Second, even if an old method cannot be used directly, the same sort of factors that resulted in the method's being recalled in the first place will enable the person to attempt to modify the old solution to fit the new problem, through the use of creative imagination.

10.9 Chess playing as problem solving

The next section of the chapter will consider some recent research in game playing, especially chess playing, to show that the same factors are in-

Problem solving

volved in these sorts of problems also. Once this has been done, we shall be able to use the general point of view to consider other research in problem solving, beginning with a brief consideration of chess-playing computer programs, and then going on to recent analyses of human chess playing. One of the important advances in understanding how chess masters play chess has come from recent attempts to specify the problem-specific knowledge which the chess master has available. We shall begin with a discussion of early attempts to program computers to play chess because there was little effort made to deal with problem-specific knowledge, and the early programs were not very successful because of it.

Complexity in chess. If one wishes to win at chess, there is one method that will maximize one's chances. One must go through all the possible move combinations and choose the move that leads to the best outcomes. This sort of a procedure is called *minimaxing,* because you choose the move that produces the minimum outcome for your opponent and the maximum for you (Newell, Shaw, & Simon, 1958). Minimaxing is the basic procedure around which chess-playing programs have been built. However, there is one practical limitation to carrying out a minimaxing analysis. There are enough moves possible at most positions in a chess game that it is impractical to reason through all the alternatives. Therefore, methods must be derived whereby the complexity of the problem is cut down to manageable size. Computer programmers attempt to reduce this complexity, and human chess players also seem to do it.

As an example, a program developed by Kister, Stein, Ulam, Walden, and Wells (1957) examined all the alternative moves that were possible from a given position. However, each move was only explored to a depth of two moves (your move → opponent's move → your move → opponent's move), which kept things reasonably manageable. The resulting situation was then evaluated on the basis of lost pieces and the mobility of the remaining pieces. In this way a value could be computed for each alternative move, and the best one could be chosen. However, in order to carry out this sort of analysis, some changes had to be made in the game. The board was reduced from 8 × 8 squares to 6 × 6, with several pieces being eliminated. In addition, some moves were eliminated from the game. These modifications served to reduce the average number of possible moves to be explored in any game from about 800,000 to about 160,000.

It is interesting to compare this sort of analysis with that of a good human chess player. It has been found that expert human players seldom explore more than 100 possible moves, total, in a normal chess game

(DeGroot, 1966). The program examines *1600 times* more moves on the average. However, the program didn't play very good chess. It is also interesting to note that this program did not take "chess knowledge" into account at all. The only factors that were used in evaluating a potential move were the lost pieces and the mobility of those that remained. These are nice neat measures, but they are based on almost no knowledge of chess. This may be the basic reason why early chess-playing programs played poor chess—no attempt was made to incorporate sophisticated chess knowledge into them. Based on the analysis of problem solving earlier in this chapter, we would expect that good chess would require extensive knowledge to serve as the basis for matching new situations.

10.10 Perception and memory in chess

As just mentioned, there is evidence that only a very small number of moves is considered by very good chess players at most points (DeGroot, 1966). The basic question then becomes how the human chess player decides on these one or two moves that should be considered further. It seems that the first step in deciding what to do is matching the pattern on the board with past experience. This may be what limits the moves that must be considered.

DeGroot's analysis. An extensive research project on chess as problem solving has been carried out by DeGroot (1965, 1966). (Aspects of this work were discussed in chapter 3.) In order to understand the differences in ability between chess masters and other players, DeGroot first attempted to find some simple quantitative differences between the play of chess masters and that of weaker players. One possibility might be that the masters would consider more moves before choosing one. This turns out not to be the case. Indeed, in one game that a master analyzed for DeGroot (1966), there seemed to be only *one or two* possible moves at each point, as far as the master was concerned. A weaker player could hardly consider fewer moves per turn than this. Another possibility might be that any proposed moves are explored more deeply by the master than by lesser players (that is, the master considers a longer string of my move → opponent's move → my move → opponent's, etc., than does the weak player), but that is not true either. Perhaps surprisingly, DeGroot could find no simple measure that would differentiate the play of the master from that of the poor player.

One difference between a master and a weaker player that DeGroot did

Problem solving

find had to do with the master's exceptional memory for chess positions, discussed in section 3.7. This result has led to the hypothesis that a master is able to recognize groups of pieces as forming a familiar pattern, or chunk. The master remembers one *chunk* for each *piece* that the beginner can remember. Thus, the master has developed a large repertoire of patterns to help him remember a new position. The weaker player has fewer patterns to apply, and they are smaller in size (Chase & Simon, 1973).

DeGroot (1966) argues that these patterns are at work in the master's play, as well as in the memory performance.

The rapid insight of the chessmaster into the possibilities of a newly shown position, his immediate "seeing" of structural and dynamic essentials, of possible combinatorial gimmicks, and so forth, are only understandable if we realize that as a result of his experience he quite literally "sees" the position in a totally different (and much more adequate) way than a weaker player. The vast difference between the two in efficiency, particularly in the amount of time to find out what the core problem is (what's cooking really) and to discover highly specific, and adequate means of thought and board action, need not and must not be primarily ascribed to large difference in "natural" power for abstraction. The difference is mainly due to differences in perception.

It is above all *the treasury of ready "experience"* which puts the master that much ahead of the others. His extremely extensive, widely branched and highly categorized system of knowledge and experience enables him, first, to recognize immediately a chess position as belonging to an unwritten category with corresponding board means to be applied, and second, to "see" immediately and in a highly adequate way its specific, individual features against the background of the category. . . .

The gist of the preceding discussion might be summarized by saying that a master *is* a master primarily by virtue of what he has been able to build up by experience; and this is: (a) a schooled and highly specific *way of perceiving*, and (b) a system of reproductively available methods, *in memory*. (DeGroot, 1965, pp.306,308)

There are a number of points to be emphasized here. First, DeGroot's use of the term *perceiving* in this excerpt seems to mean the matching of a visual pattern with one's knowledge about visual patterns. Thus, the chess master's act of perception is another example of the use of past experience as outlined earlier. In exactly the same way, one could say that a person who has experience getting candles to stand up unsupported on tables "sees" the candle problem differently than one without such experience.

Secondly, the master can recognize the important consequences likely to arise from a given position, and so can go to work directly on them. Through years of play and study, the master has come to be able to anticipate certain happenings from the pattern of pieces on the board, just as all of us have come to be able to anticipate rain from the formation of thunderclouds. The connections that the master sees may be less direct than the connection between clouds and rain, in that a number of subsequent steps may intervene before the full disaster occurs, but the principle is the same. In the same way, a person working on the candle problem could anticipate problems nailing the candle, so that that "move" might not be attempted without modification.

In summary, choosing a move in chess may provide a particularly graphic example of the interrelations among the various cognitive processes in problem solving. Solving the problem depends upon the match between the problem and memory. This in turn depends upon the knowledge that one has concerning the appearance of chess boards and what one can expect to evolve from these various configurations. The use of knowledge in perceptual processing has already been considered in several earlier chapters, and will be important in several discussions in part 5. The chess-playing example is particularly useful because it makes very clear the various processes involved and how they are interrelated. Obviously, we have only skimmed the surface of a highly complex activity here. However, the discussion serves to point out some important points of similarity between the analysis of the candle problem and DeGroot's analysis of chess playing.

10.11 Rayner's analysis of pegity (Gomoku)

DeGroot's analysis of chess playing is encouraging from our point of view, and still further encouragement comes from Rayner's (1958) study of a game called pegity in England, and Gomoku in Japan and the United States. The game is played on a square board in any of various sizes from 19×19 spaces in the Japanese version to 24×24 spaces in the English version used by Rayner. (Some recent research has used smaller boards for simplification.) The players take turns. The object of the game is to line up five of your pieces in a row while at the same time stopping your opponent from doing so. Once a piece is placed on the board, it cannot be moved.

Rayner introduced several undergraduates to the game and observed as they acquired experience by playing each other. He found various measures to indicate that as the players gained experience and skill, they were better able to plan and carry out strategies for winning while minimizing the opponent's chances to win. His explanation of the basis for this planning ability echoes very closely DeGroot's explanation of the ability to chess masters.

[If] an individual consistently carries out a certain strategy . . . then he must in all likelihood have anticipated the moves ahead. . . . However, although it seems that the individual must have anticipated the possible moves of a strategy at some time before he intentionally carried it out, there would be no necessity for him to do this on every succeeding occasion. Instead, he seems to be able to use a labor saving device. When the individual perceives a pattern of pegs from which the possible moves have been anticipated in the past, instead of anticipating again, he can refer to his memory as to what these possibilities were and what the outcome was. In this way, for instance, the percept of a pattern of pegs that in the past had been anticipated as leading to an opponent's five in a line could immediately be recognized as dangerous. By this means the player can build up a repertoire of memories of groups of pegs that had been anticipated as dangerous or potentially winning. (Rayner, 1958, p.163)

Thus, Rayner's analysis corresponds closely to that of DeGroot, and both are consistent with the present point of view. It seems that proficiency in problem solving depends upon the acquisition of a broad base of problem-specific knowledge, which can be brought forth to meet the demands of the specific situation.

10.12 Selz's Theory of Productive Thinking

Approximately fifty years ago, Otto Selz (1927, rpt. in Mandler & Mandler, 1964; Humphrey, 1963) developed a theory of productive thinking very similar to the point of view discussed here. Selz's theory is also a direct precursor of DeGroot's work. It would be fitting to end this discussion with a brief examination of Selz's theory of productive thinking.

Selz attempted to devise an explanation of productive problem solving based on the idea that past experience serves as the basis for productive thinking. In explaining how a subject uses past experience to develop a new solution, Selz postulated that several types of mental operations are available to humans. These operations can be applied to past experience so that information relevant to the specific problem at hand can be made available from memory.

In a problem situation, an organism is searching for a *means* to bring about an end. The goal is the end that is to be brought about, and the solution is a means to change the present situation into the goal. The first mental operation which can be applied to a problem is that of reproduction of task-specific knowledge. The subject tries to find knowledge from previous encounters with this specific problem, which could then be used again. If there is no such information available, a means must be *produced*. To quote Selz:

The failure of *reproductive thinking,* or reflection, that has been brought to bear upon a problem due to the absence, for example, of reproductive task-relevant knowledge-units, represents the specific conditions of elicitation for the operations of productive thinking. The primary operation of productive thinking are the operations of means-production. . . . We are concerned here with the application of previously developed methods of solution to the mastery of a task in an analogous case, whereby a new product is developed. Should the operations of means-production fail, then the operations of means-abstraction are initiated. They are designed for the discovery of new methods of solution and are arrived at by analyzing the structure of the . . . problem. (1927, quoted in Mandler & Mandler, 1964, p.232)

This needs very little elaboration in order for the relevance of Selz's ideas to our model to be seen. Thus, solution of the candle problem as an attaching problem is an example of solution through means-production. Solution of the candle problem using the box in order to rectify difficulties with an earlier solution is an example of solution through means-abstraction.

In summary, it could be said that Selz was more than fifty years ahead of his time. Other work on problem solving which has great similarities to the present point of view is that of Polya (e.g., 1945).

10.13 Problem solving without problem-specific past experience and without planning: recent research on simple move problems

The discussion so far has considered the role of problem-specific past experience in solving problems. We have considered two sorts of problems in some detail: the candle problem and picking a move in chess. As indicated earlier, chess is a very complicated "move" problem, and task-specific past experience is very important in cutting down the problem to manageable size. There has also been much research in recent years concerned with simpler move problems, such as the missionaries and cannibals problem:

Three missionaries and three cannibals come together to the bank of a river. The only method of transportation across the river is a boat that holds at most two people. The missionaries and the cannibals wish to use the boat to cross the river, but there is one difficulty: if at any time the cannibals outnumber the missionaries

Problem solving

on either bank of the river, the outnumbered missionaries will be eaten. How is it possible to get all the missionaries and all the cannibals across the river without losing anyone?

This problem, like all move problems, has several characteristics. First, there is a clearly stated *initial state,* as well as a specified *goal state.* Second, there is a set of specified moves that can be applied to the initial state, and that produce other states. For example, from the initial state, one can move two cannibals across the river, or one can move one cannibal across the river (which is a wasted move, because that same cannibal will have to bring the boat back on the next move), or one can move a missionary-cannibal pair across the river. Each of these moves produces a new state, which is different from both the initial state and the goal state; these states can be called intermediate states. From these intermediate states, one can then carry out certain further moves, each of which produces another intermediate state, and so on. Thus, in a simple move problem, one can specify all the legal combinations of moves which can be carried out. The whole set of states that results from all the legal combinations of moves is called the *problem space* (Newell & Simon, 1972). The problem space is made up of a number of "paths," each of which consists of one sequence of legal moves. The problem space for the missionaries-cannibals problem is presented in Figure 10.3. If a move problem has a solution, then at least one path in the problem space must lead from the initial state to the solution state. As can be seen in Figure 10.3, there are several solution paths in the missionaries and cannibals problem. Another move problem is shown in Figure 10.4. Research concerned with move problems has concentrated on determining how subjects search through the problem space until they solve the problem.

Some recent theorizing concerning move problems. According to Jeffries, Polson, Razran, and Atwood (1977), people work through the missionaries and cannibals, and other move problems, by first considering all the moves that are possible from a given state. The possible moves are considered in a specific order, specified by Jeffries et al. The outcome of each move—that is, the resulting state—is then evaluated by the subjects. The evaluation is based on whether or not the new state is closer to the goal then the old state was. In order for this to occur, Jeffries et al. assume that people are able to note the differences that exist between a given state and the goal, and that such differences form the basis for evaluation. If a given move results in a positively valued state—if the resulting state is closer to the goal—then there is assumed to be some probability that the move will

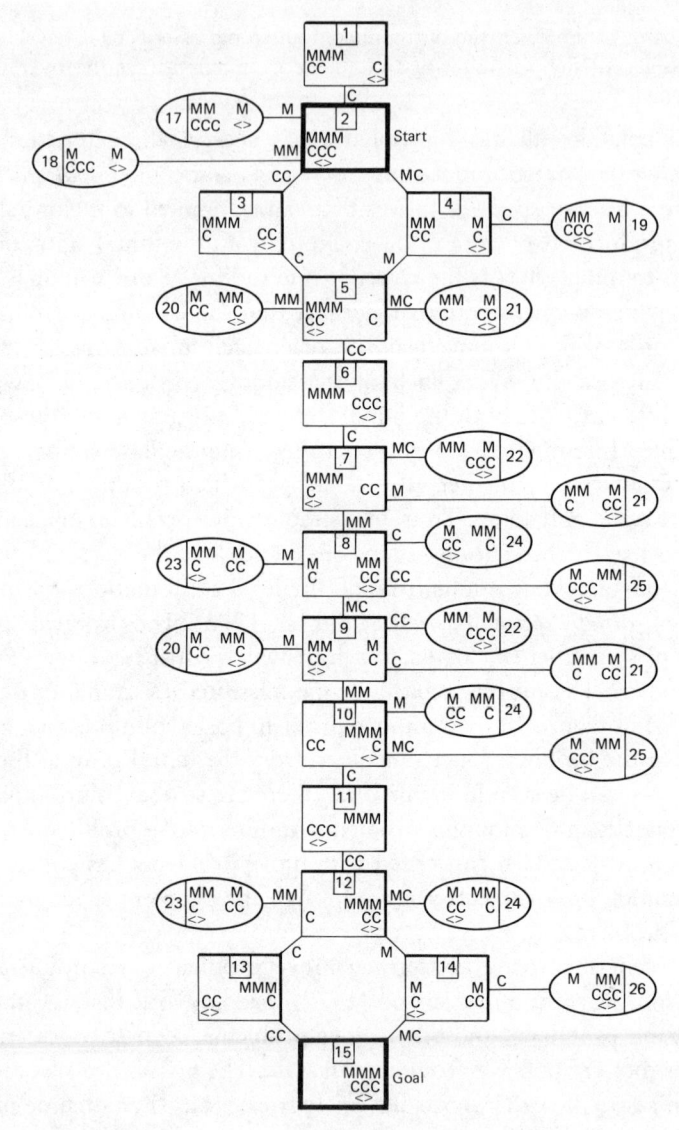

Figure 10.3. Problem space for missionaries-cannibals problem. Diagram is read as follows: The Ms in each box represent the missionaries on the left-hand and right-hand banks of the river, and the Cs represent the cannibals. The symbol < > represents the boat. Thus, in state 2, there are three missionaries, three cannibals, and the boat on the left bank; in state 21 there are two missionaries and one cannibal on the left bank, and the boat is on the other bank. The letters on the lines between states represent the move made in changing from one state to another. So, for example, from state 2 to state 3, two cannibals are moved.

Problem solving

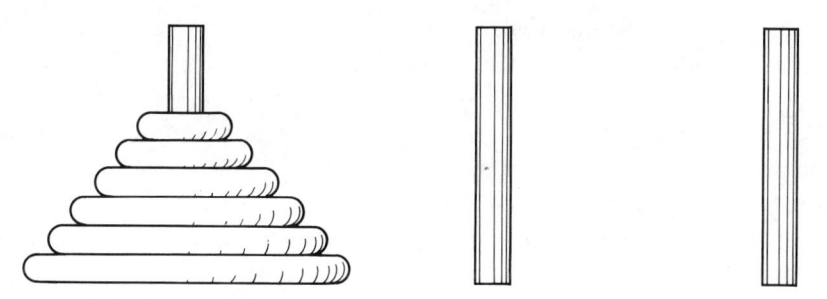

Figure 10.4. Towers of Hanoi, another move problem. The problem is to move all the disks from the left-hand peg to the peg on the right, so that the pile on the right will look exactly like the one on the left. Only one disk can be moved at a time, and a disk cannot be put on a peg if there is a smaller disk already on the peg. The middle peg can be used to hold disks temporarily, but the same rule applies: no disk can go on top of a smaller disk.

be chosen. In this way, the problem solver chooses a move at each state, until the solution state occurs.

Missionaries and cannibals and the candle problem. This discussion of the theorizing of Jeffries et al. is a bit simplified, but serves to make several points clear. The most important point for the present discussion is that Jeffries et al. assume that the only factors influencing the choice of a given move are the state that the problem solver is in and the state that the move in question produces. To put it another way, there is no long-range planning involved in selecting a move: the problem solver does not consider what might happen three or four moves later. The only factor taken into account is what will happen now if this move is made. If this analysis of move problems is correct, then there are obvious differences between move problems and the candle problem, since the latter does seem to involve planning, as discussed earlier.

It should be noted, however, that there is some controversy concerning the role of planning in the missionaries and cannibals problem. Thomas (1974) and Greeno (1974) have argued that the problem is not solved one step at a time, but that groups of steps may be dealt with at once, which is planning in advance. Jeffries et al. argue that their nonplanning model can account for Thomas's results without invoking planning, but the issue may not be completely closed yet. In any case, there may be an important difference between the candle problem and the missionaries and cannibals problem.

A second important difference between these problems involves the need for problem-specific knowledge. The first part of this chapter considered in some detail the specific knowledge involved in the candle problem. If that analysis is correct, people take into account very subtle aspects of the objects involved, aspects which are not given in the problem, but come from the problem solver's knowledge of the objects involved. One such aspect concerns whether or not a nail can be used to attach the candle to the wall. However, there seems to be no such knowledge involved in the missionaries and cannibals problem. Given that a subject can use the words in the problem instructions, then no other knowledge is needed. One does not have to know what missionaries and cannibals *are*, all one has to know is that if there are more of the latter than the former, then one is in trouble. This is not true of the candle problem—if one does not know what a candle is, in some detail, then one cannot do much more than stumble through the problem. Several other move problems have also been studied recently, and these problems also require little in the way of problem-specific knowledge.

In summary, there may be a basic difference between the candle problem and move problems. In the latter problems, the initial state, the goal state, and the possible moves are all precisely defined, and the basic task of the subject is to choose the best move at any given time. In the candle problem, on the other hand, the initial state is precisely defined, but the goal state and the "moves" are not precisely defined. That is, the subject is told to "attach the candle to the wall," but this instruction can refer to several different specific solution methods. The specific interpretation of the problem that a specific subject arrives at is a function of that subject's knowledge concerning candles and the other objects in the problem. Also, the moves that are possible in the candle problem depend on the knowledge of the subject who is working on the problem. For example, whether or not nailing the candle is a "legal move" depends upon what the person knows about candles.

Thus, the very structure of the candle problem depends on the knowledge of the problem solver, which is very different than the case with move problems. Hayes (1978, chap. 11) makes a distinction between ill-defined and well-defined problems. In a well-defined problem, the initial state, the goal state, and the permissible moves are all specified, while in an ill-defined problem the problem solver plays a part in actually defining the various aspects of the problem. Based on these criteria, move problems are well-defined, while the candle problem is not, and there seem to be some basic differences in the way these two sorts of problems are solved.

Computer simulation and ill-defined versus well-defined problems. One of the reasons that move problems are of interest to modern psychologists is that there has been some success recently in programming computers to solve such problems (Hayes, 1978, chap. 10; Newell & Simon, 1972). The most important of these programs may be the General Problem Solver (GPS) of Newell and Simon. This program is an attempt to simulate the behavior of humans by using the computer. That is, the programmers hope to write their programs in such a way so that the typed output of the computer looks like, or simulates, the verbal output of a person working on the same problem. This goal is different than the goal of simply writing a program which could carry out some task efficiently, such as bookkeeping for a corporation. If one is simply interested in having a computer carry out some task, one is interested in artificial intelligence; if one is interested in having a computer carry out a task in a way similar to that of humans, *including mistakes,* if humans make them, then one is interested in computer simulation. It has been argued that if a computer can do a good job of simulating the behavior of a human on a given task, then the program that is directing the computer at that time is a good theory of how the human carried out the task. That is, if the computer's output matches that of some person, then it is argued that the person may be working under a "program" like that controlling the computer.

GPS solves several different sorts of move problems, using methods similar to those discussed by Jeffries et al. (1977) in their discussion of human performance on the missionaries and cannibals problem. (This correspondence is not surprising, since the theorizing of Jeffries et al. was influenced by GPS.) When GPS is given a problem to solve, the problem is represented in the following way. First, the initial state, goal state, and legal moves are specified. Second, there is a way of determining how similar any two states in the problem are to each other. Finally, the program attempts to apply various moves to the initial state and any intermediate states until the goal state is produced, which means that the problem is solved. In a simplified manner, GPS chooses moves by examining the current state of the problem and comparing it with the goal state. If any difference is noted, the program tries to find a move which can be applied to eliminate this difference. This is done by searching through the problem moves until one is found which will eliminate the difference in question, which results in a new state. If any differences exist between this new state and the goal, attempts are made to eliminate these differences; if no differences exist, the problem is solved.

GPS has been applied to several different sorts of move problems, and has been successful in solving them. There is some question concerning the program's adequacy as a theory of human behavior, however, since Greeno (1974) argues that people working on the missionaries and cannibals problem have difficulties in different places than GPS does. This indicates that the program may not be solving the problem in a truly humanlike manner, since the program does not have the difficulties that humans do. Among other things, Greeno argues that humans are using planning methods to solve the problem, which GPS does not use on this problem. In response to Greeno's criticism, Jeffries et al. argue that their GPS-like model can predict where humans will have difficulties in the missionaries and cannibals problem, and that notions of planning are therefore unnecessary.

In summary, move problems have been important as an area for the development of programs that attempt to simulate human behavior. This work is important in its own right, and also because the notion of computer programs as theories of human behavior played an important role in shaping much theorizing in other areas of cognitive psychology. As one final point, it is interesting to contemplate what would be involved in programming a computer to solve the candle problem in a humanlike way. One is immediately struck by the need to give the program all sorts of detailed information about the objects in question, including their various physical characteristics. This is simply another way of pointing out the differences that may exist between move problems and practical or insight problems.

10.14 Summary

The two situations that were analyzed in detail in the first half of the chapter are very different on the surface: the candle problem is a practical problem involving the manipulation of objects, and picking a move in chess is a much more abstract intellectual problem. However, performance in both cases seems to depend upon the use of past experience as directly as possible. The degree to which a person will be able to directly apply past experience to the problem depends upon the precision of the match that can be made between the problem and situations that have been encountered in the past. To the degree that a new problem doesn't match one's specific knowledge, then one's more general knowledge must be used to fill in any gaps. This is a view that has been presented previously by a

Problem solving

number of theorists, and some of this work was considered. In addition, the processes underlying the use of past experience to solve these problems are of the same sort as those which have been considered in earlier chapters.

At the end of the chapter, a class of problems was considered that may be solved without the need for problem-specific past experience or planning. These move problems were discussed from the point of view of the performance of humans on them, as well as from the point of view of attempts to program computers to solve them in humanlike ways. The candle problem is an ill-defined problem, which requires detailed knowledge for its solution, while move problems are well-defined.

11
Task-specific knowledge and more general knowledge: a consideration of hypothesis-testing models of problem solving

11.0 Introduction

In the situations considered in detail in the last chapter, the candle problem and chess playing, the factor of crucial importance was the person's knowledge of the specific requirements and objects involved in the problem. That is, the discussion was limited almost totally to what could be called problem-specific or task-specific knowledge: knowledge about attaching objects to walls in the candle problem, and about patterns of chess pieces in chess. However, in order to understand the behavior of people when they are trying to solve problems, one must also take into account broader aspects of their knowledge. For example, if a subject in an experiment is introduced to a new problem involving novel combinations of objects, there will be relatively little task-specific knowledge that the subject will have available. In such circumstances, all the task-specific information is acquired during the subject's solution attempts, but as we shall see, the way in which the subject makes use of this task-specific information depends on more general knowledge that is brought into the laboratory by the subject. Thus, in order to understand what the subject does while working on a problem, one must become aware of this other source of information, the more general knowledge that the subject has available. It will be particularly important when we examine "insight" and "fixation" in problem solving, in the next chapter.

In order to appreciate the importance of this sort of information, let us

Task-specific knowledge

consider recent research in the area of concept formation, in which this issue has recently been of some importance. In the last chapter, it was argued that two factors are important in a problem solver's production of a novel solution to a problem. The first of these was the match between the problem and the person's knowledge. The second important factor was the person's assessment of whether a potentially useful solution would in fact work. According to the discussion in the last chapter, this assessment comes about through the person's imagining the solution being carried out. In the present chapter this imaginative factor will not be particularly important, because the problems are such that all potentially useful solutions can be attempted, since they only require that the subject write down a few numbers, or say a word or two, or point at an object. Therefore, this chapter will be concentrating almost exclusively on the kind of information that comes into play when a subject examines a problem in order to determine the sort of solution to be attempted. The main conclusion to be drawn from this chapter will be that scripts (see chapter 3) play an important role in problem-solving experiments. That is, when people come into a problem-solving experiment, or any experiment for that matter, they have definite expectations about the sorts of things that will occur—they have a script. Based on this script, subjects then interpret the events which occur in the experiment. As we shall see in this chapter and the next one, a subject's interpretation plays a large role in determining what he or she does in problem-solving experiments. Indeed, it will be argued in the next chapter that several experimental findings have been misinterpreted by psychologists because they overlooked the script that the subject was using.

Classification problems: a brief history. If one trains a group of animals on some moderately difficult two-choice discrimination, choice of the correct stimulus gradually increases in frequency over trials. For example, if monkeys are shown a black cup and a white cup, with food under the white cup, the group of monkeys will gradually learn to turn over the white cup to get the food. Based on this, it was argued by some theorists that the tendency to choose the reinforced stimulus, and to avoid the nonreinforced stimulus, was gradually being strengthened over trials (Spence, 1936). However, several other investigators argued that group curves were not meaningful summaries of the performance of individual subjects. Lashley (1929) had examined individual results from many rats learning various simple discriminations and found that there usually was a sudden switch from chance performance to virtually perfect performance. In addition, Krechevsky (1932) noted systematic response tendencies before the animals had solved the problem. For example, an animal would make mistakes by consistently picking the left hand stimulus, no matter if it was the correct response or not.

In order to deal with both the suddenness of discrimination learning, and the systematic, though incorrect, presolution behavior, Lashley and Krechevsky assumed that the animal was only using certain aspects of the stimulus to direct its behavior at any time. If the animal chose the wrong aspect of the stimulus (say the position), then it would be incorrect half the time, by accident. It would be correct only when the correct stimulus happened to be at the position that it was choosing. According to Krechevsky, the subject gradually worked its way through the various aspects of the situation until it hit upon that aspect that the experimenter had chosen. When this happened, performance would jump suddenly from a chance level to errorless performance.

Krechevsky (1932) used the term *hypothesis* to refer to the systematic response tendencies that animals exhibited before they solved discrimination problems. Thus, one might say that a "position hypothesis" was dominant at the beginning of training, because an animal consistently chose one position to respond to. Krechevsky made it clear that he was not assuming that the animals were doing anything like consciously testing hypotheses. He used the term only to refer to the response patterns that he found.

Although this hypothesis-testing model was originally formulated to account for discrimination in rats, in recent years it has been applied, with reasonable success, to the behavior of humans solving concept-formation problems. Several variations of the same basic point of view have evolved, but we shall ignore the differences and concentrate on those common features relevant to the discussion in this chapter. The model to be discussed is a distillation of the work of a number of theorists (e.g., Hunt, 1962; Levine, 1966, 1971; Restle, 1962; Trabasso & Bower, 1968). For the present discussion, the problems to be discussed will be referred to as *classification problems,* because this term both accurately describes what the subjects must do and avoids some unfortunate connotations of the term *concept formation.*

11.1 A model of classification based on hypotheses

Let us take a situation such as that in Figure 11.1. The subject is shown the first pair of stimuli and told that *a* is correct. According to the hypoth-

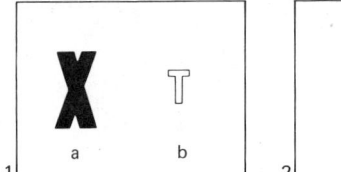

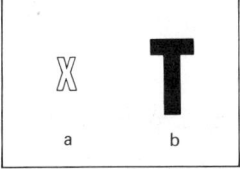

Figure 11.1. Two pairs of stimuli from a classification experiment.

esis-testing model, each of the stimuli is analyzed into a set of attributes. When the attributes of the stimuli have been encoded, the subject uses them as the basis for hypotheses-formation. Let us assume that the subject formulates the hypothesis that X is correct. A second pair of stimuli is then presented, corresponding to the second pair in Figure 11.1. The model assumes that the subject now uses the hypothesis in order to make a choice. Since the hypothesis is that X was correct, the subject will pick *a* in the second pair.

The next assumption of the model is that the subject uses the feedback from the experimenter. If the choice is correct, then the subject stays with the hypothesis. However, if the choice was wrong, a new hypothesis is formulated and the cycle starts again. The way in which the subject uses the feedback from the experimenter could be summarized as a "win-stay, lost-shift" strategy. That is, if your hypothesis about the correct stimulus enables you to pick correctly in a new pair (if you "win"), then stay with that hypothesis. If you do not pick correctly when a new pair is presented (if you "lose"), then try to formulate another hypothesis that will enable you to pick correctly. This cycle of win-stay, lose-shift continues until the subject formulates a hypothesis that happens to match the rule the experimenter is using to determine which stimulus is correct. From that point on, according to the model, the subject will make no further errors.

To summarize, according to the hypothesis-testing model, a subject's performance in a classification problem is based on the hypothesis that has been formulated about the correct stimulus. This hypothesis is used to direct further choices. If these choices are correct, then this hypothesis is retained. If an incorrect choice is made, a new hypothesis is chosen, and the cycle begins again. This continues until the correct hypothesis is chosen, at which point performance becomes perfect.

There are many predictions derivable from this model, several of which will be discussed in the remainder of this chapter. For the sake of brevity, we shall not consider various aspects of the model that are not directly relevant to the present concerns. Interested readers can consult the references listed earlier.

11.2 Formulating hypotheses

Let us now consider some of the factors that enter into a subject's choice of attributes when formulating hypotheses.

Relative salience of attributes. One way that the probability of selecting an attribute can be increased is by making the attribute more salient perceptually. For example, this can be done by physically emphasizing it in some way. One method entails coloring the relevant attribute differently, so that it stands out. Variations of this technique have been used in several studies and were effective. This basis for choosing an attribute will not be considered further, because it is probably relatively independent of past experience.

Acquired distinctiveness. It is also possible to influence a subject's choice of attributes through prior training. Assume that a group of subjects solves a problem based on the color of the objects. The objects are circles and squares, either red or black. In order for the problem to be solved, the subject must use red as the basis for choosing. As an example of specific transfer of a previously-effective hypothesis to a new problem, consider a new problem, containing diamonds and ovals, which could be red or black. It would be predicted that these prior-trained subjects would now pick the red object in each pair, based on the task-specific knowledge derived from the earlier problem.

It is also possible to produce more general transfer from problem to problem, so that the subject will use a previously relevant dimension, even if the specific attribute on that dimension is no longer relevant. For example, if subjects solved a problem by choosing the red stimulus every time, then they might pay particular attention to the colors of the stimuli in subsequent problems, even though none of them may be red. There have been several studies that have demonstrated that past experience influences the dimensions selected on a given problem. Lawrence (1949, 1950) called the generalized influence of past experience the "acquired distinctiveness" of attributes or dimensions, because they could be made more "salient" through past experience.

To summarize, the choice of a given attribute in hypothesis formation seems to be based on past experience with both the specific attribute in question and the more general dimension. These findings are consistent

Task-specific knowledge

with the discussion in the last chapter, in that they indicate that task-specific knowledge will be brought to bear on new problems.

11.3 Complicated solution rules

Selecting attributes is only the first step in solving a classification problem. One then has to combine these attributes into some rule for classifying new stimuli. Until now, the only possible rules we considered were conjunctive rules, in which one or more attributes must be present for an object to be correct. Examples of these are: triangles, black figures, and green squares. Many other solution rules are possible, and the choice of solution rule by the experimenter has a great effect on how quickly naive subjects will solve a classification problem.

Types of solution rules. At least five types of solution rules have been studied, and these are outlined in Table 11.1 A number of studies have indicated that there is an increase in difficulty in solving problems as one goes down the rules in the table. Affirmation rules are the easiest and biconditional rules are the most difficult (e.g., Bruner, Goodnow, & Aus-

Table 11.1. Conceptual rules describing binary partitions of a stimulus population

Rule name	Symbolic description*	Verbal description	Real-life examples
Affirmation	R	Every red pattern is an example of the concept	Any attribute will do: a copy editor, short, blonde, etc.
Conjunction	$R \cap S$	Every pattern which is red and a star is an example	A *volume*: large and bookish
Inclusive disjunction	$R \cup S$	Every pattern which is red or a star or both is an example	An eligible *voter*: a *resident and/or* a *property owner*
Conditional	$R \rightarrow S$	If a pattern is red then it must be a star to be an example; if it is nonred then it is an example regardless of shape	A *well-mannered male*: If a *lady* enters, *then* he will stand
Biconditional	$R \leftrightarrow S$	A red pattern is an example if and only if it is also a star; any red nonstar or nonred star is not an example	An *appropriate piece of behavior*: wearing a cummerbund *if and only if* it is a *formal occasion*

*R and S stand for red and star (relevant attributes), respectively.

tin, 1956; Hunt & Hovland, 1960; Neisser & Weene, 1962; Wells, 1963). However, there is one problem with the studies just cited (Bourne, 1966; Bourne, Ekstrand, & Dominowski, 1971). Producing a solution entails identifying the relevant attributes *and* combining them into a rule. Therefore, if one wanted to examine how difficult it was just to formulate the solution rule, then perhaps one ought to point out the relevant attributes to the subject. In addition, one could tell the subject the possible rules that might be correct. The subject would then be shown positive and negative instances of the unknown rule and would try to determine which rule it was. In this way, one would get some idea as to how difficult it was to formulate each of the various possible rules. Bourne (1967) called this procedure *rule learning*. On the other hand, one could also tell the subject the form of the rule, such that it is conditional, and ask the subject to identify the relevant attributes. This would give an idea of how easily the subject could apply the rule. Bourne called this procedure *attribute identification*.

Why are some rules harder than others? Two sorts of explanations have been offered as to why some rules are harder than others. First, it has been argued that some rules are inherently more complicated than others (Neisser & Weene, 1962). For example, biconditional rules involve both conjunction and disjunction, which should make them harder to process than simple conjunction rules. Second, others have argued that certain rules are more difficult to use because subjects had less practice in using them before they begin working on the problems (e.g., Bruner et al., 1956). The argument is that the types of rules that subjects will formulate quickly and use without error are a result of previous experience in formulating and using rules in other situations. This is based on the idea that the rule for calling certain things "people," for example, is a conjunction rule.

If experience is the crucial determinant of rule difficulty, then giving subjects extensive experience with the harder rules should make them easier to use, and perhaps should make them equivalent to the rules that were easy to begin with. A study by Bourne (1967) was addressed to this question. Subjects were given a series of either attribute-identification or rule-learning problems to solve. All the problems for a given subject were solvable by the same rule, and different subjects had to deal with different rules. As they worked through nine problems, the initially difficult rules became as easy as the others. Indeed, all subjects were performing perfectly on the last three problems. This is strong support for the idea that experience with various sorts of rules is crucial in determining the ease

Task-specific knowledge

with which a subject can use them. This is in accord with the conclusions drawn in the last chapter concerning the use of task-relevant past experience in problem solving. In sum, past experience influences the attributes that will be considered relevant and the way in which they will be combined into a hypothesis.

Strategies and rule difficulty. However, there is still the question of why the various rules are initially of differential difficulty. Bourne (1973) has recently argued that the initial differences in the various rule types comes about because a subject comes to these sorts of problems with a very specific strategy. This strategy works well for conjunctive problems, but does not work well for the other type of problems. Assume that a subject is working on a problem in which two attributes are relevant, and known to be relevant. According to Bourne, the strategy is as follows. The subject first looks for stimuli that contain both of these attributes. These stimuli are assumed to be correct. Stimuli that have neither of the attributes are incorrect, and those stimuli that have only one of the two attributes are also assumed to be incorrect. So if the problem is based on the conjunctive rule, then the subject will perform well.

With the other types of rules, though, the subject will make errors with this conjunctive strategy. For example, if the problem were based on a disjunctive rule, then the stimuli with only one of the two attributes must be called correct. However, the subject's strategy dictates that these stimuli are to be called incorrect. Thus, the subject will be told that he or she is wrong when responding to the stimuli with only one of the two attributes. In order to solve the problem, then, the subject must reorganize his or her choices. This should make disjunctive problems more difficult than conjunctive problems, as indeed they are.

Based on this sort of analysis, Bourne has shown that it is possible to predict the order of difficulty of the various sorts of rules shown in Table 11.1. The predictions are based on the idea that the difficulty of a rule depends upon the number of stimuli which will be incorrectly classified by the initial strategy. The more incorrect classifications, the more reorganization that the subject must carry out, and the more difficult a given rule should be. Supposedly, this initial strategy comes from experience with classifying objects in the real world. Most classifications we make are based on the simple presence or absence of attributes, not on complicated rules. Therefore, these simple sorts of rules will be applied here. Thus, rule difficulties are assumed to be the result of the subject's application of previously acquired "classification knowledge" to these problems.

11.4 Retaining and relinquishing hypotheses

We now have to consider what happens as a subject works through a problem. According to the hypothesis-testing model, if the subject is told that a given choice is correct, then the hypothesis will be retained. If a given choice is incorrect, then the hypothesis will be discarded. This is the win-stay, lose-shift strategy. Although it may seem obvious that any rational person would use this strategy, we shall soon see that "rationality" depends upon the assumptions one is working under.

Win-stay, lose-shift. An important study by Levine (1966) examined the win-stay, lose-shift strategy in detail. The basic design was a classification task with carefully designed stimuli, such as those shown in Figure 11.2. The stimuli were made up of four dimensions: size, brightness, position, and shape, with two attributes on each dimension. The instructions pointed out that the letters would vary on several different attributes, and the correct letter could always be chosen on the basis of *only one* of the attributes. This was emphasized so that the subject would not formulate any complicated hypotheses, but simply stay with the single attributes. The subjects also received a training program, to further insure that they stayed with one attribute at a time.

Once the subject completed the pretraining, the experiment proper began. In order to be able to determine precisely what hypothesis the subject was using, the stimuli were carefully chosen. As an example, consider the four pairs of stimuli in Figure 11.2. The specific attributes are so arranged that each hypothesis produces only one sequence of choices, and the sequence is different for each attribute. Therefore, let's say we tell the subject "correct" on the first pair *no matter what stimulus is chosen*. We can then determine which attribute the subject is using by noting which choices the subject makes on the next four cards, without feedback. The eight possible choice sequences correspond to the eight panels in Figure 11.2. If the subject produced a pattern that did not correspond to one of those in Figure 11.2, it would mean that the model was not correct.

Levine assumed that if the experimenter says "correct" on the first trial and then says nothing for the next four trials ("blank" trials), then the subject will stick with the attribute encoded on trial one. This is "win-stay." After these trials (one "correct" and four blank), the experimenter then said "wrong" on trial six. This should produce a new hypothesis on trial seven. (This is "lose-shift.") Four more blank trials (trials seven through ten) were then given, and it was predicted that the subject would

Task-specific knowledge

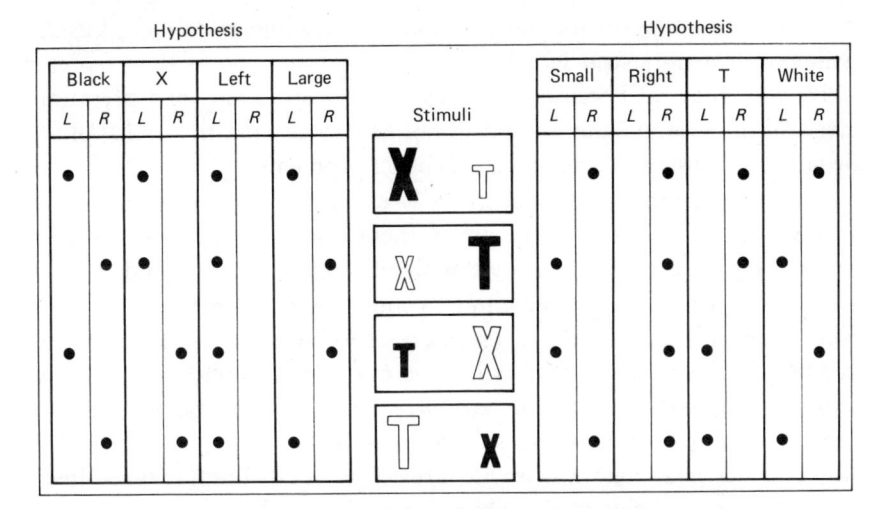

Figure 11.2. Patterns of choices corresponding to eight different hypotheses when the four stimulus pairs in the center are presented. Each column is one hypothesis. Dots represent stimulus which would be chosen (L = left-hand member of pair, R = right-hand). (After Levine, 1966.)

now choose on the basis of this new attribute. On trial 11, the experimenter said "wrong" again, with another switch expected, and four blank trials again followed. Actually, the design was a bit more complicated. We have said that on trial 1, 6, and 11, the experimenter said correct, wrong, and wrong to the subject. In actuality, half the subjects were given this feedback, and the other subjects were told the opposite. Telling the subjects that they were wrong was used to see if the attribute would be switched, and telling the subjects that they were correct was used to test the basic assumption that the subjects would stay with the successful attribute.

The results indicated that over 92 percent of the response patterns corresponded to one of the patterns in Figure 11.2. Furthermore, when the subject was told that a choice was wrong, 98 percent of the time a new attribute was chosen for the next four blank trials. When the subject was told that a choice was correct, 95 percent of the following choices were consistent with that same attribute. Thus, one wrong response "pushed" the subject immediately into a new hypothesis, and one correct response made it virtually certain that the present hypothesis would be retained.

Other examinations of win-stay, lose-shift. Although Levine's results provide strong support for the assumption that subjects do indeed use the win-stay, lost-shift strategy, there is some question as to how representative the study is. Because of the extensive instructions and pretraining given all the subjects, the study does not give us any information about the behavior of naive subjects on classification problems.

Two experiments by Williams (1971) examined the win-stay, lose-shift strategy with naive subjects by giving them a series of problems to solve. In the first experiment, there was a significant deviation found from the win-stay aspect of the strategy, in that more than one-third of the *correct* choices on the first problem of a series were followed by a *change* to a new attribute. However, by the sixth problem, almost none of the correct choices produced a change in attributes. Thus, these naive subjects only gradually came to use the win-stay portion of the strategy. As far as lose-shift is concerned, there was frequent rejection of attributes that resulted in incorrect choices being made, which supports lose-shift.

This study indicates that efficient use of a win-stay, lose-shift strategy may only come about with some practice on classification tasks. This conclusion is also supported by studies performed by White (1974). He tested subjects on a task of the sort used by Levine (1966) and shown in Figure 11.2. However, since Levine's subjects had had extensive training, White decided to look at performance on blank-trials problems as a function of previous experience with similar problems. Various groups of subjects were given from zero to four training problems, in which feedback was given for all choices. They were then given several blank-trial problems. White found that efficient use of the win-stay, lose-shift strategy was a function of previous practice. Subjects with no prior experience did not reject incorrect attributes or retain correct attributes as efficiently as did more sophisticated subjects, who had had practice problems. White argues that various strategies are available to subjects when they are working on classification problems, and one of the reasons that win-stay, lose-shift is used is that it develops out of the subject's experience with such problems.

A recent study by Matthews and Patton (1975) also indicates that dropping a hypothesis following an incorrect choice is not always a straightforward matter. They gave subjects varying degrees of success with a given hypothesis, and then suddenly told them that they were wrong. Subjects who had made many correct choices were more reluctant to give up the old hypothesis than were subjects who had only been correct a few times.

Scripts. These results concerning the win-stay, lose-shift strategy are very

Task-specific knowledge

important for our understanding of problem solving. Intuitively, it seems that all subjects ought to automatically use such a strategy. After all, what could be more rational? The subject has just been told that a choice is correct; surely any sane person would make the same choice again. In the same way, no one who has just made an incorrect choice would make the same choice again. This intuition seems to have been the basis for experimenters postulating the win-stay, lose-shift strategy in their theories.

And yet, research indicates that naive subjects, who are presumably normal and rational people, do not use this rational strategy when they start on classification problems. Why was the experimenters' intuition wrong? The crucial point, and it is a very important one, is that the win-stay, lose-shift strategy is the most rational strategy *only if one knows how classification problems are designed.* That is, if one knows that there is only one correct attribute, and that this attribute never changes, then win-stay, lose-shift is the best strategy. However, the subjects in these experiments do not know this at first, so they will try to use whatever knowledge they have in order to decide what to do on each trial, since they have no task-specific experience available.

This more general knowledge that subjects use could be called the script that the subjects bring with them into the experiment. This script is used to interpret the various events in the experiment. For example, after making a series of correct choices, a subject might suddenly make a new choice, because he or she can't believe that the task could be so simple. Thus, the subject has some expectations concerning difficulty level, which determine how the subject interprets the events in the experiment.

It must be emphasized that all the events in the experiment are essentially ambiguous. That is, the experimenter's telling a subject that a choice is correct can mean many things, only one of which is that the subject has solved the problem. The reason that the win-stay, lose-shift strategy is obvious to the experimenter is because of the script which he or she is using to interpret the events in the problem. However, this interpretation is only one of many that are possible if one doesn't have detailed knowledge about the situation. The subject's interpretation may be equally valid, and may result in behavior which is unexpected from the experimenter's point of view. However, from the subject's point of view, the behavior is completely rational.

The importance of the subject's script, as well as the experimenter's, will be emphasized in the discussion in chapter 12. It will be argued that in many cases experimenters have concluded that subjects are "fixated" or "rigid" or "lacking insight" because the experimenter is ignorant of the subject's script.

Summary. Several studies have shown that subjects do not immediately relinquish a hypothesis if it has produced incorrect choices. If an incorrect choice is made, it seems that subjects must *decide* if a hypothesis shift is warranted. If the information available to a subject indicates that it is better to stay with the same hypothesis and try again, then a shift will not occur. On the other hand, if the subject's knowledge indicates that a single incorrect choice means that a hypothesis just won't work, then the hypothesis will be dropped. Therefore, the win-stay, lose-shift strategy is just one specific example of the application of past experience to a present problem. Subjects make use of their knowledge in order to interpret the events that occur as they work on a problem.

11.5 Summary and conclusions

This chapter has been concerned with the hypothesis-testing model of performance on classification or concept formation tasks. The model assumed first that subjects formulate a hypothesis about the solution of the problem. It has been found that past experience can influence both the attribute or attributes selected for hypothesis formation, and the way in which these attributes are combined into a possible solution rule.

A second assumption of the model was that a hypothesis was retained only so long as it produced correct choices. One incorrect choice was assumed to result in immediate rejection of the hypothesis that produced it. This assumption was found to be in need of modification, because whether or not an incorrect choice results in immediate rejection of a hypothesis depends upon the past experience of the subject. Subjects who have extensive experience with classification problems, and/or who have received detailed instructions about the problems, will reject a hypothesis after one incorrect choice. Naive subjects may not do so. The reason that naive subjects do not always retain or drop hypotheses in the most efficient manner seems to be that they are applying broader knowledge to the experimental situation. So long as subjects do not possess sufficient task-specific knowledge to enable them to interpret the events in the experiment, then they will apply this broader knowledge, or script, to the experiment. This point of view will be applied to several different types of problems in the next chapter.

12
"Insight" and "fixation" in problem solving

12.0 Introduction

Chapters 10 and 11 have been a straightforward discussion of the role of past experience in problem solving. We have seen that if we take into account the various types of knowledge that people bring to problems, we can understand the things that they do when they work on problems. In some cases this knowledge is relatively problem-specific, while in other cases the knowledge is of a broader scope. It seems that the crucial determinant of whether or not a person's script comes into play is how much the person knows about the specific problem in question. As we saw in the last chapter, once people have some experience with classification problems, they then use win-stay, lose-shift. It is only when they don't have any specific knowledge, at the beginning of the experiment, that they rely on their broader experience. However, it should be noted that the literature regarding problem solving, particularly practical problem solving, is much more confusing and difficult to deal with than the discussion so far has indicated. Much of this confusion comes about because of a lack of coherent theoretical principles. At present, research in practical problem solving, or "insight" problems, is dominated by the residue of the work of Gestalt-oriented psychologists, who used quasi-perceptual explanations to account for the behavior of their subjects on various problems. However, as mentioned in chapter 10, this theorizing has not had an appreciable effect on other psychologists, and as a result, much work in practical problem solving sits in isolation from the rest of cognitive psychology.

The last two chapters have shown that it is possible to understand some aspects of problem solving in a straightforward manner, by considering what people know and how they apply this knowledge to the problem in front of them. The present chapter attempts to extend this analysis to what have been called "insight" problems, which have been the main area of interest of Gestalt-oriented psychologists. The term "insight" is sometimes taken to mean that one solves such problems by "seeing into" the structure of the problem in a flash of illumination. Supposedly, this insight enables one to produce a truly creative solution, one which is relatively independent of past experience. As indicated at the beginning of chapter 10, "insight" and several other terms are used only in explaining problem solving, and the use of these terms may have helped to isolate this area. In order to deal with this research from the present point of view, it must be demonstrated that such notions as insight are either not truly different from the concepts employed in other areas in psychology, or are not helpful in understanding problem solving. The notion of insight is really a combination of two separate ideas. We shall see that one of the uses of insight is compatible with other work in psychology. In addition, we shall argue that the second use of the term insight, which has become the dominant one, is not helpful in understanding problem solving.

The insight versus trial-and-error controversy. Over the years, there have existed two opposing philosophies of problem solving, differing in terms of the reliance placed on past experience as the explanation of problem solving. On the one hand were associationistic psychologists, who felt that problem solving entailed the rather direct use of past experience. It was assumed that a problem could bring forth past experiences in either of two ways. First, if a new situation was a repetition of an old one, then it would directly call forth experiences that had been associated with it in the past. Second, if a new situation was not a direct repetition of an old situation, but was similar to some old problem, then it would call forth past experiences through generalization. If a new problem was neither a direct repetition of an old one, nor similar to an old problem, then the problem solver would have nothing to do and would behave randomly.

Psychologists influenced by Gestalt psychology, on the other hand, were more impressed with the creative aspect of problem solving. It seemed to them that in some cases a problem solver would produce a solution not related to past experience, but totally new. In addition, in some cases subjects produced these novel solutions after sitting quietly and contemplating the problem. This indicated that problem solvers did not simply randomly behave until they hit upon a new solution. Rather, their solution attempts were directed toward the source of the difficulty, indicating that they had analyzed the problem and were directing their efforts toward the core of the problem. Let us now briefly trace the history of this dispute to enable us to draw some conclusions about one of the uses of the term insight in explaining problem solving.

12.1 Trial-and-error

The early experiments of Thorndike (1911) were presented as examples of problem-solving behavior in which solution of a *new* problem began with random, trial-and-error responses, and only gradually changed into an efficient solution. Thorndike placed hungry cats in closed cages, the doors of which could be opened in some cases by hitting a pole inside the cage that released the latch, or in other cases by pulling a string. A dish of food was visible to the cat outside the cage. Thorndike noted that the animals made many energetic responses, such as clawing the sides and roof of the cage, moving around the cages as best they could, and hissing. When the animal accidentally happened to hit the pole and so opened the door, it seemed as startled as the experimenter. The next time the cat was put into the cage, the whole sequence began again. Only after many attempts did the animal quickly go over to the pole, push it, and leave the cage. On the basis of these studies, Thorndike argued that random behavior is produced at first, and that the response that accidentally (as far as the cat is concerned) produces food is automatically strengthened.

This idea was expanded by Hull (1930, 1931) into the habit-family hierarchy, which was applied to human problem-solving explicitly by Maltzman (1955). The essential notion is that any problem situation has conditioned to it several responses (or habits) of varying strengths, based on differing numbers of past reinforcements. Thus, we have a family of habits organized into a hierarchy. Of these habits, the strongest will be elicited by the situation. If the strongest response doesn't solve the problem (doesn't produce reinforcement), it will be decreased in strength (extinguished). Sooner or later, the once-dominant response will extinguish to a level of strength less than that of the response that was initially the second strongest. This response will now be the strongest, and so will be given. This cycle continues until an originally weak response becomes strong and can be used to solve the problem. The basic assumption behind all this is that the subject has the solution available in his repertoire. The problem is just to get to it by getting the stronger responses out of the way.

As a concrete example of this type of explanation, we can consider the candle problem. If we give the candle problem to a large group of subjects, we get several different solutions given as the first solution. It would be assumed that this represents the habit-family hierarchy of previously conditioned responses. Therefore, the reason that the box solution is given infrequently is because it is a weak response to this situation. However, it might be argued that people have never nailed candles to walls, so how could this response have been previously reinforced? In answer to this, the notion of generalization is brought forth. The subject has nailed similar things, so the response generalizes to candles. This discussion is a bit simplified, but gets at the essentials of associationistic explanations of problem solving.

Criticisms of Thorndike: insight. Thorndike's work received much criticism from Gestalt psychologists, among others. These psychologists argued that animals could exhibit insight when solving new problems. As it was first used by Kohler (1917) in his discussion of animal problem solving (Mandler & Mandler, 1964), insight meant that an animal would not behave blindly: The responses that would be made would be relevant to the problem at hand.

We can, in our own experience, distinguish sharply between the kind of behavior which from the very beginning arises out of a consideration of the structure of a situation, and one that does not. Only in the former case do we speak of insight. . . . (Kohler, 1917, p.190)

Based on this notion, it was argued that Thorndike's experiments were inadequate as studies of insight in problem solving for several reasons. First, the cages were so designed that they opened in a way which was unrelated to the cat's previous experience. In such circumstances, it was difficult if not impossible for the animal to bring insight gained from past experience to bear on the problem. Second, the string that had to be manipulated by the animal was placed in such a way that it was unobtrusive, so there was little chance that it would even be noticed by the animal. Third, Thorndike's analysis of the behavior of the animals as "random"

"Insight" and "fixation" in problem solving

was questioned, because, for example, the cats spent a lot of time in the vicinity of the door of the cage, which would not seem to be random. Thus, there might have been some insight exhibited after all.

These last few points were supposedly raised by Gestalt psychologists in criticism of associationistic theories of thinking. However, if one looks at these points carefully, the most impressive thing is how similar they are to the notions advanced by associationistic theories. For example, according to the advocates of insight, the cats could not show insight because the puzzle box was too different from their previous experience. This seems to be very similar to saying that if the present situation is too dissimilar from past experiences, then no generalization will occur and random behavior will occur.

Kohler's studies of the mentality of apes. In any case, Kohler (1917) attempted to show that apes could demonstrate insight in solving complicated problems of various sorts. One such problem concerned using sticks to rake in a banana that was outside the animal's cage, beyond reach. On one occasion, one of the apes put two short sticks together to make a longer one and used this to retrieve the banana. There are two important aspects concerning this performance. First, it was argued that the "need" to make a long stick, or the insight into the problem, was directing the animal's behavior. Secondly, before using the sticks, the animal had not fiddled with them in a random, trial-and-error manner, but had sat quietly, then acted directly.

However, the demonstration of insight by Kohler's subjects may have been more dependent upon past experience than Kohler realized. His subjects had not been raised from birth in captivity. Therefore there might have been some relevant past experience that had occurred before the animals were captured. Birch (1945) attempted to replicate Kohler's findings using animals that had been raised from birth in captivity, and found no evidence for widespread insight. Most of Birch's subjects fumbled with the sticks and seemed to have no insight whatever into the potential usefulness of the sticks in solving the problem.

This seems to be a further indication that to say a solution comes about through insight into a problem is at base the same thing as saying that a solution can be transferred to a new problem through generalization.

Reproductive versus productive thought. A second point of conflict among theorists concerned with problem solving, which is very similar if not identical to the question of trial-and-error versus insight, is the distinction between *reproductive* and *productive* thought. In the former case, problem-solving is seen as involving nothing more than recall of the relevant information from memory. For example, answering the question, "What is your phone number?" is pure reproduction. On the other hand, some kinds of problems were assumed to necessitate the recombination of past experiences in ways that had never been experienced. This was productive thinking, and it was of great interest to Gestalt-oriented psychologists. For example, use of the box as a candle holder in the candle problem is productive thinking, assuming it has never been done before.

However, once again, if the point of view in chapter 10 is at least generally correct, then there is not a dichotomy between reproductive and productive thinking. Rather, there are degrees of reproductivity and productivity involved in all problem solutions. If we go back to the earlier discussion this can be clearly seen. If a problem is not recognized as being familiar, then there is a search for situations of the same general class, and so on. If match is made, then a solution will be produced which is novel for this subject in this situation. This is by definition an example of productive thought. However, the solution comes from recall of the solution of another problem, which is reproductive thought. Therefore, a productive solution involves reproductive thought, *but it is reproduction of a solution for another problem.* That is, one reproduces an earlier solution and applies it to a new problem because the new problem has some critical characteristics in common with the old problem.

Trial-and-error versus insight: summary. One of the controversies in the history of the psychology of thinking concerned the role of insight in problem solving. One difficulty with resolving this controversy comes from the fact that there have been at least two distinct uses of the term insight that have evolved over the years. On the one hand, to say that a problem solver exhibits insight is to say that the problem solver's knowledge plays a role in determining the solution that will be attempted. In this use of the term, one has insight into a problem to the degree that one has knowledge that is relevant to the problem. The present discussion was concerned with this use of the term. Thorndike's research, which allegedly did not demonstrate insightful behavior, was considered, as was some of Kohler's research, which allegedly did. It was argued that these supposedly opposite points of view were really saying the same thing, so that there was really no controversy involved. We can now consider the second use of the term insight.

12.2 Insight as sudden illumination

As mentioned, Kohler (1917) had reported that his ape subjects sometimes sat quietly for a while, "contemplating" a problem, before suddenly producing a solution. This sudden production of a solution impressed many people, and the term insight was also used to refer to it. According to this point of view, a creative or productive solution to a problem came about suddenly because the subject had a sudden insight into the structure of the problem. This usage of the term insight is almost literally "in" + "sight," in that it is assumed that the subject's perception of the problem changes.

Consider the reversible cube in Figure 12.1. This object can undergo "spontaneous restructuring" as it is looked at. In an analogous manner, Gestalt theorists argued that a problem can undergo spontaneous restructuring as it is worked on. The problem is then viewed from a "new perspective," as are the objects in the situation. When this occurs, a novel solution can quickly appear. Insightful restructuring of a problem can be interfered with by what is called "fixation" (Scheerer, 1963). "If insight is the essential element in intelligent problem solving, fixation is its archenemy. Fixation is overcome and insight is attained by a sudden shift in the way the problem or the objects involved in it are viewed" (Scheerer, 1963, p.128). The remainder of the present chapter will be concerned with an analysis of several problem situations in which fixation supposedly interferes with efficient problem solving.

Figure 12.1. A reversible cube; if viewed steadily for a short while, it will spontaneously "reverse" in depth.

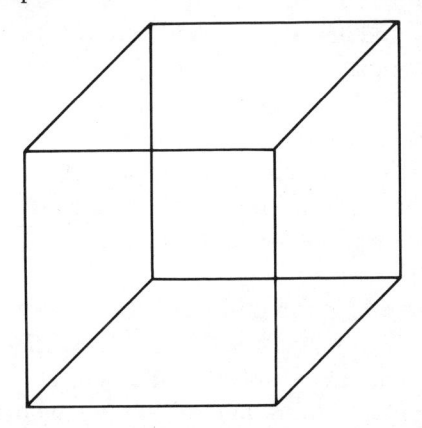

12.3 Water-jar problems

There is one type of fixation problem on which more subjects have probably been tested than on all other problems of any sort, combined. These are the famous water-jar problems, investigated extensively by Luchins (1942). In this case, the fixation is called *problem solving set*. The purpose of the present discussion is to apply the same sort of analysis to water-jar problems as was applied to classification problems in chapter 11. We shall see that we can understand what people do in this situation also if we make some plausible assumptions about their knowledge and how they attempt to apply it to the experimental situation. We shall conclude that the notions of insight and fixation are neither necessary nor helpful in understanding problem solving set. The problem for theoretical interpretation arises because sometimes the theorist disregards or is unaware of the information that the subject is using, especially the subject's script.

An example. Studies of problem solving set usually entail two groups of subjects: the set group and a control group. Both groups are first given a series of training problems. For the set group, the training problems are all solved by the same general method; for the control group, each training problem is solved by a different method. As specific examples, problems 3 through 7 in Table 12.1 are all solvable by the $B - A - 2C$ method and by no other. A control group would have a different solution for each of these problems.

After the training problems, a single series of test problems is given to both the set and control groups. In Table 12.1, the test problems are problems 8 through 12. Problems 8 and 9 can be solved in either of two ways: the set method or a more direct method. Problem 8 can be solved by $B - A - 2C$ or $A - C$, and problem 9 can be solved by $B - A - 2C$ or $A + C$. These problems are called critical problems because of their multiple solutions. Most people who have been given a set training series, such as the series in Table 12.1, solve problems 8 and 9 using $B - A - 2C$. (See "results," bottom of Table 12.1) They do not "see" the more direct $A - C$ or $A + C$ solution until it is pointed out to them. This use of an indirect solution at the expense of a more direct one is assumed to be an example of fixation.

Problem 10 in Table 12.1 is a different kind of test problem, because it cannot be solved by $B - A - 2C$. It is called an extinction problem because the set solution must be "extinguished" if the subject is to solve the problem. Control subjects have no trouble solving the extinction problem, but

"Insight" and "fixation" in problem solving

Table 12.1. Water-jar problems.
You are given jars labelled A, B, and C, and an unlimited amount of water. Use the three jars in combination to produce the required amount of water. Assume that you cannot estimate amounts: any jars must be filled to the top.

Problem	Jars (capacity in quarts) A	B	C	Required	Solution
1	29	3	—	20 quarts	A-B-B-B (Fill A, empty water into B three times; 20 quarts left in A.)
2	21	127	3	100	B-A-C-C or B-9C
3	14	163	25	99	B-A-2C
4	30	57	4	19	
5	18	43	10	5	
6	9	42	6	21	
7	20	59	4	31	
8	23	49	3	20	
9	15	39	3	18	
10	28	76	3	25	
11	18	48	4	22	
12	14	36	8	6	

Some typical results (unpublished data)

Problem	Set Group	Control Group
Critical 1 (set solution)	.84	.12
Critical 2	.82	.08
Extinction: nonsolvers	.34	.05
Critical 3 (set solution)	.30	.06
Critical 4	.25	.08

a large proportion of set subjects do not solve it. This is also assumed to be an example of fixation.

Problems 11 and 12 in Table 12.1 are also critical problems which can be solved in more than one way. As with the earlier criticals, the set subjects use $B - A - 2C$ more frequently than control subjects do.

To summarize, the phenomenon of problem solving set occurs when a previously successful solution is applied to a new problem, to the exclusion of a potentially simpler solution.

Set and fixation. Much of the research on water-jar problems has come from the Gestalt interest in insight and fixation. It has been assumed that set is one type of fixation, which interferes with productive solutions to problems (Scheerer, 1963). Luchins and Luchins (1959), for example, are interested in set because they feel that it produces rigidity in behavior. As one example of rigidity, Luchins and Luchins (1959) consider the fact that an experimental subject will use the $B - A - 2C$ solution on a critical problem, thereby being "blind" to the simpler solution that is available. Also, many experimental subjects fail to solve the extinction problem because they keep trying to apply the $B - A - 2C$ solution to it; this is another example of rigidity. The feelings of Luchins and Luchins are made clear in these passages.

Why do people persist in behavior when it is no longer useful? Why do they hold on to their accustomed patterns of behavior when other more efficient ones are available? Why do they sometimes repeatedly manifest behavior which is destructive and self-defeating? . . . Examples are legion of man acting through force of habit, of his mastering a habit so well that it in turn masters him. (p.1)

One of the objectives of modern education is to educate the individual that, while he has a repertoire of certain habits, he does not become a mechanized robot, but instead is flexible enough in his behavior to meet the need of a changing dynamic world. (p.2)

Saying that "the habit masters the individual" implies that the subject behaves without thought, simply by rote habit. We shall argue in this chapter that nothing could be further from the truth. Subjects who use the set solution, and who produce a complicated solution for a seemingly simple problem, are being totally rational and thoughtful. A rational, thoughtful, person is using all the information available in order to decide how to behave in a given situation. The reason that the experimenter might want to say that such a subject is behaving without thought is because the experimenter does not know the information that the subject is using. Once again, the problem is with the experimenter, not the subject.

12.4 The subject's interpretation of the experiment: math test scripts

Let us now consider in more detail just what might be happening as a subject works through a series of water-jar problems, all of which have a similar format and the same solution.

Repetition of B–A–2C. When the experiment begins, we instruct the subjects that we are going to present several simple math problems. It is assumed that since the subjects have not tried to solve a series of water-jar problems before, they have no knowledge about solving this exact sort of problem. However, students (who make up most of the tested subjects) have a relevant script: a series of simple math problems is a math test. Most important for the present discussion, this script tells the subject that *each problem is independent of the others.*

When the very first water-jar problem is presented, the subjects try to combine the jars in various simple ways, based on what they know about numbers, and a solution is produced. When the second problem is presented, the subjects pay little or no attention to the specific solution from the first problem and go to work on the second problem. Much to their surprise, the solution turns out to be the same. This raises a problem for the subjects, because it means that their feelings about these problems, based on past experience with somewhat similar problems, are incorrect: all the problems are not independent. The subjects now must make some sense out of that repeating solution before going further. That is, a new script is now called into play by the repetition of the $B - A - 2C$ solution.

The subject's interpretation. It is important to realize that the repetition of the $B - A - 2C$ solution is an ambiguous situation. On the one hand, if the subjects feel that this experiment must be an intelligence test, or something of that sort, then they will think that the purpose of the repetition is to see if they will discover it and use it later. Therefore, once they see that the set solution keeps repeating, they will immediately apply it to all later problems in the series, including the criticals. On the other hand, the subjects might suspect that the repetition of the $B - A - 2C$ solution is really a trick. Such subjects would carefully scan each problem to see if there is any catch involved before trying the $B - A - 2C$ solution. These subjects would then produce the direct solutions on all the test problems.

Thus, it seems that set experiments are much more complicated than usually assumed. These sorts of problems are such that subjects have relevant knowledge which can be applied to them and this knowledge influences how the subject will respond to the repetition of the $B - A - 2C$ solution. In Table 12.2, an outline is presented of the ways in which subjects might interpret the various crucial events in a series of water-jar problems. The two interpretations of the repetition of the $B - A - 2C$ solution, which were just discussed, are shown in the second column, and the subsequent behavior on the first two criticals is indicated. Table 12.2 could be looked upon as a summary of the application of various scripts to the water-jar situation.

Table 12.2. Critical events and possible interpretations.

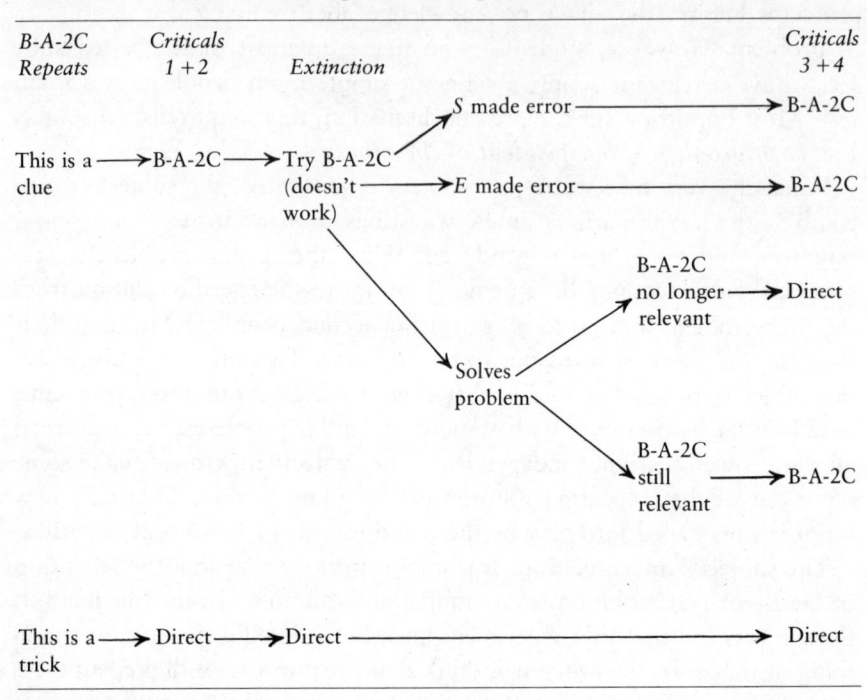

B-A-2C Repeats	Criticals 1 + 2	Extinction		Criticals 3 + 4
This is a clue	→B-A-2C→	Try B-A-2C (doesn't work) → S made error → E made error → Solves problem	B-A-2C no longer relevant → B-A-2C still relevant →	B-A-2C B-A-2C Direct B-A-2C
This is a trick	→ Direct →	Direct		Direct

12.5 Extinction of a set

The next important event is the extinction problem, as far as the subjects who have adopted the set are concerned. (For the subjects who assume that the whole thing is a trick, then there really is not an extinction problem at all.) The subjects who have adopted the set will try to use the $B - A - 2C$ solution, and then will find that it does not work on the extinction problem. This calls for a new interpretation. There seem to be at least three alternative interpretations possible for the failure of $B - A - 2C$ on the extinction problem, as outlined in Table 12.2 At first, most subjects seem to think that they must have made a simple computational error and they therefore try the solution again. Since there is a limited amount of time given on each problem, some subjects will still be trying to make sure their calculations are done correctly when time runs out. These subjects will assume that they have made a math error, and the set solution will still be relevant. They will then use it on the next two criticals. In essence, their set has not been extinguished.

If the subjects feel that they made no error in their calculations, they may decide that the experimenter made an error in designing the problem and that this problem has no solution. The extinction problem has not extinguished the set in this case either.

Finally, there are subjects who do solve the extinction problem. However, this simple fact may not mean that the set is abandoned once and for all. The subjects still must interpret this new piece of information; that is, the $B - A - 2C$ did not work on the last problem after having worked on all the others. Once again, there seem to be two possible interpretations here (see Table 12.2). First, the subjects might assume that this failure of the $B - A - 2C$ solution means that it will no longer be relevant. They will then probably revert to the method that they brought into the experiment with them, which was to try to combine the jars in various simple ways in order to produce the desired amount. These subjects will then solve the other two criticals directly. On the other hand, subjects might assume that even though the set solution was not correct on one problem (the extinction problem), that problem was put in by the experimenter to try to throw them off. Therefore, the set solution might still be relevant. These subjects would then first try the set solution on the other two criticals, and when it works they would never produce the direct solution.

12.6 Relevant data

This position brings with it many predictions concerning the behavior of subjects in these sorts of experiments. First of all, the basic prediction is that if one knew the subjects' attitudes toward the experiment, then one could predict which subjects would resist using the set solution because of their suspicions of a trick. Two experiments have attempted to do this. One study concerned anagram sets (Rees & Israel, 1935) and the other concerned water-jar problems (Luchins & Luchins, 1959). Both studies found that "accepting" subjects produced more set solutions on critical problems than "suspecting" subjects did, which supports the present interpretation.

Instructions and set use. If it is true that subjects' assessments of ambiguous events are critical in determining whether our set will be adopted, and if subjects were instructed about the significance of these various events before they occurred, so they were no longer ambiguous, then there should be strong effects on their behavior. Luchins and Luchins (1959, chap. 13) report several experiments of this sort. In one experiment, subjects were given detailed descriptions of exactly what was going to occur in the experiment, so that the "trap" in the criticals was clearly demonstrated as something to be avoided. This almost totally eliminated the use of the set solution. In other experiments reported by Luchins and Luchins (1959 chap. 11), subjects were explicitly told that the set solution was a rule for solving all the problems. Under these conditions, schoolchildren showed very strong set effects. In addition, one group of elementary school children were told that there was a simple rule for solving all the problems that they would see. They were given only *one* set-training problem, followed by criticals and an extinction problem, and very strong set effects were found. Thus, if one can provide a reasonable interpretation of the repetition of the set solution, which implies that the solution is of value, then it will be used almost exclusively on critical problems, and subjects will have great difficulties in solving an extinction problem.

In summary, there are several experimental results available that support the present interpretation, in that factors that seemingly influence the subjects' interpretations of the experiment also influence set use. It also follows from the present interpretation that if subjects came into the laboratory with no expectations about what would happen on a string of problems, then a set should be established very quickly. Let us consider some research from a related area which is relevant to this prediction.

Learning-set research with monkeys and humans. Harlow (1949) investigated the performance of animal subjects on a series of similar discrimination problems. Adult rhesus monkeys were given 344 two-choice discrimination problems, spread out over several sessions. In such a problem, two objects are presented, say, a circle and a square, and food is always under one of them, say, the square. The subject must learn to pick up the square all the time to get rewarded all the time. These sorts of problems are similar to the classification problems discussed in the last chapter. In the study to be considered, each problem was presented for a total of six trials. If the subject was not performing perfectly after the alotted number of trials, the next problem was presented anyway. It is conceivable that when the alotted trials were completed, the subject still might not have solved the problem. If so, this would mean that the subject would not have much additional knowledge in memory to apply to subsequent problems. No attempt was made to control the stimuli; they were chosen randomly for each of the various problems.

The results of this well-known experiment showed that on the later problems, the animals made no efforts after the first trial. If the correct

"Insight" and "fixation" in problem solving 301

stimulus were accidentally chosen on the first trial, then the animal stayed with it for the rest of the trials. If the object chosen on the first trial did not produce food, then the animal chose the other stimulus on all the remaining trials. This improvement in performance over a series of learning problems is called a learning set.

Harlow also presented results from experiments with children, in which it was shown that they could also acquire a learning set. There have been many studies that have further investigated learning sets with humans. One particularly important study from our point of view was carried out by Reese (1965) using preschool children as subjects, and discrimination problems. The first problem was presented until the subject was correct on five consecutive responses. Only then was the second problem presented, and so on. Under these conditions, it only took *one problem* to bring the children up to perfect performance on subsequent problems. This finding is exactly what would be predicted based on the present interpretation. Since the subjects were preschool children, they had no expectations about either discrimination problems or experiments. Therefore, the only relevant information would be what was acquired from the first problem, which should lead to perfect performance on the second problem. Bourne (1967) reported a similar finding with human adults, which was discussed in section 11.3.

12.7 Direct solutions by control subjects: what does the subject bring to the experiment?

One phenomenon concerning set experiments that has only been discussed in passing is the performance of the control subjects. Most of the control subjects, who have had a training series with varied solutions, solve critical problems by producing the more direct solution, and have no trouble with an "extinction" problem. (Obviously, it is not really an extinction problem for these control subjects, because by definition they have nothing to extinguish). However, when examined closely, the performance of control subjects raises a question. It is often pointed out that the *set* subjects do not "see" the simple solutions to the critical problems until they are pointed out. But no one ever asks *why the control subjects do not "see" the $B - A - 2C$ solutions to the same criticals*. It is probably exactly the same reason as why the set subjects do not see the direct solutions.

Using problem 12 from Table 12.1 as an example, the values are A:13, B:35, C:3, get 16. A control subject examines the sizes of the jars and immediately produces $13 + 3 = 16$, thereby solving the problem. (This problem is also solvable by $B - A - 2C$.) How and why does the control subject go through these simple manipulations? One thing control subjects seem to try to do is to combine jars in pairs, or three at a time, in order to produce the required amount. They also try to subtract one jar from another to determine if the required quantity is thereby produced. To put it a slightly different way, control subjects use their knowledge of numbers. (This idea was suggested to me by Louis Scavo.) That is, the subjects make estimates concerning the relative magnitudes of A, B, C, and the solution, and from this estimate what kind of an operation is needed. These estimations and operations are part of the subjects' knowledge concerning arithmetic problems in general.

If this reasoning is correct, then we come to an interesting conclusion concerning control subjects, as was mentioned earlier. *The control subjects are also influenced by a set.* They are also using past knowledge, or a script, to work on a present problem. The experiment is interpreted as an arithmetic test, and there is no reason to change the interpretation while working. Therefore, one could argue that there is no real difference between set subjects and control subjects.

Set and fixation. As indicated earlier, much set research stems from interest in fixation (Scheerer, 1963). As an example of this point of view, here is what Ray (1967) has to say about set: "under a certain . . . set the subject carries out arithmetic procedures on given numbers *but he does not stop to think what he is doing*" (p.49). However, based on the discussion in the last section, it is obvious that control subjects are behaving no differently than the subjects who automatically use the set solution. It is just that the control subjects are using *less efficient* solution methods, because their past experience does not fit the present problem specifically enough. Therefore, the set subjects are performing on a much more sophisticated level, and much more efficiently. The reason that the control subjects must "stop and think" is because the solution method they are using forces them to do so. That is, if the method being used by control subjects is something like: "Compare each jar with the required amount, and take the jar that is closest in value," then the subjects will sit quietly and "think about what they are doing." But they are still using past experience, just like the set subjects who immediately try $B - A - 2C$.

Therefore, it seems to be incorrect to conclude that subjects who use the set solution automatically are not thinking. They are thinking, and very efficiently, too. The reason for saying that set subjects are not thinking seems

"Insight" and "fixation" in problem solving   303

to be the result of shortsightedness on the part of the experimenter. The *experimenter* knows about the possibility of simple solutions to some problems, and therefore is surprised when the subjects do not realize that they exist also. But how could the subjects come to such a realization? They could reach this realization by examining the values in each problem carefully and trying to combine them in simple ways. But we have just presented several problems to convince the subjects that all they should do is consider the gross characteristics of the problem and then apply $B - A - 2C$, so of course a direct solution is never seen. Once again, it seems that the subject is being nothing if not reasonable and "thoughtful." One reason that fixation may be attractive as an explanation of the performance of set subjects is because it seems necessary to deal with facts like the following: set subjects can look at 20 and 3 and not see that they equal 23 (see problem 8 in Table 12.1). Surely some external factor must be blocking the automatic recognition of such an obvious solution to a problem. However, this orientation overlooks that fact that "seeing" that 20 and 3 are 23 is not a completely automatic process; and since the set subjects are thinking about another aspect of those numbers, their simple sum will not be noticed. Once again, it is not that the set subjects are not thinking, it is just that they are thinking about something other than the simple sum of the numbers.

Much recent research has been conducted by Levine and his colleagues (e.g., Levine, 1966; Fingerman & Levine, 1974) on "unsolvable" problems and the partial reinforcement effect. Levine's work is very similar to the position advocated here.

12.8 Levine's research on unsolvable problems

Consider the following problem. A subject is presented with a card with two letters on it, A and B. The subject's task is to pick the correct letter every time. The solution is simple: pick A. If such a problem is presented to a naive subject, it is solved easily. However, it is easy to make it very difficult to solve the "pick A" problem. Before giving the simple problem to subjects, Levine (1966; Fingerman & Levine, 1974) presented several other problems. In these problems, the solution is always some complicated position sequence, such as left-left-right-left-right-right-right. This sequence would recycle throughout the problem. If the subject did not solve any of these early problems, the solution was demonstrated. The simple pick-A problem was then presented, and a large majority of experienced subjects *failed to solve it*. Levine (1974) argues that the reason that subjects with prior experience fail to solve the problem is because of the information they have available from the early problems. From the early problems, the subjects have concluded that these problems are solvable only by complicated sequences of choices. They then try to work out some complicated sequence that will solve the pick-A problem. Obviously, there is no such sequence, but the subjects do not know this. Furthermore, since there are very many possible sequences that can be tested, the subjects work and work and never solve the problem.

One interesting aspect of these results is that when subjects try to work out complicated sequences for the simple pick-A problem, they will pick A and be correct about half the time by chance. However, these reinforcements do not increase the tendency that A will be chosen on later trials. At first glance, this finding may seem paradoxical, because if picking A is the only choice that is ever reinforced, perhaps subjects should start to pick A all the time, since B is never reinforced. Apparently, however, the important thing is not the specific choice that is being made, but rather the sequence that is being worked on. So long as the subject believes that some correct sequence will produce *errorless* performance, the fact that one stimulus is reinforced more than the other is irrelevant and has no effect on subsequent choices.

The partial-reinforcement extinction effect. Another seemingly paradoxical situation investigated by Levine (1974) concerns the effect of partial reinforcement on the extinction of a simple choice response. Assume that subjects are presented with cards with two letters on them. The subjects are to pick the correct letter on each card. For one group of subjects, the solution is to pick the A every time. For a second group, each of the two letters is correct on 50 percent of the trials, and on each trial the correct letter is chosen randomly. Therefore, this version of the problem is impossible to solve, although the subjects are not told this. The group with the pick-A problem solves it easily. The other group works through the random sequence, trying to solve the problem. Of course they cannot do this, and they are correct for picking A about half the time and correct for picking B about half the time.

After this experience, all subjects are switched to a problem in which B is always correct. Based on their earlier training, the pick-A subjects have received many reinforcements for picking A. According to a straightforward reinforcement notion, it ought to be much harder for the pick-A subjects to switch to the pick-B solution, because A has been reinforced so many times. The random group received relatively small numbers of reinforcements for picking either A or B. Therefore, the pick-A response is not very strong, which should make it easier for it to be extinguished. Thus, based on reinforcement alone, one would predict that the random subjects should extinguish their weak pick-A response faster than the other group.

The paradoxical finding is that this does not occur. The group that has been consistently reinforced for picking A now switches to picking B significantly faster than the group that wasn't consistently reinforced for either choice. Levine (1974) explains this result by assuming that the pick-A subjects have learned that a very simple solution is possible on these problems. Therefore, when pick-A is no longer correct, they switch to another simple solution: pick-B. The random subjects, on the other hand, have already tried and rejected simple solutions to the first problem. Therefore, they will not now return to simple solutions, but will keep trying to crack the code in a complex way. This explanation is the same as that advanced in the last section. Meyers (1969) has proposed a similar type of explanation for phenomena of this sort.

In summary, Levine argues that subjects use information from earlier problems in a manner similar to that proposed here. If they get a series of complex problems, they assume that the remaining problems will be complex, and this can result in failure to solve a problem that the experimenter knows is very simple.

12.9 Problem solving set: summary

An attempt was made in these sections to demonstrate how one could account for the major facts concerning problem solving set on the basis of the decisions that subjects might make as they worked through a series of water-jar problems. These decisions are important because there are several ambiguous events which occur in set experiemnts, and naive subjects must use their more general knowledge to decide what these events mean. This general knowledge corresponds to the scripts discussed in the last chapter and in chapter 3.

12.10 Insight problems and fixation

The water-jar problems are not the only situation in which Gestalt-oriented psychologists argued that fixation was occurring. Over the years, a group of "insight" problems has appeared in the literature. Although these problems are not uniform as regards subject matter, it has been argued that similar processes are involved in the solution of all of them. Basically, it is argued that one solution to each of these problems is different than the others because production of that solution requires true "insight" into the problem.

The analysis of these problems will be based on several factors. First, it will be shown for several problems that the reason the subject is late in producing the "insightful" solution is because the subject is too busy solving the problem. That is, the Gestalt psychologists were so busy looking for insight or the lack of it that they overlooked what their subjects were doing. Second, it will be shown that one does not need to postulate insight in order to explain why some subjects produce the "insight" solution to these problems. Plausible explanations can be produced that are based on the more or less direct use of past experience. Third, it sill be shown that for some problems it is highly unlikely that naive subjects could ever produce the insight solution, because that solution is in reality a very complex one. Therefore, the subjects do not possess the relevant task-specific knowledge, and invoking fixation to explain the lack of this solution would seem to be beside the point. Fourth, it will be shown that, in their eagerness to demonstrate fixation, the Gestalt-oriented investigators sometimes designed problems that could not be solved with the insight solution, if the subject followed the instructions. Once again, the notion of insight is not helpful in such circumstances. Finally, it will be shown that in some problems the production of the insight solution depends on the subject's making a critical assumption about the usefulness of the various objects in the situation. However, in most cases, subjects would not make this assumption, because of the script that they bring with them to the problem, and thereby would not solve the problem. Once again, the difficulty is that the psychologists have overlooked the knowledge that the subjects are applying to the problem.

12.11 The two-string problem

This problem, illustrated in Figure 12.2, requires that the subject tie together two pieces of string hanging from hooks in the ceiling. The strings are set far enough apart so that it is impossible to reach one while holding the other, but the subject isn't told this. Various objects are available, such as a ball of twine, a weight, a 12-inch ruler, and a bar of soap. After sev-

"Insight" and "fixation" in problem solving

Figure 12.2. The two-string problem.

eral futile attempts at grasping the second string, the subject realizes that the simple reaching operation cannot be performed.

Maier, who has done much research with this problem, has classified the solutions usually obtained into four types (Maier, 1930):

1. *Anchor.* One string is tied to a heavy object, such as a chair, which is used to hold it at a midpoint, and the second string is brought over to it.
2. *Extension.* One of the strings is lengthened, as with an extension cord, and the other is reached with the hand.
3. *Hook.* Something is used to increase the subject's reach, so that the second string can be reached.
4. *Pendulum.* Something is tied to one string to make it serve as a pendulum, and the other string is brought to the middle, where the pendulum string is caught. This solution, which is relatively infrequent, is looked upon as a solution based on "insight." According to Maier, the subjects must perceive the string not as a string, but as a pendulum. This can

come about supposedly when the subjects "restructure" the situation, and perceive the problem as one in which they must get the string to come to them rather than reaching for the string.

According to the present point of view, all these various solutions would arise directly from the subjects' attempt to solve the "reaching" problem. The extension and hook solutions are straightforward, in the sense that when one wants to get something that is out of reach, there are only a couple of methods which come to mind: reaching for it with some instrument to extend one's reach or pulling it in towards you by attaching a string to it. These two solutions then follow relatively directly. The anchor solution is a bit more complicated, and may arise as the subject works on the problem. For example, a subject who is in the position in Figure 12.2 might imagine what would happen if the first string were momentarily let go while reaching for the second. The need for an anchor then follows immediately.

Since these solutions follow relatively directly from the way in which the problem is presented, then most subjects will begin with them. Therefore, any other solution, such as the pendulum, must wait until subjects are finished with these more direct solutions. As with the box solution in the candle problem, subjects may never get to the pendulum solution because other solutions "get in the way."

Pendulum solution. There seem to be two ways in which the pendulum solution might arise. In the first place, let us consider again the subject who is reaching for the second string and not having success. "Leaving" the first string in the center will not work since the string will not stay, because it is a string. But given this knowledge about the hanging string, one also realizes that when the string is released it will swing away and then swing back a bit. Thus, the two strings can be brought to the center at the same time, if one is efficient. So here is a relatively straightforward basis for the pendulum solution. It arises from what any reasonably sophisticated human being would seem to know about hanging strings.

A second way in which the pendulum solution might arise can be seen more clearly if we change Maier's terminology a bit. The pendulum solution could more easily be conceived of as a *swing* solution. It does not seem far-fetched to assume that in this problem, with the requirements of bringing the string closer, a hanging string would remind subjects of previous situations in which they were standing waiting for a swing to come to them. The pendulum solution would then follow rather directly.

"Insight" and "fixation" in problem solving 309

In summary, our analysis indicates that there seem to be two plausible and testable hypotheses for production of the pendulum solution. In addition, it can be argued that subjects who do not produce the pendulum solution for the problem aren't fixated at all. Rather, they are using their knowledge to produce other solutions which solve the problem just as well.

12.12 Hat rack problem

This problem has also been extensively investigated by Maier (1945), and is presented in Figure 12.3. The subject is given two boards, of unequal length, and a C-clamp. The task is to make a hat rack strong enough to

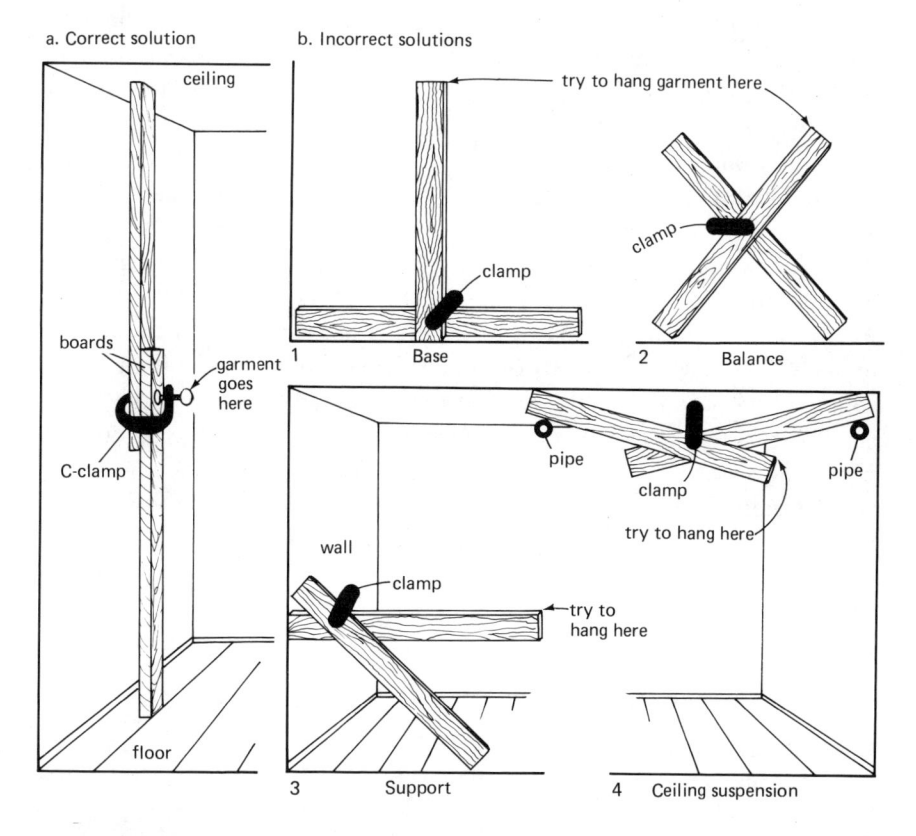

Figure 12.3. a. Correct solution to hat rack problem. b.1–4. Incorrect solutions frequently attempted.

hold a heavy garment without falling. (The problem should be called the "clothes rack" problem.)

This problem has only one correct solution. The solutions usually attempted are also shown in Figure 12.3. The floor-ceiling solution, the only workable solution, is either produced late or not at all by most subjects. Only about 50 percent of college students solve the problem, and only 10 percent do so on their first solution attempt.

This problem is a good example of how an interest in fixation in problem solving influences the choice of problems that one works on. The incorrect solutions in Figure 12.3 (base, balance, support, ceiling suspension) follow from attempts to model structures from past experience, and the problem is so designed that they will not work. Once again, early solutions must be eliminated before the crucial solution can come to the surface.

Here again there is reasonable speculation possible about how the floor-ceiling solution might come about. First of all, this solution is very infrequently given as an initial solution. Therefore, it may ultimately arise as a modification of an earlier solution seen as inadequate.

In addition, when this solution is considered in some detail, it seems very unlikely that most people would simply think of it directly. First of all, making a longer board out of two short ones is probably not something that would be thought of directly because most of us have never had occasion to do this. Second, as the problem is presented, there is no reason for the subject to believe that a long pole is needed, which also makes it unlikely that such a construction would be thought of. The floor-ceiling solution is very complex, and the fact that many subjects do not produce it is not surprising. If one examines the situation from the subject's point of view, one sees that many different pieces must fit together, both literally and figuratively, before this solution will be produced. Thus, saying that the subject is fixated overlooks all these factors.

To summarize, in this problem also there may be relatively direct explanations for the production or lack of production of the really novel solution.

12.13 Scheerer's studies of fixation

In an article which has been widely referred to, Scheerer (1963) examines several problems in which it is assumed that insightful problem solving is interfered with by fixation. Although he does not present many data on several of these problems, they are intriguing problems, and it is interesting to examine them.

Connect-the-dots. This problem is presented in Figure 12.4. The goal is to connect all the dots by drawing four continuous straight lines without lifting the pencil from the paper. The lines may cross each other. The only requirement is that there be four continuous straight lines, drawn without lifting the pencil from the paper.

The reason most people never solve this problem, according to Scheerer, is that they assume that the lines must stay within the outlines of the figure formed by the dots. This is an incorrect assumption, and is the basis for the fixation, from Scheerer's point of view. According to Scheerer, if this incorrect assumption could be eliminated, the nine-dot problem should become very easy to solve. However, let us look at the problem from the subjects' point of view: even if the subjects decide that simply connecting the dots as in a children's game will not solve the problem, *they still don't know what will solve the problem.* When one considers it, it is really very sophisticated to set up a line at just the right angle, and so on. Indeed, even after they have been shown how to solve this problem, many subjects cannot later reproduce the solution. This is evidence for the complexities involved. Thus, we have here an apparent example of the experimenter mistakenly taking for granted that the insightful solution is easy; but this doesn't seem to be so at all. In addition, there is experimental evidence to support these criticisms. Two studies (Burnham & Davis, 1969; Weisberg & Alba, 1979) have demonstrated that the nine-dot problem is not a simple problem made difficult by "fixation" on the shape of the dot pattern. In both these studies, some subjects were told that the only way to solve the problem was to go outside the square. This instruction did eliminate the fixation, in that all subjects did go outside the borders of the

Figure 12.4. Nine-dot problem and solution.

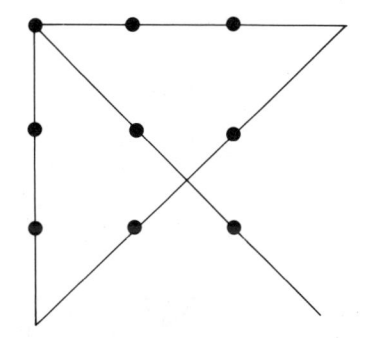

square with their lines. However, 80 percent of these subjects still did not solve the problem, indicating that the nine-dot problem is in reality a very difficult problem, and fixation on the shape of the square is not a crucial aspect of the problem.

Triangles. The problem is to make four triangles, using six wooden matches, with a match being a side of a triangle. The matches cannot be broken. The solution is shown in Figure 12.5. Again, very few people solve this problem. Indeed, from our discussion, it would be predicted that very few people would ever solve this problem without external help. The only way in which past experience might be relevant would be if the subject had knowledge concerning the geometry of a tetrahedron. There is experimental evidence to support this analysis also (Weisberg & Alba, 1979).

In sum, in these last three problems, the hat rack, nine-dot, and triangles problems, the lack of the insight solution seems to be due at least in part to the complexity of that solution, rather than "fixation" on the part of the subject.

12.14 Duncker's radiation problem

Duncker (1945) also investigated insight and fixation in problem solving. He developed a number of different problems that were used to study how subjects arrived at solutions when their past experience was not directly applicable. One of these, the radiation problem, is presented in Figure 12.6.

One point of particular interest is that Duncker's presentation of the ra-

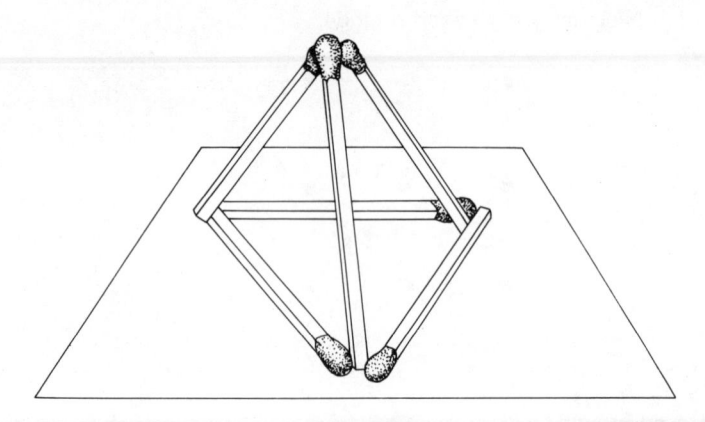

Figure 12.5. Solution to triangles problem.

"Insight" and "fixation" in problem solving

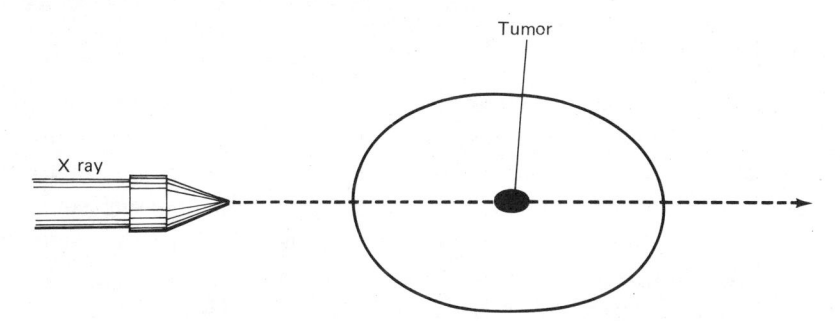

Figure 12.6. Tumor or X-ray problem. A person is suffering from an inoperable tumor. That is, if the person is cut in any way, he or she will die. All that is available are X rays, which at sufficient intensity will kill the tumor. However, at this intensity the X rays will also kill healthy tissue, which will also kill the patient. Is there any way to destroy the tumor and save the patient?

diation problem itself produces a very important difficulty: if the instructions are followed to the letter, then the "correct" solution is impossible to carry out. Duncker sometimes presented the diagram shown in Figure 12.6 to the subjects working on the problem. But, according to the diagram, it is impossible to solve the problem in the way Duncker considers best, which is to use two weak bundles of X rays, crossed just at the tumor, because the diagram shows only a single source of X rays. This is an example of an experimenter's bias getting in the way of his or her consideration of the situation that is presented to the subject.

According to the present point of view, solution of the radiation problem should proceed in the following way. Most people have some familiarity with the use of X rays to destroy cancerous tumors, so that knowledge would be used. However, subjects should assume that only one X-ray source is available, because when most of us have been in the presence of X-ray equipment, such as in a doctor's or dentist's office, there is only one machine present. This makes the problem unsolvable. So it would be predicted that the subject would first have to be told that more than one source of X rays is available before any real progress could be made, and even then progress could be limited by people's lack of knowledge about what can be done with X rays. There is some evidence to support this contention (Weisberg, 1979).

In summary, both the subject's knowledge and the way this problem is usually presented make the problem unsolvable.

12.15 Functional fixation

There are several other types of "fixation" which have also been investigated. One of these is assumed to come about because of the prior use of an object. If a common object is first used by the subject in its usual way as part of a problem, then it turns out to be more difficult to subsequently use this object in a novel way in order to solve the problem. This could be called fixation by function, or functional fixation.

An experiment by Scheerer (1963), presented in Figure 12.7, will be used as an example of the alleged influence of functional fixation on problem solving. (Duncker, 1945, also did research in this area.)

The insightful solution to the problem in Figure 12.7 is to tie the two sticks together with the piece of string that is holding up the object on the far wall. When the problem is presented with the string simply hanging over the nail on the wall, all subjects solve the problem (Scheerer, 1963). However, if the string is used to hold up a current calendar, a usable mirror, or a "No Smoking" sign, over 50 percent of the subjects failed to use the string. If the string holds up a piece of blank cardboard, an *old* calendar, or a cloudy mirror, however, then everyone uses the string to tie the two sticks together. Scheerer (1963) mentions that all the subjects quickly noted that a string would solve the problem, but even so, subjects still spend 20 minutes without using the "obvious" string if it was holding up something useful.

In this experiment, the functional fixation effect would presumably occur when the subject is searching the environment for a string, as reported by Scheerer (1963). Although Scheerer doesn't consider it, it is reasonable to assume that this search of the environment must be based on the implicit assessment as to whether or not a given object is to be assumed to be part of the problem. For example, the subject will probably not use the shoelace of the experimenter to tie the two sticks together. This is because when the experimenter says "Use anything," they don't really mean *anything;* they mean "any of these objects that have been made available to you." Therefore, if it looks as if an object has a prior purpose, the subject will assume it is not relevant to the problem.

In this way, Scheerer's results can be tentatively explained. When the string holds up a "No Smoking" sign, etc., then the subject assumes that it is not relevant to the experiment. In the case of an old calendar, or a blank piece of cardboard, or dull mirror, there would seem to be more chance

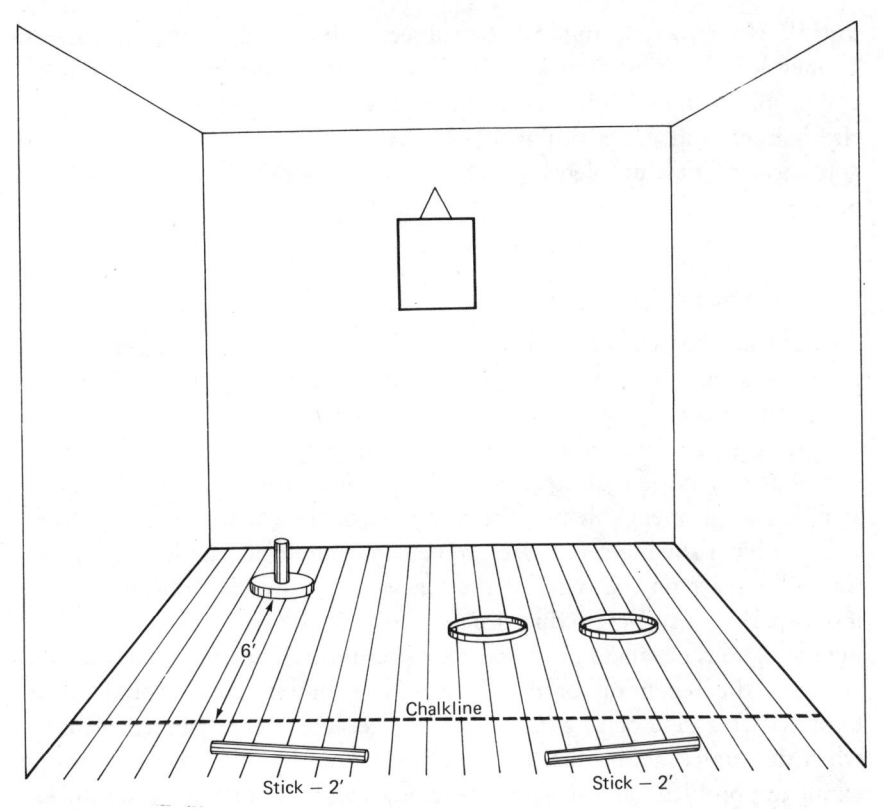

Figure 12.7. Scheerer's functional fixation problem. The problem is to get the two rings on the peg, without throwing them or moving the peg, while standing behind the chalk line. The individual sticks are not long enough to reach the peg while standing behind the line. While working on the problem, the subject is free to move around the room. However, when actually putting the rings on the peg, the subject must be behind the chalk line.

that the subject would see no purpose in the object, and so assume that it is relevant to his present problem.

If these speculations are correct, then the notion of functional fixation should be changed to one concerning "assumed relevance to the problem at hand." Thus, we have here a case in which the subject does not use the critical object because the subject is using a different script than that of the experimenter. However, it must be emphasized that the subject's script is at least as reasonable as that of the experimenter, and perhaps is more reasonable. Therefore, saying that the subject is fixated seems to be incorrect. As mentioned earlier, Duncker (1945) also examined performance on several problems in which functional fixation was alleged to occur (the paperclip, gimlet, and pliers problems). However, the present analysis is also applicable to these problems, which were not discussed here for the sake of brevity.

12.16 Summary

This chapter has examined a number of problems that were assumed to require insight for solution. If subjects did not produce the "insightful" solutions for these problems, the lack of success was attributed to fixation of various sorts. The main theoretical conclusion drawn from this chapter was that the notion of fixation does not add anything to our understanding of problem solving. The first part of the chapter was concerned with problem solving set. It was argued that one could understand problem solving set on the basis of the scripts that subjects bring with them into experiments. These scripts are used to make several decisions concerning ambiguous events in the water-jar experiment. The first major decision concerns the repetition of the $B - A - 2C$ solution, which could be interpreted as a clue or as a trap. Similar decisions were assumed to occur when the subject found that the $B - A - 2C$ solution did not work on the extinction problem, and when another problem was presented after the extinction problem. A number of different sorts of evidence were discussed that support this viewpoint, and it was concluded that set subjects should not be described as being fixated.

The analysis of other insight problems indicated that there were several different reasons for subjects either not producing the "insightful" solution at all for a given problem, or producing it late. First, most of these problems could be solved in multiple ways. If a subject chose a "noninsightful" method and it proved effective, the subject might stop at that point and never get to the "insightful" solution. The subject was not fixated, he or she was just successful and satisfied. Second, in some cases the "insightful" solution was very complex, and its production was beyond the capacity of a naive subject. Third, in some cases the physical appearance of the problem implied that certain objects were not available to the subject for use in solutions. If the insightful solution depended upon the use of this object, the solution would never be produced. Once again, the notion of fixation seems to be misplaced here. Finally, in some cases the insightful solutions

"Insight" and "fixation" in problem solving 317

could not be produced if the subject correctly followed the instructions. Once again, attributing the lack of these solutions to fixation indicates a misunderstanding of what the subject was trying to accomplish. In conclusion, it seems possible to understand much of what subjects do on these problems simply through a consideration of what the subjects know and what they are trying to do.

12.17 Summary of part 4

To summarize the discussion of the last several chapters, it seems that as subjects work through problems, they are constantly using their knowledge to decide what to do next. These decisions depend upon the match that can be made between the problem and the information stored in memory. In some cases, the match is relatively exact, as when a subject possesses relevant task-specific knowledge. In other cases, there is no task-specific knowledge available, so subjects must rely on more general knowledge, acquired in other situations. This knowledge, to borrow Shank's term (1975), is called a script.

FIVE
Cognitive development

13
Cognitive development I: thinking in infancy

13.0 Introduction to part five

The area of cognitive development has been of great interest to psychologists recently, for several reasons. One important issue concerns the question of qualitative differences in cognitive functioning between children and adults. The main impetus in this area has been Piaget's work in cognitive development. As is well known, Piaget argues that qualitative changes occur during cognitive development: infants think differently than young children, who in turn think differently than older children and adults.

The main purpose of this chapter and the next one is to examine some selected topics in cognitive development from the point of view developed in the earlier chapters. We shall argue against Piaget, that there are no basic differences between adults and children as far as thought processes are concerned, except that children may be less efficient than adults are. In addition, in some cases children behave differently than adults do because they lack the information available to adults. The discussion will be very similar in spirit to the analysis of problem solving in part 4. It will be argued that in order to understand what infants and children do, one must first take into account what they know, and one must also consider what infants and children can do with what they know.

One problem with a discussion of this sort is that the distinction between qualitative and quantitative change is very hard to make. That is, two people can look at the same results, and one person will see qualitative change where the other sees only quantitative change. Therefore, the point of the next few chapters is to present a reasonably simple and coherent point of view, so that the reader at least has an alternative viewpoint on some phenomena in cognitive development. The mode of argument in the next two chapters will be to analyze several phenomena in order to demonstrate that the reason that children behave differently than adults in various situations is that they lack the necessary knowledge. For several of the phenomena in question, plausible reasons will be advanced as to why the children lack this knowledge. In addition, it will be argued that the processes whereby children deal with the environment, and whereby they "think about" the environment, are no different than those of adults, which have already been extensively discussed. The ultimate choice will then be up to the reader.

The present chapter will be concerned with cognitive development in infancy, the next with the development of concrete operations during childhood. Chapter 15 will apply the present analysis to language development, another important area in cognitive development. It will be argued that the development of language depends upon the development of the child's ability to efficiently process sentences, in terms of pattern recognition, and on the child's capacity to efficiently produce words as needed. The fact that children produce utterances that sound exotic from an adult point of view is because they have less available to say because of their limited processing capacities. Finally, chapter 16 will present the outline of a model of the internalization of thought, which will center on infancy, and will attempt to tie together several themes developed so far.

13.1 A brief outline of Piaget's theory

Piaget began his scientific career as a biologist, and his theory of mental development is strongly biological in its philosophy. For Piaget (1966), the development of intelligence is considered to be the highest form of the adaptation of an organism to its environment, which entails two subprocesses: assimilation and accommodation. Consider a familiar example of adaptation in the biological world. An amoeba comes in contact with a particle of food and extends pseudopods in order to encircle it. Once this is completed, the food is broken down and incorporated into the amoeba. This entire act is one of adaptation of the amoeba to the environment, and it can be broken down into the components of assimilation and accommodation. The ultimate breakdown and incorporation of the food by the amoeba is assimilation. That is, the amoeba assimilates the food into itself. However, the assimilation could not have occurred unless the amoeba had first accommodated itself to the food particle. This accommodation permits the complete assimilation of the environmental object.

There is also one further component which is prior to the active accommodation of the amoeba to the food particle. If the amoeba was not sensitive to the presence of the food particle in the first place, then nothing further would have occurred. This sensitivity to the presence of food can be looked upon as a primitive assimilation of the external object, because the object is "taken in," in the sense that it produces activity in the amoeba. This activity comes about because the structure of the amoeba is such that a food particle nearby produces an irritation that results in the extension of pseudopods, and so forth. So the complete cycle is: primitive assimilation, accommodation, complete assimilation.

This analysis can also be applied to the development of intelligence in human beings. The basic mechanisms whereby primitive assimilation comes about are the reflexes with which humans are born. If the appropriate environmental stimulus is presented, the reflex will occur. Since the reflex does not occur to just any input, Piaget argues that the environmental situation must match the structure of the organism before the reflex is given. In Piaget's terms, the environmental event must be assimilated to the structure of the organism before a response can be given. According to this reasoning, it is meaningless to say that a given environmental event is the "stimulus" for a response. If the organism was not constructed in the way that it is, then there would not be a response given in that situation.

The further development of intelligence comes about through the elaboration of these reflexes into schemas. A schema is a class of responsees which evolves out of a reflex. For example, the reflex of visual fixation evolves into the schema of looking, and the reflex of sucking evolves into the schema of sucking. These schemas serve as the basis for responding to new objects. Presentation of an object to a three- or four-month-old infant results in the infant's reaching for and grasping the object, looking at the object, shaking it, putting it in his mouth. The object is responded to through its being assimilated to the various schemas. This occurs because the object meets the requirements for application of the various schemas.

However, once a schema, such as the sucking schema, has been applied to a new object because of the object's being assimilated to the schema, the schema must still be accommodated to meet the specific characteristics of the new object. Thus, the initial assimilation of the object to the schema results in the schema's accommodation to the object. This accommodation, or change in the application of the schema, results in the new object's being completely assimilated. After some experience with the new object, the infant will automatically respond to it in the way that just fits it. This interplay of assimilation and accommodation occurs throughout life, as new situations are constantly being encountered and adapted to.

At first glance, Piaget's theorizing would seem to be very similar to the position being advocated here, in the sense that Piaget sees behavior as being the result of the interaction of the child's knowledge and the external situation. However, this similarity is misleading, because Piaget wishes to argue that qualititave changes occur with development in the ways that children deal with the world. One important consequence of Piaget's biological orientation is that development is seen as a progression through a series of stages, or periods, similar to those that are seen in the development of an embryo. In cognitive development, three major periods have been isolated. They are: sensorimotor intelligence (0–2 years), preoperational and operational thought (2–11 years), and formal operations (11+ years). Each of these large periods is divided into a number of smaller stages and substages. In the present chapter the various stages as outlined by Piaget will be used as convenient markers, without dealing with the question of whether it is possible to actually parcel cognitive development into stages.

13.2 Sensorimotor development: the major phenomena

The newborn infant can be considered to be at a point of zero intelligence. Two years later, the young child can deal effectively with the physical objects in the environment, and also gives evidence of being able to "think about" objects that are not present; that is, in Piaget's terms, to symbolize objects.

Stage I: reflexes (0–1 month). As already mentioned, the human infant comes into the world equipped with some simple reflexes, such as sucking, grasping, and visual following. The very first time a reflex is produced, it is simply a mechanical response to an appropriate event in the environment. Thus, in theory, there is no adaptation here, because the events that are responded to are determined by the inherited structure, and the response that is produced is simply the mechanical reflex. In actuality, however, this

Cognitive development I: thinking in infancy 325

so-called zero point in intelligence is really impossible to isolate, because one sees modification of the basic reflexes from the very beginning. As an example of the adaptation that quickly takes place in the use of reflexes, Piaget (1963) discusses the changes exhibited by his son Laurent in sucking. Immediately after birth, Laurent began to suck whenever his own hands accidentally touched his lips. Thus, the reflex is set off by contact of the lips with an object. On the third day, Laurent's lips touched the skin surrounding the nipple, but not the nipple itself. He then began to search for the nipple with his mouth open (the "rooting reflex"), but his movements were misdirected. However, at 12 days of age, when his lips touched the skin of the breast, he quickly rejected it. He then searched in the correct direction until he found the nipple. Thus, by about two weeks of age, if sucking was not followed by a full mouth and swallowing, the hungry child stopped sucking and began searching to find another object to suck. In these episodes, one can see the beginnings of adaptation and intelligent behavior.

Stage II: the primary circular reactions (1–4 months). In the second stage, one sees clear evidence of the modification of actions in order to accommodate them to the specific environmental situation. In this way, the specific environmental event can be assimilated. The ultimate response that is produced in such a situation is one that was not produced before; it is one that was "created" to meet the special needs of the present situation, although the new response is only a small step from the old one.

One new development seen in this period is the primary circular reactions. The general term *circular reactions* refers to responses that are repeated again and again. The primary circular reactions are repeated acts centered around the infant's own body. For example, early in life, most infants begin to suck on their own lips, protrude their tongues, and drool saliva. These are primary circular reactions that evolve out of the sucking reflex. Similar things occur with other responses. For example, crying evolves into circular reactions of sound production. The reflexive closing of the hand when the palm is touched evolves into grasping, and also into the circular reactions revolving around the child's touching his or her own body.

One very important point to note about the all circular reactions is that initially they occur by accident. The child will produce some result by chance, such as drooling saliva while nursing. Due to the repetitive, reproductive nature of these response systems, the activity will be repeated again and again, as a primary circular reaction. Ultimately, the response will become a firmly established schema. A second important aspect of all the circular reactions is that they stop almost as suddenly as they start. An infant may spend a large proportion of its waking hours doing something like kicking its feet, when it suddenly stops doing it. A new reaction will then occur.

One other very important phenomenon that occurs during this stage is the beginning of intercoordination of various schemas, such as grasping and sucking, and vision and grasping. The initial primary circular reactions involving grasping are independent of other schemas. For example, the child will grasp something that the hand comes into contact with and will look at something in the environment. However, the child will not try to grasp what he or she is looking at. The beginnings of what Piaget calls reciprocal assimilation among schemas can be seen with grasping and sucking: objects that are in the mouth are touched. This becomes a complete reciprocal assimilation between sucking and grasping: anything that is sucked is touched, and vice versa.

In summary, out of the primitive attempts at accommodation with which the stage begins, the primary circular reactions form the basis for the beginnings of interrelationships among the various response systems.

Stage III: secondary circular reactions (4–8 months). The secondary circular reactions are repetitive actions, like the primary circular reactions. They differ from the primary circular reactions in that they are directed toward the environment, rather than the child's body.

The secondary circular reactions evolve out of the primary circular reactions. Piaget argues that in carrying out the primary circular reactions of pulling, shaking, and so on, the child must come to realize that the rattle he or she is grasping also makes a sound. Once this surprising event occurs, the new response will be repeated. It will then become a secondary schema.

These secondary circular responses provide the basis for an important development in the child's ability to deal with objects: motor recognition. When the child sees a familiar object, instead of actually performing actions on the object, the child may only outline the actions that would be performed. Piaget argues that the child at this point cannot recognize objects by simply thinking about them. The schema that serves as the basis for recognition must be carried out, at least in part. This is the precursor of recognition by thought alone.

Stage IV: the coordination of secondary schemas and their application to new situations (8–12 months). In this stage, the child begins to combine

Cognitive development I: thinking in infancy

two previously separate secondary circular reactions in order to solve simple problems. For example, if a desired toy is seen extending from under a blanket, the child will remove the blanket to get at the toy. In order to carry out such a coordination, the child must have established a means-end relationship between the two secondary reactions. The pushing aside of the blanket is the means to the end of grasping the toy. Thus, a good deal of planning is involved here, and one can see clear evidence of intention on the part of the child.

Stage V: tertiary circular reactions and the discovery of new means by active experimentation (12–18 months). The tertiary circular reactions are still another class of repetitive reactions, which involve repetition with variation. The child begins by carrying out some familiar secondary circular reaction, but breaks off in the middle to try out some variant of it. This is especially useful in the coordination of schemas in order to solve a problem. The Stage IV child simply coordinates old schemas to try to solve the problem. If they do not work, they will simply be tried again and again until the child loses interest or cries. In Stage V, if an initial coordination of schemas does not solve a problem, then the child will actively accommodate the schemas to meet the needs of the situation. One sees trial-and-error problem solving here, just like with animals or adult humans in situations in which they do not have specific knowledge that can be applied.

Stage VI: invention of new means through mental combination (18–24 months). In Stage V, as discussed, the child produces novel solutions to problems by actively accommodating the schemas while working on the problem. This is seen by an observer as overt trial-and-error behavior. In Stage VI, however, the child no longer responds to a problem by actively trying out variations on what he or she initially started with. If something the child is trying to do will not work, the child now is able to sit and think about the problem, and to invent a solution through covert, rather than overt, activities. Piaget argues that in order to do this, the child must be able to represent objects and actions internally, so that those "internalized objects" can be "manipulated" in a manner analogous to the actual manipulation that occurred in Stage V.

There are two points that should be mentioned here. First, there are obvious similarities between this analysis and the discussion of practical problem solving in chapter 10, particularly section 10.8, when we considered how problem solvers assess the adequacy of a potential solution to a problem. In that case also it was argued that people use their knowledge to "think out" a solution before actually attempting it, and this knowledge was assumed to arise from actual experience manipulating the objects in question.

The second point concerns Piaget's "symbolist" conception of thinking. Piaget argues that the ability of a child to mentally solve a sensorimotor problem depends on the ability to symbolize the objects in question, so they can be manipulated in the child's imagination. Based on the extensive discussion in part 3, especially chapter 7, it should be noted that one does not have to believe that images serve a symbolic function in order to believe that imagination is important in problem solving. One can work out a solution in one's imagination without "contemplating" one's images. Thus, there are two issues here, one concerning imagination and the other concerning symbolization, that should be kept separate.

In summary, the sensorimotor period ends with the child able to think, at least about actions and objects in the physical world. However, this ability comes about as the result of a long period of activity, which starts with mechanical reflexes and only gradually develops.

13.3 The object concept

As already emphasized, Piaget argues that cognitive development evolves out of the interaction of the organism and the environment. If so, then the adult's conception of the physical world, consisting of separate objects occupying space and existing independently over time, must be the result of the development of many levels of schemas over the course of the adult's development. Therefore, infants, whose schemas are much less differentiated and integrated than those of adults, should not conceive of the world in the same way as adults do.

According to Piaget, it is only at the end of the sensorimotor period that children have the concept of a world made up of physical objects, with the child's own body as one of these objects. At the beginning of sensorimotor intelligence, it is not possible for the infant to conceive of separate objects that have an independent existence. This state, wherein there is no differentiation of the self from the external world, is called egocentrism. The infant is egocentric because the primitive schemas have not become differentiated enough to permit the child to conceive of external objects that have an independent existence. Piaget analyzes the development of the object concept according to the six substages of the sensorimotor period.

Stages I and II: reflexes and primary circular reactions (0–4 months). Although the infant in these stages can be described as acting upon objects,

Cognitive development I: thinking in infancy   329

one would not want to conclude that from the infant's point of view there are objects that are being acted upon. According to Piaget, environmental events cease to exist when the infant is not interacting with them. When an object that the child has been playing with is removed, the child makes no attempt to recover it. During the first few months, the child may not even follow it visually for more than an instant.

Stage III: secondary circular reactions (4–8 months). During this stage, the child will reach for visible objects and will go after an interesting object if it is partially hidden. However, if an object is completely covered, the child will not search for it, even if he or she has just been playing with the object in question. The following observation from Piaget presents a graphic example of the sort of thing that occurs.

Obs. 28. At 0;7(28) [0 years; 7 months; 28 days] Jacqueline tries to grasp a celluloid duck on top of her quilt. She almost catches it, shakes herself, and the duck slides down beside her. It falls very close to her hand but behind a fold in the sheet. Jacqueline's eyes have followed the movement, she has even followed it with her out-stretched hand. But as soon as the duck has disappeared—nothing more! It does not occur to her to search behind the fold of the sheet, which would be very easy to do (she twists it mechanically without searching at all) . . . I then take the duck from its hiding-place and place it near her hand three times. All three times she tries to grasp it, but when she is about to touch it I replace it very obviously under the sheet. Jacqueline immediately withdraws her hand and gives up. (1954, pp.36–37)

Stage IV: coordination of secondary schemas (8–12 months). At the beginning of this stage, the child has become able to search for completely hidden objects. However, there is still evidence that the object does not have an existence totally independent of the child's actions. Let us say the child has been successful in recovering a hidden object from one place. As the child watches, the object in question then is hidden in another place. When the child looks for the missing object, he or she may look in the initial location from which the object was retrieved earlier, even after having seen that the object has not been placed there. This indicates to Piaget that the existence of the object still depends upon the actions that the child has performed on it. Here is another relevant observation by Piaget.

Obs. 52. Let us cite an observation made not on our own children but on an older cousin . . . Gerard, at 13 months, knows how to walk, and is playing ball in a large room. He throws the ball, or rather lets it drop in front of him and, either, on his feet or on all fours, hurries to pick it up. At a given moment the ball rolls under an armchair. Gerard sees it and, not without some difficulty, takes it out in order to resume the game. Then the ball rolls under the sofa at the other end of the room. Gerard has seen it pass under the fringe of the sofa; he bends down to recover it. But as the sofa is deeper than the armchair and the fringe does prevent a clear view, Gerard gives up after a moment. He gets up, crosses the room, goes right under the armchair and carefully explores the place where the ball was before. (1954, p.59)

Thus, in a situation in which there is conflict between what the child has seen and what the child has done earlier to recover the ball, the previously successful recovery actions win out.

Stage V: tertiary circular reactions (12–18 months). By this stage, the child is able to restrict manual search to the location in which the object was seen to disappear, and there is no return to scenes of past successful recoveries. However, there is still some indication that objects are not yet assumed to have a totally independent existence. As an example, if a child sees you hide a small object in your hand so that it cannot be seen, he or she will open your hand to retrieve the object. However, if you hide the object in your hand and then put your hand in your pocket, the child will look for the object only in your hand. It will not occur to the child that the object could have been removed from your hand while it was in your pocket. If the path of the object is not seen, it cannot be deduced by the child. Thus, the *perceptible* disappearance is more important than the *inferable* journey (Flavell, 1963, p.133).

Stage VI: mental combinations (18–24 months). By this stage, children deal with objects in a way more or less similar to that of adults, at least on the level of these sensorimotor actions. Children seem to know that objects exist independently, and this would indicate that they know that they themselves are simply one of the many objects in the world. They know the characteristic "behaviors" exhibited by objects and how to deal with them.

Summary of Piaget's research on object concept. Piaget discovered that infants do not deal with objects in the way that adults do. Perhaps the most important and striking finding is that of perseverative search in Stage IV. Perseverative search occurs when the child perseveres in searching for an object in the place in which the object was found earlier, even though the child has seen the object being placed somewhere else. Piaget takes data of this sort to mean that the child thinks that objects only exist when he or she acts upon them.

These early findings of Piaget were based on his own informal observations of his own three children, as well as more controlled observations

Cognitive development I: thinking in infancy   331

that he conducted with each child. Given the small number of subjects and the problems with measuring the fine grain of behavior solely by eye, it is remarkable that Piaget's findings have proven so robust. However, due to those limitations, there are various aspects of the object concept and related behavior which Piaget did not explore. For example, one particularly interesting area of research concerns the behavior of infants in Stages I and II. According to the relatively gross measures used by Piaget, these infants have essentially no object concept at all. Recent techniques have made it possible to obtain new types of data from these very young infants, which are interesting in their own right, and which raise some new issues concerning the object concept. These new results will serve as the starting point for our analysis of these phenomena.

13.4 Development of visual tracking

Bower and his associates (summarized in Bower, 1973, chaps. 6 & 7) have conducted a number of studies examining the sophistication of the infant's visual following of an object, or visual tracking. Bower has investigated whether young infants would search visually for objects before they would search manually for them. In the basic situation, a train moves along a track in front of the child, goes into a tunnel, and reappears at the far end of the tunnel after a few seconds. Thus, the train is "covered" by the tunnel. The infant would show "visual search" by looking toward the far end of the tunnel before the train came out, thus anticipating the train's reemergence. This could be taken as evidence that the child still believed that the train existed while it was in the tunnel.

A number of studies have examined the infant's visual tracking in these situations, and a consistent pattern of results emerges (Bower, 1971; Nelson, 1971). When the train first begins to move, infants of about two to three months of age have trouble just following it, even when the train is completely visible. Very quickly, though, the children become able to follow the train whenever they can see it.

The first time the train moves into the tunnel, the infant's eyes simply stop at the end of the tunnel at which the train disppeared. When the train emerges at the far end of the tunnel, the child is still looking at the other end. The infant's eyes now catch up to the train and follow it again. Thus, at the very beginning, the infant is not able to track a moving object, or anticipate its reappearance after it disappears.

Once the child has some experience with the train entering and leaving the tunnel, he or she begins to anticipate the reappearance of the train. These results indicated to Bower that perhaps these infants possessed the object concept, since they could so quickly begin to search visually for objects that had disappeared. However, according to Bower (1973, chap. 7), one other interpretation of the eye-movement results was possible. Perhaps the infants kept moving their eyes across the tunnel after the train went into it because they simply could not stop moving their eyes. If so, it would look as if the infants were tracking the object in the tunnel and anticipating its reemergence, when all that was happening was a failure to stop head and eye movements.

In order to test this alternate explanation, the same design was used, except the tunnel was removed, and this time the train simply stopped in full view of the infant. To Bower's surprise, the infant kept "tracking" the train, even when it stopped in full view. This indicated that the earlier results were simply the result of the infant's tendency to keep tracking a moving object even if it stops in full view.

13.5 Objects and movements

Given these surprising findings, Bower conjectured that perhaps infants do not equate the moving object with the same object when it is stationary. Let us say a three-month-old infant is presented with the following sequence of events. A train is first seen at location A, directly in front of the infant. The train then moves to the right a few feet to location B and stops there for 10 seconds. It then goes back to A and stops there for 10 seconds. The train makes ten of these A-B-A cycles. From the results just considered, one would expect the infant to qucikly become able to track the object and anticipate its path. The important manipulation comes after the tenth cycle is completed. The train now starts to move again, *but this time it goes off in the opposite direction, to location C.*

What eye movements are to be expected under these circumstances? Let us follow Bower's reasoning in his own words. First, what does the infant "see" for the ten A-B-A cycles?

Initially, the infant should see a stationary object in a particular place. Then the object would disappear and a new moving object would appear. Then the moving object would disappear and a stationary object would appear in a new place. After a time that too would disappear and a new moving object would appear, which in turn would give way to the original object in the original place again. To the infant the cycle would seem to involve perhaps four objects, whereas in reality there is

Cognitive development I: thinking in infancy   333

only one. An infant quickly learns to look from one place to another as an object moves between them. If our hypothesis is correct, the infant is not following an object from place to place; rather he is applying a rule in the form, "Object disappears at A, object will reappear at B." (p.35)

If the infant is using this rule as the basis for tracking, what now happens when the train moves to C?

A subject who was following a single object would have no trouble. If an infant is applying the rule above, he should make an error. Specifically, when the stationary object moves [to C] for the first time, thereby disappearing at the middle, the infant should look for the stationary object [in location B] where it has reappeared before. (pp.35–36)

The results supported Bower's predictions. All the infants looked for the object at B on the eleventh cycle, even though the object was sitting at C. Furthermore, "the infant looked [at B] and stared at the empty space. Meanwhile the train with its flashing lights was in full view [at C]" (p.36).

In summarizing all this research, one could say that the visual tracking of infants is based on a very primitive knowledge about objects and what they can do. Bower concludes from this that the young infant does not yet possess the concept of a permanent object as a unified whole that can move around the world. This conclusion supports that of Piaget, based on his earlier studies of manual search.

13.6 Adult visual tracking and the object concept

Perhaps not surprisingly, Bower and others (e.g., Harris, 1975) have placed great emphasis on the tracking errors of young infants. They conclude from these errors that such infants do not deal as adults do with objects in the world. Of course, there is an assumption underlying this conclusion, although it is not stated explicitly by either Bower or Harris. This is that adults, who obviously possess a complete object concept, would not make the sorts of errors that young infants undoubtedly make when tracking objects. Therefore, it might be valuable to consider these tracking tasks from the point of view of adult processing.

We can begin with the ability to track an object as it moves to an unexpected location, or as it stops unexpectedly. Bower (1971, p.35) says: "A subject who was following a single object would have no trouble." However, following a moving object means that one attends to the object as it changes position over time. Based on the models of attention discussed in chapter 6, this tracking must depend at least in part on the person's knowledge and expectations. Therefore, the more one knows about how an object is going to move, the better one ought to be able to predict where it is going to be at the next moment, and the better one ought to be able to track it. This point of view leads to the prediction that adults ought to make tracking errors also, if the actual movement of the objct does not conform to their expectations of where the object is going to be. In such a case, the adult should look at the place where the object *ought* to be. Only when the adult sees that the object is not there will there be a search for the actual location of the object.

There are experimental data that support the prediction that adults will make tracking errors of the sort reported by Bower for infants (Weisberg & Chromiak, 1979). The study examined undergraduates tracking an object that moved back and forth in front of them, and then suddenly stopped in the middle of one of its cycles. Rather than tracking an electric train, the undergraduates tracked a small dot that moved regularly back and forth across a television screen in front of them. At one point, the dot unexpectedly stopped right in front of them, in full view, as in Bower's study in which the train stopped in full view of the infants. However, contrary to Bower's assumptions, the adults kept on tracking, just like Bower's infants did. Furthermore, there was evidence that the undergraduates got more efficient in tracking the dot as the session progressed, just as infants do. Thus, on the basis of these data, no qualitative distinction can be made between the visual tracking of infants and that of adults. Therefore, on the basis of these data, there is no basis here for saying that the infants think any differently about objects than adults do.

We are also presently investigating Bower's A-B-A-B-C design, in which the object goes back and forth between A and B, and then unexpectedly goes off to location C. Preliminary results indicate that adults may make errors in this situation also. When the dot moves to C, some adults first move their eyes in the direction of A, and only then find the dot moving to C. Other adults don't actually look in the direction of C, but they may take longer to follow the dot to C than to B. Once again, the adults make errors comparable to errors made by infants. The basic differences seem to be that the adults make errors of smaller magnitude and can correct these errors very quickly. The differences between the behavior of infants and adults may be due to one factor: the greater knowledge possessed by adults concerning how objects can move. This knowledge comes about because adults have more experience watching objects than infants do.

Cognitive development I: thinking in infancy

In discussing the results of Bower's (1973) tracking studies, Harris (1975) says: "Such errors suggest surprisingly that past expectations override perceptually available data . . ." (p.335). However, it ought not be surprising that errors are brought about by past expectations. Since past expectations play a role in errorless normal perception, it is not surprising that they play a role in errors also. Also, Harris's statement seems to imply that adults do not make such errors, and that adult perception is based only on the available data. This implication is incorrect.

13.7 Manual search and the object concept I: out of sight, out of mind

Piaget's original analysis of object concept development was based on errors made by infants when searching manually for objects. Two particularly striking bits of behavior have been extensively studied in recent years. These are the lack of search for a covered object in Stage III and the perserverative search in Stage IV. The results are summarized in the left-hand column of Table 13.1. We shall next consider the possible sources for these sorts of errors, because they are also relevant to the question of whether infants think differently than do older people.

Uncovering objects. The Stage II infant does not search for objects that are covered, even if the object is one that the infant has just been playing with (Harris, 1975). Bower (1973, chap. 7) considers two possible explanations for the lack of active search by the infant. First, there is the hypothesis that the child thinks that the object no longer exists when it is out of sight. This is the explanation based on the lack of the object concept. A second possibility is that the infant still thinks that the object is there, but simply does not have the motor skill to remove the cover. Such an infant would also not try to remove the cover, but in this case the reason would not be the lack of the object concept.

If the above reasoning is correct, some additional source of data is needed which does not suffer from the potential problems that grasping and removing a cover may suffer from. Let us say that an interesting object is presented to an infant in Stage III. While the infant is looking at the object, it is covered. This should make the infant lose interest in the object. What happens if we now remove the cover and *the object has disappeared*? According to Piaget's theory, the infant should not take note of this at all. If the object ceases to exist when it is covered, then removal of the cover to reveal nothing under it is not an extraordinary event. But if

Table 13.1. Object search summary

	Piaget's results	Other results
Stage III 4 *mos.*	Cover hand holding object—object released.	Infant will continue reaching *in the dark* for an object that has disappeared.
7 *mos.*	Infant will remove hand & object, but will not reach under cloth if hadn't been grasping object when it was covered.	Infant shows surprise when cover removed & object is gone. Infant will push aside screen to get object from behind it.
Stage IV 8 *mos.*	Retrieves objects, but has to have grasped object shortly before it was covered.	
12 *mos.*	Removes cover even if only looking at object when covered. However, searches at place where object was retrieved earlier—perseverative search.	No perseverative search with very short delays. If a *new* toy is hidden at new location, infant still searches at old location (still "perseveres").

Cognitive development I: thinking in infancy

the infant does not think that the object has disappeared, then there should be surprise when the cover is removed and the object is gone.

Two studies (Bower, 1966; Charlesworth, 1966) have tried to measure an infant's surprise in such circumstances. In both studies, the disappearance of the object when the cover was removed produced evidence of surprise when compared with the condition in which the object was still there when the cover was removed. These studies therefore indicate that the infant does indeed have some information available about the object that was there.

A related finding was reported by Bower and Wishart (1972). They took infants who had failed to search for a covered object, and presented each of them with a desirable object. As the infant was reaching for the object the lights went out. The infants were able to continue reaching and to grasp the vanished object in the dark, indicating that they remembered something about the object, which survived the object's disappearance due to the sudden darkness. These results are also summarized in Table 13.1.

Thus, at face value these results indicate that Piaget's notion that the object concept only gradually develops over the first two years may be wrong. At the very least, it is in need of some modification, since Stage III infants do have some information available to them about objects that they cannot see. However, this does not mean that we can simply conclude that very young infants know all about objects and that they just do not know about removing covers. There are several other pieces of evidence that argue against this conclusion. First of all, the infants show no signs of distress when the desired object is covered in the first place. If they really knew that the object was there they ought to fuss and complain.

Secondly, there is other evidence that infants in this stage can remove covers. One of Bower's students has shown that infants in Stage III will push aside a *screen* to get a hidden object, which is displacement of a cover of a sort (Bower, 1973, chap. 7). However, these same infants will not lift up a cup or a blanket that covers an object. Also, if the object is covered by a *transparent* cup, Stage III infants will remove the cup to get the object, although it takes them a while to do it.

Let us briefly summarize the results of these interesting studies (see Table 13.1). 1. If an object is covered by a blanket or a cup, an infant in Stage III will show no interest in it and will make no attempt to remove the cover. 2. If an object is covered and then surreptitiously removed from under the cover, an infant in Stage III will show surprise when the cover is lifted and the object is not there. 3. If an object is put behind a screen, or if the room is made dark, infants in Stage III will now work to get the object. In short, it seems that the one situation in which infants do not respond is when the object is covered by a cloth or a cup, even though they seem to be able to remove the cover. However, removal of the cover by someone else seems to make the infant expect the reappearance of the object.

Thus, the crucial point here seems to be that the only time a Stage III infant no longer responds to an object is when it is covered by a cloth or cup. Bower (1973), chap. 7) notes that these are the only cases in which the cover and the object occupy the same position in space. Based on this, Bower argues that the infant's concept includes information that two objects cannot be in the same place simultaneously. Therefore, if the cover is in that place, then the original object cannot be. However, this explanation runs into a problem, because when the cover is removed, the infant expects the original object to be there. It seems that the original object has not been wiped out by the cover, it has simply been covered.

Memory and search for a covered object. Let us examine this situation from the point of view of interference in memory, because we may be able to explain the lack of search by a Stage III infant for a covered object in terms of mechanisms with which we are familiar. From the point of view of interference, this search task could be looked upon as a paired-associate situation, comparable to the A-B, A-D paradigm discussed in section 1.8. We could conceive of the position of the object as A, and the object itself as B. The infant's seeing the object in that place corresponds to A-B. The cover (D) is then placed in the same place. This corresponds to A-D, which should interfere with recall of A-B, and the infant should respond as if the original object no longer exists.

However, when the cover is removed, A as a cue should produce recall of B, so there should be some surprise elicited when object B has been removed from under the cover. Also, when a screen is placed between the infant and the object, the screen is not in location A, so there should be much less interference with the infant's concentration on A-B. Therefore, the infant should try to get the object when it is screened. The same sort of reasoning is involved in dealing with the situation in which the lights go out. There should be no blockage involved.

Bower briefly considers the possible role of memory in the development of the object concept, and he concludes that lack of memory is probably not a valid explanation. He argues that infants are able to remember their previous experiences in the laboratory, which may have occurred days before. Therefore, their memories are too good to explain the lack of the object concept as a failure of memory. However, the fact that the infant can remember things from a few days ago says nothing about what will happen in an interference situation. As happens with adults, interference can produce a performance deficit even though a good memory is involved.

Overcoming the interference: encoding "inside." Given that young infants do not search for hidden objects because of retroactive interference from the cover, we are still faced with a problem. Older infants overcome this interference and are able to search under covers for hidden objects. By what means is this interference overcome? If an adult has to learn an A-B pair, followed by an A-D pair, one way to reduce retroactive interference from the A-D pair is to incorporate the D item into the A-B pair. One way to do this is to have the subject integrate A,B, and D into a sequential image (Bower, 1972; Bugelski, 1970). In an analogous way, perhaps at some point infants learn something that enables them to deal with the cover plus the object as one integrated pair of objects, rather then two separate objects. Bower (1973, chap. 7) discusses one possible way in which this could come about; it concerns the child's learning about *inside*. At about this time, children seem to be very interested in putting objects inside other objects and taking them out again. Bower cites several observations made by Piaget (1954, Obs. 111–13) of his own children, and Bower provides some evidence of his own.

Assume for the sake of discussion that an infant has become familiar with ways in which objects can be put into other objects, how they can be taken out, or dumped out, and many other related phenomena. We now place a cup over a small toy that the child was playing with. It does not seem too farfetched to argue that when the cup is going over the toy, the visual pattern can now be recognized as a familiar one. If that cup-over-toy sequence is indeed familiar, it can serve as a cue to enable the child to retrieve a method for getting the toy back.

In summary, one may be able to explain the lack of manual search by Stage III infants by assuming that their knowledge is too limited. Because the infants have not had that much experience manipulating objects, their interpretation of certain situations may be impoverished from our point of view. That is, these infants do not know what it looks like when one thing goes inside another. This ignorance makes them susceptible to memory problems that do not plague more sophisticated people. If so, then infants do not think differently about objects, they simply know less about them.

13.8 Manual search and the object concept II: perseverative search

At the end of Stage III, the infant will remove a cover in order to retrieve an object at location A. However, development is not yet complete, because the infant will still search incorrectly under certain circumstances. If one now covers the same object at location B, while the infant watches, the infant will search for it at A. The infant will *pesevere* in searching for the object at the place in which it was found originally.

Piaget's explanation for perseverative search. Piaget (1954) explains these results in terms of the developing object concept: infants believe that the object's existence and appearance depend upon their actions. Since the object was found once at location A, from then on the child thinks of that object as "object to be found at location A." The location B is not even registered, because previous experience finding the object at location A precludes the storage of the new information. Piaget also considered the possibility that the infant's behavior might be analogous to that of an "absent-minded" adult. For example, one leaves one's keys in a new location, and one then searches for the keys in the place they usually are put. Piaget rejects this possibility because his own children immediately turned to location A after watching the object being hidden at B. Therefore, they did not even register B, or so it seemed to Piaget. Also, the infants had found the object previously at A only once or twice. Therefore, persevering at A would not seem to be comparable to going back to the place where one always keeps one's keys. However, as we shall see, the reasons for rejecting the "absent-minded" explanation are not as clear as Piaget thought them to be.

Recent studies of perseverative search. A number of recent studies of perserverative search indicate that the child does register location B in memory, contrary to Piaget. For example, Gratch, Appel, Evans, LeCompte, and Wright (1974) tested nine-month-old infants in a manual search task. They first hid an object (a toy) in location A as the infant watched. The infant then retrieved the object. The object was then hidden at A again, and again the infant found it. The object was then hidden at B while the infant watched, and the infant was then allowed to search for it. However, different groups of infants were given various delay intervals before they were allowed to search; the delays used were 0, 1, 3, and 7 seconds. The important finding was that the group with the zero interval performed almost perfectly, while the infants in the delay groups produced many perseverative errors. Thus, the problem was not that the infants did not register B. Rather, the memory that the object was at B was effective only for a very short amount of time.

Also, Piaget's explanation of perseverative search is based on the assumption that the infant thinks of the toy as "object I found at location A." When the same object is hidden at B, the infant goes to A because that is what is remembered about the object. However, Evans and Gratch (1972) tested infants who saw a *different* toy being hidden at B after finding an earlier toy at A. These infants also searched at A, even though the new toy had never been found there. This indicates that the *object* is not the crucial thing. Rather, location A seems to be the crucial thing.

To summarize, these studies indicate that Piaget's rejection of the absent-mindedness hypothesis may have been premature. Evidence indicates that Stage IV infants do register information about the new hiding place (see Table 13.1, bottom). This information is effective if the infant is allowed to search immediately. If a delay is imposed, this information loses its effectiveness, although the information may still be available in memory. Finally, the information producing perseverative search may be information that a toy was found at location A.

Proactive interference and perseverative errors. Consider the following: (1) The infant is shown an object hidden at location A. The infant can retrieve it. (2) The infant then sees the same object, or a different object, hidden at B. The infant searches for the object at A. (3) The longer the delay, the greater the tendency to search at A. When looked at it in this way, these findings may remind one of proactive interference in a memory situation. In such an experiment, subjects are given a series of recall trials with similar materials. On the first trial, recall is good, even with a relatively long retention interval. On subsequent trials, recall gets worse, especially with long retention intervals. With short retention intervals, little or no recall decrement occurs. This is directly comparable to what occurs in these search situations. Performance is good on the first trial (location A) and gets worse on subsequent trials (location B) if there is a delay interval.

Harris (1973) argued that perseverative errors are the result of proactive interference. According to Harris, the delay interval results in the earlier retrieval success at location A interfering with performance. This model predicts that the infant should do well on trial 1 (hiding at A), and do poorly on trial 2 (hiding at B), especially if A and B are similar and confusable locations, and if there is a delay before the infant can search. We have already seen some evidence in support of this model. Obviously, this sort of a model would fit in well with the point of view of the present discussion. This is especially true since it was argued that retroactive interference is important in the lack of search for covered objects by infants in Stage III. However, there is at least one difficulty in extending the proactive interference model to try to deal with perseverative search.

The problem comes from a situation in which one finds perseverative errors without any memory problems. Harris (1974) changed the usual manual search task by placing the object behind one of two transparent plexiglass doors (location A). The subjects, one-year-old infants, retrieved the object without any problem. The object was then placed behind the other transparent door (B), so that it was still in full view of the infant. However, door B was locked, so that the object could not be retrieved. All the infants reached for the object at location B, but could not get the door open. All the infants then went back to the A door and opened it, as if they were expecting to retrieve the object there. So we have here what seem to be perseverative errors even though the object is still clearly visible at B. Harris (1974, 1975) argues that such results mean that interference in memory cannot be an adequate explanation of perseverative errors. If interference was the only basis for perseverative errors, then the infant should not search at location A if the object can be seen at B.

However, there are some questions that can be raised about Harris's interpretation of his study. First, one could argue that these infants really had not made a perseverative error. All the infants began by trying to open door B. *It was only after door B did not open that they switched to A.* Consider the situation from the point of view of the infants. They are seated in front of this apparatus that they have never seen before, and a toy is placed behind one door. The infant opens the door and gets the toy. The toy is then placed behind a second door and the infant reaches to get it, but the door does not open. What does the infant know now? The infant knows that you can retrieve toys by opening door A and reaching in there. (Recall the discussion of the Evans & Gratch study, 1972, in the last section.) The infant also knows that you cannot retrieve a toy by opening door B. So the infant goes back to A to try to get the toy from there. This does not seem to be making an error. Rather, it seems to be a case of trying your best possibility. Thus, this study is really irrelevant to perseverative search errors. The infants seem to know just what to do at the beginning, and when that does not work, they do the next best thing. Even though the infants can see the toy at B, they cannot get it, so they search at A. It is true that the infant can't see a toy at A, but this information alone may not be sufficient to stop the infant from opening the door at A. For example, an adult might open door A in order to try to reach the toy at B

Cognitive development I: thinking in infancy

from the side. A year-old infant may not be able to reason at this high a level, but there is still something reasonable about going back to A.

To summarize, the basic notion that memory plays a role in perservative errors seems to be worth pursuing. One can explain much of the data if one assumes that the infant stores information about location B, but that this information can serve to direct the infant's search for only a very short time.

Absent-mindedness in adults. Let us say I come into the house and stop to look at the mail on the kitchen table. As I pick up an envelope, I put down my keys. After browsing through the bills, I go inside and hang up my coat. Later, I want to go out, but the keys are nowhere to be found. I search where they usually are, but they are not there. I then try to retrace my steps; I might be able to recall that the keys are on the table, or I might not. In any case, the important point is that the information that is directing my search is not the information from when I put the keys down. Rather, the search is being directed by my knowledge about where my keys are likely to be. This knowledge is activated by the problem that I am trying to solve, that of finding my keys. However, if I had been asked where my keys were immediately after I put them down, or very shortly thereafter, I would be able to find them directly. I have stored the information about where my keys are, but this information is effective for only a very short while.

This analysis can be extended to the Stage IV child. In addition to the recency of the hiding at B, the second important factor is the situation itself. The infant had a toy, and the toy was taken away and hidden. This could be looked upon as a problem—the infant now wants to get the toy back. Just as in the key-finding example, this serves as a retrieval cue for the infant. The infant has only had one or two experiences in finding the toy in this situation, but they are unambiguous—search at A. So if the delay is long enough so that the recent memory of B is no longer effective, the infant will search at A.

To summarize, if we can look at the hiding situation as a problem, then we can explain perseverative search by using the memory model developed earlier.

13.9 Summary and conclusions

One of the basic assumptions of Piaget's theorizing is that great changes take place in the way in which humans think as they develop. Supposedly, the young infant deals with the world in a way that is very different from the way in which adults do. A prime example of this difference is usually assumed to be the way in which infants behave with regard to external objects. The lack of the object concept supposedly makes the infant's experiences and way of thinking very different from those of adults. However, the analysis in the last half of the present chapter indicated that the same factors may be influencing the behavior of infants and adults. For example, the tracking errors produced by young infants may not be qualitatively different from those produced by adults. Also, the errors produced by infants during manual search, such as the perseverative error, are also produced by adults in comparable sorts of situations. On the basis of these sorts of comparisons, one could conclude that infants are more ignorant than adults, but not that their basic information-processing schemes are any different. They are using attention and memory in the same ways that adults do, it is just that they have less information available to work with.

14
Cognitive development II: thinking in childhood

14.0 Introduction

In the last chapter we considered some of the wide-ranging changes that occur in the sensorimotor period of infancy. Piaget argues that after infancy there are additional great changes that occur in cognitive development. A major part of Piaget's research has been concerned with many areas in which young children's thought appears to be very different from that of adults, and Piaget concludes that some of the most obvious and taken-for-granted aspects of adult thinking are beyond the capacities of young children. Piaget uses these results to argue that the thought of young children is qualitatively different from that of older children and adults. The first part of the present chapter will review some of Piaget's findings concerning differences in thinking between young children and adults. The remainder of the chapter will be concerned with Piaget's analysis of how children come to think like adults. As in the last chapter, we shall argue that young children do not think differently than adults do. The things that "preoperational" children say and do on Piaget-type tasks are due merely to ignorance on the part of the child, and are not related to a primitive mode of thought at all. For each of several specific phenomena, there is strong reason to believe that the experience of young children would lead them to respond in certain ways to the questions posed to them by

Piaget and his followers. Hence the claim that ignorance is at the heart of the primitive thought of young children.

14.1 Schemas to operations

The discussion will focus on Piaget's analysis of the development that occurs between the ages of two and eleven years. According to Piaget (1966), this period can be divided into three stages of development: preconceptual thought, intuitive thought, and concrete operational thought. Most of the discussion in this chapter will be concerned with intuitive thought and concrete operations, beginning with a brief consideration of the differences between the sensorimotor child and the operational child. (We shall not consider formal operations, the last stage of development.)

Schemas versus operations. Piaget (1966, chap. 5) argues that the sensorimotor schemas are not true instruments of thought. First of all, sensorimotor schemas are concerned with transforming one state of the world into another. If this is so, then each schema is tied up only with the events immediately preceding and immediately following its application. However, one characteristic of true thought is that there can be a representation of a whole sequence of interconnected actions. In order to represent such a sequence of actions as a unit, all the parts of the act must be present simultaneously. Piaget argues that this can occur because with repetition, the internal carrying out of an act can become faster and faster, until the parts of the act are essentially simultaneous (Hunt, 1961). This speeding up of the internal representation of an action, relative to the actual overt response, is necessary for the act to become an object of thought.

Secondly, sensorimotor intelligence is concerned only with acts and goals. There is no interest in *knowledge* independent of the act and the surrounding circumstances. Therefore, according to Piaget, before real thought can develop, the child must begin to contemplate the mechanisms involved in carrying out these actions. Thought must be reflective, and sensorimotor intelligence is not. Finally, there is a great difference in the scope of sensorimotor intelligence versus the scope of true thought. Sensorimotor intelligence is concerned with actual objects in the real world. Thought, however, can deal with things that are not of the physical world, and perhaps not even imaginable in concrete terms.

To summarize, Piaget argues that the development of true thought occurs on a plane above that of sensorimotor intelligence. Sensorimotor acts are not simply internalized to become objects of thought. Rather, a whole new system of representations must be constructed, with sensorimotor actions being simply one sort of object which can be represented. In order for this to occur, thought must become free from the concrete here and now, and must quicken and broaden at the same time. The reader may recall that a crucial step in sensorimotor development was the child's breaking out of primitive egocentrism. This egocentrism was brought about by the lack of differentiation and integration of the primitive response systems that humans are born with. According to Piaget, an equivalent egocentrism will be present when the construction of the operations of true thought begins. In this case, egocentrism occurs when the thinker takes it for granted that his or her way of thinking about things is the only way possible. No other points of view are considered because the child is incapable of even conceiving of the existence of alternative points of view. The discussion in this chapter will concern the development from preoperational, egocentric thought to an operational system of decentralized, logical thought (Piaget, 1966, chap. 5).

14.2 The child's understanding of relations

Much of adult thinking is based on the ability to understand and use relations. We can deal with the *bigger* of two things, we know what it is for one person to be another's *assistant,* and so on. In order to deal with such terms in a general way, one must be able to think about the relation independently of any specific situation in which it is exemplified. As a concrete example, consider the terms *left* and *right*. As used by adults, these terms are based on the positions of pairs of objects relative to each other and to an observer. That is, object A can be to the left of object B while at the same time being to the right of object C. Furthermore, in any given pair, the application of left and right depends upon the point from which one views the pair. The object that is on the left from my point of view may be on the right when viewed from the position that you are in.

In one of his investigations, Piaget (1968a) studied children's understanding of various relational terms. He consistently found that children use these terms in ways that are very different from the way that adults use them. First and foremost, children use relational terms as if they were absolutes. Thus, children will be able to show you their left and right hands, but will label your hands incorrectly if you are facing them. This inability to use the terms relatively stems from the children's egocentrism. Everything is considered from their own point of view, so left and right are determined only by their left and right.

Older children may be able to label your hands correctly, but there will still be gaps in the ability to use the terms. If three objects are presented in a line, the children will say that the object on one end is on the left, the one on the other end is on the right, and the third object is in the middle. The children cannot break the series into pairs and consider the pairs separately; they can only deal with the series as a whole. An adult can break the series into two pairs of objects, and see that the middle object is on the right in one pair and on the left in the other pair. The fact that the children cannot break the series of three objects into two overlapping pairs exemplifies another expression of the egocentrism of the thought of the young child: this thought is not *reversible*. That is, in order to deal with the series A-B-C as the pairs A-B and B-C, the object B must be put in one pair and then put into the second. In order to do this, a child must be able to "undo" the operation of forming A-B and now make the pair B-C. The egocentric child is not able to do this, so a series can only be viewed as one whole configuration. Ultimately the older child can deal with left and right in the adult manner.

Piaget also examined many other relational terms, such as foreigner, brother, sister, family, and friend. The use of these relations developed in a way similar to that just discussed for left and right. For example, if a five-year-old girl has a younger sister, the five-year-old will correctly answer you if you ask her if she has a sister. However, if you ask her if her younger sister has a sister, she will tell you that she doesn't. The five-year-old cannot put herself into her younger sister's place and view the relation from her point of view. For all these terms, one sees a shift from usage based on some absolute definition to a comprehension of the relation involved. The absolute definition is totally egocentric, and the true understanding of the relation evolves slowly.

14.3 The child's thinking about reality

In addition to the adult's ability to consider things like relations in the abstract, we also possess more concrete knowledge about the world and the things in it. Once again, Piaget finds that children do not think about phenomena in the world in any way similar to the way adults do. More specifically, three types of thinking are found when young children are questioned about natural phenomena: realism, animism, and artificialism. As we shall see, each of these ways of thinking is found in different subject areas. However, although they seem to be very different, Piaget argues that the same processes are involved in all of them, they are simply different expressions of the child's egocentrism.

Realism. A child is said to exhibit realism in thought when the child argues that psychological or mental phenomena have an existence in the physical world. Piaget (1967) reported a number of different examples of this. One investigation concerned the child's beliefs about dreams. The youngest children (ages 5–6), when questioned about where dreams originated and whether or not they were real, seemed to think that dreams were events in the real world. The children have no idea that dreams might be creations of their own, with no independent physical existence. Here are two examples of the children in this stage according to Piaget, with Piaget's comments in parenthesis.

Barb (5½): Do you ever have dreams?—Yes, I dreamt that I had a hole in my hand.—Are dreams true?—No, they are pictures (images) we see (!)—Where do they come from?—From God.—Are your eyes open or shut when you dream?—Shut.—Could I see your dream?—No, you would be too far away.—And your mother?—Yes, but she lights the light.—Is the dream in the room or inside you?—It isn't in me or I shouldn't see it (!)—And could your mother see it?—No, she isn't in the bed. Only my little sister sleeps with me. (1967, p.94)

Engl (8½): Where do dreams come from?—I don't know.—Say what you think.—From the sky.—How? . . . Where do they come?—To the house.—Where is the dream whilst you are dreaming?—Beside me.—Are your eyes shut when you dream?—Yes.—Where is the dream?—Over there.—Can you touch it?—No.—See it?—No.—Could someone beside you see it?—No.—What do we dream with?—The eyes. (1967, p.95)

In these two examples one can see places in which the children seem to attribute objective reality to dreams.

At a later stage (7–8), according to Piaget, children realize that in some way they produce the dream, but they still think that it possesses some objective reality in the physical world. Finally, the child realizes that dreams are products of thought and have no objective reality in the physical world.

A similar sort of progression occurs with the child's knowledge about the use of names (Piaget, 1967). When young children are asked about the origin of names, they exhibit realism of thought—they regard names as belonging to things. Furthermore, the name in some way comes from the thing itself.

Clouds are called clouds, aren't they? Where does the name of the clouds come from?—The name? That is the name.—Yes, but where does it come from?—The clouds.—What do you mean when you say it comes from the clouds?—It's the name they've got.—But how did the name happen? How did the name begin?—By itself. . . . (1967, p.64)

It is only gradually that the child gets to the adult level of understanding, which conceives of names as established by convention among people, and not inextricably linked to the objects.

Animism. As we have just seen, in realism, mental processes and products are given objective reality. In *animism,* mental processes are attributed to inanimate objects (Piaget, 1967, chap. 5). For instance, a young child will attribute consciousness to all things: the wind feels it when it blows against a mountain, and a button feels it when it is pulled off a shirt. At a later stage, only those things that can move are assumed to be conscious. The wind and a bicycle can feel things at this stage, but the button no longer can. The next stage restricts consciousness only to things which are spontaneously active: the clouds would still feel things, but the bicycle wouldn't. Finally, only animals are assumed to be capable of feeling.

Once again, the egocentrism involved here is obvious. Since the child feels it when the wind blows, then the wind feels it when it blows against something.

Artificialism. When young children are asked about the origins of natural phenomena, their thought exhibits a third characteristic tendency: artificialism, which is the tendency to believe that natural phenomena have been made by people, and that the only reason that natural phenomena exist is to serve us. Here are several examples of artificialism.

Hub (6½): Has the sun always been there?—No, it began.—How?—With fire.—How did it start?—With a match.—How?—It was lighted.—How did that happen?—By striking the match.—Who struck it?—A man.

Fran (9): People took little stones and made them into little stars.

Grang (7½): What are the stars?—Round things.—Made of what?—Made of fire! It is God who made them. (1967, pp.266–67)

The same sorts of explanations are given for the origin of the sun and moon, trees, lakes, and so on. In some cases it is God who was the creator, but sometimes it is mommy or daddy, or "people." It is interesting to note that at first children will attribute creation of the sun, say, to their parents. For this reason, Piaget (1967) argues that formalized religious teaching is

Cognitive development II: thinking in childhood

not the cause of artificialism. If religious training were the cause, then children ought to start with God as the creator, but they don't. They only transfer the creative powers from their parents to God when it becomes implausible that parents could do some of the things under consideration.

Thinking about reality—summary. The young child's thinking about the world is dominated by three modes of thought: realism, animism, and artificialism. Young children think in these terms because they have not yet made a complete differentiation of the objects in the world into their various classes. From their point of view, there is no basic difference between people and animals and other physical objects. Therefore, it is natural that children think that all physical objects think and feel as they.

14.4 Mathematical and logical reasoning

Perhaps the most important discoveries of Piaget in the area of conceptual thinking have been under the general topic of mathematical and logical reasoning.

Conservation. A young child is shown two identical glasses, which are filled to the same height with liquid. We ask the child if both glasses contain the same amount to drink, or if one has more. The child examines the two glasses carefully, and tells us that both glasses have the same to drink. We then take one of the glasses and, as the child looks on, we pour the liquid into a short wide glass. The child is now asked again if the two glasses (the original one and the new one) have the same amount to drink, or if one has more. First of all, the child examines the two glasses very carefully, comparing their relative heights and widths. Secondly, the child will invariably decide that both glasses do not contain the same amount to drink. The child will say either that the original glass has more because it's higher, or that the new glass has more because it's wider. It is a universal finding that young children do not conserve liquid when it is poured from one container into one of a different shape. Lack of conservation also occurs in many other areas, as is well known. The preoperational child does not conserve number, quantity, length, or volume. As an example, if a child who does not conserve number is shown two rows with, say, three objects in each row, the child will say that the rows don't have the same number of objects if one row is more spread out. As with liquid, the appearance is more important than the actual amount.

Piaget's explanation of the development of conservation. In order to discuss Piaget's explanation of the development of conservation, let us use conservation of liquid as a representative example (Piaget, 1965, chap. 1). Three stages can be found in the development of conservation of liquid. At the lowest level, the child argues that one glass contains more than the other, and the conclusion is based on only one of the dimensions of the two glasses. Some children will use the difference in heights as the basis for their judgments, saying that one glass has more because it is taller, while others will use width as their criterion. In either case, the child *centers* on only one dimension, and uses it as the basis for the decision. According to Piaget, one further characteristic of preoperational egocentric thinking is that of *centration:* the child can deal with only one aspect of a situation at a time. In order for conservation to develop, *decentration* or decentering must occur, because there can be no conservation so long as the child focuses on only one of the dimensions.

One sees the beginning of decentering in the second stage. The child still does not conserve, but one observes a vacillation between the two dimensions of height and width before the child settles on a conclusion. A child might say: "This one has more because it's higher. But . . . it's skinnier than the other too. But it's a lot higher, so it must have more." The child has begun to take both dimensions into account, indicating that he or she no longer exclusively centers on one. This is a large step towards conservation. Finally, at the last stage, decentering is complete, and *compensation* occurs. The child now realizes that not only is one glass taller but skinnier, but also that its increase in height is exactly compensated for by its decrease in width. Once the child realizes this, then conservation develops.

To summarize, the child goes from simply considering one dimension at a time, to trying to deal with more than one dimension, to realizing that the changes in dimensions compensate for one another. Once this occurs, the child will ignore the dimensions and conserve liquid because he or she knows that if nothing is added or taken away, the amounts will stay the same.

Transitive inferences. A related area concerns the child's ability to reason using transitive relations and make inferences from them. There are many relations of this sort that we use in thinking all the time, such as bigger, smarter, more creative, fatter, more pleasant.

In order to study the child's ability to use such relations, the child is given a group of three objects, and is asked to order them on the basis of, say, weight (Flavell, 1963, chap. 9). The child is allowed to heft the objects, but can only compare them two at a time. When young children attempt to solve problems of this sort, they are deficient in various ways. In some cases they do not test all the pairs needed to determine the correct ordering of the objects. The child will determine that $A<B$ and $C<B$, and will conclude that $A<C<B$ or $C<A<B$, neither of which is established from $A<B$ and $C<B$. On the other hand, the child may have found that $A<B$ and $B<C$, which is sufficient information to infer that $A<C$. This produces the ordering $A<B<C$. However, the child often will not make the inference, and will either test the remaining pair or will order the stimuli incorrectly. According to Piaget, young children fail to make transitive inferences because they cannot take the two pieces of information that are available ($A<B$ and $B<C$) and coordinate them in order to reach a further conclusion.

14.5 The development of concrete operations: summary

We have now reviewed a number of situations in which there are large changes in performance between younger and older children. Piaget argues that a child's inability to deal with these situations stems from egocentrism of thought. In contrast to the operational thought of an older child or an adult, the younger child's egocentric thought has the following characteristics. The child cannot conceive of there being any other point of view but his or her own. This shows itself in the child's inability to understand certain relational terms and the realism, animism, and artificialism in his or her beliefs about the world. In addition, the child's thought is not flexible and mobile, as is an adult's. This lack of mobility and flexibility is seen as *centration* and *irreversibility* in various tasks. They are seen in a child's problems with conservation and transitive inferences. Egocentric thought gradually evolves into operational thought through the child's continuous interaction with the people and objects in the world.

The remainder of this chapter will critically analyze Piaget's explanation of these various developments. It will be argued that one can explain the behavior of young children without assuming that they think differently from adults. This conclusion will parallel those drawn in chapter 13 concerning thinking in infancy.

The discussion will be in several parts. First, we shall consider the notion that the "egocentric" answers given by young children to Piaget's questions are the result of rational humans working with impoverished data. That is, young children don't think differently, they are just ignorant. Second, the conservation task will be analyzed in some detail, to show that Piaget's explanation of conservation is incorrect, and to present an alternative point of view, based on the child's learning to use terms like *more, less,* and *same.*

14.6 Egocentrism and ignorance

Many of the child's egocentric responses to Piaget's questions seem very rational when one considers what it is that the four- or five-year-old child knows.

Animism: stones and pains. A young child will say that a stone feels it if we kick it. This would seem to be a perfect example of pure egocentrism at work. However, consider why an adult would say that the stone wouldn't feel anything. If we forget about reasons based on specialized knowledge about nervous systems, one reason that adults don't attribute feelings to stones is because stones don't exhibit any of the characteristics which we associate with being a sentient organism. Stones don't wince, cry, or say anything about their pain. Animals, of course, do several of these things, so we will attribute feelings to them. The young child hears various mental-type words being used with reference to humans and animals in various sorts of situations. The child probably hears these terms also used toward other objects on occasion, as when one "feels sorry" for a flower that one has accidently trampled. Under such circumstances, it is not at all surprising that the child would extend such terms farther than adults would. Thus, the explanation for animistic thought may simply be that the child hasn't learned to use certain terms correctly.

Realism: names and dreams. Young children say that a name is an objective feature of an object; one can simply look at a cloud and see that it is to be called by that name. Once again, let us consider why the child might say these sorts of things. Children constantly ask for the names of objects, and adults usually have little difficulty in supplying names. How is it that adults know so much? The child hasn't seen the adults being taught the names, so the adults must have some other source of information as to what name goes with what object. What might this source of information be? This is the essence of the question asked by Piaget.

It seems reasonable to assume that children would use their own experience with words to answer the question. Take the word *yellow* as an example. How do children tell if something is yellow? They simply examine the object and they know. Furthermore, if a child cannot remember the specific experience of learning to use this word, which most of us cannot, then it could appear to the child that the connection between the word and

Cognitive development II: thinking in childhood 355

the characteristic must be self-evident. That is, one *calls* it yellow because it *is* yellow. The child then extends this reasoning to answer the question of how adults know the names that they supply. Adults must be able to tell that something is a cloud in the same way that the child can tell that something is yellow. The adults just look at the cloud and they know what it is to be called. Thus, the child's answer could be the result of a reasonable extension of knowledge to cover what seems to be a similar situation. Such children aren't egocentric, they are just ignorant.

Piaget also says that dreams have an objective reality for young children. It is important to note that one often hears adults talk about the realism of their dreams. If it is true that children's dreams contain the same sorts of episodes, then there is ample reason for the belief that dreams are in some sense real. So this aspect of the child's belief isn't egocentric at all. However, things are a bit more complicated than this. If the experiences that one has during dreams are very similar to those that one has when awake, then why is it that we adults differentiate dreams from waking experiences?

There would seem to be at least four sorts of factors pushing us into separating dream experiences from waking experiences. On the one hand, one sometimes wakes up in the middle of a dream, in a very excited state, to find that one is in bed. This could mean that one must be able to switch back and forth from one place to another instantaneously, if both the dream and the bedroom are real. As the child gets more information about the possibilities of going from one place to another, then a suspicion might grow that the instantaneous change from a dream to one's own bedroom is not the sort of thing that usually happens, and the objective reality of the dreams becomes suspect.

Another factor that might influence the child's beliefs about dreams is information picked up from others. Simply hearing others talk about their dreams might provide additional information to help the child comprehend what happens during dreams. Also, an adult often tries to explain things to a child who wakes up crying from a nightmare. Third, the child might have occasion to witness someone waking up and describing a dream. The fact that the child saw the person sleeping here, and yet the person is describing some happening in some other place, would point the child to the conclusion that dreams are something that happens to us during sleep and are not real at all. Finally, the extraordinary things that occur only in dreams may lead children to believe that what occurs after going to bed is different from what occurs before. This point of view could be summarized by saying that if an adult had been raised from birth in total isolation, that adult could conceivably think what we call dreams are really happening in the world.

Given this description of what young children ought to know about dreams, based on their experiences, their hunches, and what they pick up from others around them, one would expect that more than anything else the children would be confused. It now becomes interesting to reexamine the protocols about dreams which were given in section 14.2 from this point of view. There were a number of self-contradictions in each protocol, such as one child saying that one's eyes are closed when one dreams and yet someone else can see the dream. Piaget (1967) argued that at this stage the young child thinks that dreams have objective reality. However, if one looks at the protocols carefully, it seems more reasonable to conclude that the children aren't quite sure just what dreams are, and so they vacillate from one conclusion to another. They don't seem to be in the grips of egocentrism so much as they are caught in confusion. Once again, we have ignorant children trying to answer an especially difficult question.

Artificialism: parental omniscience and omnipotence. When young children are asked to explain the origins of natural phenomena, their thought exhibits artificialism: they think that natural phenomena were made by humans. According to Piaget (1967, pp.376–85), one of the reasons for this way of thinking is that children consider their parents to be possessed of extraordinary powers. This belief in the omniscience and omnipotence of parents stems from the fact that children are totally dependent upon parents, and therefore believe that parents have organized the world just for them.

Once again, though, it is possible to ask if this sort of thinking on the part of children is really because they think differently than adults do. The first point to be noted about this omnipotence and omniscience of parents is that young children often behave as if their parents are anything but godlike. When young children think they know what they are doing, they do not hesitate to assert themselves and tell adults just what to do. And yet, "there are many instances on record of children attributing *extraordinary powers* to their parents. A little girl asked her aunt to make it rain" (Piaget, 1965, p.378; my italics).

So we seem to have a paradox here. How can the child attribute extraordinary powers to the very same people that are targets for criticism at other times? One way to resolve the paradox is to consider the supposedly "extraordinary powers" attributed to parents in more detail. Why is it that making the stars, say, requires extraordinary power? Extraordinary powers are required because we know what the stars are, how far away they are, how old they are, and so on. So, *from the point of view of reasonably sophisticated adults,* making the stars must require extraordinary power. But what if some ignorant person doesn't know much about stars, except what can be seen by *looking* at them? The stars are little lights in the sky. They are up high, but perhaps not much higher than a moderately tall building. That is, they might be in reach without an extraordinary amount of work. In addition, let's say that this ignorant person has seen someone take care of lights that are high up, like putting new bulbs in ceiling fixtures, at the top of Christmas trees, and so on. In these sorts of cases, there is no light, then that someone goes to work, and there is light. Would it be so strange for this naive person to think that the worker could have brought about those other lights also; that is, the stars?

Thus, one could resolve the paradox if one assumed that the child does not think that making stars is something extraordinary at all. If the child thinks that it is simply a do-it-yourself chore of some sort, then the child's parents, the do-it-yourselfers that the child knows best, must have done it. The same thing can be said about other so-called extraordinary powers. If someone knows how to turn showers and baths on and off, and to make water come out of a hose, then why shouldn't that person know how to produce that water that is called rain? Indeed, when someone attaches a lawn sprinkler to a hose and turns it on, one does make it rain, in a way. And again, if someone puts in plants, takes them out, feeds the grass, makes it grow, cuts it, and so on, then why shouldn't this person be capable of making trees and woods and maybe even mountains? Can't parents dig holes and pile up dirt? What's a mountain, if not a big pile of dirt?

In summary, we may once again have a situation in which ignorance leads the child to say things that sophisticated adults misinterpret. The child is drawing straightforward inferences; based on what the *experimenter* knows, the child is saying strange things. But that is more the experimenter's problem than the child's.

Piaget also points out that children sometimes start by attributing creation to their parents, and only later switch the credit to God. This seems to be a very rational thing to do. As the child begins to learn the limits of things that parents and other adults can do, and as the child learns more about natural phenomena, then something like creation of the stars becomes extraordinary. It then follows that a being with superhuman powers must have done these great things, if normal people can only do more mundane things.

Relational terms: foreigners and people from somewhere else; brothers and sisters. Young children say that foreigners are people who are different than they. In order to understand this conclusion, think of the times that children have heard the word *foreigner*. Surely, the great majority of the times young children hear the word, it is used in exactly the way they define it for Piaget. That is, children hear *foreigner* used to refer to people who come from a place that they do not come from and who talk and perhaps dress differently than they do. Therefore, why should we expect anything else from the children? In order for someone to know that a term is to be used relationally, then one must have heard the term used in a broad enough set of contexts so that the relational aspects of its use can be appreciated. If someone hears a relational term in only one type of situation, then for this listener, the term will be limited in its meaning to the sort of situation in which it has been heard.

The same sort of argument may hold for terms like *brother* and *sister*. Consider a girl who has a smaller sister. When is this child likely to hear the term *sister* used? The great majority of the time it will refer to her sister. She would be much less likely to hear the term used to refer to herself, because when she is present the speaker will probably use her name to refer to her. Therefore, she will quickly learn that the little girl who lives in the same house as she does is called sister, but she won't learn nearly as quickly, or as easily, that she herself is also called sister.

Thus, at least for some terms, it is not too implausible to argue that the child's egocentric understanding of the terms stems not from egocentric throught per se, but rather from the information that is available.

Egocentrism as a description versus an explanation. The argument repeated several times in the last few sections has been that children's egocentric responses are not the result of egocentric thought. Rather, the children's knowledge is limited and their answers are based on what they know. Thus, the answers will be egocentric. Therefore, we could say that the term egocentric is adequate as a *description* of what children produce, but it is not adequate as an *explanation* of why they say these things. This whole discussion could be summarized in the following question: Why shouldn't young children say what they do? If an adult knew only what young children know, wouldn't that adult say the same things?

Cognitive development II: thinking in childhood   359

14.7 The development of conservation

As far as Piaget's theory is concerned, the development of conservation is important because it marks a major step forward toward truly operational thinking. Conservation comes about when the child has developed a whole system of operations which can be used to analyze the pouring of a liquid from one glass to another. This system of operations enables the child to break away from the physical appearance of the glasses, and deal with the amount of liquid.

Piaget's stages. To briefly review, Piaget postulates three stages in the development of conservation. In the first stage, there is no conservation, because the child focuses on only one dimension of the transformed liquid. In the second stage, the child also considers the other dimension. This second stage marks a large step forward, because once the child notices the second dimension and tries to deal with it, it opens the way for a consideration of both dimensions at once.

In the third stage, the child becomes capable of reasoning about the two dimensions. The child's consideration of the two dimensions leads to the discovery that the change in one dimension is compensated for the change in the other. This then leads the child away from the dimensions, to conservation.

As a further example of the importance attributed to this discovery of compensation in Piagetian theory, consider the following excerpt from one of the leading experts in this area.

Piaget would use his equilibration model to explain the development of conservation of liquid quantity, for example, in roughly the following manner. . . . [The] non-conserver usually focuses his attention only on the greater height of the liquid column in the taller, thinner glass, and therefore concludes that it has more liquid than the standard. His thinking about this problem is said to be in equilibrium, albeit at an immature, non-conservation level.

Suppose, however, that at some point he also notices that the new column is thinner, a fact that by itself would incline him to conclude that the new glass contains less liquid than the standard. If he finds both of these conclusions plausible at the same psychological moment, his cognitive system has moved from a stage of equilibrium to one of cognitive conflict with respect to this problem. According to Piaget, states of cognitive conflict and disequilibrium impel the child to make cognitive progress. In this case, the child achieves a new, more intellectually advanced equilibrium state by conceptualizing both the height increase and the width decrease as predictable, mutually compensatory changes in a process of physical transformation that leaves liquid quantity unchanged. A developmental advance has been made by means of a process of equilibration composed of these major steps: (1) cognitive equilibrium at a lower developmental level; (2) cognitive disequilibrium or conflict, induced by awareness of contradictory, discrepant, "nonassimilable" data not previously attended to; (3) cognitive equilibrium (or reequilibration) at a higher developmental level caused by reconceptualizing the problem in such a way as to harmonize what had earlier been seen as conflicting. (Flavell, 1977, pp.241–42)

In sum, we have a new conceptualization brought about by discrepant data, namely, the child's empirical discovery that the dimensions compensate for each other. The conceptual change is brought about by the empirical discovery. Thus, let us examine whether the empirical discovery of compensation can do what Piaget wants it to.

The arithmetic of empirical compensation. It seems that the crucial empirical discovery on the part of the child is that the two dimensions compensate each other when the liquid or clay changes shape, because it is the one new piece of data that the child has at the point of transition from nonconservation to conservation. Younger children know various other things about the liquid, but they don't conserve. Therefore, they don't have adequate data available to result in a new equilibration of thought structures. From all this, it is obvious that this "discovery" bears careful scrutiny. If such empirical compensation did not actually occur, then there would be nothing for the child to discover, and any further discussion of equilibration as an explanation for the development of conservation would be incorrect.

Let us assume that we have two tall thin glasses filled with liquid to a height (h_1) of 100 cm; the glass is 2 cm wide (w_1). Assume that the liquid is poured from one of these glasses into another (w_2) that is 4 cm wide. This step is then repeated with $w_3 = 8$ cm and $w_4 = 16$ cm. How high would the column of liquid be in each of these glasses?

When most people are asked to compute what the height of the liquid would be when poured into the other glasses, they usually produce the following answers: $h_2 = 50$ cm; $h_3 = 25$ cm; and $h_4 = 12.5$ cm. These numbers, when combined with the changes in height, neatly compensate each other. For example, from glass$_1$ to glass$_2$, the width doubles, but the height decreases by half, so everything stays the same. Thus, we have changes in one dimension compensated for by changes in the other.

The only difficulty is that when the liquid is poured into glasses$_{2-4}$, those values (50 cm, 25 cm, and 12.5 cm) are *not* the values that the height will take. The three obvious answers just given are incorrect. Most people imagine the cross-sections of the glasses, see that they are rectangles, and then solve for h by multiplying h × w. Since $h_1 \times w_1 = 200$, then h_2

must be 50, since $200 \div 4 = 50$. The same is done for h_3 and h_4. However, we are not dealing with rectangles here; we are dealing with glasses, and although glasses have rectangular cross-sections, they are cylinders. Therefore, the volume of liquid in glass$_1$ is not equal to 100×2. Rather, to determine the amount of liquid, one must use the formula $V = \pi r^2 h$, with $r = \frac{1}{2}(2) = 1$. If we do this, then we find that the volume in glass$_1$ is equal to $100\ \pi$, and $h_2 = 25$, $h_3 = 6.25$ and $h_4 = 1.56$. If we then take these numbers and try to find some compensation, we see that *there is no compensation of the change in height by the change in width*. For example, from glass$_1$ to glass$_2$, the width becomes *twice* as large, but the height decreases by a factor of *four*. So these changes do not compensate each other. From glass$_1$ to glass$_3$, the width is *four* times greater, but the height as decreased by a factor of *16*. From glass$_1$ to glass$_4$, the width is *eight* times greater, but the height has decreased by a factor of *64*. Thus, there is no way that the child can "grasp" or "discover" that the differences compensate each other, because they don't.

It is not hard to see where Piaget's emphasis on empirical compensation as the disequilibrating factor came from. When one watches young children working on a conservation test, the nonconservers examine the heights and widths carefully, and make their judgments as a result of their comparisons of these dimensions. Secondly, as the children get older, one now sees them begin to try to deal with both dimensions. Then the children become able to conserve. This would lead one to try to devise an explanation for conservation that took into account the child's use of the height and width.

To summarize, it seems that the child's discovery of empirical compensation cannot be a factor in bringing about the new equilibration that results in conservation, because such compensation cannot be discovered by the child, since it does not occur. This indicates that the nonconserver never gets into the state of cognitive disequilibrium necessary to bring about the development of the new operational structure which produces conservation, and if disequilibrium never comes about, then neither can equilibration.

14.8 Changing the child's mind: learning about being the same while looking different

We have seen that the nonconserver seems to be in a state of equilibrium, in Piaget's terms: the child's way of looking at things, although incorrect from an adult point of view, is consistent as far as the child is concerned.

The child does not see the inconsistency, because the child does not know what adults know. Furthermore, as was mentioned earlier, when one looks at the glasses, it looks as if the amount of liquid does indeed change. So not only is the child's reasoning consistent, there is also some "evidence" to support it. Thus it is no surprise that children do not conserve for several years after they first come into contact with liquids. However, some time around the age of seven, children abandon this nonconservation belief system and "spontaneously" become conservers. The crucial question seems to be why children would begin to believe that two amounts of liquid are really equal although they look unequal.

Counting. What we need, once again, is a situation in which it is possible to show objectively that two amounts of liquid that look very different are really equal. One related situation in which this could occur, if not the only one, concerns collections of objects that can be *counted*. This is one way that one can see that the amounts aren't different even though they may look different—all one has to do is count the arrays.

So here we have a potential bit of evidence that could push the child toward conservation. Let's say that a child knows that two arrays are equal if they both have the same number of objects. Therefore, the child can now count the arrays after various operations have been performed on them. The child can then learn what sorts of operations increase or decrease amount, and what sorts of operations leave it unchanged. From this, the child can learn that the only operations that change amount are those that add or subtract objects from the array. The child can then pay attention only to the original equality of the arrays and the operations performed on them. No further counting is needed as long as no objects have been added or taken away.

Counting and conservation. Once the child has learned to judge *more* and *less* on the basis of adding and taking away, it becomes relevant to conservation of liquid. Here, too, we have a situation in which the child must judge *more, less,* and *equal/same,* and here, too, is a situation in which the objects in question are simply rearranged, without anything being added or subtracted. Therefore, the child ought to judge the amounts of liquid still equal, on the basis of knowledge from the number situation.

To summarize, it is argued that conservation of liquid is the result of the child's extension of knowledge derived from numbers to another domain, because of the similarities between what occurs in the two situations. To repeat, the reason this explanation is worth considering is because it pro-

Cognitive development II: thinking in childhood

vides a way whereby the child could come across objective evidence that amounts do not always change when appearances change. This would result in the child's dropping a reliance on physical appearance because the child knows that other factors must also be taken into account. This in turn would result in a reliance on previous equality or inequality of the liquid and what has happened to the liquid since then.

14.9 Some relevant data: conservation of number and conservation of quantity

This model of the development of conservation of liquid makes one clear prediction: the conservation of number must occur before the conservation of liquid.

Age of acquisition of conservation of number versus conservation of liquid. Elkind (1970) presents data on the average age of acquisition of conservation of number versus other types of conservation. Number is the earliest, as demanded by the model. However, Elkind's data are only averages across groups of subjects. A study by Brainerd and Brainerd (1973) examined the relationship of conservation of number and conservation of liquid in individual children, and the results strongly supported the sequence predicted by the present analysis: conservation of number developed before conservation of liquid in a large majority of their subjects. Also, Smedslund (1961) examined the relationship between conservation of continuous quantity (modeling clay) and conservation of discontinuous quantity (piles made out of small pieces of linoleum—very similar, if not identical, to conservation of number). He found that conservation of discontinuous quantity developed earlier than conservation of continuous quantity in a large majority of children, also supporting the present position.

Teaching conservation of liquid through conservation of number. Another prediction that comes from the present model is that accelerating the child's number development ought to accelerate the development of conservation of liquid. A study by Gelman (1969) tried to accelerate conservation in this way. The subjects were a group of kindergarten children who were nonconservers of number, length, liquid, and mass (clay) on the basis of standard conservation tests. The experimental group was given a series of problems designed to make them focus on the dimensions relevant to conservation. The problems involved number and length, and in each problem there were three sticks or three rows of objects. On each trial in the stick problems, the child was asked either to show the experimenter two sticks that were the same length, or to show the experimenter two sticks that were different in length. The sticks were arranged so that the child could not simply examine whether or not the ends coincided in order to make the choice. The whole length of the sticks had to be considered. For the number problems, the child had to show the experimenter two rows that had the same number of things in them, or two rows that had different numbers of objects. As with the length problems, the rows were so arranged that the child could consistently choose correctly only by concentrating on the actual number of objects present. Half the time, the children were asked to pick out two stimuli that were the same in number, and half the time they were asked to pick out two stimuli that were different in number. The child was told whether the choice was correct, then the stimuli were rearranged for the next trial and the questions asked again. Each problem was presented separately, and there were six trials on each problem. A total of 32 six-trial problems were presented, 16 number and 16 length.

There were two control groups, also made up of nonconserving kindergartners. One group had 32 problems in which they had to pick the stimuli that were the same or different, but the stimuli were things like stars and circles. These stimuli have nothing to do with conservation. The second control group received the same number and length problems as those presented to the conservation training group, and were asked the same questions. However, these children were not given any feedback as to whether their choices were correct or not.

After the 32 training problems, all the children were given the four types of conservation tests again. The training group that had received the feedback now performed almost perfectly on the tests for conservation of number and length. In addition, about 60 percent of these children now conserved liquid and mass, even though they had not been trained in those areas. This supports the prediction from the present model. Also, the children were retested after three weeks, and no decrease in conservation performance was found. The two control groups showed almost no increase in conservation performance, indicating that the specific number and length tests plus the feedback were crucial here. Gruen (1965) also found that training in conservation of number generalized to conservation of quantity, although neither the effectiveness of the number conservation training, nor the amount of generalization to conservation of quantity, was as great as that reported by Gelman (1969).

Basis for conservation: summary. To summarize, there are some experimental data that support the notion that conservation of liquid develops only after the child learns that certain sorts of operations do not change amount. This in turn only comes about in domains in which the child has some objective way of determining whether the changed object does indeed contain more or less, or whether it is still the same although it looks as if it changed.

From this point of view, one would not say that conservation is the result of a new way of thinking on the child's part (i.e., Piaget's concrete operations). Rather, just as in the other areas discussed earlier in this chapter, the child is simply using different information than that available to adults. Once the child gets enough information to see what adults mean by *more, less,* and *same,* then adultlike performance should occur.

14.10 Memory problems in concrete-operational tasks

We have seen that in order to conserve liquid, the child must know that (a) the two liquids were equal originally, and (b) nothing has been added or subtracted since. When looked at in this way, there is a further potential problem for conservation development. The child who doesn't conserve might not be able to recall the fact that the amounts were equal before being poured into the different-sized glasses. If so, the child would be faced with the two different-sized glasses, and we have already concluded that from this evidence alone even adults would not conserve, especially if they used the cross-section as the basis for their judgments.

Forgetting that the amounts are equal. One reason that the child might not be able to remember that the two amounts of liquid were originally equal is because the child might not be able to encode this information. Some evidence that a nonconserver has problems remembering the initial amount of liquid comes from an unpublished study by Weisberg, Urbanski, and Sloane (1975). Memory for the initial pair of glasses was tested by covering the glasses and asking the children to pick out a picture that showed how the glasses looked. The choices were a group of several pictures, all of which contained pairs of glasses with various amounts of liquid in them. The children had some problems picking the correct picture when the glasses had been covered, although they could pick the correct picture reasonably well when the glasses were uncovered in front of them. These results support the idea that young children may not conserve in part because they don't have the necessary information (that the two amounts were equal) still in memory when they need it.

Interference. Another reason that the child might not use the information that the amounts of liquid were equal is that the standard conservation test is a retroactive interference situation (see section 1.8.) The table in front of the child is analogous to the A word, and the original pair of identical glasses with equal amounts of liquid in them is analogous to B. The situation after the liquid had been poured into the short, wide glass is analogous to D. If so, then we have an A-B, A-D situation, and it might be expected that the child would have difficulty in retrieving the information about the two amounts being equal originally (Weisberg, Urbanski, & Sloane, 1975). In another condition the child's recognition of the *original* glasses was tested *after* the liquid had been poured into the short, wide glass. The new glasses were left standing in front of the child. Pouring the liquid made memory for the original glasses worse than when the original glasses were simply covered. This is the hypothesized interference effect.

Of course, this discussion leaves us with the question of why it is that a nonconserver's memory is interfered with by pouring, while that of a conserver is not. One reason for this may be that the nonconserver can't predict what it will look like when the water is poured into the short, wide glass as well as the conserver can (e.g., Gelman and Weinberg, 1972). The new situation would then be expected to capture his or her attention, and might thereby interfere with recall of the original pair. This would indicate that experience handling and observing liquids may be indirectly relevant to conservation of liquids.

14.11 Summary and conclusions: do young children think differently than adults do?

This chapter was concerned with the question of whether it is necessary to assume the development of concrete operations in order to explain the changes in thinking that occur as children get older. First, it was argued that the notion of egocentrism didn't help to explain the young child's responses in various situations. While it is true that young children understand things by interpreting them in terms of what they know, this does not necessarily mean that their thinking is locked in by egocentrism. Rather, children's responses may be egocentric because they have only limited experience with the various phenomena in question. Because of this, the children's responses would be egocentric, but their "thought processes" wouldn't be.

The development of conservation was also considered in some detail, in order to examine the adequacy of the explanations based on concrete operations. On the one hand, Piaget's explanation of the development of conservation was shown to be unable to explain it. An alternative explanation was tentatively outlined, which assumed that the basic problem of nonconservers was due to lack of knowledge concerning the use of *more, less,* and *same,* as well as inadequate encoding and retrieval of information from memory.

If these sorts of explanations are valid, then younger children may not think differently than older children or adults. The same simple information-processing operations may be involved in each case. The only difference would be in the way in which information is handled, and this would be due to the broader experiences of older children and adults.

15
Cognitive factors in language development

15.0 Introduction

The recent surge of interest in cognitive psychology has been called a scientific revolution of the sort described by Kuhn (1970). That is, it has been argued that the cognitive point of view has displaced learning theory as the dominant mode of thought for most psychologists, much like one ideology replacing another as the result of a political revolution (e.g., Palermo, 1978, Introduction). If so, then one of the major battle fields of that revolution was the area of developmental psycholinguistics, for it was here that traditional psychological theorizing was subject to strong criticism. It was argued that language development was a unique phenomenon, limited to humans. Attempts were made to show that human language was different from other sorts of behaviors in such a way that models based on conditioning and reinforcement principles could not explain how humans acquired the capacity to produce and understand sentences (e.g., Chomsky, 1957, 1968; McNeill, 1966, 1970). As an alternative to traditional psychological theories based on learning, it was proposed that the capacity to speak is innate to humans and limited to humans. Thus a whole new point of view was being advocated, and many psychologists adopted it wholeheartedly. (See, for example, Palermo, 1978.)

However, as often occurs in psychology, the pendulum of opinion is beginning to swing back toward the more traditional sorts of analyses of language use and language development. The basic orientation of the present chapter will be that the development of language can be analyzed in terms of the processes developed earlier in the book. It will be argued that the reason young children speak differently than adults is because they are not able to process language as efficiently as adults. This means, not surprisingly, that when children try to talk, they will not be able to say what an adult would say in the same circumstances. However, what the children *do* say will therefore be related to what they have heard others say, but somewhat indirectly. The model of perception and attention discussed in part 2 will be important in understanding the problems faced by children when they are learning to speak.

When we talk, we often talk about our experiences. This is especially true of young children; they are almost always talking about perceptible events in the world. Thus, the first step in learning to talk is becoming able to produce and understand verbalizations that correspond to events in the physical environment. In other words, at least part of our verbal knowledge consists of a mapping of perceptual information to verbal descriptions. The reverse also occurs; we become able to pick out relevant events in the environment based on someone else's description. The important point to emphasize is that we learn the relationship between verbalizations and events. Language is not learned independently of the world, nor is it used independently of the world. Furthermore, it is important to keep in mind that speech is also an event in the world, and must be processed like all such events.

The discussion in this chapter will follow language development chronologically, from the first isolated words through combinations of words. While such a sequence is most logical from a developmental point of view, it is not the sequence that the researchers in the area followed over the last few years. For reasons to be elaborated later, interest in two-word combinations came before interest in single-word utterances. Therefore, there may be a bit of backtracking involved in getting all the conceptual threads straightened out.

15.1 The first words: semantic features

Children acquire their first words by listening to others talk, by observing the circumstances in which others talk, and by observing what happens when others talk. In recent years, much interest has centered on the sort of information the child takes from the world and uses as the basis for production of the first words. We shall consider the work of two investigators, Clark (1973) and Nelson (1974), in some detail.

The acquisition of semantic features. According to Clark, the full meaning of a word consists of a set of basic meaning elements called semantic features. The child acquires semantic features initially by observing the situations in which adults use the word. Furthermore, since the meanings of words consist of several features, the child will not be able to pick up all the features at once. Therefore, the child's meaning of a given word will be impoverished with respect to the meaning known by adults, and the use of the word will be wider than that of adults.

As an example of this, assume that the child hears an adult use the word *dog*. Based on Clark's analysis, there are several features which an object must possess before it can be called a dog, but the child is able to store only one of these features. Let us say that the child stores the feature "four-legged." At this point, then, the child will use the word *dog* to refer to anything with four legs, such as cows and zebras.

In order to provide evidence that semantic features are acquired only one at a time, Clark reviewed a number of "diary" studies of the first words of young children. In these studies, the child's parent, usually a linguist or a psychologist, kept a diary of the utterances produced by the child, and the context in which each utterance was produced. The semantic features hypothesis predicts that the first words should be used in an overextended manner, and the overextensions should fit the idea that the child is only using a limited number of features, rather than the complete set used by adults.

Some examples of the overextensions reported in diary studies are shown in Table 15.1, which supports one prediction of the semantic features hypothesis. However, simply finding overextensions does not necessarily support the second part of the hypothesis, that these overextensions are due to the child's use of only one or two features. Rather, on close examination of Table 15.1, one can see several problems with the notion that the child's meaning for a word is based on one or two semantic features, to be discussed shortly. There is an even more basic problem, however, which has to do with the adequacy of the semantic feature notion itself. Let us discuss this latter issue first.

Semantic features and perceptual features. Several linguists have argued that semantic features are based on the functioning of the human perceptual apparatus (e.g., Bierwisch, 1969; Postal, 1966). These features would then be innate to all humans and would come about because of the way in which humans are able to process information. If the discussion of

Cognitive factors in language development

Table 15.1. Overextensions taken from diary studies by E. Clark (1973)

Source	Item	First referent		Extensions and overextensions in order of occurrence
Kenyeres (1926)	titi	animals	>	(pictures of animals)>(things that move)
Leopold (1949)	sch	sound of train	>	(all moving machines)
Pavlovitch (1920)	dzin-dzin	moving train	>	(train itself)>(journey by train)
Pavlovitch (1920)	tutu	train	>	(engines)>(moving train)>(journey)
Schulte (cited in Prayer, 1889)	ass	goat with rough hide on wheels	>	(things that move, e.g., animals, sister, wagon)>(all moving things)> (all things with a rough surface)
Chamberlain & Chamberlain (1904)	mooi	moon	>	(cakes)>(round marks on window) >(writing on window and in books) >(round shapes in books)>(tooling on leather book covers)>(round postmark)>(letter O)
Guillaume (1927)	nenin (breast)	breast, food	>	(button on garment)>(point of bare elbow)>(eye in portrait)>(face of person in photograph)
Idelberger (1903)	bow-wow	dog	>	(fur piece with glass eyes)>(father's cuff links)>(pearl buttons on dress) >(bath thermometer)
Leopold (1949)	tick-tock	watch	>	(clocks)>(all clocks and watches)> (gas-meter)>(fire hose wound on spool)>(bath scale with round dial)
Pavlovitch (1920)	bébé	reflection of child (self) in mirror	>	(photograph of self)>(all photographs)>(all pictures)>(all books with pictures)>(all books)
Rasmussen (1922)	vov-vov	dog	>	(kitten)>(hens)>(all animals at zoo) >(picture of pigs dancing)
Kenyeres (1926)	baba	baby	>	(adults in pictures)>(pictures in books)
Moore (1896)	fly	fly	>	(specks of dirt)>(dust)>(all small insects)>(his own toes)>(crumbs of bread)>(a toad)

features in chapter 5 is correct, however, then there is no set of simple visual features which will exclusively characterize all dogs, say, which means that the meaning of a word does not consist of some small set of perceptually-based features.

A second problem for the semantic features hypothesis comes from the notion that semantic features are based on the built-in operation of the perceptual systems of humans. A feature such as four-legged could only be taken in as the result of a series of fixations, and if one wishes to say that a feature like four-legged is innate, one would have to assume that humans come into the world with a complicated eye-movement sequence built in.

In addition, some of the postulated semantic features are of a very abstract nature, such as animate versus inanimate. For such features, it is difficult to see how they could be based directly on perceptual information at all.

One or two features as the basis for overextensions. Further problems for the notion that children use only one or two features as the basis for their use of words comes from some of the overextensions in Table 15.1. Consider first Pavlovitch's report on the use of *bébé*. The child first used it to refer to the child's own reflection. It was then used to refer to a photograph of the child. At the very least, some face-type features were involved here. The use of the word then shifts, though, to all photographs. The next big step is to books with pictures, and then to books. These different types of information are each more complex than one or two features, and they seem to be used in succession, indicating that the child is changing the basis for use of the word as time goes on, and not simply taking one little bit of information and gradually adding to it.

With the exception of *sch, mooi,* and *fly,* all the items in Table 15.1 are further examples of this. They seem to entail a stringing of uses one onto another, by shifting criteria in midstream, as it were. Vygotsky (1962) talked about a similar occurrence in the early concepts of children. It seems that the child has a relatively large body of information available about when to use each word. The decision as to whether or not to use a given word in a given situation is based on this information, but it is not always based on the same specific subset of this information.

A different analysis of overextensions. As an alternative to the semantic features hypothesis, let us assume that the child takes in a good deal about the situations in which words are used, and that the child doesn't know just which information is relevant to the use of the word in question. If a child hears the word *dog* used while a dog is walking by, the child can't tell just what the word is referring to, assuming that the child knows no other words. The only way in which the child could begin to approximate adult usage is either through being explicitly corrected by adults or by learning other words, which will result in the narrowing of the use of the words learned earlier.

Let us go through some hypothetical experiences to see how a child could produce overextensions even though more than one or two semantic features are stored. Let's say a child hears the word *dog* used in a situation in which the child's attention is focused on a dog running by. The child has seen dogs before and so is able to take in information about what the dog looks like and what it is doing. On the basis of this information, the child now must decide whether or not to use *dog* in new situations. The only basis the child will have is the overlap between the new situation and what is stored in memory. There are several important points here. First, there are some situations that are so different from a dog running that there will be no match made at all, so the child will say nothing. Second, some situations will perhaps be very close to the original, such as when the same dog runs by again. These situations will produce *dog* from the child. Third, there will be some intermediate situations, which overlap with parts of the child's information, but not all of it. For example, the child could see a dog standing still, or a horse running through a field. Given the sorts of information stored by the child, any number of new situations will produce a partial match. If we assume that a partial match can be effective, then the child will use the word in an overextended manner. This will result even if the child has perfect storage of the earlier situation. The crucial point here is that he or she has no way of knowing the limits of the word's use.

However, as soon as the child hears other words being used, changes in overextension will occur. Let's say the child now goes to the zoo, sees zebras for the first time, and learns their name. The child examines the zebra, which means that some physical differences in appearance and action between zebras and dogs will be noted. Therefore, neither *dog* nor *zebra* will now be as overextended as *dog* was when it was the only word the child knew. That is, the range of situations that fall "between" the child's knowledge of zebras and dogs will now be divided up. Some of them will be called zebras and some will be called dogs. If the same situations had occurred before the child learned *zebra*, he or she might have called all of them dogs.

To summarize, it may be possible to account for the early overextended use of words without assuming that the child stores only one or two semantic features. In addition, there are some logical questions that can be raised about the basic notion of semantic features.

15.2 Nelson's analysis of first-word acquisition: functional concepts

Nelson (1974) has presented an alternative to the notion that the child learns the meaning of words by acquiring semantic features one at a time. She criticizes the semantic features hypothesis because it argues that the beginnings of concepts depend upon the child's hearing others talk about things. According to Nelson, the child has available a set of concepts long before the first words are learned. He or she has information available about objects, the things that objects do, and things that one can do with objects. This is conceptual information which the child brings to the language-learning situation, which the semantic features hypothesis ignores.

A second criticism that Nelson raises concerning the semantic features hypothesis is that it assumes that all knowledge about objects is in terms of perceptual attributes. Nelson argues that there is another important way in which things can be grouped—on the basis of their functional characteristics. That is, one can group things together as a single concept because they can be acted upon on the same way. Once the child has grouped objects together on the basis of their functional characteristics, he or she can then note physical similarities among them. These would then be the physical features used to classify new objects without actually carrying out operations on them.

As an example of how this learning takes place, let us consider Nelson's analysis of the development of the concept *ball*. The child and the mother are playing with a ball. From this interaction, the child pulls out the actions and relations that the ball goes through. That is, the new physical object can be rolled and bounced, it goes under the couch, mother picks it up and throws it, and so on. Throughout the child's interaction with the mother, the activities are constantly changing. The only constant in the situation, except for the child and the mother, is the ball. Thus, from the very beginning, the child has detailed information about the ball, according to Nelson.

The child does not yet have a concept, though, because only a single object is involved. However, at a later time he or she notices some children playing with a different ball at the playground. Since certain actions are the same—the ball is thrown and it rolls, for example—the two situations will be combined. In this way, one begins to get a grouping of objects on the basis of the kinds of actions that the objects can take part in. Also, the child begins to carry out an analysis of the features present in the two objects, which can serve to identify new members of the *ball* class on the basis of physical appearance alone. Nelson seems to view this feature storage in a way similar to that of Clark (1973). "As instances have been added, a set of identifying features has been abstracted and stored with the concept" (Nelson, 1974, p.280).

Nelson argues that this feature analysis is secondary to the grouping of the objects that came about because the same actions were involved with each, which is where she differs from Clark. According to Nelson's point of view, it seems that the child wouldn't at first notice that the ball from home and the ball on the playground are similar, at least in shape. This may be an overemphasis, because it seems more reasonable to assume that from the child's very first sight of a ball and the things that it can do, the child would use physical characteristics as the basis for dealing with new objects. That is, it seems probable that a child would respond appropriately to the new ball in the park simply on the basis of its physical similarity to the ball at home, even if the child didn't see children playing with the ball in the park. It is not unreasonable to assume that a child would run to an idle ball in the park and start to play with it, on the basis of its physical appearance alone. If so, then the physical characteristics of the objects are important from the very beginning, and they shouldn't be considered in any way secondary to the functional characteristics, as Nelson seems to want to do. In addition, it is not at all clear that functional aspects of objects are different from perceptual aspects. For example, the function "graspable" is based on the size and shape of the object relative to the child's hand. This seems to be perceptual information.

In any case, according to Nelson, when the child begins to learn to use words, there are already available these action-based concepts that have evolved out of the child's interactions with objects. Names are then attached to these functional concepts. Based on this analysis, Nelson argues that the first use of words on the child's part will be based on the interactions that serve to define the various concepts possessed at this time. So, for example, it would be predicted that the child would only use *ball* to refer to an object that is acting in the way that he or she has seen balls act in the past. Only later would the concept be separated from the specific actions, and only then would the name be applied to the relevant object even if not actions were being carried out on it.

To summarize Nelson's model, she argues that concept formation is carried out independently of language, and that the child has much information available about objects before words are learned. This information about objects is acquired through the child's interaction with objects. These actions form the basis for the early concepts; the perceptual characteristics of the objects are assumed to be extracted secondarily, only after objects have already been classified on the basis of actions.

A possible problem for a functional analysis of early concepts: "there's Mommy." There is a very common phenomenon in the acquisition of the first words that raises some interesting questions about Nelson's word-acquisition model. Most, if not all, children overextend the words *Mommy* and *Daddy;* they call other adults by these names very frequently. However, while the child will use the name *Mommy* to refer to a strange female, that same child will not approach this strange female in order to be picked up and cuddled. That is, there is often a sharp distinction made by the child concerning how far the word can be extended versus how far other responses can be extended.

This phenomenon seems to raise problems for Nelson's model of early concepts, for the following reason. According to Nelson, the child's first use of words would be based on the action core of the early concepts. Therefore, the earliest uses of words would be based on the action that the object would be undergoing, and not its physical characteristics. If this were true, then the child should not use the word *Mommy* to refer to someone with whom the child wouldn't interact in the way it would with its mother. However, just such a use of *Mommy* and *Daddy* seems to occur frequently. This seems to argue against the notion that everything depends on action. The child in this hypothetical but plausible example seems to be using perceptual features alone, which means that Nelson's model may not be able to explain the behavior.

Furthermore, it will not help to argue that the child may be using perceptual features because he or she has already extracted them from interaction with the mother. If this were true, then these features ought to serve as the basis for the extension of other responses to any individual that can be called *Mommy*. According to Nelson's model, it seems that one must argue that all responses will be transferred on the basis of this conceptual core. Therefore, one should not find only some "Mommy-appropriate" responses transferring to other people; all responses should transfer, or no responses should.

Why are words generalized when other actions aren't? At this point, we ought to briefly try to deal with this transfer of verbal responses, but not other responses, to new objects. The first thing to note is that there is a

Cognitive factors in language development

period in the first year of life during which young children will indeed play with strangers just as they will with their parents. At the age of six to nine months, children begin to show distress when other people try to pick them up or come close to play with them, and the children will no longer reach toward strangers to be picked up. Before we can understand why the child will call these strangers *Mommy,* when he or she begins to talk, let us first consider a greatly oversimplified explanation of why the child starts to lose interest in them during the latter part of the first year of life.

One could argue that the child who wants to be picked up or played with has a problem to solve. The problem is how to be picked up or played with. The child then raises its arms or crawls over to a person in order to solve the problem. Now, let us assume that the child gradually comes to want to get that particular set of feelings that corresponds to being held by its mother. This means the child will carry out those responses that in the past have brought about those feelings. When the child becomes capable of discriminating the mother from others, then the child will only approach the mother. This will come about because only the features corresponding to the mother are always followed by the right sorts of feelings. The important point to note is that the child has a basis on which to make a discrimination here, because the various sorts of features are relevant to one of at least two different outcomes.

When the child hears *Mommy* used in the mother's presence, he or she will be able to remember the situation, and that memory may be reasonably detailed, as discussed in section 15.1. When a somewhat similar-appearing person is seen next, the child will say "Mommy" because no other words are available to match that situation better. The crucial point is the same as that raised concerning the early overextension of *dog.* So long as *Mommy* is one of the child's first words, and no alternatives are available, then it will be used much more widely than any other responses that the child could produce at the same time. This is because the child knows much more about the domains of these various responses than he or she does about these first words.

The first words: summary. These last few sections have argued that the acquisition of word meaning doesn't begin with the learning of words. Rather, as Nelson (1974) argues, learning words is superimposed upon what the child already knows about objects. Thus, the semantic features hypothesis seems to be incorrect. However, it also seems to be true that the production of words can sometimes be independent of the production of other responses. This may be due to the fact that the child cannot tell beforehand the domain of any given word; that is, the set of situations to which the word can be applied. This can only be determined by acquiring other words, which gradually narrows down the domain of each of them. Therefore, although Nelson seems to be correct in arguing that the child has action concepts available before the first words are learned, it is also true that learning how words are to be used is at least somewhat independent of them, as Clark (1973) argues.

15.3 Expressing semantic relations in two-word utterances

Obviously, one-word utterances are followed by two-word utterances in the normal course of development. However, the recent surge of research in language development began with two-word utterances, and only later were the single-word utterances considered in earnest. This initial interest in two-word utterances was a result of the influence of structural linguistics on the psychology of language. Chomsky (e.g., 1965) and his followers in linguistics and psychology (e.g., Miller, 1963) were interested in formulating the set of rules needed to characterize the grammatical sentences of English. This point of view was adopted by many developmental psycholinguists, who set out to make a comparable analysis of the utterances of children. If one hopes to formulate the rules describing the structure of children's utterances, then one must obviously begin with utterances that have the potential for structure. That is, one must begin with multi-word utterances, since single-word utterances have no syntactic structure. Therefore, developmental psycholinguistics began with two-word utterances and only later got to the developmental precursor, one-word utterances.

Pivot-open grammars and their problems. The first attempts at structural analyses of children's utterances produced the pivot-open grammar, one of the most well-known phenomena in modern psychology. This was built on the assumptions that: (a) one could analyze children's utterances into grammatical classes, and (b) one could formulate a set of rules that would specify how words from the grammatical classes were to be combined to produce the utterances that the child produced. The specification of grammatical classes was to be the result of distributional analysis of the child's speech. That is, words were put into the same grammatical class if they appeared in the same positions in utterances (Brown & Fraser, 1963). It was hoped that the only criterion for analysis of utterances would be the distributional data. In this way, a purely syntactic analysis could be carried out, parallel to that being advocated by Chomsky (e.g., 1957, 1965) concerning adult utterances.

Cognitive factors in language development

The first analyses were encouraging, because they indicated that the early two-word utterances of children had some internal structure, and this structure was more or less constant across the dozen or so children whose speech had been analyzed (Braine, 1963b; Brown & Fraser, 1963; Miller & Ervin, 1964). Two grammatical classes were found and many of the two-word utterances were made up of one word from each of these classes. The two classes were the pivot class and the open class, and there seemed to be a number of distributional criteria for distinguishing them. The pivot class contained a small number of words, each of which could appear in either position of a two-word utterance, but not both. Also, no two-word utterances were found that contained two pivot words. In addition, pivot words could not appear alone, as one-word utterances. The open class consisted of many more words than the pivot class. The open words could appear in either position in a two word utterance; two open words could be combined to form a two-word utterance; and one open word could appear alone as a single-word utterance. For example, consider the following utterances: See Daddy; See Mommy; See milk; See car; Want Daddy; Milk there; Milk here; Daddy here; Mommy here. In this oversimplified example, *see* would clearly be a pivot word, since it appears in only one position, as would *here; Mommy, Daddy* and *Milk* would be open words, since they appear in either position. *Want, there* and *car* are ambiguous in this sample, but there is some indirect evidence that the first two are pivots and the last is an open word. For example, *want* appears with *Daddy,* clearly an open word. If that is the only position that *want* appears in, then it would be a pivot. As already mentioned, the early investigations seemed to indicate a great deal of regularity in the structure of two-word utterances from child to child. The specific words in the pivot and open classes might change from child to child, but the basic pivot-open structure seemed to be universal among children.

However, soon after the first pivot-open grammars were formulated, there was evidence that they might not be adequate as a description of the two-word utterances of children. Two sorts of problems arose. First, it turned out that not all words could be unambiguously placed in either the pivot or open class (Bowerman, 1973). Second, it was pointed out by Bloom (1970) that the relationships among words in children's utterances were much richer than those dealt with by pivot-open grammars.

As a well-known example, Bloom discussed the production of the utterance *Mommy sock* by one of the children whose speech she recorded. In one sample of speech, the child said *Mommy sock* on two separate occasions. According to a pivot-open analysis, these two utterances would have the same structure, since the same combination of words was involved. However, Bloom also noted the circumstances in which the utterance was produced each time, and the circumstances indicated to her that two very different structures were involved. In the first case, *Mommy sock* was said when the child picked up her mother's sock. In the second case, the mother was putting the child's sock on the child's foot. Therefore, even though the same words were involved each time, the utterances were not really the same.

Bloom argued that in order to more completely understand and analyze children's utterances, it was necessary to take into account the circumstances in which an utterance was produced. She tried to do this by keeping a running record of the contexts of the child's utterances. This was a step beyond the strictly syntactic analysis on which pivot-open grammars were based. Bloom's analysis was a semantic analysis, in that it took the meaning of an utterance into account when the utterance was analyzed.

Semantic relations in early utterances. Recent analyses of the semantic aspects of the speech of young children have indicated that they are attempting to express a number of different relations with their first two-word utterances. Some examples are shown in Table 15.2. The first three relations are interesting in that when they are combined they make up the

Table 15.2. Relations expressed in two-word utterances

Relation	Example
agent & action	Bambi go mail come
action & subject	see sock want more
agent & object	Eve lunch (Eve is eating lunch) Mommy sandwich (Mommy will have a sandwich)
modifier & head	pretty boat my stool
negation	no wash no wet (I am not wet)
datives (indirect object)	throw daddy (Throw it to daddy)
ostension (identification)	it ball there book
locative	sat wall baby highchair (baby is in the highchair)

standard *agent + action + object* form which is very typical in English. However, the child does not express all this information at once: only one of the relations is expressed in any given utterance. An interesting question that immediately arises is why the child's utterance is shorter than the corresponding adult utterance. Assuming that the child knows the words involved, why doesn't he or she say "Mommy is eating lunch," or at least "Mommy eat lunch"? We shall consides this question in a later section.

The *modifier + head* relationship is also expressed in the manner of adult speech, with the modifier coming first. This would seem to indicate that adult speech served as a model, since all the various types of examples in Table 15.2 follow the format of adult speech (Schlesinger, 1971). The same is true of the ostensive utterances, datives, and locatives.

Summary. A child's first two-word utterances are used to express the same sorts of relations that are expressed by adult utterances (Bloom, 1970). However, adult utterances usually express multiple relations, while the child's early two-word utterances only express one relation at a time. He or she seems to learn to express relations by producing pairs of words in the appropriate order. These pairs of words seem to be integrated in some way as the child develops, to produce complete sentences.

15.4 Communication and context

Bloom, among others, argues that the basis for production of an utterance is the semantic relation or relations which the speaker wishes to express. However, a difficulty arises here because there are many different ways of expressing exactly the same relation. So far, we have said nothing about how a speaker chooses among these possible utterances.

Emphasis and choice of utterance. One factor that is important in determining how a given relation will be expressed is the aspect of the situation that the speaker wishes to emphasize. Turner and Rommetveit (1968) gave subjects sentences to memorize, such as "The rabbit eats the carrot" or "The carrot is eaten by the rabbit." Both of these sentences express the same relations, with the rabbit being the agent of *eat,* and the carrot being the object. At recall, the subjects were given pictorial cues. Some subjects were shown a picture of only the agent (i.e., the rabbit in the above example), which others were shown a picture of the object (the carrot in the example). The cue given the subject strongly influenced the sentence that was recalled. When the picture of the object was given as a cue, subjects tended to produce passive sentences, whether or not they had originally heard them. In the same way, subjects given the agent as a cue tended to produce active sentences. Thus, depending upon what is being emphasized in the situation, different utterances will be produced to express the same relations.

The set of objects to be discriminated. Even though one specific object is being emphasized or discussed in a situation, the utterances used to describe this object can still vary greatly, depending upon other aspects of the situation (Olson, 1970). For example, consider the various sets of objects in Figure 15.1. Assume that a person is given one of the sets of objects, with a gold star placed under one of them. The person's task is to tell someone else which figure the star is under. In the first case, the description might be "the white one," but this description wouldn't work for the other two cases. "The round one" would be helpful in the second case, but more would be needed in the third case.

Olson argues that utterances are used to assist the listener in picking one event (the referent) out of some set of alternatives. Therefore, the specific utterance that a speaker will produce in order to describe a given referent will depend upon the other objects that the referent must be differentiated from. The examples just discussed are a case in point. According to Olson, a speaker always has much more perceptual information available about a referent than is expressed in any utterance. Before all this information is put into words, however, the speaker determines the set of objects that the listener must pick the referent from. The only features of the referent that

Figure 15.1. Olson's communication task. In each line, the star is always under the left-most object. The message used to describe that object will probably change, depending on the other objects that are present.

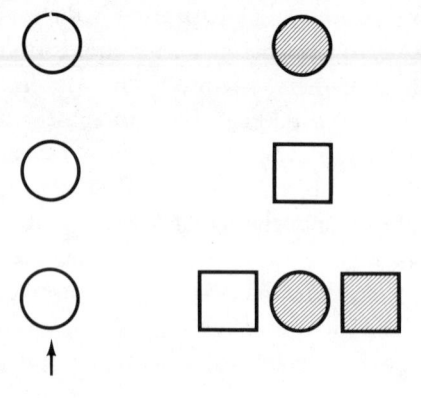

Cognitive factors in language development

will then be mentioned are those that will serve to differentiate it from the other objects in the environment.

If Olson is correct, then one cannot explain the production of an utterance by taking into account only the referent to be described. One must also know the objects that the referent is to be differentiated from. This means that for an utterance to be effective, both the speaker and listener must be entertaining the same set of alternatives. This is no difficulty if the objects in question are physically present. Often, however, this is not the case: one could be describing something that occurred yesterday to someone else who did not witness it. Since the speaker and listener do not have the referent physically present before them, the speaker must base the utterance on an inferred set of alternatives. If the speaker can accurately infer the set of alternatives that the listener will be considering, then the speaker's utterance will be effective in giving the listener information. If the speaker cannot accurately infer the set of alternatives being contemplated by the listener, then the utterance will not be effective. The more knowledge that the speaker and listener have in common, then the greater the chance that the speaker will produce an utterance that is informative to the listener. This will be discussed further in a later section.

To summarize Olson's theorizing, the realization of an utterance does not depend only upon the event to be described. Another crucial factor is the other events from which the referent must be discriminated. Therefore, it seems that the semantic relations to be expressed are not the sole determinant of the utterance that will be produced.

15.5 The development of communication skills

With so many factors to take into account in producing an utterance, one might expect that it would take a while before children could communicate effectively, and there is some evidence that this is so.

Examples of communication inadequacy in young children. Piaget (1955) conducted a number of influential investigations of children's ability to communicate. As was discussed in chapter 15, Piaget was interested in communication because he argued that at one point in life children are egocentric in their thinking, which means that they are capable of seeing any situation from only one point of view: their own. If this is so, then one area in which this would be expected to be evident would be communication, since, as we have seen, adequate communication requires that the speaker be sensitive to the needs of the listener. In one task, a child was told a simple story by the experimenter, and the child then attempted to communicate the story to another child, who had not heard it. The basic finding was that children six to eight years of age did a poor job of communicating the story to the other child. Here is the story and the version produced by one child.

Story told by experimenter: Once upon a time, there was a lady who was called Niobe, and who had 12 sons and 12 daughters. She met a fairy who had only one son and no daughter. Then the lady laughed at the fairy because the fairy only had one boy. Then the fairy was very angry and fastened the lady to a rock. The lady cried for ten years. In the end she turned into a rock, and her tears made a stream which still runs today. (Piaget, 1955, p.99)

Story told by Gio (8 years old) with Piaget's comments in parenthesis: Once upon a time there was a lady who had twelve boys and twelve girls, and then a fairy a boy and a girl. And then Niobe wanted to have some more sons (than the fairy. Gio means by this that Niobe competed with the fairy, as was told in the text. But it will be seen how elliptical is his way of expressing it.) Then she (who?) was angry. She (who?) fastened her (whom?) to a stone. He (who?) turned into a rock, and then his tears (whose?) made a stream which is still running today. (Piaget, 1955, p. 116–17)

If one only heard the child's version, one would not come away with the incident that the original story described. The child never makes the rivalry explicit, and he never uses enough nouns, so that the pronouns are almost always ambiguous. This child seems to know very little about the fine points of communication. The child's rules for introducing pronouns, for example, do not seem to be based on whether or not the listener has sufficient information available to determine the referent of the pronoun.

Other studies by Piaget (1955), in which children had to describe simple mechanisms to other children, produced the same results. The children could not communicate information to others, even though they understood what it was that had been communicated. Piaget's findings have been replicated by other investigators (e.g., Flavell, Botkin, Fry, Wright, & Jarvis, 1968), and similar findings have come from studies using other types of tasks (e.g., Glucksberg, Krauss, & Weisberg, 1966).

Communication adequacy in young children. From the studies reviewed, one gets the feeling that young children are totally incapable of communicating effectively. However, some recent studies have found that this is not true. Young children do communicate less effectively than adults do, but they are not totally insensitive to the demands of the communicative situation that they are in. Schatz and Gelman (1973) had four-year-old children communicate information to other children who were either two years old or ten years old. The children spoke differently to the younger and older listeners: they used simpler words and sentences, and more gestures, when speaking to the two-year-olds. The speakers seemed to be making sure that the younger listeners would be able to understand everything being told to them.

From this study, as well as others (e.g., Maratsos, 1973), it seems that relatively young children are able to modify their messages somewhat to meet the needs of the situation. Therefore, the most reasonable conclusion seems to be that young children are not totally ineffective as communicators. However, there do seem to be clear differences between the capabilities of young children and those of older children and adults.

One question that remains is why some studies find that young children are reasonably effective communicators, while others find a total lack of communicative competence in young children. An important factor here must be the communication situation itself, and the demands that it puts on the child. That is, if a child is in an unfamiliar experimental situation, this newness must make it harder to communicate effectively. On the other hand, effective communication should be much more frequent in a familiar situation.

15.6 The creativity of language: creating new utterances as problem solving I: Words

One aspect of human language which has greatly impressed many theorists is its creativity. New sentences are constantly being produced to meet the demands of new situations, and these new sentences are easily understood by people hearing them for the first time. We have not yet considered in detail how people can produce novel sentences at will, or why it is that these sentences meet the demands of the situations in which they are produced.

One sort of creation of a new utterance entails creation of new words. For example, a middle-class three-year-old child might say "He cut hisself," "I goed to the zoo yesterday," "It's the gooder one," or "I have two foots." In most middle-class households, the probability of the child's hearing such words as *hisself, goed, gooder,* and *foots* is very low. Therefore, these words must be inventions on the part of the child. Furthermore, as anyone who has been around young children can testify, such truly invented words are not isolated phenomena; all children produce them, and they do it more than once. Let us consider two such creations and where they might come from.

Foots. There is evidence that children acquire general knowledge about how plurals are formed soon after they begin to speak (Berko, 1958; Ervin, 1964). If children of two or three years of age are given nonsense words that they have never heard before, they can form the plurals correctly. Assume that we show a child a picture of an animal and say "This is a wug." We then show the child a picture with two of these animals, and the child will say "There are two wugs," using the correct form.

A more interesting demonstration of the development of general knowledge on the part of the child concerns the few words in English that are irregular in the plural: woman, women; foot, feet; sheep, sheep; etc. Children invariably say things like *foots* and *sheeps,* which they probably have not heard from their parents (Ervin, 1964). So we have the creation of really new words *in the face of the experience of having heard the correct forms produced by adults.* If the only factor involved in producing a word was having heard it previously, then *feet* should always be produced, but this does not happen.

Comed and Goed. A similar phenomenon occurs with verbs. The verbs in English can be divided into two classes, sometimes called strong verbs and weak verbs. The strong verbs are the ones used most frequently, such as *to come, to go, to do,* and *to be.* Each of these verbs is irregular in the past tense: come-came, go-went, do-did, be-was. The weak verbs are the less frequent verbs, such as *to watch, to polish, to argue, to confirm.* For the sake of discussion, let us generalize that all weak verbs form their past tense by adding *ed,* although the specific pronunciation varies, depending on how the verb ends.

We thus have two sorts of verbs, the frequent and irregular versus the infrequent and regular. Since the strong verbs are so frequent (i.e., the child hears them so much), these are the first past-tense verbs that are learned (Ervin, 1964). It is important to note again that each of these verbs is more or less independent of the others. Knowing that the past tense of *go* is *went* doesn't help you in forming the past tense of *come.* This means that each of these past tense forms must be learned as a separate item. What happens during this time is that the child learns things such as: if you are talking about the past, and the action involves someone's arrival, then say *came;* if the action involves someone's leaving, say

Cognitive factors in language development

went; and so on, one for each verb. In essence, each situation is separate from all the others.

All the while this correct usage of strong verbs is going on, the child is also coming across weak verbs, in both the present and past tense. The child begins to use these weak verbs correctly in the past tense, as they have been used by others. In addition, the child now begins to produce "corrupted" forms of the strong verbs in the past tense. One hears children say things like "He *comed* here yesterday." This is a form that most middle-class children have never heard, and yet they spontaneously produce it and many other such forms.

Obviously, the crucial factor in the creation of these new forms for strong verbs is the regularity in the formation of the past tense in the weak verbs that the child is beginning to learn. Unlike the strong verbs, forming the past tense of one weak verb is basically the same as forming the past tense of any other weak verb. This could pave the way for the formation of some generalized knowledge about speaking about the past, and this knowledge could turn out to be dangerous as far as the strong verbs are concerned. For example, let's say a child hears "I planted roses yesterday," and then hears "I painted the house last week." Assume further that the child witnessed the two incidents in question, and that when the sentences were heard, each served to retrieve the related incident. Given these hypothetical events, this child has learned some things about using the past tense: (a) when you are talking about a recalled incident of planting flowers, then say *planted;* (b) when you are talking about a recalled incident of painting a house, say *painted.*

Furthermore, we also have a third piece of information which comes out of the two of these: when you are talking about something that you remember doing, say what you would say if the action were actually happening and add *ed* to it. We have here a generalized rule about talking about the past. (Obviously, there are some unanswered questions here, such as whether remembering an incident is crucial for use of past tense, and if it is, just how remembering works in actual sentence production. These sorts of questions must be left unanswered for now. They may not be crucial to the present discussion, so long as it be granted that the speaker has some way of distinguishing between those situations that call for the present versus past tense.) Now let us place our hypothetical child speaker in a situation in which he or she is describing an experience already taken place, and the verb involved is *go*. From the experience with this verb alone, the child knows to say *went*. However, from the experience producing past-tense sentences recently, the child knows to say *verb + ed*. We thus have two potential responses available, and sometimes *goed* wins out and sometimes *went*.

One thing that might be important here is the relative frequency that the two forms have been used and heard in the past. For instance, let's say that the child has heard and used *went* a given number of times in the past. Perhaps when the total number of regular verbs that have been used and heard is about the same as the total number of *wents,* then *goed* will begin to appear. One problem with this is that it doesn't explain how the child could ever stop producing the regular form and get back to the correct irregular form. According to this frequency model, the generalized rule should just keep increasing and increasing in frequency relative to the specific rules, because the new verbs that the child learns are almost all regular in form.

One way to deal with this is to make two further assumptions. First, let us assume that as the irregular form is used more and more frequently, it is produced faster and faster each time. It is probably true that the regular form also gets faster with experience. However, it cannot be that the regular form and the irregular form get faster to the same degree as they are used again and again. If so, then the irregular form could never come to dominate over the regular form in those cases in which it is correct. Thus, let us also assume that ultimately the form corresponding to the specific rule will be produced faster than the form corresponding to the general rule, even though each specific irregular form is produced less frequently than the total number of general regular forms.

The question that remains here is why the specific form ultimately gets faster than the form based on the regularity. One reason for this might be the way information in memory is activated. For example, since the specific rule is related more closely to the specific situation, that rule might be activated more quickly than the general rule. If the child is asked "Did you see it?" then the rule *see* → *saw* fits this situation more closely than *verb* → *verb + ed*. This might account for the ultimate difference in speeds, although this is obviously speculative.

Producing words: summary. In these last few sections, we have seen that a consistent pattern is found in the development of the child's ability to create words. The irregular forms may be produced correctly at first, but they are then corrupted by the child's developing general knowledge. At a later point the irregular forms will emerge again. Several factors that might be important in this reemergence of irregular forms were considered.

15.7 Creating new utterances II: sentences

The second sort of creativity in speaking concerns production of novel sentences. A number of theorists have presented models of sentence production in which production of a novel utterance is analogous to the production of a novel solution to a problem as we discussed it earlier. As an oversimplification, let us begin with the hypothetical child discussed by Quine (1959). The child has learned the following utterances: "My hand hurts," "This is my hand," and "This is my foot." We shall assume that the child knows how to use each of these sentences in a small number of relevant situations. Now, the child's foot is stepped on and the child says "My foot hurts." For the sake of this discussion, we shall assume that this is a new utterance; the child has never produced it before and has never heard it before. The question to be considered is where this novel sentence comes from.

The child is in a situation in which he or she has been injured and is experiencing a pain in a specific bodily part. The child has never said anything in a situation of exactly this sort. However, the child has said "My hand hurts" in a similar situation involving injury and a pain in a bodily part. This sentence cannot be produced in the present situation, though, because it does not fit in this situation, since the hand isn't what is hurting.

Given that the child knows "This is my hand" and "My hand hurts," he or she can pull out "my hand" as the part of the sentence that deals with the object in question. "———hurts" must then deal with the injury and pain. Since he or she also knows "This is my foot," by comparing it with "This is my hand" the child can tell that "my foot" refers to the object in question there. Now the child can combine the knowledge of what to say when he or she has been injured and has a pain in a bodily part with the knowledge of what to say when talking about the part in question. This leads the child to say: "My foot hurts." To put it briefly, the child determines that "———hurts" is used when there is a pain in a bodily part and the blank is to be filled in with whatever verbalization has been used to talk about that body part in the past. Parts of this argument have been raised by various psychologists (e.g., Skinner, 1957; Braine, 1963a; Jenkins & Palermo, 1964; Hayes-Roth & Hayes-Roth, 1977).

In summary, one's knowledge about the sorts of things to say in certain situations parallels one's knowledge about the sorts of things to use in certain situations, as discussed in part 4. Production of a novel sentence is a function of two processes. First, one must compare the situation that one is now in with comparable past situations in order to find something to say. Second, one must modify what one said in the past in order to produce something that meets the particular needs of the present situation.

15.8 Why are young children's sentences telegraphic?

In the last section, it was argued that people produce new sentences by taking what they have heard around them and modifying it to fit the circumstances of the moment. According to this sort of an analysis, children's sentences must be based at least in part on the sentences of adults, since adult sentences are what they hear most. Therefore, any sentence that a child produces ought to be similar to some adult sentences. However, the earliest "sentences" produced by children aren't very similar to adult sentences. First of all, the utterances are much shorter than normal adult utterances. Secondly, not only are the utterances shorter, they aren't complete. Words and phrases are missing in some places, and some parts of words are also missing, such as plural endings on nouns and verbs. Finally, some of the utterances contain combinations of words that don't seem to be related to adult utterances at all. It is hard to think of any adult sentence from which a child could have derived an utterance like *More high*, but young children do produce utterances of this sort. If one wants to argue that children's sentences are based on adults' sentences, then one has to explain why the earliest sentences of children are so different from those of adults. These early utterances have been called "telegraphic" because they are similar to the sorts of shortened sentences that adults produce when they send telegrams. This is a useful description of these shortened early utterances, but it tells us nothing about the basis for this sort of speech.

Analogy and memory. One point that was not mentioned earlier, and which now becomes important, is the role of memory in the production of new sentences. It was argued that if a given situation matches something from the past, then a sentence would be recalled. Depending upon the match between the present situation and earlier ones, this sentence would either be uttered as is, or it would be modified to fit the new situation. This description is only partially true. To put it more precisely, the child's utterances depend not upon the utterances that the child hears, but on *what the child remembers* from the utterances that have been heard. Therefore, a child could produce utterances that are very different from adult utter-

Cognitive factors in language development

ances, even though the child is using adult utterances as models, simply because the child cannot completely remember the adult utterances.

This sort of phenomenon is not uncommon with adults who are not fluent in a foreign language and who listen to native speakers of that language. One experiences a blur of sound, with an occasional word suddenly jumping out. Therefore, immediately after one hears an utterance, all one has available is the few words that one was able to fish out of the torrent that went by. In a later situation of the same sort, if one tried to speak to someone else, one's utterance would be very primitive, even though it was based on an utterance from a native speaker. The problem is that one's limited knowledge of the language places great constraints on what can be extracted from any utterance. The same situation should occur with young children (Brown & Fraser, 1963).

There is some evidence that children cannot completely process even the relatively simple sentences that they hear around them. Brown and Fraser (1963) asked children between two and three years of age to repeat simple sentences of various sorts. The younger children consistently made errors in their repetitions, and the errors were not simply random omissions of words. First of all, there was a serial position curve found that is similar to the serial position effect found with lists of words. The last word in the sentence was almost always recalled, while words in other positions were recalled less well.

A second important result was that different sorts of words were repeated with differing degrees of success. Nouns, adjectives, and verbs—the content words—were imitated best. On the other hand, articles (*a, the,* etc.), forms of *to be,* and other function words were not imitated at nearly so high a rate.

In summary, this is evidence that children may not be storing all the words from the sentences that they hear around them. Therefore, one should not assume that, if children's speech is based on that of adults, it must sound just like adult speech. The information that a child has about what to say may be a very distorted version of what actually was said.

Processing, recognizing, and storage. Let us briefly consider why children might not be able to completely process the sentences that they hear around them. The reader may recall the discussion in chapters 5 and 6 of models of attention and perception based on knowledge and expectations, especially those of Hochberg (1969) and Neisser (1976). The same notions are relevant here. Let us assume that what one hears in a sentence depends on the match that one is able to make as one attempts to listen. (The reader may recall the "resonance" metaphor—section 5.5.) These ideas can now be used as the basis for some speculations about why children do not process sentences completely. First of all, it seems reasonable to assume that, all other things being equal, children should be slower at recognizing words when they hear them. As the word frequency effect demonstrates, the more times one hears a word, the easier it is to hear it later on (see section 5.3). Since young children have had much less experience simply listening to speech, they should be much less efficient at recognizing words. Therefore, they should be less able to hear words in sentences, when one word follows closely upon another. The last word in a sentence might be in a better position than the other words in this respect, because there may be significantly more "processing time" after it. This could at least partially account for the serial position effect obtained by Brown and Fraser (1963).

Slobin (1973) has recently argued that one can explain the sorts of things that children extract from what they hear if one assumes that children use certain strategies in order to process verbal input. Two such strategies might be: "Listen to ends of words first" and "Listen to ends of sentences first." Postulating such strategies can enable one to explain various aspects of language development, but one is still left with the problem of where the strategies came from. It may be simpler and more direct if one ignores such intervening levels as processing strategies, and goes instead directly to the basic capacities assumed to underlie all extraction of information from environmental events. For example, if one simply assumes (a) that word recognition is extended in time, and (b) that later words can interfere with the recognition of earlier words if the listener is relatively inefficient, one can directly explain why children pull more information out of the ends of sentences.

The second important finding from the Brown and Fraser study was that content words are repeated more frequently than function words. One factor that undoubtedly influenced this was that content words were invariably at the end of the sentences. In addition, content words are often stressed as sentences are spoken, meaning that they are louder, which would be expected to make their processing easier. Also, the content words that children hear usually refer to concrete things in the environment. This means that the things that the child sees as the sentence is spoken may serve as cues to the content words that will be heard. This might help processing. Finally, many of the concrete words are those that the child has learned as separate items. They have been heard many times by the child in isolation from other words, or close to it. The function words, on the other hand, are almost never heard alone, which means that they must be identified from the stream of sound. This would seem to depend upon the listener's being able to begin to break the stream into parts. This in turn would depend upon having some potential units available, which would be the already familiar content words. There is evidence to support this last contention from a study by Scholes (1969).

To summarize, there are several possible reasons why children do not process even relatively simple sentences perfectly. Although the reasons are of various types, they seem to have a common core, in that they are all based on the ease with which a child can recognize the words in a spoken sentence. Given that children do indeed process adult sentences imperfectly, we now have a basis for the nonadultlike sentences that they sometimes produce. Let us now consider a hypothetical example of how a child might come to produce an utterance that seems to be totally unrelated to anything the child has heard.

"More high": a creation based on past experience. Consider a child who is being tossed up in the air by her father. The father may say something like "Let's throw you up high." Since the child can't get much out of the sentence, we shall assume that she hears "high" or "throw high." Soon the father stops, but the child wants him to continue, so she must produce a sentence which will bring that about. The child knows the word "more" and has used it to request that something be repeated. For example, "More milk" means that the parent should pour milk into the child's cup again. So the child knows that "More————" is used to get an action repeated. She also knows that the action to be repeated is referred to as "high" or "throw high," so she says "More high" or "More throw high." In either case, we have an example of an utterance that doesn't seem to be related to adult utterances at all, an utterance that seems to be a pure creation on the part of the child. The analysis in this section, although speculative, has shown how such utterances could be firmly based on what the child has heard about her, even though they don't sound as if they are.

Possible output effects. The discussion so far has assumed that children produce childlike utterances at least in part because they are inefficient in processing the utterances that they hear around them. This could be called an input effect—a distortion of adult sentences occurs at input. There might also be output effects contributing to the childlike utterances produced by children, and these should be briefly mentioned. Consider a situation in which a child is witnessing some event and attempts to describe it. It has been argued earlier that some words are processed by the child more efficiently than others, for various reasons. In the same way, it is probably true that some words are *produced* by the child more efficiently than others, if only because the child uses some words much more frequently than others. Therefore, when attempting to describe a scene, some words might "come to mind" more quickly than others. Therefore, the child may produce a primitive utterance because not all the words were available when the child started to speak. Even though the child knows other words, they take longer to produce, and so the child starts to speak before they become available for production.

An analogy can help make this clear. When a train pulls into a station, many would-be passengers may run to catch it. However, some people may not run fast enough, or are too far away, and so will be left behind. Therefore, the train pulls out of the station with only a select number of the people who wanted to get on it. In the same way, the speech mechanism "pulls out of the station" with only those words that were made avilable by the child's viewing the situation. If one assumes that there is some sort of "speaking schedule" initiated by the viewing of the scene, then only those words that can meet the demands of this schedule will be produced. Therefore, one would expect that the early utterances of children would consist of those words most readily available to describe the situation at hand. As the child gets more linguistic experience, more words should become able to meet the scheduling demands involved in speech, and so the child's speech should become more complex.

In summary, there are at least two possible reasons for childlike utterances, even though children's speech is based on that of adults: distortion of adult sentences at input, and inefficiency of production at output.

15.9 Why does child speech become more complex?

Perhaps the most obvious fact concerning language development is that children's utterances get longer and more complex as they get older. This phenomenon is in need of explanation, obviously, and there is some question as to just what the explanation might be (Brown, 1973, pp.411–12).

Selective reinforcement. One explanation that was often proposed to account for language development, as well as any other development, was based on reinforcement. It was argued that selective reinforcement by parents of the child's more complex and adultlike utterances resulted in the child's overall level of speech becoming more complex, until adult complexity was reached.

One secondary finding from studies of child language is that this explanation is very probably incorrect (Brown & Hanlon, 1972). As part of the task of recording the spontaneous utterances of children, one also gets many adult utterances on tape. This enables one to test the hypothesis that the most complex and grammatically correct utterances of children are the utterances that are responded to most positively by adults. Brown and Hanlon found that this was not the case. Adults are just as likely to correct a child's speech after a grammatically correct sentence as after a grammatically incorrect sentence, and adults are just as likely to respond with a sentence of their own to a grammatically incorrect sentence as to a correct sentence. As an example, if a child says: "I think it's Tuesday," the adult will correct the child if it's Wednesday. In the same way, if the child says: "It Wednesday" on Wednesday, the adult will say something like: "Yes it is." Both correction by adults and adult communicative responses have been postulated as possible reinforcers (one negative and one positive) to shape correct speech. The finding that adults don't differentially reinforce correct utterances in either of these ways raises problems for reinforcement theories.

Brown and Hanlon found that the most important factor in determining whether or not a child would be corrected was whether or not what the child said was true. A child could produce a garbled sentence, but if the adult could make sense of it, and if the sentence was appropriate, the adult would respond to it with further conversation. Thus, one factor that has often been assumed to be crucial for development of any skill, that of selective reinforcement, turns out not to be relevant to language development. As Brown (1973) notes, such a finding raises some problems, because the "selection pressure" that pushes the child to develop more complex speech then becomes obscure.

Information processing capacity and language development. From the point of view advocated in the last few sections, a search for "selection pressure" is misdirected. We have argued that children's utterances are simplified at least in part because they can't process sentences efficiently enough to recognize all the words. If so, then as word recognition becomes more efficient with experience in listening to speech, the child should become able to recognize more words in sentences. This should make the child's memory for what has been said in various situations more complete, which should in turn result in more complex utterances from the child.

Therefore, we may be able to explain the complexity that comes with age if we simply assume that language production is based on what the child has heard others say, and that hearing what others say is a skill that improves with time, because it uses knowledge based on earlier listening. This conclusion assumes that no reinforcement effects whatever are important in language acquisition. This may be too strong an assertion, because the interaction between child and parents is very complex, and there are many possible reinforcing events that could be influencing language development. However, the purpose of the present discussion was to point out that one can develop a model of language acquisition that is strongly based on past experiences and yet does not depend on the notion of reinforcement.

15.10 Summary

This chapter has examined language development from a cognitive point of view. A number of important phenomena were analyzed, and in each case an attempt was made to determine what sort of information the child had available and how this information was being used by the child. Recent analyses of the acquisition of the first words by children indicate that two factors are involved in determining the breadth of usage of these words by the child. First, based on preverbal experience with objects, the child is able to extract detailed information about the situations in which words are used. However, the child may still use a word differently than an adult would, because the child knows so few words. Acquiring new words cuts down the range of application of the earliest words.

The production of two-word utterances likewise is a function of several factors. First, there is evidence that young children are expressing semantic relations with their earliest multiple-word utterances. These semantic relations have been extracted by the child from the situation in which words are heard. However, additional factors are involved here, because it is possible to express the same relation in many different ways. Communication skills and their development were briefly considered.

The discussion then turned to the creative aspects of language, the ability to produce novel utterances as needed. The creation of novel words and sentences was examined, and it was argued that these creations come out of the knowledge of the child concerning how to say certain things in certain situations. This knowledge serves as the basis for creation of new utterances to fit other situations.

The chapter ended with a discussion of the unique structure of child language. It was argued that children's utterances are firmly based on what they hear around them. However, due to processing inefficiencies, children are not able to store a complete record of what they hear. Therefore, they will say things that will not sound as if they were based on adult utterances, although they are. This same argument can be used to explain why children's utterances become more complex. Since listening skill would be expected to increase with increasing linguistic experience, then the child will be able to store more of the utterances that he or she hears. This will result in more information being available to serve as the basis for the child's production of utterances, which will bring the child's utterances into closer correspondence to adult utterances.

At the beginning of the chapter, it was noted that some theorists have argued that language could not be acquired through learning, and that language was therefore innate in humans and restricted to humans. There are several grounds now available for questioning this conclusion. First, based on the discussion in this chapter, it does not seem that we are dealing with any phenomena that preclude learning. There are complexities involved in language, to be sure, but their acquisition does not seem to be outside the realm of learning. In addition, since the position advocated in section 15.8 does not base learning on direct reinforcement, it avoids some of the difficulties encountered by reinforcement models. Thus, it seems premature to categorically conclude that language cannot be acquired through learning.

There are also questions that can be raised concerning the claim that language is limited to only the human species. This claim was based on several early studies that attempted to teach chimpanzees to talk, and that failed (e.g., Hayes & Hayes, 1951). However, several more recent studies have reported great success in teaching chimps to communicate using American Sign Language (e.g., Gardner & Gardner, 1969, 1971) and various other sorts of symbol systems (e.g., Premack, 1971). These studies, which could not be reviewed here due to space limitations, are important because they indicate that the linguistic gap between humans and other animals is not as wide as had been recently suggested.

In conclusion, recent work indicates that language development, while still an important phenomeneon, is not out of the realm of psychological theorizing.

16
Internalization of overt responses: outline of a model of thinking

16.0 Introduction

There have been a number of major themes that have appeared and reappeared throughout the earlier chapters. These various themes can now be used as the basis for a sketch of a model of human thinking.

Thinking and behaving. The first of these ideas was that there is a great deal of similarity between overt behavioral acts and covert or mental acts. This idea has been advocated in various forms by many theorists, as mentioned in earlier chapters. Sechenov (1863, rpt. 1952) argued that thinking is the first two-thirds of a reflex, with the only difference between thinking and acting being that in thought the overt act was inhibited (see chap. 9). Sechenov's model included both central and peripheral components. The central nervous system was assumed to play a role in all reflexes and, accordingly, in all thought. In addition, he assumed that some activity in the peripheral nerves and muscles was necessary for thought to occur, even though this activity couldn't be seen without special recording techniques. This sort of a model is still being advocated by Russian psychologists (e.g., Sokolov, 1972). In the United States, Watson (1924) also argued that mental phenomena were simply overt behaviors of a very small magnitude. Watson's peripheralist model was essentially identical to the peripheral half of Sechenov's model, since Watson based all thought on movements which were supposedly peripheral in origin.

Piaget (e.g., 1968) has also argued that concrete operations are closely related to sensorimotor schemas (see chap. 14). According to Piaget, the operations evolve out of internalized schemas, although Piaget argues that the schemas are changed in the process of internalization. Piaget's model is probably not a peripheral one like those of Sechenov and Watson, although Piaget does not discuss things in these terms.

Thus, we have here the same basic idea, that thought is behavior that is not expressed as actual large-scale movements, being advocated by theorists from very different traditions. Based on the discussion in chapter 9, especially section 9.6, a solely peripheral theory of thinking is probably not tenable. The reader may recall the study by Smith et al. (1947), in which a subject was given an injection of curare, which eliminates all movement and feedback from the periphery. The subject in this study reported that he had been fully conscious throughout the experiment, and there was objective evidence to support that claim. Therefore, peripheral feedback does not seem to be necessary for conscious thought. Other evidence reviewed in chapter 9 also supports this conclusion. However, even though we reject peripheral models of thinking, this does not mean that we must also reject the notion that thinking is closely related to behavior. The model which will be sketched out later in the chapter will attempt to make explicit the relation between overt behavioral acts and covert mental acts, especially as regards the basis for internalization of overt behavior.

Perception as action. The second important theme was that perception could be looked upon as a behavioral act, rather than simply a recording of information in the manner of a tape recorder or a camera. Once again, this is an idea that has been advocated by theorists from different traditions. For example, Hochberg's recent model of attention and perception (Hochberg, 1969, 1970) is based on the assumption that people are constantly sampling and interpreting information from the environment. The interpretation of this information entails matching it with information already in memory. Thus, if one attends to a sentence, the process of attention entails matching this sentence with a sentence of one's own. Here again we see a close link between mental processes, or mental acts or thoughts, and overt behavior. The ability to listen to some sentence may be the same ability that allows one to imagine oneself hearing the sentence. Furthermore, the ability to imagine oneself hearing the sentence spoken by oneself may be the basis for much verbal thought.

Past experience as the basis for creativity. A third theme concerned the role of the past experience in the creation of novel responses. It was argued that creation of a response was based on a modification of some old response that had been produced in some similar situation. In order for the new response to meet the specific demands of the new situation, the old response would have to be modified to take into account the characteristics of the new situation that were not present when the response had been made originally. However, these characteristics were also dealt with in terms of relevant past experience.

This sort of analysis was applied to a number of different situations in the earlier chapters. It was the basis for the discussion of research in problem solving in part 4. In addition, it was argued that the same use of knowledge about the visual world is the basis for our ability to create novel visual images (see chap. 7). Other sorts of imagery were assumed to have similar bases. The production of novel sentences by children and adults was also seen as the result of modification of past experience (see chap. 15). In this case, the experience concerned hearing and producing sentences in various situations, and the results brought about by these sentences.

No changes from children to adults. In the last few chapters, it was argued that "egocentrism" in the thought of infants and young children was the result of a lack of knowledge, not the result of different thought processes. Thus, these chapters argued that all human beings think in the same way. The only change that occurs with age is in the quantity of knowledge that the person has available. Not surprisingly, adults, with their wider knowledge, will be able to deal effectively with many more situations than will children. Because of their insufficient knowledge, children will have a tendency to behave in nonadult, or "childlike," ways. Based on this reasoning, the model of thinking to be presented in this chapter will use sensorimotor development as a representative phenomenon for all of human thought.

Thinking is not a unique activity. According to the classical theory, thinking is an activity that involves contemplation or manipulation of special mental objects, which are concepts (Price, 1953, chap. X). This sort of view is still prevalent in modern psychology (see chap. 8). Many theorists argue that human knowledge is made up of networks of concepts, and that acquiring new knowledge means adding to these networks. These conceptual networks can be manipulated to produce new knowledge. Furthermore, answering questions about events that one witnessed, or about any facts that one knows, would come about through the examination of these networks. This is very similar to the classical act of contemplation,

Internalization of overt responses

although it is often argued by modern theorists that all this manipulation of concepts is an unconscious activity. Much of thinking would be assumed to entail such activities.

The notion that thinking is some specific and unique activity that involves either the conscious or unconscious manipulation of things called concepts has been criticized on several grounds in earlier chapters. First, there is the assumption that concepts are mental objects analogous to physical objects. One reason for rejecting this notion is the finding that it is not possible to specify the features that define any given concept or pattern. If so, it means that all features are involved in all concepts, which also means that there is nothing "inside" to stand for the object that is outside (see the discussion in part 2). Recent research in memory also raises problems for this view (see part 1), as does work in imagery and in sentence processing and storage (see part 3).

A second and perhaps more important criticism of the classical theory of thinking arises if one accepts the notion that mental or covert acts are simply ordinary behavioral acts with the final response inhibited, as just discussed. Consider the following sequence of events. Two tennis players are in the midst of a point, when one of the players hits a weak shot. The opponent, upon seeing the ball lazily floating across the net, says to himself "Not too big a backswing now, and deep to the backhand." He then does just this and wins the point. In this example, at first glance, it seems reasonable to argue that the player first *thought* about how he could win the point, and then *acted* in the appropriate way. The verbal thought was the basis for, or the cause of, the nonverbal actions that followed. However, if the "verbal thought" is simply an inhibited verbalization, then it is hard to see why it should be given a privileged status in all this (see chap. 9). The basis for the verbalization is the same as that for the other actions that the tennis player carried out, so that postulating the verbal image as the cause of the later responses does not really add anything. Therefore, if this argument is accepted, when one sits and "contemplates" some situation, one is simply doing what one would do if one was actually talking about that situation with someone else. One is not carrying out some special activity called thinking.

From this point of view, the important question is the following: Why is it that sometimes we actually behave, while other times we only sit and talk about behaving, if only to ourselves? We have already said something about this in chapters 9, 10, and 15, and the discussion in this chapter will add to that. The chapter will be concerned basically with the question of how and why overt responses can become internalized, where they are experienced as mental events, or thoughts.

As already mentioned, we shall use sensorimotor development as the paradigm example of human thinking. We shall consider three separate but related phenomena: (1) the selectivity of infant responsiveness; (2) the generalization of the early circular reactions; and (3) the internalization of the sensorimotor schemes. In the course of the discussion, we shall touch upon findings from a number of different areas.

16.1 Initiation and selectivity of reactions

The phenomenon to be considered first is the selectivity of the reflexes. Why is it that the infant sucks when something touches its lips and not when something touches its foot? One answer that comes to mind is that, since the reflexes are present at birth, it must be innately determined that sucking occurs when only certain specific conditions occur. There has been much research conducted on inherited behavior patterns in many species of animals other than humans. Let us consider some of this research in order to see what it can tell us about the capacities of humans.

Some examples of species-specific behavior in lower animals. As part of his extensive review of animal behavior, Hinde (1970) has discussed many studies that examined the stimulus conditions necessry for the elicitation of various species-specific responses. One example of species-specific behavior that has been extensively studied is the courtship behavior of the three-spined stickleback, a small fish. In the spring, the males and females of this species go through a long series of interconnected behaviors that result in mating, protecting and hatching the eggs, and caring for the young. At the earliest stage, in the spring, the males establish territories and build nests in them. In his territory, a male acts aggressively toward other males that cross its boundaries. However, a male is less aggressive to females that enter the territory and sooner or later he will court one of them.

One question that immediately arises here is the basis for the territory-owner to exhibit aggression versus courtship. In one study, a series of models was presented to males in their own territories. The models ranged from lifelike replicas of sticklebacks to simple oval and circular shapes. The effectiveness of the various models in eliciting aggression and/or courtship was the variable of interest. Intuitively, it would seem that the lifelike models would be most effective in eliciting these behaviors, but in neither case was this so. As far as aggression was concerned, a model of almost any shape would be effective, so long as its underside was red. In the spring, when they begin to stake out territories, the underside of the male stickleback turns red, and this serves as a sign for other males. After the mating season is over, the male loses his red color on the underside, so that there is little or no aggression exhibited for the remainder of the year. Thus an input is analyzed. Such an input will be even more effective if it takes a "head-down" posture, which is typical of that adopted by trespassers when the territory-owner moves out to meet them.

A similar pattern holds as far as courtship is concerned. A very realistic female model was ineffective in releasing courtship if it did not have a swollen abdomen, while a very unstickleback-looking model would elicit courtship if it had a swollen "abdomen." In the spring, when a female produces eggs, her abdomen swells, so there is a good reason for the male's selectivity. In addition, the swollen-abdomen model is even more effective if it is presented in the relatively upright position in which swollen females usually swim.

To summarize this research, it seems that the species-specific courtship and aggressive behaviors of the stickleback depend upon the presence of certain attributes in environmental objects. Therefore, if it is true that these behaviors occur without prior learning, then these organisms must come into the world already able to analyze stimuli in order to determine if they contain these attributes. In addition, since the courtship and aggressive responses are also not learned in this species, once these attributes have been found, they serve to set off the relevant responses. And all this occurs only in the spring, indicating that some changes in the general bodily state of the stickleback probably also play a part in making the organism ready to respond in just this way to just those attributes. That is, if there are some prewired circuits involved here, they are operating only during the spring.

This behavior in the stickleback is only one of a large number of behaviors that have been analyzed in this way by ethologists, who are students of animal behavior in natural settings. As is well known, the results parallel those just discussed. Hinde (1970) provides summaries of many other examples.

FAPs and releasers. In their analysis of species-specific behaviors, ethologists have found that complicated behavioral sequences can often be broken down into units, called fixed-action patterns (FAPs). The FAP is the building block of species-specific behavior. It is a relatively rigid and unchanging response that is inherited and is elicited by a relatively specific set of conditions. The stimulus which elicits the FAP is called the *releaser* for the FAP. As an example of the combination of FAPs and releasers in a complicated behavioral sequence, consider again the courtship behavior in the stickleback. The first step in courtship involves the male's swimming up to a female in a particular way. This zigzag courtship dance of the male is the FAP, and the swollen abdomen of the female, oriented upward, is the releaser. The male's zigzag dance then serves as a releaser for the female's FAP of swimming toward him with her body still tilted upward. This in turn releases the male's swimming toward the nest, and so on. The entire complicated sequence is built up out of a series of smaller pieces and the whole thing is held together because each FAP contains elements that serve to release the next one in the sequence. Furthermore, it is argued that each FAP is elicited by a specific releaser because part of what is inherited are circuits of nerve cells. Therefore, when a specific event occurs, this sets off a sequence of nervous impulses that results in the sequence of motor responses corresponding to the FAP. At the risk of oversimplification, we could say that part of the "design" of lower animals is that circuits are set up during the development of the nervous system. These circuits result in certain patterns of excitement in sensory nerves resulting in transmission to motor centers, which results in the motor movements corresponding to various FAPs.

Reflexes, FAPs, and releasers. An analysis of the selectivity of reflexes in human infants can now be briefly outlined. Reflexes would seem to be FAPs in humans. If one considers the reflexes at that hypothetical point at which the infant is yet to have any experience, then the reflexes are segments of behavior that are available at birth, are fixed in form, and are elicited by specific environmental events. They are directly comparable to the FAPs in animals discussed in the last few sections. If so, then the selectivity of the reflexes comes about because of the fact that each reflex can be elicited only by a relatively specific releaser. Thus, the selectivity of human responding at birth comes about because we arrive on the scene with certain "circuits" already "wired." These circuits could be looked upon as a series of instructions of the form: in circumstance x, do y, where x is the releaser and y is the reflex or FAP.

16.2 Generalization of reflexes

Given that human reflexes are FAPs at birth, as soon as the infant begins to use the reflexes, they become very different from the "pure" FAPs in

Internalization of overt responses 405

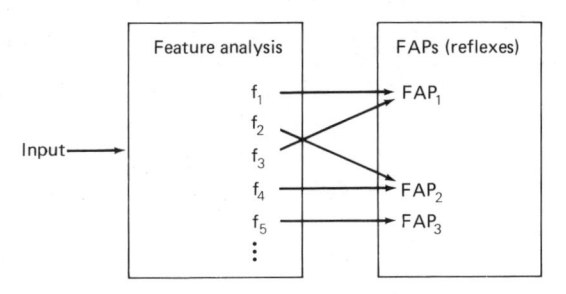

Figure 16.1. Situation at birth: a set of FAPs ready to go.

lower animals. The most important difference for the present discussion is that human reflexes evolve into schemas, and the schemas are applied to a wider and wider range of objects as the infant grows older. This doesn't happen to FAPs in animals, although many animals are also able to elaborate on inherited behavior patterns in a manner similar to humans.

An outline of the situation in the human infant at birth is presented in Figure 16.1. Each of the various reflexes is related to a cluster of features, or a primitive pattern map, that describes the sort of event that will result in the reflex being produced. As we saw in the discussion of the stickleback, the inherited releaser is usually not a detailed description of a real environmental event. Rather, the releaser is a set of attributes that are more like a very simplified caricature of an environmental event. In order for the reflex to be applied to a broader range of situations, the releaser must be "filled in" to include more information. In this way, formerly irrelevant objects could become effective releasers. One further point about this broadening is that it only occurs gradually. The first new stimuli that become effective are only slightly different from those that were effective at birth. There is a slow "oozing" of a schema from the original releaser to a broader spectrum of objects.

In order to account for the broadening of releasers, it is reasonable to assume that infants remember their encounters with the world, or the various episodes of their lives. What children remember can then serve as the basis for a broadening of the range of application of a schema. Let us expand the model in Figure 16.1 in the following way. We already have the connections between various primitive pattern maps and the reflexes that evolve into schemas. When a given object is presented, and it matches one of the pattern maps, the relevant reflex will be produced. Assume that as a result of this, the infant will remember the following: (a) something

Cognitive development

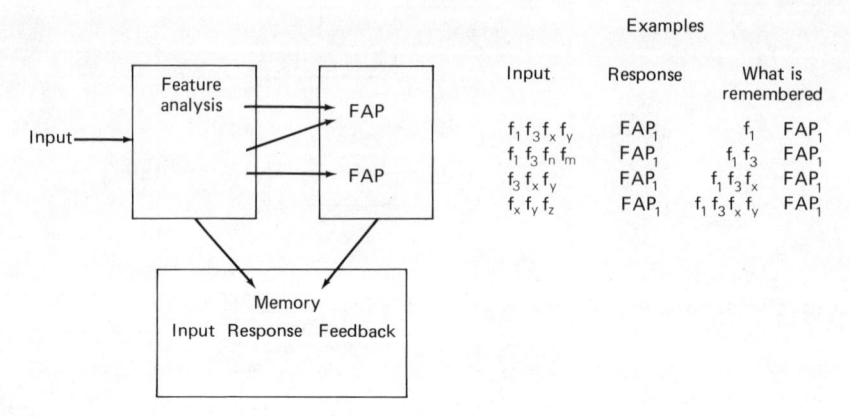

```
                                              Examples
                                    Input      Response   What is
          ┌──────────┐                                    remembered
          │ Feature  │──→ FAP
          │ analysis │              f₁ f₃ fₓ f_y   FAP₁    f₁        FAP₁
Input ──→ │          │              f₁ f₃ fₙ f_m   FAP₁    f₁ f₃     FAP₁
          │          │──→ FAP       f₃ fₓ f_y      FAP₁    f₁ f₃ fₓ  FAP₁
          └──────────┘              fₓ f_y f_z     FAP₁    f₁ f₃ fₓ f_y FAP₁
                ↓  ↑
          ┌──────────────┐
          │   Memory     │
          │Input Response Feedback│
          └──────────────┘
```

Figure 16.2. The organism now remembers something about its past actions, and the information gets more and more removed from the built-in "releasers."

about the object; (b) something about the response that was made; and (c) something about what happened, or the feedback from the response. This expanded model is shown at the top of Figure 16.2. (In the present discussion, we shall be concerned only with the information about the stimulus. The other aspects, especially the feedback, will become important shortly.) The model then works as shown in the figure for several hypothetical situations. The child remembers these various episodes. Since these situations contain more information than that directly relevant to the reflex that was initiated, sooner or later this other information will be stored. For the present, it doesn't matter just how much of the information about a stimulus situation is stored at once. In Figure 16.2 it has been assumed that not all the information about a stimulus is stored at once. This seems a reasonable assumption to make, given that we are talking about an infant, for whom every situation is essentially novel. In the last chapter it was argued that lack of familiarity would hamper the child's linguistic processing, based on the model of pattern recognition developed in part 2. The same logic applies to the present discussion: the child's initial unfamiliarity with the world should severely limit the information which can be "resonated to" at any given time.

In any case, given that the child is learning something about environmental events, then a wider and wider range of features will be encountered, so one will have a distribution of features in relation to the various responses. Now, when a new stimulus is presented, a response will be selected for it, based on how well its features match those of the various episodes that have been encountered. Thus, we have the capacity to generalize reflexes to broader and broader ranges of stimuli. As can be seen in Figure 16.2, by the time that the four episodes have occurred, an event containing the features x and y could release the response in question, although these features could not do so immediately after birth.

To summarize, it may be possible to account for the generalization of reflexes by assuming that the inherited connections between pattern maps and reflexes is only the first step. If one also assumes that infants are able to remember something about the stimuli that release the reflexes, then one gets a basis for generalization. Again, this discussion would also be relevant to animals in many situations.

16.3 The waning of responsiveness

According to the model in Figure 16.2, infants should just go happily on, applying schemas to objects, for the rest of their lives. This does not happen, of course. Sooner or later, there comes a point at which the infant no longer responds to a previously effective object with some given schema. The object is no longer an adequate releaser. Since the model in Figure 16.2 cannot deal with this sort of phenomenon, it will have to be elaborated a bit further. This is an especially important phenomenon, since it may be the basis for internalization of actions. That is, we may now be speculating about the basis for "thoughts."

The orienting reflex. The orienting reflex, discussed in chapter 6, is a group of responses made when a novel stimulus occurs. It seems to serve the purpose of orienting the organism toward the new stimulus so that it can be identified and responded to. If the stimulus has occurred several times, and so long as the stimulus has no important consequences, the orienting reflex drops out, or habituates.

Humans of all ages show habituation of orienting reflexes when a once-novel stimulus is made commonplace through repetition. This habituation does not come about because the peripheral receptors are no longer working. Rather, it seems that the stimulus is still being registered, it just is no longer capable of eliciting an orienting reflex. The strongest evidence for this comes from studies that have shown that an orienting reflex will occur when a heretofore repeated stimulus is omitted or when a stimulus of a given duration fails to end at the usual time.

Habituation and knowledge. As mentioned in chapter 6, Sokolov (1963) has argued that habituation of an orienting reflex comes about because the organism develops knowledge about the stimulus, or develops a "model" of the stimulus. If there is no match between a stimulus and the model, that is, if the stimulus is unexpected, then an orienting reflex occurs. If the model matches the stimulus, then no orienting reflex occurs and the stimulus is ignored. One could perhaps paraphrase Sokolov's theory by saying that if an organism knows what is going to happen if it attends to a stimulus, then the organism will not attend to the stimulus at all. Familiarity breeds habituation.

The waning of circular reactions and the development of knowledge. With this discussion of orienting reflexes as a background, we can now return to the main topic of this section, the waning of circular reactions. It was assumed in section 16.2 that several sorts of information are stored in memory as the infant works its way through the sensorimotor period (see Fig. 16.2). The infant stores information about the stimulus, the response that was given, and the feedback that occurred, or what happened. The information is of the sort: When such-and-such a situation occurred, I did this, and that happened. We can now use this knowledge in order to produce the waning of the circular reactions, or one might even say the habituation of the circular reactions: a circular reaction might no longer be applied to an object once the infant becomes capable of predicting what is going to happen if that reaction is carried out. That is, if one can predict what will happen if something is done, then it will not be done.

In order to make this notion more concrete, consider the situation in Figure 16.3. We have a subject who has information in memory about what has happened when a given schema has been applied to a given ob-

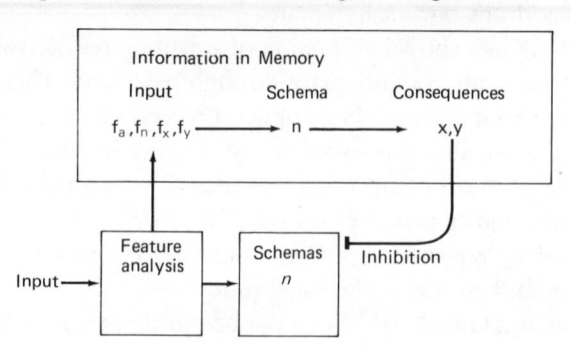

Figure 16.3. Output is inhibited in a knowledgeable organism.

ject. The object is now presented again, and the following occurs. The object matches the requirements for activation of the schema (arbitrarily called schema n), so the schema is released. In addition, the object results in a previous episode being recalled. If we can assume that this information from memory has an inhibitory effect on responding, then the habituation of the schema can be explained. In essence, this model argues that there is a race of a sort going on between the information in memory and the activation of the schema. If the information is activated before the motor message gets going, then no response will occur. Initially, since the organism has no experience with the object in question, there is no information available to block the response. However, as the object is responded to more and more, additional information is stored. Furthermore, with this increased experience with the object, one might expect that the information in memory would get activated more and more quickly when the object is presented. Therefore, one might find that initially the response in question would be given completely. With more experience, the response would be "turned off" after it got started, because the information in memory was activated, but not quickly enough to cut the response off completely. With still more experience, and still-faster activation of the information in memory, the response should be cut off more and more quickly. Therefore, one would see less and less of the response, until it wouldn't be seen at all.

16.4 Internalization, habituation, and thinking

Before going on to consider how it is that behavior is brought about in a knowledgeable subject, the question of internalization of schemas must be considered further. At the end of the sensorimotor period, the infant is able to sit quietly and think about solving a problem. Earlier in this period, the infant actually carried everything out, which resulted in any really new solution being stumbled upon through overt trial and error. In Stage VI, however, the schemas have been internalized and overt responding is not necessary. New solutions can be formulated covertly.

Based on the discussion in the last section, it seems reasonable to argue that habituation of reflexes and internalization of schemas are one and the same. A schema becomes internalized when an object that was an effective releaser loses its effectiveness. This is the same as saying that internalization equals habituation. If this is so, then any internalized "thinking" that goes on at the end of the sensorimotor period is essentially the same as the overt responding that took place in the substage just before. Thus, thinking is not a separate process that can be sharply distinguished from actual behavior. At the very least, thinking entails using the knowledge based on previous behavior. This means that the kinds of activities carried out internally would be the same as the activities which could be carried out externally.

However, we have to add one further aspect to the notion that thinking is simply internalization based on knowledge. This knowledge is not simply knowledge of what has been done in the past. The child is also able to use this knowledge to design new responses internally. Therefore, this knowledge is of a sort that enables the creation of a new response without its actually being carried out. This would seem to be very similar to the processes discussed in the earlier chapters on adult problem solving. That is, new responses are produced because of the match that is made between the new problem and past experience. In addition, once a match has been made, the child can predict what will happen and use these predictions to modify the response before it is ever given. This ability to predict the consequences internally, however, is still very directly based on the active accommodations that the Stage VI child has been making for almost two years.

Thus, the ability to predict the consequences of responding is important in two ways. It results in overt responding being eliminated, and it enables the child to formulate new solutions internally. This means that the same thread may be underlying the behavior of young children in the sensorimotor stage and adults solving problems. These processes were discussed in detail in chapter 10.

As mentioned earlier, over one hundred years ago Sechenov (1863, rpt. 1952) argued that thinking was the first two-thirds of a reflex. Sechenov assumed that all behavior was the result of reflex activity, including complicated human behavior. A reflex consisted of a sensory message produced by a stimulus, which activated some center in the cortex, which in turn resulted in some outflow that produced the response that was seen by an observer. In thinking, according to Sechenov, a sensory message activated the cortical center, but no outflow occurred, so there was no overt response. This was the first two-thirds of the reflex. Obviously, the ideas briefly outlined in this section and the last one are very similar to those expressed by Sechenov many years ago.

16.5 Behavior in knowledgeable organisms

We are now relatively advanced developmentally. We have an organism who is knowledgeable enough to be able to predict what will happen if he or she does any of a number of things to any of a number of objects. Thus, according to the model in Figure 16.3, we should all spend most of the rest of our lives in catatonic states, not responding to anything, once we reach the last stage of sensorimotor development. Why, then, do knowledgeable organisms behave? One reason which is obvious is that although we are knowledgeable, we are not omniscient: we don't know everything, and we are always running across objects which we cannot immediately assimilate. Therefore, we will still behave, at least occasionally.

However, there are other times in which we seem to behave *because we know what will happen,* not because we don't. When I reach to pick up a pencil in order to start to write, I know what will happen, and that is just the reason that I picked up the pencil. Thus, there would seem to be one time in which one's knowledge would serve to *select* the response in question, rather than inhibit it: when the consequences of a given response match the solution requirements for some problem that the person is working on.

In order to bring this about, an addition such as that in Figure 16.4 is needed. We have here a subject who is working toward some goal. The subject now scans the environment, and some object in the environment

Figure 16.4. Output is disinhibited (output occurs) in an organism working toward a goal when the desired goal matches remembered result of carrying out some response schemes (schema).

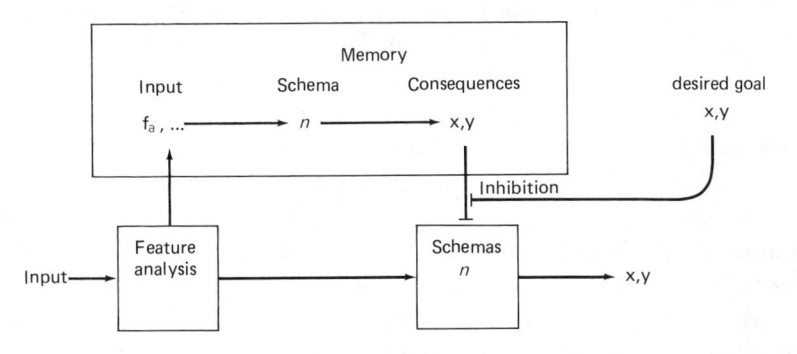

can be used to bring this goal about. Ordinarily, the object would not be responded to, because the person can predict what will happen. However, at the present time, the goal itself gets in the way. It blocks the activation of the knowledge from memory, or, to put it another way, it overcomes the inhibition brought about by the knowledge from memory. In either case, the response will not be blocked any longer. It can be carried out, precisely because it will bring about the goal in question.

This raises one further requirement, which is that there must be some way to activate the goal. One way in which goals are activated in adults is by other people's requests. If you are asked to do something, then a goal is automatically available (assuming that you are willing to carry out the request). In some cases these methods will also work with children, because in Stage VI of sensorimotor development most children can understand some language and can be requested to do things.

However, goals do not only become activated through the intervention of others. For example, sometimes a person, either an adult or a child, may walk into the kitchen to get something to eat, without anyone else being around or saying anything. One way in which a food-getting goal might be activated is through bodily changes. That is, the goal of eating food is activated by the changes that occur in one's body as one gets hungry (see Lindsay & Norman, 1972, chap. 17). These changes serve to activate information in memory concerning how this hunger had been eased in the past. This could then serve as the goal in a problem solving attempt.

One final point concerns the relation between the present discussion and that in chapter 9 concerning speech-for-self during problem solving. At that time, an "overflow" hypothesis was presented, which argued that speech gets released during problem solving because a person who is busy working on a difficult problem does not have enough capacity available to keep his or her mouth shut. At first glance, the present discussion seems to contradict that hypothesis, because it has just been argued that the accumulation of knowledge automatically results in an overt motor response being inhibited. The only way a response can be released is if the response can bring about some goal that the person is working toward.

This issue is in need of further elaboration in order to determine if a contradiction is indeed involved. First, the speech-for-self situation in chapter 9 is much more complicated than the sensorimotor situation being considered here, because in the former there are several sorts of responses involved, one superimposed on the other. First, young children are initially reinforced for talking to anyone, and then the range of stimuli is narrowed. Therefore, the speech-for-self situation involves at least two responses (talking versus not talking). Also, a person is present in the problem solving situation, which makes the situation a quasi-communication situation, and which adds to the complexity. The presence of a person would serve to make speech more probable, all other things being equal. Second, it might also be true that if an infant were placed in a cognitively taxing situation, then previously habituated secondary reactions might be released due to the overload. This would be comparable to what happens with verbal responses during problem solving. Given the highly speculative nature of the present discussion, nothing further can be said about this, except to emphasize the complexity of the questions involved and how little is known about the answers.

Behaving without goals. There are still two problems remaining. One has to do with problem solving that seems to be related to neither external instructions nor internal bodily changes. For example, you may be sitting watching television when you suddenly remember that you have to hang a picture, so you go off to get a hammer. One often thinks about things that must be done "out of the blue"; that is, without any help from the environment. Once one thinks of the problem, then one can start behaving; but the question remains as to how one would think of the problem in the first place. Second, there seem to be cases in which one doesn't really have a problem to solve at all. An example of this would be going to the library to get a mystery story. If one spontaneously thinks of doing this, then one could argue that there hasn't really been an explicitly formulated problem. This section has been filled with enough speculation, so these points will not be pursued further. However, it is obvious that they are very important points, and they must be dealt with if the ideas in this section are to have broad relevance to human behavior.

Summary. This section has argued that the waning of responsiveness comes about because infants acquire information about what will happen if a response is carried out. When the consequences of a response can be predicted, the response will be inhibited. However, when the consequences of a given response match the solution requirements for some problem that the person is working on, then the response will not be inhibited. Any input that then matches the requirements for the response will release it. Questions were raised about certain situations that are not simply conceived of as problems.

16.6 Thoughts as the cause of actions

It is usually taken as a hallmark of voluntary actions in humans that they come about as the result of conscious thoughts (Kimble & Perlmutter, 1970). A voluntary act is one that is consciously thought about before it gets carried out. Involuntary acts are those that are carried out without any conscious involvement. Given that thoughts cause voluntary actions, the next question is just how this comes about. James's model (1890) will serve to represent what has been called the "classical theory" of volition. We shall first outline this point of view, and then criticize it and outline an alternative conception of the relationship between thoughts and actions.

Images and acts. According to James, the cause of a voluntary act is the thought or image of the consequences of that act. For example, if one thinks about the consequences of lifting one's arm, that act will be carried out. There are two sorts of consequences that are important with an act such as raising one's arm. There is first of all the feedback from the muscles and joints when one has moved the arm. This is what would ordinarily be called the feeling of having moved one's arm. Second, there is the visual feedback after the arm has been moved. Imagining either of these two things is supposedly sufficient to bring about voluntary movement of the arm. An additional question which arises is why we sometimes imagine acts without them actually occurring. From James's model, the act ought to be carried out if we have imagined what it would be like to carry it out. James deals with this potential problem by arguing that at the same time one is imagining an act, one may have in mind the thought that the act is not to be carried out. This conflicting thought stops the imagined act from occurring.

Not long after James formulated his model, Woodworth (1906, cited in Kimble & Perlmutter, 1970) raised a cogent criticism. James had formulated his model on the basis of his own introspections. Woodworth used the same sort of data and came to a conclusion different from that of James. Woodworth found that many voluntary acts were carried out without the images that James had argued for.

If I wish to cut a stick, my intention is not that of making a certain back and forth movement of my arm, while simultaneously holding the fingers pressed tightly towards each other; my intention is to cut that stick. When I voluntarily start to walk, my intention is not that of alternately moving my legs in a certain manner; my will is directed toward reaching a certain place. I am unable to describe with any approach to accuracy what movements my arms or legs are to make; but I am

Internalization of overt responses

able to state exactly what result I design to accomplish. . . . It is not so much a supply of ideas of the various movements that are possible as a knowledge of the various effects that can be produced that is the first prerequisite of the voluntary life. (Woodworth, 1906, p.375, cited in Kimble & Perlmutter, 1970, p.369)

Woodworth argues that one does not consciously think about the fine points of the act to be carried out, as James claimed. Rather, one thinks of the effect one wishes to bring about, in general terms, without being conscious of the exact way in which this effect is to be brought about. One can agree with Woodworth's general claim, but it seems that he may have not gone far enough.

One example from my own experience raises further questions about the role of thoughts in causing actions. A while ago, when our son was just beginning to feed himself, he naturally dropped a lot of food on the floor. We tried to pick up what he dropped, but we didn't get it all. This would result in one's squashing peas and corn by accident as one walked around the kitchen after supper. One time, he dropped some peas off his tray, and I reached down to pick them up. Since I had recently been thinking about James's model of volition, just after I finished picking up the peas I was struck by the thoughts that accompanied the act. When I first bent down to pick up the peas, I had no thoughts whatever. However, as I reached down, I got a clear image of a shoe squashing the peas I was reaching for. Thus, my thoughts were different from the effects discussed by Woodworth. I was thinking about what would happen if I hadn't carried out the act. I am as sure as I can be that I had no thoughts of a clean floor as I reached for the peas. So if this report of mine is accurate, then neither James nor Woodworth is correct.

A second important aspect of this example is that I am sure that those thoughts about shoes squashing peas didn't occur until *after I had started reaching*. Before that I had done nothing but see the peas falling and start to reach. If so, then this obviously voluntary act was carried out without being consciously thought about beforehand. This goes against both James and Woodworth, and raises problems for all models that argue that conscious thoughts are the causes of voluntary acts.

The causes of thoughts. Based on the discussion in several of the earlier chapters, it would be argued that thoughts do not cause actions. In chapter 9, for example, it was concluded that verbal imagery is simply a sentence which is not spoken overtly. If so, then the verbal thought is brought about by the same causes that produce any other motor act. The same is true of nonverbal imagery, as discussed in chapter 7 for visual images. Therefore, if one says "I must get out of bed" to oneself just before getting out of bed, this does not mean that the thought caused the act. All it means is that at that time one was able to say that sentence to oneself while not getting out of bed, and that one got out of bed soon thereafter. Just as it is possible to talk aloud about doing things without doing them, it is possible to talk to oneself about doing things without doing them. If one then actually carries out the act, it is not because one talked to onself. Rather, it is because whatever had been interfering with the motor act is doing so no longer. For example, anticipating the cold floor could stop one from getting out of bed, but it wouldn't stop one from talking to oneself about getting out of bed. If it got late enough, so that one would be late for an important appointment if one stayed in bed any longer, then one would get out of bed. But this wouldn't necessarily be because one had had earlier verbal thoughts about getting out.

Thus, the important questions are not how and why thoughts cause actions. Rather, the important questions concern how and why motor acts and images occur. If we knew that, then we could explain why images sometimes occur before motor acts, sometimes during motor acts, sometimes after motor acts, and sometimes not at all, and why the image is sometimes of the act itself, sometimes of the effect of the act, and sometimes of something else. This issue was briefly considered in chapter 10, when we considered the role of imagination in problem solving. At that time, a distinction was made between a situation in which one simply carried out a solution to a problem and a situation in which one first imagined a potential solution being carried out. It was argued that one important factor was the completeness of the match between a problem and the problem-solver's knowledge. If the problem solver knew that the goal in question had been brought about with the available objects, then no "thought" would occur, and the solution would simply be carried out. However, if the exact goal had not been brought about before, then imagination would be brought into play, and the subject would have to "think" about the solution. From the point of view of the present discussion, one could say that if the problem solver can imagine the goal being brought about, that will result in the solution being "released," as in Figure 16.4.

Although this is obviously only the barest beginning, perhaps the point of view outlined in the present chapter will make it easier to understand the relationship between "thought" and "behavior."

16.7 Summary

This chapter attempted to sketch a model of thinking, defined as the internalization of overt responses. This internalization is clearly seen during sensorimotor development in infants, so this was the period that was analyzed. The discussion centered on three main areas. First, the selectivity of the reflexes and schemas was explained by analogy to the FAPs found in lower animals. Second, the generalization of the early schemas was explained with reference to the storage of information about environmental events. Finally, internalization of schemas was explained through the use of the concept of inhibition. A modification of Sechenov's model was presented, in which inhibition of a response was brought about if the organism could predict the outcome of the response. Relevant evidence from several areas was also discussed. Finally, the notion of volition was considered, especially the idea that thoughts cause actions. It was argued that thoughts do not cause actions, because thoughts are actions themselves.

Obviously, the model outlined in this chapter is at best a very small step as far as an understanding of thinking is concerned. As indicated in the discussion, these topics have been of interest to scientists for over a hundred years, at least back to Sechenov. However, very little actual research in this has been carried out over the years, and that is still true today. About the only research that has specifically considered conscious action and volition has descended directly from the classical model, as outlined by James (e.g., Greenwald, 1970). Very little attention has been paid to alternative conceptions of conscious action and volition, at least as far as cognitive psychologists have been concerned. It is hoped that more psychologists who are interested in cognitive processes will soon begin to reconsider the basic mechanisms which lie behind our thoughts themselves.

16.8 Summary of part 5.

The last four chapters have attempted to apply the ideas from the earlier discussion to some important issues in cognitive development. The basic point being argued was that the cognitive processes discussed in the earlier parts of the book are also directly relevant to the understanding of the behavior of infants and children in various situations. That is, it was argued that the same processes were involved in a child's and an adult's interactions with the world: pattern recogntion and retrieval of information from memory, and the modification of this information to meet the demands of the present situation. In addition, it was argued that infants and children differed from adults because they are less efficient in dealing with environmental events, and because their specific knowledge may be deficient in certain areas.

In chapters 13 and 14, this point of view was applied to recent research and theorizing based on Piaget's ideas. Piaget's very influential theory argues that humans go through several stages before their thought processes become like those of adults. We first considered evidence for this point of view from the behavior of infants. The various sensorimotor substages were discussed in chapter 13, and the development of the object concept was discussed in some detail. An alternative explanation for the infant's behavior was then presented based on the notion that infants don't know very much about the behavior of objects, and their behavior reflects this ignorance.

In chapter 14, the development of concrete operations was considered. Here again Piaget has argued that there are differences in thought processes between children and adults, and the first part of the chapter reviewed Piaget's findings. As in chapter 13, it was argued that there might be an alternative explanation for the differences in performance between children and adults on Piaget's tasks. For several specific phenomena, it was argued that children's ignorance would lead them to answer Piaget's questions in a nonadult manner. For example, one reason that children think that their parents made the stars is because they don't know enough about either what stars are or what their parents can and cannot do. Given this ignorance, it is not surprising that they answer Piaget's questions in the way that they do. Similar hypotheses were offered to explain children's "preoperational" performance in several other areas, including the lack of conservation of liquid. In summary, the purpose of chapters 13 and 14 was to demonstrate that one might be able to provide a coherent explanation of cognitive development using the concepts developed from the consideration of adult performance in the earlier chapters.

Chapter 15 considered recent research in language development from this point of view. An attempt was made to account for the "childlike" characteristics of children's sentences by examining the processing limitations of young children who are beginning to speak. It was argued that children's speech is based on the speech they hear around them, but the relationship is only indirect. The basic reason for this is that children may not remember everything they hear, which means that what they say will not sound exactly like what they hear. Children's inability to remember ev-

Internalization of overt responses

erything that they hear was explained on the basis of their lack of experience hearing things. The increasing complexity of children's speech with increasing age was also linked to their increasing capacity to process sentences.

Finally, the present chapter attempted to sketch an outline of the processes whereby action evolves into thought. It was suggested that the acquisition of knowledge about the consequences of one's actions may serve to inhibit the actual performance of these actions unless there is a need to carry them out. This conception is an elaboration of Sechenov's notion that thought is the first two-thirds of a reflex.

16.9 Memory, thought, and behavior: summary and conclusions

We have now completed our survey of human thought in its multiple facets. We began with a consideration of memory processes, because it was argued that memory is central to all thinking, and the discussion made its way through perception and attention, thinking and the question of the medium thought, problem solving, and cognitive development, concluding with a discussion of the "internalization" of thought. The following is a brief review of the major themes from these various discussions.

Part 1: memory. The discussion of memory centered on two related issues: the basic mechanisms involved in recall, and the "form" of the information stored in memory. As far as the first issue was concerned, it was argued that recall depended upon a person's ability to isolate the to-be-recalled item from all the potentially interfering items in memory. The first chapter contained a discussion of interference in memory, and the role of retrieval cues in recall. Chapters 2 and 3 examined the storage of information in memory, and it was concluded that one does not store "items" in an abstract sense, but that one remembers the episodes that one experiences, more or less completely. The term "encoding" was used to refer to the events that occurred during the presentation of a to-be-recalled item, and on which later recall seems to depend. In chapter 3, these encodings were considered further, in the context of a discussion of memory for prose. Followers of Bartlett have argued that what we remember about a prose passage may be very far removed from the actual passage that was presented, but recent research indicates that people remember both the details of passages and the things which a passage may make them think of. Depending upon how recall is tested, one's recall may give evidence for reconstruction or reproduction. The importance of "scripts," or one's knowledge about a given class of events, in comprehension and recall of verbal material was emphasized.

Chapter 4, the last chapter in part 1, presented a discussion of the possible importance of our ability to order events in time. It was suggested that the "glue" that holds episodes together is related to the "background" information that may be used to order events in time. The importance of this information in retrieval was also discussed.

Part 2: perception and attention. These two chapters were really two views of the same phenomenon, if current thinking is correct. The emphasis in these chapters was that perception and attention are two sides of the same coin: the sequential or cyclical processing of information postulated by several different theorists. This view emphasizes the importance of one's knowledge and expectancies in perception and attention, which implicates memory in these processes also, and which parallels the use of knowledge in recall tasks, discussed in part 1.

Part 3: the medium of thought. The important conclusions from these chapters were several. First, it was concluded that there was no single medium of thought, in that it seems that various sorts of information can be used by thinkers, depending on the task being carried out. Secondly, it was argued that the commonsense "symbolist" conception of thought was incorrect, because our thoughts, be they images or subvocal speech, do not serve to symbolize anything for us, in the way that a picture or someone else's speech can be symbolic. It was also argued that "concepts" do not serve as a medium of thought because "having a concept" is not the same sort of thing as "having a thought." Based on this viewpoint, suggestions were made concerning how images and subvocal speech played a part in cognitive activities.

Part 4: problem solving. These chapters examined the role of task-specific and more general knowledge in problem solving. It was argued that creation of a solution for a novel problem is based on the match that is made between the problem and one's knowledge. The problem serves as a cue to retrieve relevant past experience from memory, and this experience serves as the basis for construction of a novel solution. In addition to problem-specific experience, often acquired in the experiment itself, problem solvers also possess scripts about the probable structure of psychological experiments, and these scripts play an important role in the interpretation of the events that occur in an experiment. It was suggested that the behavior of subjects on water-jar problems, for example, could be understood in terms of the scripts brought to the experimental situation by the

Internalization of overt responses

subjects. Questions were raised about the use of concepts such as "insight" and "fixation" in explanations of problem solving success and/or failure.

Part 5: cognitive development. In these chapters, it was argued that the concepts which were applied to adults in the earlier chapters could also be applied to children. That is, the same cognitive processes may be present in children and adults, and differences in performance between children and adults may be brought about because of lack of knowledge on the part of children. This lack of knowledge is important in two ways. On the one hand, children's concepts are impoverished because they have not had the experience necessary for a mature understanding of such things as dreams and the origins of natural phenomena. Secondly, children's inexperience results in inefficient processing of certain types of information, such as speech. This inefficiency results in differences between the performance of children and that of adults, even though the same mechanisms are involved. The final chapter sketched a model of the relationship of behavior and thought based on the role of knowledge in the inhibition of overt behavior.

In sum, the close relationship between memory, thought, and behavior was emphasized throughout the book. Thought was seen as developing from the internalization or inhibition of behavior, based on what one remembered about past behavioral episodes.

References

Anderson, J. R. Verbatim and propositional representation of sentences in immediate and long-term memory. *Journal of Verbal Learning and Verbal Behavior,* 1974, *13,* 149–162. (a)

Anderson, J. R. Retrieval of propositional information from long-term memory. *Cognitive Psychology,* 1974, *6,* 451–474. (b)

Anderson, J. R. *Language, memory, and thought.* Hillsdale, N.J.: Erlbaum, 1976.

Anderson, J. R. Arguments concerning representations for mental imagery. *Psychological Review,* 1978, *85,* 249–277.

Anderson, J. R., & Bower, G. H. Recognition and retrieval processes in free recall. *Psychological Review,* 1972, *79,* 97–123.

Anderson, J. R., & Bower, G. H. *Human associative memory.* Washington, D.C.: V. H. Winston, 1973.

Anderson, R. C., & Pichert, J. W. Recall of previously unrecallable information following a shift in perspective. *Journal of Verbal Learning and Verbal Behavior,* 1978, *17,* 1–12.

Anisfeld, M. False recognition of adjective-noun phrases. *Journal of Experimental Psychology,* 1970, *86,* 120–122.

Anisfeld, M., & Knapp, M. Association, synonymity, and directionality in false recognition. *Journal of Experimental Psychology,* 1968, *77,* 171–179.

Atkinson, R. C., & Shiffrin, R. M. Human memory: A proposed system and its control processes. In K. W. Spence and J. T. Spence (Eds.), *The psychology learning and motivation: Advances in research and theory* (Vol. 2). New York: Academic Press, 1968, pp. 89–195.

Atwood, G. An experimental study of visual imagination and memory. *Cognitive Psychology,* 1971, *2,* 290–297.

References

Austin, J. L. *How to do things with words.* New York: Oxford University Press, 1965.
Austin, J. L. Are there *a priori* concepts? Orginally published in 1939. Reprinted in J. O. Urmson & G. J. Warnock (Eds.), *J. L. Austin: Philosophical papers* (2nd ed.). London: Oxford University Press, 1970, pp. 32–54.
Baddeley, A. D. The trouble with levels: A reexamination of Craik and Lockhart's framework for memory research. *Psychological Review,* 1978, *85,* 139–152.
Bartlett, F. C. *Remembering: A study in experimental and social psychology.* Cambridge, Eng.: Cambridge University Press, 1932.
Bartram, D. J. The role of visual and semantic codes in object naming. *Cognitive Psychology,* 1974, *6,* 325–356.
Beng, T. H., Richards, D. W., III, & Chute, D. L. (Eds.), *Drug discrimination and state dependent learning.* New York: Academic Press, 1978.
Berkeley, G. *The principles of human knowledge.* Originally published in 1710. Reprinted in G. J. Warnock (Ed.), *George Berkeley.* Cleveland, Ohio: Meridian Books, 1963, pp. 41–146.
Berko, J. The child's learning of English morphology. *Word,* 1958, *14,* 150–177.
Bernbach, H. A. Processing strategies for recognition and recall. *Journal of Experimental Psychology,* 1973, *99,* 409–412.
Bierwisch, M. Some semantic universals of German adjectivals. *Foundations of Language,* 1967, *3,* 1–36.
Birch, H. G. The relation of previous experience to insightful problem solving. *Journal of Comparative Psychology,* 1945, *38,* 367–383.
Bjork, R. A. Positive forgetting: The noninterference of items intentionally forgotten. *Journal of Verbal Hearing and Verbal Behavior,* 1970, *9,* 255–268.
Block, R. A. Effects of instructions to forget in short-term memory. *Journal of Experimental Psychology,* 1971, *89,* 1–9.
Bloom, L. *Language development: Form and function in emerging grammars.* Cambridge, Mass.: MIT Press, 1970.
Bobrow, S. A. Memory for words in sentences. *Journal of Verbal Learning and Verbal Behavior,* 1970, *9,* 363–372.
Bock, J. K., & Brewer, W. F. Reconstructive recall in sentences with alternative surface structures. *Journal of Experimental Psychology,* 1974, *103,* 837–843.
Boring, E. G. *A history of experimental psychology* (2nd ed.). New York: Appleton-Century-Crofts, 1950.
Bourne, L. E., Jr. *Human conceptual behavior.* Boston: Allyn & Bacon, 1966.
Bourne, L. E., Jr. Learning and utilization of conceptual rules. In B. Kleinmuntz (Ed.), *Concepts and the structure of memory.* New York: Wiley, 1967, pp. 1–32.
Bourne, L. E., Jr., An inference model for conceptual rule learning. In R. L. Solso (Ed.), *Theories in cognitive psychology: The Loyola symposium.* Potomac, Md.: Erlbaum, 1974, pp. 231–256.
Bourne, L. E. Jr., Ekstrand, B. R., & Dominowski, R. L. *The psychology of thinking.* Englewood Cliffs, N.J.: Prentice-Hall, 1971.
Bousfield, W. A. The occurrence of clustering in the recall of randomly arranged associates. *Journal of General Psychology,* 1953, *49,* 229–240.

Bower, G. H. Organizational factors in memory. *Cognitive Psychology,* 1970, *1,* 18–46. (a)

Bower, G. H. Analysis of a mnemonic device. *American Scientist,* 1970, *58,* 496–510. (b)

Bower, G. H. Stimulus-sampling theory of encoding variability. In A. W. Melton & E. Martin (Eds.), *Coding processes in human memory.* Washington, D.C.: Winston, 1972, pp. 85–124. (a)

Bower, G. H. Mental imagery and associative learning. In L. W. Gregg (Ed.), *Cognition in learning and memory.* New York: Wiley, 1972, pp. 51–88. (b)

Bower, G. H., Clark, M., Lesgold, A. & Winzenz, D. Hierarchical retrieval schemes in recall of categorized word lists. *Journal of Verbal Learning and Verbal Behavior,* 1969, *8,* 323–343.

Bower, G. H., & Holyoak, K. Encoding and recognition memory for naturalistic sounds. *Journal of Experimental Psychology,* 1973, *101,* 360–366.

Bower, G. H., Lesgold, A. M., and Tieman, D. Grouping operations in free recall. *Journal of Verbal Learning and Verbal Behavior,* 1969, *8,* 481–493.

Bower, G. H., Munoz, R., & Arnold, P. G. On distinguishing semantic and imaginal mnemonics. Unpublished manuscript, 1972. Cited in R. Klatzky, *Human memory: Structures and processes.* San Francisco: Freeman, 1975.

Bower, G. H., & Winzenz, D. Comparison of associative learning strategies. *Psychonomic Science,* 1970, *20,* 119–120.

Bower, T. G. R. Object permanence and short-term memory in the human infant. Unpublished manuscript, 1966. Cited in T. G. R. Bower, *Development in infancy.* San Francisco: Freeman, 1973.

Bower, T. G. R. The object in the world of the infant. *Scientific American,* 1971, *225,* 30–38.

Bower, T. G. R. *Development in infancy.* San Francisco: Freeman, 1973.

Bower, T. G. R., & Wishart, J. G. The effects of motor skill on object permanence. *Cognition,* 1971, *1,* 163–172.

Bowerman, M. *Early syntactic development.* Cambridge, Eng.: Cambridge University Press, 1973.

Braine, M. D. S. On learning the grammatical order of words. *Psychological Review,* 1963, *70,* 323–348. (a)

Braine, M. D. S. The ontogeny of English phrase structure: The first phase. *Language,* 1963, *39,* 1–13. (b)

Brainerd, C. J. & Brainerd, S. H. Order of acquisition of number and quantity conservation. *Child Development,* 1972, *43,* 1401–6.

Bransford, J. D., & Franks, J. J. The abstraction of linguistic ideas. *Cognitive Psychology,* 1971, *2,* 331–350.

Bransford, J. D., & Johnson, M. K. Contextual prerequisites for understanding: Some investigations of comprehension and recall. *Journal of Verbal Learning and Verbal Behavior,* 1972, *11,* 717–726.

Bregman, A. S. Perception and behavior as compositions of ideals. *Cognitive Psychology,* 1977, *9,* 250–292.

Broadbent, D. E. *Perception and communication.* London: Pergamon Press, 1958.

Broadbent, D. E. Word frequency effect and response bias. *Psychological Review,* 1967, *74,* 1–15.

References

Broadbent, D. E. *Decision and stress.* New York: Academic Press, 1971.

Brooks, L. R. Spatial and verbal components of the act of recall. *Canadian Journal of Psychology,* 1968, *22,* 349–368.

Brown, R. *A first language: The early stages.* Cambridge, Mass.: Harvard University Press, 1973.

Brown, R., & Fraser, C. The acquisiton of syntax. In C. N. Cofer & B. S. Musgrave (Eds.), *Verbal behavior and learning.* New York: McGraw-Hill, 1963, pp. 158–197.

Brown, R., & Hanlon, C. Derivational complexity and order of acquisition in child speech. In J. R. Hayes (Ed.), *Cognition and the development of language.* New York: Wiley, 1970, pp. 155–207.

Bruner, J. S., Goodnow, J. J., & Austin, G. A. *A study of thinking.* New York: Wiley, 1956.

Bugelski, B. R. Words and things and images. *American Psychologist,* 1970, *25,* 1002–1012.

Burnham, C. A., & Davis, K. G. The 9-dot problem: Beyond perceptual organization. *Psychonomic Science,* 1969, *17,* 321–323.

Charlesworth, W. R. Persistence of orienting and attending behavior in infants as a function of stimulus-locus uncertainty. *Child Development,* 1966, *37,* 473–491.

Chase, W. G., & Simon, H. A. Perception in chess. *Cognitive Psychology,* 1973, *4,* 55–81.

Chastain, G., & Burnham, C. A. The first glimpse determines the perception of an ambiguous figure. *Perception and Psychophysics,* 1975, *17,* 221–224.

Cherry, E. C. Some experiments on the recognition of speech with one and two ears. *Journal of the Acoustical Society of America,* 1953, *25,* 975–979.

Chomsky, N. *Aspects of the theory of syntax.* Cambridge, Mass.: MIT Press, 1965.

Chomsky, N. *Language and mind.* New York: Harcourt, Brace, and World, 1968.

Chomsky, N. *Syntactic structures.* The Hague: Mouton, 1957.

Clark, E. V. What's in a word? On the child's acquisition of semantics in his first language. In T. E. Moore (Ed.), *Cognitive development and the acquisition of language.* New York: Academic Press, 1973, pp. 65–110.

Conrad, C. Cognitive economy in semantic memory. *Journal of Experimental Psychology,* 1972, *92,* 149–154.

Cooper, L. A., & Shepard, R. N. Chronometric studies of the rotation of mental images. In W. G. Chase (Ed.), *Visual information processing.* New York: Academic Press, 1973.

Craik, F. I. M. The fate of primary memory items in free recall. *Journal of Verbal Learning and Verbal Behavior,* 1970, *9,* 143–148.

Craik, F. I. M., & Lockhart, R. S. Levels of processing: A framework for memory research. *Journal of Verbal Learning and Verbal Behavior,* 1972, *11,* 671–684.

Craik, F. I. M., & Tulving, E. Depth of processing and the retention of words in episodic memory. *Journal of Experimental Psychology: General,* 1975, *104,* 268–294.

Cramer, P. Associative strength as a determinant of mediated priming. *Journal of Verbal Learning and Verbal Behavior,* 1970, *9,* 658–664.

Crowder, R. G. The relation between interpolated-task performance and proactive inhibition in short-term retention. *Journal of Verbal Learning and Verbal Behavior*, 1968, 7, 577–583.

Crowder, R. G. *Principles of learning and memory*. Hillsdale, N.J.: Erlbaum, 1976.

De Groot, A. D. *Thought and choice in chess*. The Hague: Mouton, 1965.

De Groot, A. D. Perception and memory versus thought. In B. Kleinmuntz (Ed.), *Problem solving*. New York: Wiley, 1966.

Dodge, R. Motoric speech production. Cited in G. Humphrey, *Thinking: An introduction to its experimental psychology*. New York: Wiley Science Editions, 1963.

Dong, T., & Kintsch, W. Subjective retrieval cues in free recall. *Journal of Verbal Learning and Verbal Behavior*, 1968, 7, 813–816.

Dooling, D. J., & Mullet, R. L. Locus of thematic effects in retention of prose. *Journal of Experimental Psychology*, 1973, 97, 404–406.

Duncker, K. On problem-solving. *Psychological Monographs*, 1945, 58(5 Whole No. 270).

Earhard, M. Cued recall and free recall as a function of the number of items per cue. *Journal of Verbal Learning and Verbal Behavior*, 1967, 6, 257–263.

Edwards, P. (Ed.). *The encyclopedia of philosophy*. New York: Macmillan, 1972.

Egeth, H. E. Parallel versus serial processes in multidimensional stimulus discrimination. *Perception and Psychophysics*, 1966, 1, 245–252.

Elkind, D. Cognitive development. In H. W. Reese & L. P. Lipsitt (Eds.), *Experimental child psychology*. New York: Academic Press, 1970, pp. 479–508.

Elmes, D. G., Adams, C., & Roediger, H. L. Cued forgetting in short-term memory: Response selection. *Journal of Experimental Psychology*, 1970, 86, 103–107.

Epstein, W., Rock, I., & Zuckerman, C. B. Meaning and familiarity in associative learning. *Psychological Monographs*, 1960, 74(4, Whole No. 491).

Ervin, S. M. Imitation and structural change in children's language. In E. H. Lenneberg (Ed.), *New directions in the study of language*. Cambridge, Mass.: MIT Press, 1964, pp. 163–189.

Estes, W. K. The statistical approach to learning theory. In S. Koch (Ed.), *Psychology: A study of a science* (Vol. 2). New York: McGraw-Hill, 1959.

Estes, W. K. Structural aspects of associative models for memory. In C. Cofer (Ed.), *The structure of human memory*. San Francisco: Freeman, 1975, pp. 31–53.

Evans, W. F., & Gratch, G. The stage IV error in Piaget's theory of object concept development: Difficulties in object conceptualization or spatial localization? *Child Development*, 1972, 43, 682–688.

Fingerman, P., & Levine, M. Nonlearning: The completeness of the blindness. *Journal of Experimental Psychology*, 1974, 102, 720–721.

Fillenbaum, S. Words as feature complexes: False recognition of antonyms and synonyms. *Journal of Experimental Psychology*, 1969, 82, 400–402.

Flagg, P. W. Semantic integration in sentence memory? *Journal of verbal Learning and Verbal Behavior*, 1976, 15, 491–504.

References

Flavell, J. H. *The developmental psychology of Jean Piaget.* Princeton, N.J.: Van Nostrand, 1963.

Flavell, J. H. *Cognitive development.* Englewood Cliffs, N.J.: Prentice-Hall, 1977.

Flavell, J. H., Botkin, P. T., Fry, C. L., Jr., Wright, J. W., & Jarvis, P. E. *The development of role-taking and communication skills in children.* New York: Wiley, 1968.

Flexser, A. J., & Tulving, E. Retrieval independence in recognition and recall. *Psychological Review*, 1978, *85*, 153–171.

Frege, G. On sense and nominatum. Originally published in 1892. In E. Nagel & R. B. Brandt (Eds.), *Meaning and knowledge: Systematic readings in epistemology.* New York: Harcourt, Brace, & World, 1965, pp. 69–77.

Friedman, M. J., & Reynolds, J. H. Retroactive inhibition as a function of response-class similarity. *Journal of Experimental Psychology*, 1967, *74*, 351–355.

Furth, H. G. *Thinking without language: Psychological implications of deafness.* New York: Free Press, 1966.

Furth, H. G., & Youniss, J. The influence of language and experience on discovery and use of logical symbols. *British Journal of Psychology*, 1965, *56*, 381–390.

Gaarder, K. R. *Eye movements, vision and behavior.* Washington, D.C.: Hemisphere, 1975.

Gardiner, J. M., Craik, F. I. M., & Birtwhistle, J. Retrieval cues and release from proactive inhibition. *Journal of Verbal Learning and Verbal Behavior*, 1972, *11*, 778–783.

Gardner, B. T., & Gardner, R. A. Two-way communication with an infant chimpanzee. In A. Schrier & F. Stollnitz (Eds.), *Behavior of nonhuman primates* (Vol. IV). New York: Academic Press, 1971, pp. 117–184.

Gardner, R. A., & Gardner, B. T. Teaching sign language to a champanzee. *Science*, 1969, *165*, 664–672.

Gelman, R. Conservation acquisition: A problem of learning to attend to relevant attributes. *Journal of Experimental Child Psychology*, 1969, *7*, 167–187.

Gelman, R., & Weinberg, D. H. The relationship between liquid conservation and compensation. *Child Development*, 1972, *43*, 371–383.

Gever, B., & Weisberg, R. Spontaneous verbalization of children during problem solving: Effects of task difficulty, age and social class. *Proceedings of the 78th American Psychological Association Convention*, 1970, 297–298.

Glanzer, M., & Cunitz, A. R. Two storage mechanisms in free recall. *Journal of Verbal Learning and Verbal Behavior*, 1966, *5*, 351–360.

Glucksberg, S., Krauss, R. M., & Weisberg, R. Referential communication in nursery school children: Method and some preliminary findings. *Journal of Experimental Child Psychology*, 1966, *3*, 333–342.

Goggin, J., & Riley, D. Maintenance of interference in short-term memory. *Journal of Experimental Psychology*, 1974, *102*, 1027–1034.

Gratch, G., Appel, K. J., Evans, W. F., LeCompte, G. K., & Wright, N. A. Piaget's stage IV object concept error: Evidence of forgetting or object conception? *Child Development*, 1974, *45*, 71–77.

Greeno, J. G. Hobbits and orcs: Acquisition of a sequential concept. *Cognitive Psychology*, 1974, *6*, 270–292.

Greenwald, A. A choice reaction time test of ideomotor theory. *Journal of Experimental Psychology*, 1970, *86*, 20–25.
Grice, G. R. Do responses evoke responses? *American Psychologist*, 1965, *20*, 282–294.
Gross, A. E., Baresi, J., & Smith, E. E. Voluntary forgetting of a shared memory load. *Psychonomic Science*, 1970, *20*, 73–75.
Gruen, G. E. Experiences affecting the development of number conservation in children. *Child Development*, 1965, *36*, 963–979.
Haber, R. N. How we remember what we see. *Scientific American*, 1970, *222*, 104–115.
Harlow, H. F. The formation of learning sets. *Psychological Review*, 1949, *56*, 51–65.
Harris, P. L. Perseverative errors in search by young children. *Child Development*, 1973, *44*, 28–33.
Harris, P. L. Perseverative search at a visibly empty place by young infants. *Journal of Experimental Child Psychology*, 1974, *18*, 535–542.
Harris, P. L. Development of search and object permanence during infancy. *Psychological Bulletin*, 1975, *82*, 332–344.
Hasher, L., & Griffin, M. Reconstructive and reproductive processes in memory. *Journal of Experimental Psychology: Human Learning and Memory*, 1978, *4*, 318–330.
Hayes, J. R. *Cognitive psychology: Thinking and creating*. Homewood, Ill.: Dorsey, 1978.
Hayes, K. J., & Hayes, C. Intellectual development of a home-raised chimpanzee. *Proceedings of the American Philosophical Society*, 1951, *95*, 105–109.
Hayes-Roth, F., & Hayes-Roth, B. The prominence of lexical information in memory representations of meaning. *Journal of Verbal Learning and Verbal Behavior*, 1977, *16*, 119–136.
Heath, P. L. Concept. In P. Edwards (Ed.), *Encyclopedia of Philosophy*. New York: Macmillan, 1972, pp. 177–180.
Hebb, D. O. *Organization of behavior*. New York: Wiley, 1949.
Hilgard, E. R., & Bower, G. H. *Theories of learning* (4th ed.). Englewood Cliffs, N.J.: Prentice-Hall, 1975.
Hinde, R. A. *Animal behavior: A synthesis of ethology and comparative psychology* (2nd ed.). New York: McGraw-Hill, 1970.
Hintzman, D. L., & Block, R. A. Memory for the spacing of repetitions. *Journal of Experimental Psychology*, 1973, *99*, 70–74.
Hochberg, J. In the mind's eye. In R. N. Haber (Ed.), *Contemporary theory and research in visual perception*. New York: Holt, Rinehart, and Winston, 1968, pp. 309–331.
Hochberg, J. Attention, organization, and consciousness. In D. I. Mostofsky (Ed.), *Attention: Contemporary theory and analysis*. New York: Appleton-Century-Crofts, 1970, pp. 99–124. (a)
Hochberg, J. Components of literacy: Speculations and exploratory research. In H. Levin & J. P. Williams (Eds.), *Basic studies on reading*. New York: Basic Books, 1970, pp. 74–89. (b)

References

Hochberg, J. E. *Perception* (2nd ed.). Englewood Cliffs, N.J.: Prentice-Hall, 1978.

Hochberg, J., & Galper, R. E. Recognition of faces: I. An exploratory study. *Psychonomic Science*, 1967, 9, 619–620.

Homa, D., Cross, J., Cornell, D., Goldman, D., & Schwartz, S. Prototype abstraction and classification of new instances as a function of number of instances defining the prototype. *Journal of Experimental Psychology*, 1973, 101, 116–122.

Hull, C. L. Knowledge and purpose as habit mechanisms. *Psychological Review*, 1930, 37, 511–525.

Hull, C. L. Goal attraction and directing ideas conceived as habit phenomena. *Psychological Review*, 1931, 38, 487–506.

Humphrey, G. *Thinking: An introduction to its experimental psychology*. New York: Wiley Science Editions, 1963.

Hunt, E. B. *Concept learning: An information processing problem*. New York: Wiley, 1962.

Hunt, E. B. The memory we must have. In R. Schank & K. Colby (Eds.), *Computer models of thought and language*. San Francisco: Freeman, 1973, pp. 343–371.

Hunt, E. B., & Hovland, C. I. Order of consideration of different types of concepts. *Journal of Experimental Psychology*, 1960, 59, 220–225.

Hunt, J. Mc V. *Intelligence and experience*. New York: Ronald Press, 1961.

Hutcheon, E. G. An investigation into stimulus classification under varying instructions. Unpublished M.A. Thesis, Dundee University, 1970. Cited in D. J. Bartram, The role of visual and semantic codes in object naming. *Cognitive Psychology*, 1974, 6, 325–356.

Hyde, T. S., & Jenkins, J. J. Recall of words as a function of semantic, graphic, and syntactic orienting tasks. *Journal of Verbal Learning and Verbal Behavior*, 1973, 12, 471–480.

Jacobson, E. Imagination of movement involving skeletal muscle. *American Journal of Physiology*, 1930, 91, 567–608.

Jacobson, E. Imagination, recollection and abstract thinking involving the speech musculature. *American Journal of Physiology*, 1931, 97, 200–209. Reprinted in F. J. McGuigan (Ed.), *Thinking: Studies of covert language processes*. New York: Appleton-Century-Crofts, 1966. (a)

Jacobson, E. Variation of specific muscles contracting during imagination. *American Journal of Physiology*, 1931, 96, 115–121. (b)

Jacoby, L. Encoding processes, rehearsal, and recall requirements. *Journal of Verbal Learning and Verbal Behavior*, 1973, 12, 302–310.

James, W. *The principles of psychology* (Vol. 1). New York: Henry Holt, 1890.

Jarvis, P. E. Verbal control of sensory-motor performance: A test of Luria's hypothesis. *Human Development*, 1968, 11, 172–183.

Jeffrey, W. E. Transfer. In H. W. Reese & L. P. Lipsitt (Eds.), *Experimental child psychology*. New York: Academic Press, 1970, pp. 223–262.

Jeffries, R., Polson, P. G., Razran, L., & Atwood, M. E. A process model for missionaries-cannibals and other river-crossing problems. *Cognitive Psychology*, 1977, 9, 412–440.

Jenkins, J. J. Remember that old theory of memory? Well, forget it! *American Psychologist,* 1974, *29,* 785–795.

Jenkins, J. J., & Palcimo, D. S. Mediation processes and the acquisition of linguistic structure. In U. Bellugi & R. W. Brown (Eds.), *The acquisition of language.* Monograph of the Society for Research in Child Development, 1964, *29,* no. 1, pp. 141–169.

Johnson, M. K., Bransford, J. D., & Solomon, S. K. Memory for tacit implications of sentences. *Journal of Experimental Psychology,* 1973, *98,* 203–205.

Kahneman, D. *Attention and effort.* Englewood Cliffs,N.J.: Prentice-Hall, 1973.

Kaplan, R. M. On process models for sentence analysis. In D. A. Norman, D. E. Rumelhart, and the LNR Research Group, *Explortions in cognition.* San Francisco: Freeman, 1975, pp. 117–135.

Katz, S. Role of instructions in abstraction of linguistic ideas. *Journal of Experimental Psychology,* 1973, *98,* 79–84.

Keppel, G., & Underwood, B. J. Proactive inhibition in short-term retention of single items. *Journal of Verbal Learning and Verbal Behavior,* 1962, *1,* 153–161.

Kimble, G. A., & Perlmutter, L. C. The problem of volition. *Psychological Review,* 1970, *77,* 361–384.

Kintsch, W. Models for free recall and recognition. In D. A. Norman (Ed.), *Models of human memory.* New York: Academic Press, 1970, pp. 333–373.

Kintsch, W. *Memory and cognition* (2nd ed.). New York: Wiley, 1977.

Kister, J., Stein, P., Ulam, S., Walden, W., & Wells, M. Experiments in chess. *Journal of the ACM,* 1957, *4,* 174–177.

Kohlberg, L., Yaeger, J., & Hjertholm, E. Private speech: Four studies and a review of theories. *Child Development,* 1968, *39,* 691–736.

Kohler, W. *The mentality of apes* (2nd ed.). New York: Harcourt Brace, 1927, p. 190.

Kolers, P. A. Specificity of operations in sentence recognition. *Cognitive Psychology,* 1975, *7,* 289–306.

Kolers, P. A., & Ostry, D. Time course of loss of information regarding pattern analyzing operations. *Journal of Verbal Learning and Verbal Behavior,* 1974, *13,* 599–612.

Konorski, J. *Integrative activity of the brain.* Chicago: University of Chicago Press, 1967.

Kosslyn, S. M. Information representation in visual images. *Cognitive Psychology,* 1975, *7,* 341–370.

Kosslyn, S. M., & Pomerantz, J. R. Imagery, propositions, and the form of internal representations. *Cognitive Psychology,* 1977, *9,* 52–76.

Krechevsky, I. "Hypotheses" in rats. *Psychological Review,* 1932, *39,* 516–532.

Kuenne, M. R. Experimental investigation of the relation of language to transposition behavior in young children. *Journal of Experimental Psychology,* 1946, *36,* 471–490.

Kuhn, T. S. *The structure of scientific revolutions* (2nd ed.). Chicago: University of Chicago Press, 1970.

LaBerge, D., & Samuels, S. J. Toward a theory of automatic information processing in reading. *Cognitive Psychology,* 1974, *6,* 293–324.

References

Lambert, W. E., & Paivio, A. The influence of noun-adjective order on learning. *Canadian Journal of Psychology,* 1956, *10,* 9–12.

Lashley, K. S. *Brain mechanisms and intelligence.* Chicago: University of Chicago Press, 1929.

Lawrence, D. H. Acquired distinctiveness of cues: I. Transfer between discriminations on the basis of familiarity with the stimulus. *Journal of Experimental Psychology,* 1949, *39,* 770–784.

Lawrence, D. H. Acquired distinctiveness of cues: II. Selective association in a constant stimulus situation. *Journal of Experimental Psychology,* 1950, *40,* 175–188.

Levine, M. Hypothesis behavior by humans during discrimination learning. *Journal of Experimental Psychology,* 1966, *71* 331–338.

Levine, M. Hypothesis theory and nonlearning despite ideal S-R reinforcement contingencies. *Psychological Review,* 1971, *78,* 130–140.

Levine, M. A transfer hypothesis, whereby learning-to-learn, Einstellung, the PREE, reversal-nonreversal shifts, and other curiosities are elucidated. In R. L. Solso (Ed.), *Theories in cognitive psychology: The Loyola symposium.* Potomac, Md.: Erlbaum, 1974, pp. 289–305.

Liberman, A. M. The grammars of speech and language. *Cognitive Psychology,* 1970, *1,* 301–323.

Lindsay, P. H., & Norman, D. A. *Human information processing.* New York: Academic Press, 1972.

Lindsay, P. H., & Norman, D. A. *Human information processing* (2nd ed.). New York: Academic Press, 1977.

Locke, J. *An essay concerning human understanding.* London: Basset, 1690. Excerpted in J. M. Mandler & G. Mandler (Eds.), *Thinking: From association to Gestalt.* New York: Wiley, 1964, pp. 26–49.

Lockhart, R. S., Craik, F. I. M., & Jacoby, L. Depth of processing, recognition and recall. In J. Brown (Ed.), *Recall and recognition.* New York: Wiley, 1975.

Loess, H., & Waugh, N. C. Short-term memory and intertrial interval. *Journal of Verbal Learning and Verbal Behavior,* 1967, *6,* 455–460.

Loftus, G. R. Eye fixations and recognition memory for pictures. *Cognitive Psychology,* 1972, *3,* 525–551.

Loftus, G. R., & Patterson, K. K. Components of short-term proactive interference. *Journal of Verbal Learning and Verbal Behavior,* 1975, *14,* 105–121.

Luchins, A. S. Mechanization in problem solving: The effect of *Einstellung. Psychological Monographs,* 1942, *54*(6, Whole No. 248).

Luchins, A. S., & Luchins, E. H. *Rigidity of behavior: A variational approach to the effect of Einstellung.* Eugene, Oregon: University of Oregon Press, 1959.

Luria, A. R. *The role of speech in the regulation of normal and abnormal behavior.* New York: Liveright, 1961.

Madigan, S. A., & McCabe, L. Perfect recall and total forgetting: A problem for models of short-term memory. *Journal of Verbal Learning and Verbal Behavior,* 1971, *10,* 101–106.

Maier, N. R. F. Reasoning in humans: I. On direction. *Journal of Comparative Psychology,* 1930, *12,* 115–143.

Maier, N. R. F. Reasoning in humans: III. The mechanisms of equivalent stimuli and of reasoning. *Journal of Experimental Psychology,* 1945, *35,* 349–360.

Maltzman, I. Thinking: From a behavioristic point of view. *Psychological Review,* 1955, *66,* 367–386.

Mandler, G. Organization and memory. In K. W. Spence & J. T. Spence (Eds.), *The The psychology of learning and motivation: Advances in Research and Theory* (Vol. 1). New York: Academic Press, 1967, pp. 328–372.

Mandler, G. Association and organization: Facts, fancies, and theories. In T. R. Dixon & D. L. Horton (Eds.), *Verbal behavior and general behavior theory.* Englewood Cliffs, N.J.: Prentice-Hall, 1968, pp. 109–119.

Mandler, G. *Mind and emotion.* New York: Wiley, 1975.

Mandler, J. M., & Mandler, G. *Thinking: From association to Gestalt.* New York: Wiley, 1964.

Maratsos, M. P. Nonegocentric communication abilities in preschool children. *Child Development,* 1973, *44,* 697–700.

Marbe, K. The psychology of judgments. Originally printed in German in 1901. Excerpted in J. M. Mandler & G. Mandler (Eds.), *Thinking: From association to Gestalt.* New York: Wiley, 1964, pp. 143–146.

Massaro, D. W. *Experimental psychology and information processing.* Chicago: Rand McNally, 1975.

Matthews, L. J., & Patton, J. H. Failure to shift following disconfirmation in concept identification. *Journal of Experimental Psychology: Human Learning and Memory,* 1975, *1,* 91–94.

Max, L. W. An experimental study of the motor theory of consciousness III: Action-current responses in deaf-mutes during sleep, sensory stimulation and dreams. *Journal of Comparative Psychology,* 1935, *19,* 469–486. Reprinted in F. J. McGuigan (Ed.), *Thinking: Studies of covert language processes.* New York: Appleton-Century-Crofts, 1966, pp. 86–96.

Max, L. W. An experimental study of the motor theory of consciousness IV: Action-current responses in the deaf during awakening, kinesthetic imagery and abstract thinking. *Journal of Comparative Psychology,* 1937, *24,* 301–344.

Mayer, A., & Orth, J. The qualitative investigation of associations. Orginally published in German in 1901. Reprinted in J. M. Mandler & G. Mandler (Eds.), *Thinking: From association to Gestalt.* New York: Wiley, 1964, pp. 135–142.

McGeoch, J. A. Forgetting and the law of disuse. *Psychological Review,* 1932, *39,* 352–370.

McGuigan, F. J. (Ed.). *Thinking: Studies of covert language processes.* New York: Appleton-Century-Crofts, 1966.

McGuigan, F. J. Covert oral behavior during the silent performance of language tasks. *Psychological Bulletin,* 1970, *74,* 309–326.

McGuigan, F. J. Electrical measurement of covert processes. In F. J. McGuigan & R. A. Schoonover (Eds.), *The psychophysiology of thinking.* New York: Academic Press, 1973, pp. 343–375.

McGuigan, F. J., & Bailey, S. C. Longitudinal study of covert oral behavior during silent reading. *Perceptual and Motor Skills,* 1969, *28,* 170.

McGuigan, F. J., Keller, B., & Stanton, E. Covert language responses during silent reading. *Journal of Educational Psychology,* 1964, *55,* 339–343.

References

McGuigan, F. J., & Rodier, W. I., III. Effects of auditory stimulation on covert oral behavior during silent reading. *Journal of Experimental Psychology*, 1968, *76*, 649–655.

McGuigan, F. J., & Tanner, R. G., Covert oral behavior during conversational and visual dreams. *Psychonomic Science*, 1971, *23*, 263–264.

McNeill, D. Developmental psycholinguistics. In F. Smith & G. A. Miller (Eds.), *The genesis of language*. Cambridge, Mass.: MIT Press, 1966, pp. 15–84.

McNeill, D. *The acquisition of language*. New York: Harper & Row, 1970.

McNulty, J. A. An analysis of recall and recognition processes in verbal learning. *Journal of Verbal Learning and Verbal Behavior*, 1965, *4*, 430–436.

Medin, D. L., & Schaffer M. M. Context theory of classification learning. *Psychological Review*, 1978, *85*, 207–238.

Meyers, J. Sequential choice behavior. In G. H. Bower (Ed.), *The psychology of learning and motivation* (Vol. 4). New York: Academic Press, 1970, pp. 109–170.

Miller, G. A. Some psychological studies of grammar. *American Psychologist*, 1962, *17*, 748–762.

Miller, G. A., Galanter, E., & Pribram, K. *Plans and the structure of behavior*. New York: Holt, Rinehart, and Winston, 1960.

Miller, G. A., Heise, G. A., & Lichten, W. The intelligibility of speech as a funtion of the context of the test materials. *Journal of Experimental Psychology*, 1951, *41*, 329–335.

Miller, S. A., Shelton, J., & Flavell, J. H. A test of Luria's hypothesis concerning the development of verbal self-regulation. *Child Development*, 1970, *41*, 651–665.

Miller, W., & Ervin, S. M. The development of grammar in child language. In U. Bellugi & R. Brown (Eds.), *The acquisition of language*. Monograph of the Society for Research in Child Development, 1964, *29*, no. 1, pp. 9–34.

Minsky, M. A framework for representing knowledge. In P. Winston (Ed.), *The psychology of computer vision*. New York: McGraw-Hill, 1975.

Mischel, W. *Introduction to personality* (2nd ed.). New York: Holt, Rinehart, and Winston, 1976.

Moeser, S. D., & Bregman, A. S. The role of experience in the acquisition of a miniature artificial language. *Journal of Verbal Learning and Verbal Behavior*, 1972, *11*, 759–769.

Moray, N. Attention in dichotic listening: Affective cues and the influence of instructions. *Quarterly Journal of Experimental Psychology*, 1959, *11*, 56–60.

Morris, C. D., Bransford, J. D., & Franks, J. J. Levels of processing versus transfer appropriate processing. *Journal of Verbal Learning and Verbal Behavior*, 1977, *16*, 519–533.

Morton, J. A functional model for memory. In D. A. Norman (Ed.), *Models of human memory*. New York: Academic Press, 1970, pp. 203–254.

Murdock, B. B., Jr. An analysis of the recognition process. In C. N. Cofer & B. S. Musgrave (Eds.), *Verbal behavior and learning: Problems and processes*. New York: McGraw-Hill, 1963, pp. 10–21.

Natsoulas, T. Consciousness. *American Psychologist*, 1978, *33*, 906–914.

Neisser, U. *Cognitive psychology*. New York: Appleton-Century-Crofts, 1967.

Neisser, U. *Selective reading: A method for the study of visual attention.* Paper presented to the 19th International Congress of Psychology, London, 1969.
Neisser, U. *Cognition and reality.* San Francisco: Freeman, 1976.
Neisser, U., & Weene, P. Hierarchies in concept attainment. *Journal of Experimental Psychology,* 1952, 64, 640–645.
Nelson, K. Concept, word, and sentence: Interrelations in acquisition and development. *Psychological Review,* 1974, 81, 267–285.
Nelson, K. E. Accommodation of visual tracking patterns in human infants to object movement patterns. *Journal of Experimental Child Psychology,* 1971, 12, 182–196.
Nelson, T. O. Repetition and depth of processing. *Journal of Verbal Learning and Verbal Behavior,* 1977, 16, 151–172.
Newell, A., Shaw, J. C. & Simon, H. A. Chess-playing programs and the problem of complexity. *IBM Journal of Research and Development,* 1958, 2, 320–335.
Newell, A., & Simon, H. *Human problem solving.* Englewood Cliffs, N.J.: Prentice-Hall, 1972.
Nickerson, R. S. Short-term memory for complex meaningful visual configurations: A demonstration of capacity. *Canadian Journal of Psychology,* 1965, 19, 155–160.
Norman, D. A. *Memory and attention* (2nd ed.). New York: Wiley, 1976.
Norman, D. A., & Bobrow, D. G. On the role of active memory processes in perception and cognition. In C. N. Cofer (Ed.), *The structure of human memory.* San Francisco: Freeman, 1975, pp. 114–132.
Norman, D. A., & Rumelhart, D. E. Memory and knowledge. In D. A. Norman, D. E. Rumelhart, and the LNR Research Group, *Explorations in Cognition.* San Francisco: Freeman, 1975, pp. 3–32.
Noton, D., & Stark, L. Scanpaths in eye movements during pattern perception. *Science,* 1971, 171, 308–311.
Noton, D., & Stark, L. Eye movements and visual perception. *Scientific American,* 1972, 227, 35–43.
Olson, D. Language and thought: Aspects of a cognitive theory of semantics. *Psychological Review,* 1970, 77, 257–273.
Paivio, A. *Imagery and verbal processes.* New York: Holt, Rinehart, and Winston, 1971.
Palermo, D. S. *Psychology of language.* Glenview, Ill.: Scott, Foresman, 1978.
Palmer, S. E. Visual perception and world knowledge: Notes on a model of sensory-cognitive interaction. In D. A. Norman, D. E. Rumelhart, and the LNR Research Group, *Explorations in cognition.* San Francisco: Freeman, 1975, pp. 279–307.
Perfetti, C. A., & Goodman, D. Semantic constraint on the decoding of ambiguous words. *Journal of Experimental Psychology.* 1970, 86, 420–427.
Peterson, L. R., & Peterson, M. J. Short-term retention of individual verbal items. *Journal of Experimental Psychology,* 1959, 58, 193–198.
Piaget, J. *The construction of reality in the child.* New York: Basic Books, 1954.
Piaget, J. *The language and thought of the child.* Cleveland, Ohio: World, 1955.
Piaget, J. *The origins of intelligence in children.* New York: Norton, 1963.
Piaget, J. *The child's conception of number.* New York: Norton, 1965.

Piaget, J. *The psychology of intelligence.* Totowa, N.J.: Littlefield, Adams, 1966.
Piaget, J. *The child's conception of the world.* Totowa, N.J.: Littlefield, Adams, 1967.
Piaget, J. *Judgment and reasoning in the child.* Totowa, N.J.: Littlefield, Adams, 1968. (a)
Piaget, J. *Six psychological studies.* New York: Vintage Books, 1968. (b)
Pintner, R. Inner speech during silent reading. *Psychological Review,* 1913, *30,* 129–153.
Pollack, I. Interference, rehearsal, and short-term retention of digits. *Canadian Journal of Psychology,* 1963, *17,* 380–392.
Polya, G. *How to solve it.* Princeton: Princeton University Press, 1945.
Posner, M. I. Abstraction and the process of recognition. In G. H. Bower & J. T. Spence (Eds.), *The psychology of learning and motivation* (Vol. 3). New York: Academic Press, 1969, pp. 44–96.
Posner, M. I. *Cognition: An introduction.* Glenview, Ill.: Scott, Foresman, 1973.
Posner, M. I., & Keele, S. W. On the genesis of abstract ideas. *Journal of Experimental Psychology,* 1968, *77,* 353–363.
Posner, M. I., & Keele, S. W. Retention of abstract ideas. *Journal of Experimental Psychology,* 1970, *83,* 304–308.
Posner, M. I., & Snyder, C. R. R. Attention and cognitive control. In R. Solso (Ed.), *Information processing and cognition: The Loyola symposium.* Hillsdale, N.J.: Erlbaum, 1975.
Postal, P. Review of *Elements of general linguistics* by André Martinet. *Foundations of Language,* 1966, *2,* 151–186.
Postman, L. The temporal course of proactive inhibition for serial lists. *Journal of Experimental Psychology,* 1962, *63,* 361–369.
Postman, L., Jenkins, W. O., & Postman, D. L. An experimental comparison of active recall and recognition. *American Journal of Psychology.* 1948, *61,* 511–520.
Postman, L., & Kruesi, E. The influence of orienting tasks on the encoding and recall of words. *Journal of Verbal Learning and Verbal Behavior,* 1977, *16,* 353–370.
Postman, L., & Phillips, L. W. Short-term temporal changes in free recall. *Quarterly Journal of Experimental Psychology,* 1965, *69,* 111–118.
Potter, M. C. Meaning in visual search. *Science,* 1975, *187,* 965–966.
Potter, M. C. Short-term conceptual memory for pictures. *Journal of Experimental Psychology: Human Learning and Memory,* 1976, *2,* 509–522.
Premack, D. Language in chimpanzee? *Science,* 1971, *172,* 808–822.
Price, H. H. *Thinking and experience.* London: Hutchinson, 1953.
Pylyshyn, Z. What the mind's eye tells the mind's brain: A critique of mental imagery. *Psychological Bulletin,* 1973, *80,* 1–24.
Quine, W. V. O. *Word and object.* Cambridge, Mass.: MIT Press, 1959.
Rand, G. & Wapner, S. Postural status as a factor in memory. *Journal of Verbal Learning and Verbal Behavior,* 1967, *6,* 268–271.
Ray, W. S. *The experimental psychology of original thinking.* New York: Macmillan, 1967.
Rayner, E. H. A study of evaluative problem solving. Part I: Observation on adults. *Quarterly Journal of Experimental Psychology,* 1958, *10,* 155–165.

Rayner, K. The perception span and peripheral cues in reading. *Cognitive Psychology*, 1975, 7, 65–81.

Razran, G. The observable unconscious and the inferable conscious in current Soviet psycho-physiology: Interoceptive conditioning, semantic conditioning, and the orienting reflex. *Psychological Review*, 1961, 68, 109–119.

Reed, S. K., & Johnsen, J. A. Detection of parts in patterns and images. *Memory and Cognition*, 1975, 3, 569–575.

Rees, H. J., & Israel, H. E. An investigation of the establishment and operation of mental sets. *Psychological Monographs*, 1935, 46 (6, Whole No. 210).

Reese, H. W. Discrimination learning set and perceptual set in young children. *Child Development*, 1965, 36, 153–161.

Reicher, G. M. Perceptual recognition as a function of the meaningfulness of the material. *Journal of Experimental Psychology*, 1969, 81, 275–280.

Reitman, J. S., & Bower, G. H. Storage and later recognition of exemplars of concepts. *Cognitive Psychology*, 1973, 4, 194–206.

Restle, F. The selection of strategies in cue learning. *Psychological Review*, 1962, 69, 329–343.

Reynolds, A. G., & Flagg, P. W. *Cognitive psychology.* Cambridge, Mass.: Winthrop, 1977.

Rizzolo, A. Unpublished doctoral dissertation, Columbia University, 1931. Cited in G. Humphrey, *Thinking: An introduction to its experimental psychology.* New York: Wiley Science Editions, 1963.

Robins, C., & Shepard, R. N. Spatio-temporal probing of apparent rotational movement. *Perception & Psychophysics*, 1977, 22, 12–18.

Rosch, E. Cognitive representations of semantic categories. *Journal of Experimental Psychology: General*, 1975, 104, 192–233. (a)

Rosch, E. The nature of mental codes for color categories. *Journal of Experimental Psychology: Human Perception and Performance*, 1975, 1, 303–322. (b)

Rosch, E., & Mervis, C. B. Family resemblances: Studies of the internal structure of categories. *Cognitive Psychology*, 1975, 1, 573–605.

Rosch, E., Mervis, C. B., Gray, W. D., Johnson, D. M., & Boyes-Braem, P. Basic objects in natural catregories. *Cognitive Psychology*, 1976, 8, 382–439.

Rumelhart, D. E. *Introduction to human information processing.* New York: Wiley, 1977.

Rundus, D. Analysis of rehearsal processes in free recall. *Journal of Experimental Psychology*, 1971, 89, 63–77.

Ryle, G. *The concept of mind.* New York: Barnes & Noble, 1949.

Sachs, J. D. S. Recognition memory for syntactic and semantic aspects of connected discourse. *Perception and Psychophysics*, 1967, 2, 437–442.

Schank, R. C. Conceptual dependency: A theory of natural language understanding. *Cognitive Psychology*, 1972, 3, 552–631.

Schank, R. C. Identification of conceptualizations underlying natural language. In R. C. Schank & K. M. Colby (Eds.), *Computer models of thought and language.* San Francisco: Freeman, 1973, pp. 187–248.

Schank, R. C. The role of memory in language processing. In C. Cofer (Ed.), *The structure of human memory.* San Francisco: Freeman, 1975, pp. 162–189.

References

Schank, R. C., & Abelson, R. P. Scripts, plans, and knowledge. *Proceedings of the Fourth International Joint Conference on Artificial Intelligence,* Stanford, Calif., 1975.

Scheerer, M. Problem-solving. *Scientific American,* 1963, *208,* 118–128.

Schlesinger, I. M. Production of utterances and language acquisition. In D. I. Slobin (Ed.), *The ontogenesis of grammar.* New York: Academic Press, 1971, pp. 63–101.

Schneider, W., & Shiffrin, R. M. Controlled and automatic human information processing: I. Detection, search, and attention. *Psychological Review,* 1977, *84,* 1–62.

Scholes, R. J. The role of grammaticality in the imitation of word strings by children and adults. *Journal of Verbal Learning and Verbal Behavior,* 1969, *8,* 225–228.

Sechenov, I. *Reflexes of the brain.* Originally published in 1863. Reprinted in K. Koshtoyants (Ed.), *I. Sechenov: Selected physiological and psychological works.* Moscow: Foreign Languages Publishing House, 1952, pp. 31–139.

Segal, S., & Fusella, V. Influence of imaged pictures and sounds on detection of visual and auditory signals. *Journal of Experimental Psychology,* 1970, *83,* 458–464.

Selfridge, O. G., & Neisser, U. Pattern recognition by machine. *Scientific American,* 1960, *203,* 60–68.

Sellars, W. *Science, perception, and reality.* London: Routledge & Kegan Paul, 1963.

Selz, O. The revision of the fundamental conceptions of intellectual processes. Originally published in German in 1927. Excerpted in J. M. Mandler & G. Mandler (Eds.), *Thinking: From association to Gestalt.* New York: Wiley, 1964, pp. 225–234.

Shatz, M., & Gelman, R. The development of communication skills: Modification in the speech of young children as a function of listener. *Monographs of the Society for Research in Child Development,* 1973, 38(5, Serial No. 152).

Shepard, R. N. Learning and recall as organization and search. *Journal of Verbal Learning and Verbal Behavior,* 1966, *5,* 201–204.

Shepard, R. N. Recognition memory for words, sentences, and pictures. *Journal of Verbal Learning and Verbal Behavior,* 1967, *1,* 156–163.

Shepard, R. N. The mental image. *American Psychologist,* 1978, *33,* 125–137.

Shepard, R. N., & Chipman, S. Second-order isomorphism of internal representations: Shapes of states. *Cognitive Psychology,* 1970, *1,* 1–17.

Shepard, R. N. & Metzler, B. Mental rotation of three dimensional objects. *Science,* 1971, *171,* 701–703.

Shiffrin, R. M. Capacity limitations in information processing, attention and memory. In W. K. Estes (Ed.), *Handbook of learning and cognitive processes: Memory processes* (Vol. 4). Hillsdale, N.J.: Erlbaum, 1976.

Shiffrin, R. M., McKay, D. P., & Shaffer, W. O. Attending to forty-nine spatial positions at once. *Journal of Experimental Psychology: Human Perception and Performance,* 1976, *2,* 14–22.

Shiffrin, R. M., & Schneider, W. Controlled and automatic human information processing: II. Perceptual learning, automatic attending, and a general theory. *Psychological Review,* 1977, *84,* 127–190.

Shuell, T. J. Retroactive inhibition in free-recall learning of categorized lists. *Journal of Verbal Learning and Verbal Behavior,* 1968, *1,* 797–805.

Simon, H. A. What is visual imagery? An information processing interpretation. In L. W. Gregg (Ed.), *Cognition in learning and memory.* New York: Wiley, 1972, pp. 183–204.

Simon, H. A., & Barenfeld, M. Information-processing analysis of perceptual processes in problem solving. *Psychological Review,* 1969, *76,* 473–483.

Simon, H. A., & Gilmartin, K. A simulation of memory for chess positions. *Cognitive Psychology,* 1973, *5,* 29–46.

Skinner, B. F. *Verbal behavior.* New York: Appleton-Century-Crofts, 1957.

Slobin, D. I. Cognitive prerequisites for the development of grammar. In C. A. Ferguson & D. I. Slobin (Eds.), *Studies of child language development.* New York: Holt, Rinehart, & Winston, 1973, pp. 175–208.

Smedslund, J. The acquisition of conservation of substance and weight in children: VI. Practice in problem situations without external reinforcement. *Scandanavian Journal of Psychology,* 1961, *2,* 203–210.

Smith, E. E., Shoben, E. J., & Rips, L. J. Structure and process in semantic memory: A feature model for semantic decision. *Psychological Review,* 1974, *81,* 214–241.

Smith, S. M., Brown, H. O., Toman, J. E. P., & Goodman, L. S. Lack of cerebral effects of D-tubocurarine. *Anesthesiology,* 1947, *8,* 1–14.

Sokolov, A. N. *Inner speech and thought.* New York: Plenum, 1972.

Sokolov, Ye. N. *Perception and the conditioned reflex.* New York: Macmillan, 1963.

Spence, K. W. The nature of discrimination learning in animals. *Psychological Review,* 1936, *43,* 427–449.

Standing, L. Learning 10,000 pictures. *Quarterly Journal of Experimental Psychology,* 1973, *25,* 207–222.

Standing, L., Conezio, J., & Haber, R. N. Perception and memory for pictures: Single-trial learning of 2560 visual stimuli. *Psychonomic Science,* 1970, *19,* 73–74.

Strange, W., Keeney, T., Kessel, F. S., & Jenkins, J. J. Abstraction over time of prototypes from distortions of random dot patterns: A replication. *Journal of Experimental Psychology,* 1970, *83,* 508–10.

Sutton-Smith, B. *Child psychology.* New York: Appleton-Century-Crofts, 1973.

Thomas, J. C., Jr. An analysis of behavior in the hobbits-orcs problem. *Cognitive Psychology,* 1974, *6,* 257–269.

Thompson, M. C., & Massaro, D. W. Visual information and redundancy in reading. *Journal of Experimental Psychology,* 1973, *98,* 49–54.

Thomson, D. M., & Tulving, E. Associative encoding and retrieval: Weak and strong cues. *Journal of Experimental Psychology,* 1970, *86,* 255–262.

Thorndike, E. L. *Animal intelligence.* New York: Macmillan, 1911.

Thorson, A. M. The relation of tongue movements to internal speech. *Journal of Experimental Psychology,* 1925, *8,* 1–32.

Till, R. E., & Jenkins, J. J. The effects of cued orienting tasks on the free recall

of words. *Journal of Verbal Learning and Verbal Behavior,* 1973, *12,* 489–498.
Titchener, E. B. *Lectures on the experimental psychology of the thought-processes.* New York: Macmillan, 1909. Excerpted in J. M. Mandler & G. Mandler (Eds), *Thinking: From association to Gestalt.* New York: Wiley, 1964, pp. 167–184.
Trabasso, T. R., & Bower, G. H. *Attention in learning: Theory and research.* New York: Wiley, 1968.
Treisman, A. M. Contextual cues in selective listening. *Quarterly Journal of Experimental Psychology,* 1960, *12,* 242–248.
Treisman, A. M. Verbal cues, language, and meaning in selective attention. *American Journal of Psychology,* 1964, *77,* 206–219.
Tulving, E. Subjective organization in free recall of "unrelated" words. *Psychological Review,* 1962, *69,* 344–354.
Tulving, E. Theoretical issues in free recall. In T. R. Dixon & D. L. Horton (Eds.), *Verbal behavior and general behavior theory.* Englewood Cliffs, N.J.: Prentice-Hall, 1968. pp.2–36.
Tulving, E. Episodic and semantic memory. In E. Tulving & W. Donaldson (Eds.), *Organization and memory.* New York: Academic Press, 1972, pp.381–403.
Tulving, E. & Pearlstone, Z. Availability versus accessibility of information in memory for words. *Journal of Verbal Learning and Verbal Behavior,* 1966, *5,* 381–389.
Tulving, E., & Thomson, D. M. Encoding specificity and retrieval processes in episodic memory. *Psychological Review,* 1973, *80,* 352–373.
Turner, E. A., & Rommetveit, R. Focus of attention in recall of active and passive sentences. *Journal of Verbal Learning and Verbal Behavior,* 1968, *1,* 543–548.
Underwood, B. J. Retroactive and proactive inhibition after five and forty-eight hours. *Journal of Experimental Psychology,* 1948, *38,* 29–38.
Underwood, B. J. Interference and forgetting. *Psychological Review,* 1957, *64,* 49–60.
Underwood, B. J. False recognition produced by implicit verbal responses. *Journal of Experimental Psychology,* 1965, *70,* 122–129.
Underwood, B. J., & Freund, J. S. Effect of temporal separation of two tasks on proactive inhibition. *Journal of Experimental Psychology,* 1968, *78,* 50–54.
Underwood, B. J., & Schulz, R. W. *Meaningfulness and verbal learning.* Chicago: Lippincott, 1960.
Vendler, Z. *Res cogitans: An essay in rational psychology.* Ithaca, N.Y.: Cornell University Press, 1972.
Vinacke, W. E. *The psychology of thinking* (2nd ed.). New York: McGraw-Hill, 1974.
Vygotsky, L. S. *Thought and language.* Cambridge, Mass.: MIT Press, 1962.
Wallace, W. P. Incidental learning: The influence of associative similarity and formal similarity in producing false recognition. *Journal of Verbal Learning and Verbal Behavior,* 1968, *7,* 55–57.
Wallas, G. *The art of thought.* New York: Harcourt, Brace, 1926.
Walsh, D. A., & Jenkins, J. J. Effects of orienting tasks on free recall in incidental learning: "Difficulty," "Effort," and "Process" explanations. *Journal of Verbal Learning and Verbal Behavior,* 1973, *12,* 481–488.
Watkins, O. C., & Watkins, M J. Buildup of proactive inhibition as a cue-

overload effect. *Journal of Experimental Psychology: Human Learning and Memory*, 1975, *1*, 442–452.

Watson, J. B. Psychology as the behaviorist views it. *Psychological Review*, 1913, *20*, 158–177.

Watson, J. B. *Psychology from the standpoint of a behaviorist.* Philadelphia: Lippincott, 1919.

Watson, J. B. *Behaviorism.* Chicago: University of Chicago Press, 1930.

Weimer, W. B. Psycholinguistics and Plato's paradoxes of the *Meno. American Psychologist*, 1973, *28*, 15–33.

Weisberg, R. W. Solutions to a problem as indirect expressions of knowledge. Unpublished manuscript, 1979.

Weisberg, R. W., & Alba, J. W. An examination of the alleged role of "fixation" in the solution of several "insight" problems. Unpublished manuscript, 1979.

Weisberg, R. W., & Chromiak, W. The role of expectations in visual pursuit in adults. Unpublished manuscript, 1979.

Weisberg, R. W., & Fish, R. E. Low levels of recall after structural orienting tasks: Cue overload? Unpublished manuscript, 1979.

Weisberg, R. W., & Suls, J. M. An information-processing model of Duncker's candle problem. *Cognitive Psychology*, 1973, *4*, 255–276.

Weisberg, R. W., Urbanski, B., & Sloane, S. The role of memory in the development of conservation of liquid. Unpublished manuscript, 1975.

Wells, H. Effects of transfer and problem structure in disjunctive concept formation. *Journal of Experimental Psychology*, 1963, *65*, 63–69.

Wheeler, D. D. Processes in word recognition. *Cognitive Psychology*, 1970, *1*, 59–85.

White, R. M., Jr. Hypothesis behavior as a function of amount of pretraining. *Journal of Experimental Psychology*, 1974, *102*, 1053–1060.

Wickelgren, W. A. Phonemic similarity and interference in short-term memory for single letters. *Journal of Experimental Psychology*, 1966, *71*, 396–404.

Wickelgren, W. *Learning and memory.* San Francisco: Freeman, 1975.

Wickens, D. D. Encoding categories of words: An empirical approach to meaning. *Psychological Review*, 1970, *77*, 1–15.

Wickens, D. D., & Gittis, M. M. The temporal course of recovery from interference and degree of learning in the Brown-Peterson paradigm. *Journal of Experimental Psychology*, 1974, *102*, 1021–1026.

Wilder, L. The role of speech and other extra-signal feedback in the regulation of the child's sensorimotor behavior. *Speech Monographs*, 1969, *36*, 425–434.

Williams, G. F. A model of memory in concept learning. *Cognitive Psychology*, 1971, *2*, 158–184.

Winograd, E. Retention of list differentiation and word frequency. *Journal of Verbal Learning and Verbal Behavior*, 1968, *7*, 859–863.

Wittgenstein, L. *Philosophical investigations* (3rd ed.). New York: Macmillan, 1958.

Wollen, K. A. Effects of relevant or irrelevant pictorial mediators upon forward and backward recall. Paper presented at the meeting of the Psychonomic Society, St. Louis, 1968. Cited in A. Paivio, *Imagery and verbal processes.* New York: Holt, Rinehart, and Winston, 1971.

References

Woods, W. A. Transitional network grammars for natural language analysis. *Communications of the ACM,* 1970, *13,* 591–606.

Woodworth, R. S. The cause of a voluntary movement. In J. H. Tufts, E. B. Delabarre, F. C. Sharp, A. H. Pierce, & F. J. E. Woodbridge (Eds.), *Studies in philosophy and psychology.* Boston: Houghton-Mifflin, 1906. Cited in G. A. Kimble, & L. C. Perlmutter, The problem of volition. *Psychological Review,* 1970, *77,* 361–384.

Woozley, A. D. Universals. In P. Edwards (Ed.), *Encyclopedia of philosophy.* New York: Macmillan, 1972, pp. 194–206.

Yates, F. A. *The art of memory.* Chicago: University of Chicago Press, 1966.

Yntema, D. B., & Trask, F. P. Recall as a search process. *Journal of Verbal Learning and Verbal Behavior,* 1963, *2,* 65–74.

Zeiler, M. D. Stimulus definition and choice. In L. P. Lipsitt & C. C. Spiker (Eds.), *Advances in child development and behavior* (Vol. 3). New York: Academic Press, 1967, pp. 126–156.

Author index

Abelson, R. P., 53, 54, *437*
Adams, C., 28, *426*
Alba, J. W., 311, 312, *440*
Anderson, J. R., 26, 42, 60, 73, 75, 165, 169, 175, 176, 183–86, 196, 197, *422*
Anderson, R. C., 61, *422*
Anisfeld, M., 35, *422*
Appel, K. J., 340, *427*
Aristotle, 146, 158
Arnold, P. G., 183, 196, *424*
Atkinson, R. C., 9, *422*
Atwood, G., 159, *422*
Atwood, M. E., 267, *429*
Austin, G. A., 279, *425*
Austin, J. L., 189, 204, *423*

Baddeley, A. D., 38, 39, *423*
Bailey, S. C., 223, *432*
Barenfeld, M., 65, *438*
Baresi, J., 28, *428*
Bartlett, F. C., 45–48, 62, 68, 69, *423*
Bartram, D. J., 107, *423, 429*
Berkeley, G., 109, 110, 112, 148–50, 188, 189, *423*
Berko, J., 386, *423*
Bernbach, H. A., 32, *423*
Bierwisch, M., 370, *423*
Birch, H. E., 291, *423*
Birtwhistle, J., 11, *427*
Bjork, R. A., 27, *423*

Block, R. A., 27, 28, 41, *423, 428*
Bloom, L., 379–81, *423*
Bobrow, D. G., 115, *434*
Bobrow, S. A., 35, *423*
Bock, J. K., 50, *423*
Boring, E. G., 151, *423*
Botkin, P. T., 384, *427*
Bourne, L. E., Jr., 280, 281, 301, *423*
Bousfield, W. A., 16, *423*
Bower, G. H., 15, 17, 18, 26, 27, 36, 42, 51, 73, 75, 76, 79, 154–56, 159, 165, 176, 183–86, 196, 197, 276, 339, *422, 424, 428, 436, 439*
Bower, T.G.R., 331–33, 335, 337, 338, *424*
Bowerman, M., 379, *424*
Boyes-Braem, P., 90, *436*
Braine, M.D.S., 204, 379, 389, *424*
Brainerd, C. J., 363, *424*
Brainerd, S. H., 363, *424*
Bransford, J. D., 39, 48, 50–53, 57–59, *424, 430, 433*
Bregman, A. S., 187, 234, *424, 433*
Brewer, W. F., 50, *423*
Broadbent, D. E., 102, 103, 116, 118, 119, 121, 132, 134, 135, 138, *424, 425*
Brooks, L. R., 159, *425*
Brown, H. O., 225, *438*
Brown, R., 378, 379, 391, 392, 394, 395, *425*
Bruner, J. S., 279, 280, *425*

Bugelski, B. R., 339, *425*
Burnham, C. A., 99, 311, *425*

Charlesworth, W. C., 337, *425*
Chase, W. G., 63, 263, *425*
Chastain, G., 99, *425*
Cherry, C. E., 117, *425*
Chipman, S., 147, *437*
Chomsky, N., 368, 378, *425*
Chromiak, W., 334, *440*
Clark, E., 370, 371, 375, 378, *425*
Clark, M., 15, *424*
Conezio, J., 29, *438*
Conrad, C., 107, *425*
Cooper, L. A., 99, 160, *425*
Cornell, D., 113, *429*
Craik, F.I.M., 11, 13, 38–40, 103, *425, 427, 431*
Cramer, P., 35, *425*
Cross, J., 113, *429*
Crowder, R. G., 8, 236, *426*
Cunitz, A. R., 13, *427*

Davis, K. G., 311, *425*
DeGroot, A. D., 63, 262–65, *426*
Descartes, R., 144
Dodge, R., 225, *426*
Dollard, J., 216
Dominowski, R. L., 280, *423*
Dong, T., 17, *426*
Dooling, D. J., 59, *426*
Duncker, K., 248, 251, 260, 312, 314, 316, *426*

Earhard, M., 14, *426*
Edwards, P., 190, *426, 428, 441*
Egeth, H. E., 98, *426*
Ekstrand, B. R., 280, *423*
Elkind, D., 363, *426*
Elmes, D. G., 28, *426*
Epstein, W., 157, *426*
Ervin, S. M., 379, 386, *426, 433*
Estes, W. K., 68, 75, 76, 79, 82, *426*
Evans, W. F., 340–42, *426, 427*

Fillenbaum, S., 35, *426*
Fingerman, P., 303, *426*
Fish, R. E., 40, *440*
Flagg, P. W., 4, 51, *426, 436*
Flavell, J. H., 229, 330, 352, 360, 384, *427, 433*
Flexser, A. J., 34, 42, 103, *427*
Franks, J. J., 39, 48, 50–53, 59, *424, 433*
Fraser, C., 378, 379, 391, 392, *425*
Frege, G., 169, *427*
Freund, J. R., 29

Freund, J. S., 21, *439*
Friedman, M. J., 22, *427*
Fry, C. L., Jr., 384, *427*
Furth, H. G., 219, 228, *427*
Fusella, V., 160, *437*

Gaarder, K. R., 92, *427*
Galanter, E., 155, *433*
Galper, R. E., 99, *429*
Gardiner, J. M., 11, *427*
Gardner, B. T., 397, *427*
Gardner, R. A., 397, *427*
Gelman, R., 363, 365, 366, 385, *427, 437*
Gever, B., 227, *427*
Gilmartin, K. A., 63, 64, *438*
Gittis, M. M., 7, *440*
Glanzer, M., 13, *427*
Glucksberg, S., 384, *427*
Goggin J., 7, *427*
Goldman, D., 113, *429*
Goodman, D., 35, *434*
Goodman, L. S., 225, *438*
Goodnow, J. J., 279, *425*
Gratch, G., 340–42, *426, 427*
Gray, W. D., 90, *436*
Greeno, J. G., 269, 272, *427*
Greenwald, A., 417, *428*
Grice, G. R., 229, *428*
Griffin, M., 61, *428*
Gross, A. E., 28, *428*
Gruen, G. E., 364, *428*

Haber, R. N., 29, *428, 438*
Hanlon, C., 395, *425*
Harlow, H. F., 300, 301, *428*
Harris, P. L., 333, 335, 341, 342, *428*
Hasher, L. A., 61, *428*
Hayes, C., 397, *428*
Hayes, J. R., 270, 271, *428*
Hayes, K. J., 397, *428*
Hayes-Roth, B., 61, 196, 389, *428*
Hayes-Roth, F., 61, 196, 389, *428*
Heath, P. L., 190, *428*
Hebb, D. O., 94, *428*
Heise, G. A., 102, *433*
Hilgard, E. R., 76, *428*
Hinde, R. A., 402, 403, *428*
Hintzman, D. L., 41, *428*
Hjertholm, E., 227, *430*
Hochberg, J., 95, 97–99, 101, 115, 122, 124, 125, 128, 129, 132, 133, 139, 391, 399, *428, 429*
Holyoak, K., 36, *424*
Homa, D., 113, *429*
Hovland, C. I., 280, *429*
Hull, C. L., 215, 289, *429*

Author index

Humphrey, G., 144, 151, 152, 215, 224, 225, 265, *429*
Hunt, E. B., 103, 276, 280, *429*
Hunt, J. McV., 346, *429*
Hutcheon, E. G., 107, *429*
Hyde, T. S., 37, 38, *429*

Israel, H. E., 299, *436*

Jacobson, E., 222, *429*
Jacoby, L., 13, 27, 32, 38, 103, *429, 431*
James, W., 138, 414, 415, 417, *429*
Jarvis, P. E., 229, 384, 427, *429*
Jeffrey, W. E., 216, *429*
Jeffries, R., 267, 269, 271, 272, *429*
Jenkins, J. J., 37, 38, 40, 112, 389, *429, 430, 438, 439*
Jenkins, W. O., 31, *435*
Johnsen, J. A., 168, *436*
Johnson, D. M., 90, *436*
Johnson, M. K., 50, 52, 57–59, *424, 430*

Kahneman, D., 121–23, 132, *430*
Kaplan, R. M., 201, *430*
Katz, S., 52, *430*
Keele, S. W., 111, 112, *435*
Keeney, T., 112, *438*
Keller, B., 223, *432*
Keppel, G., 5–7, 23, *430*
Kessel, F. S., 112, *438*
Kimble, G. A., 414, 415, *430, 441*
Kintsch, W., 17, 25, 26, 202, *426, 430*
Kister, J., 261, *430*
Knapp, M., 35, *422*
Kohlberg, L., 227, 237, *430*
Kohler, W., 290–93, *430*
Kolers, P. A., 60, 61, *430*
Konorski, J., 185, 190, *430*
Kosslyn, S. M., 153, 159, 166–69, 196, *430*
Krauss, R. M., 384, *427*
Krechevsky, I., 276, *430*
Kruesi, E., 41
Kuenne, M. R., 218, *430*
Kuhn, T. S., 368, *430*
Kulpe, O., 152

LaBerge, D., 135–36, *430*
Lambert, W. E., 153, *431*
Lashley, K. S., 275, *431*
Lawrence, D. H., 278, *431*
LeCompte, G. K., 340, *427*
Lesgold, A. M., 15, 17, *424*
Levine, M. A., 276, 282–84, 303–5, *426, 431*
Liberman, A. M., 123, *431*
Lichten, W., 102, *433*
Lindsay, P. H., 88, 176, 179–82, 412, *431*

Locke, J., 109, 110, 148, 149, 173, 187–89, *431*
Lockhart, R. S., 38–40, 103, *425, 431*
Loess, H., 7, *431*
Loftus, G. R., 10, 11, 29, 30, *431*
Luchins, A. S., 294, 296, 299, 300, *431*
Luchins, E. H., 296, 299, 300, *431*
Luria, A. R., 211, 212, 217, 228–30, 236, *431*

Madigan, S. A., 13, *431*
Maier, N.R.F., 307–9, *431, 432*
Maltzman, I., 289, *432*
Mandler, G., 14, 15, 18, 135, 136, 146, 148, 152, 188, 265, 266, 290, *431, 432, 439*
Mandler, J. M., 146, 148, 152, 188, 265, 266, 290, *431, 432, 439*
Maratsos, M. P., 385, *432*
Marbe, K., 152, *432*
Massaro, D. W., 106–7, *432, 438*
Matthews, L. J., 284, *432*
Max, L. W., 222–23, *432*
Mayer, A., 152, *432*
McCabe, L., 13, *431*
McGeoch, J. A., 19, 20, *432*
McGuigan, F. J., 214–15, 222–24, 235, 237, *429, 432, 433*
McKay, D. P., 98, *437*
McNeill, D., 368, *433*
McNulty, J. A., 31, *433*
Medin, D. L., 113, *433*
Mervis, C. B., 90, 191, *436*
Metzler, B., *437*
Meyers, J., 305, *433*
Miller, G. A., 102, 155, 378, *433*
Miller, N. E., 216
Miller, S. A., 229, *433*
Miller, W., 379, *433*
Minsky, M., 104–5, 115, *433*
Mischel, W., 147, *433*
Moeser, S. D., 234, *433*
Moray, N., 117, 119, *433*
Morris, C. D., 39, *433*
Morton, J., 102–3, 121, *433*
Mullet, R. L., 59, *426*
Munoz, R., 183, 196, *424*
Murdock, B. B., Jr., 31, *433*

Natsoulas, T., 137, *433*
Neisser, U., 40, 88, 90, 94, 98, 115, 122–26, 128, 133, 137–38, 159, 162, 165, 172, 280, 391, *433, 434, 437*
Nelson, K., 370, 374–77, *433*
Nelson, K. E., 331, *433*
Nelson, T. O., 38, 39, *433*
Newell, A., 248, 261, 267, 271, *433*
Nickerson, R. S., 30, *434*

Norman, D. A., 88, 115, 128, 176, 179–82, 412, *430, 431, 434*
Noton, D., 92, 94, 95, 98, 99, *434*

Olson, D. R., 382–83, *434*
Orth, J., 152, *432*
Ostry, D., 60, *430*

Paivio, A. U., 153–56, *431, 434, 440*
Palermo, D. S., 187, 368, 389, *430, 434*
Palmer, S. E., 105, 115, *434*
Patterson, K. K., 10, 11, *431*
Patton, J. H., 284, *432*
Pavlov, I. P., 77, 129–30, 210–11
Pearlstone, Z., 15, 17, *439*
Perfetti, C. A., 35, *434*
Perlmutter, L. C., 414–15, *430, 441*
Peterson, L. R., 4, 5, 22, 23, *434*
Peterson, M. J., 4, 5, 22, 23, *434*
Phillips, L. W., 13, *435*
Piaget, J., 321–31, 333, 335, 339–41, 343, 345–51, 353–61, 365, 367, 383–84, 399, 418, *434, 435*
Pichert, J. W., 61, *422*
Pintner, R., 224, *435*
Plato, 186, 187, 189
Pollack, I., 22, *435*
Polson, P. G., 267, *429*
Polya, G., 266, *435*
Pomerantz, J. R., 153, 167, 168, 196, *430*
Posner, M. I., 4, 110–12, 122, 134–36, 190, *435*
Postal, P., 370, *435*
Postman, D. L., 31, *435*
Postman, L., 13, 21, 31, 41, *435*
Potter, M. C., 109, *435*
Premack, D., 397, *435*
Pribram, K., 155, *433*
Price, H. H., 4, 43, 144, 146, 149, 400, *435*
Pylyshyn, Z., 153, 166, 169, 175, *435*

Quine, W.V.O., 389, *435*

Rand, G., 76, *435*
Ray, W. S., 302, *435*
Rayner, E. H., 264, 265, *435*
Rayner, K., 102, *436*
Razran, G., 130, 211, 217, *436*
Razran, L., 267, *429*
Reed, S. K., 168, *436*
Rees, H. J., 299, *436*
Reese, H. W., 301, *429, 436*
Reicher, G. M., 106, *436*
Reitman, J. S., 51, *436*
Restle, F., 276, *436*
Reynolds, A. G., 4, *436*

Reynolds, J. H., 22, *427*
Riley, D., 7, *427*
Rips, L. J., 89, 91, 107, *438*
Rizzolo, A., 224, *436*
Robins, C., 161, *436*
Rock, I., 157, *426*
Rodier, W. I., III, 223, 235, *433*
Roediger, H. L., 28, *426*
Rommetveit, R., 381, *439*
Rosch, E., 90, 191–94, *436*
Rumelhart, D. E., 127, 176, 180, 202, *430, 434*
Rundus, D., 77, *436*
Ryle, G., 158, 195, 209, *436*

Sachs, J. S., 48–50, 52, 60, *436*
Samuels, S. J., 135–36, *430*
Scavo, L., 302
Schaffer, M. M., 113, *433*
Schank, R. C., 53–56, 104, 105, 176, 179–83, 197, 317, *436, 437*
Scheerer, M., 293, 296, 302, 310, 314, *437*
Schlesinger, I. M., 381, *427*
Schneider, W., 98, *437*
Scholes, R. J., 393, *437*
Schulz, R. W., 154, *439*
Schwartz, S., 113, *429*
Sechenov, I., 172, 210–11, 213–15, 398, 410, 417, 419, *437*
Segal, S. J., 160, *437*
Selfridge, O. G., 90, *437*
Sellars, W., 205, *437*
Selz, O., 250, 265–66, *437*
Shaffer, W. O., 98, *437*
Shatz, M., 385, *437*
Shaw, J. C., 261, *434*
Shelton, J., 229, *433*
Shepard, R. N., 28–30, 99, 146–47, 160–61, 166, 169, 170, 425, *436, 437*
Shiffrin, R. M., 9, 98, 132, 422, *437*
Shoben, E. J., 89, 91, 107, *438*
Shuell, T. J., 22, *438*
Simon, H. A., 63–65, 156, 175, 248, 261, 263, 267, 271, *425, 434, 438*
Skinner, B. F., 389, *438*
Sloane, S., 365–66, *440*
Slobin, D. I., 392, *437, 438*
Smedslund, J., 363, *438*
Smith, E. E., 28, 89, 91, 107, *428, 438*
Smith, S. M., 225, 399, *438*
Snyder, C. R., 122, 134–36, *435*
Sokolov, A. N., 208, 213, 223–24, 398, *438*
Sokolov, Ye. N., 130–31, 407–8, *438*
Solomon, S. K., 50, 52, 59, *430*
Spence, K. W., 275, *438*
Standing, L., 29, *438*

Author index

Stanton, E., 223, *432*
Stark, L., 92, 94, 95, 98, 99, *434*
Stein, P., 261, *430*
Strange, W., 112, *438*
Suls, J. M., 260, *440*
Sutton-Smith, B., 190, *438*

Tanner, R. G., 224, *433*
Thomas, J. C., Jr., 269, *438*
Thompson, M. C., 106, *438*
Thomson, D. M., 32, 33, *438*, *439*
Thorndike, E. L., 289, 292, *438*
Thorson, A. M., 238, *438*
Tieman, D., 17, *424*
Till, R. E., 37, *438*
Titchener, E. B., 151, 152, *439*
Toman, J.E.P., 225, *438*
Trabasso, T. R., 276, *439*
Trask, F. P., 72–74, 76, *441*
Treisman, A. M., 116, 119, 120, *439*
Tulving, E., 14–18, 25, 32–34, 38, 42, 45, 67, 79, 80, 103, *425*, *427*, *438*, *439*
Turner, E. A., 381, *439*

Ulam, S., 261, *430*
Underwood, B. J., 5–7, 20, 21, 23, 34, 35, 154, *430*, *439*
Urbanski, B., 365–66, *440*

Vendler, Z., 144–45, *439*
Vinacke, W. E., 249, *439*
Vygotsky, L. S., 211–12, 226–28, 230, 236–37, 372, *439*

Walden, W., 261, *430*
Wallace, W. P., 35, *439*
Wallas, G., 248, *439*

Walsh, D. A., 37, *439*
Wapner, S., 76, *435*
Watkins, M. J., 10, 11, *439*
Watkins, O. C., 10, 11, *439*
Watson, J. B., 146, 153, 214, 398, *440*
Waugh, N. C., 7, *431*
Weene, P., 280, *434*
Weimer, W. B., 187, *440*
Weinberg, D. H., 366, *429*
Weisberg, R. W., 40, 227, 260, 311–13, 334, 365–66, 384, *427*, *440*
Wells, H., 280, *440*
Wells, M., 261, *430*
Wheeler, D. D., 106, *440*
White, R. M., Jr., 284, *440*
Wickelgren, W. A., 21, 82, *440*
Wickens, D. D., 7, 9, *440*
Wilder, L., 229, *440*
Williams, G. F., 284, *440*
Winograd, E., 74, *440*
Winzenz, D., 15, 184, 196, *424*
Wishart, J. G., 337, *424*
Wittgenstein, L., 189, 204, 207, 220, *440*
Wollen, K. A., 157, *440*
Woods, W. A., 201, *441*
Woodworth, R. S., 414–15, *441*
Woozley, A. D., 190, *441*
Wright, J. W., 384, *427*
Wright, N. A., 340, *427*

Yaeger, J., 227, *430*
Yates, F. A., 154–55, *441*
Yntema, D. B., 72–74, 76, *441*
Youniss, J., 219, *427*

Zeiler, M. D., 219, *441*
Zuckerman, C. B., 157, *426*

Subject index

abstract attributes, in pattern recognition, 113
abstract ideas
  generic images, 149
  and images, 147
  Locke vs Berkeley, 110, 148–49
  in pattern recognition, 109–10
  prototype studies, 110–13
abstraction
  as basis for knowledge, 187–88
  and defining features, 107–9
accommodation, in cognitive development, 321–24. *See also* Piaget's theory.
actions
  as basis for events, 179
  as basis for representations, 176
  and images, 414–16
  and thought, 414–16
ambiguous figures, 99
animism, in child thought, 350. *See also* Piaget's theory.
artificialism, in child thought, 350. *See also* Piaget's theory.
assimilation, in cognitive development, 321, 323. *See also* Piaget's theory.
associations, and psychological state, 77–79
attitudes
  in hypothesis formation in problem solving, 278
  in problem solving, 299

Bartlett's reconstructive theory of recall, 46–47
behaving, and thinking, 389–99
behavior, and goals, 411–13
behaviorism, and imagery, 153
Berkeley vs Locke on images as abstract ideas, 148–49
bottom-up processing, in pattern recognition. *See also* top-down processing. filter model, 118
box problem. *See* candle problem.

candle problem, 251–60, 290
capacity, and consciousness, 134–37, 139
categories. *See* concepts.
categories, as cues in recall, 15, 18–19, 63
category clustering, in recall, 15–16
centration, in child thought, 353. *See also* Piaget's theory.
chess
  perception and memory, 262
  as problem solving, 261–64
chess master
  knowledge, 263–64
  memory, 62–67
chess-playing programs, 261–62
child's thinking about reality, 348, 350. *See also* Piaget's theory.
child's understanding of relations, 347–48. *See also* Piaget's theory.

448

Subject index

classification problems, 275–86
 discrimination learning, 275–76
 hypotheses, 277–78
 scripts, 284–86
 solution rules, 279–81
 win-stay, lose-shift strategy, 277, 282–84
clustering, in recall, 15–16
cognitive capacity, and speech for self, 239–41
cognitive development. *See* Piaget's theory.
communication
 egocentrism, 383–84
 emphasis and utterances, 381
 objects to be discriminated, 382
 skills development, 383–84
comprehension
 in memory for sentences, 53–57
 scripts, 53–57
computer chess playing, 261–62
computer simulation of problem solving, 271–72
concept formation. *See* classification problems.
concepts, 175–201
 as basis for inferences, 183
 as basis for knowledge, 176
 as basis for paraphrase, 182
 conceptualism, 186
 defined by abstract features, 185
 defined by properties, 176
 defined by relations to other concepts, 176
 and family resemblances, 190–93
 and language, 209, 212, 216–17, 220–21
 logic of having a concept, 195
 as meanings of words, 185
 as mental elements, 185
 nominalism, 186, 188–89
 and patterns, 114
 philosophical analysis, 184
 Plato's forms, 186
 and propositions, 183
 question of essences, 91
 realism, 185
 sentence comprehension, 180, 196
 sentence recognition, 200
 and thought, 401
conceptual networks, 176–81
 alternative descriptions, 198–99
conceptual primitives, as medium of thought, 190
conceptual thinking, in the deaf, 219
conscious thought, vs unconscious, 145
consciousness
 in filter model, 118
 and imagery, 171–72
 and limited capacity, 134
 multiple dimensions, 137

selective attention, 134–37
 and speech, 234
conservation
 of liquid, 351–52
 memory, 365–66
 past experience, 361–65
 Piaget's analysis, critique, 355–65
conservation training, 361–65
context, in recall of verbal material, 57, 59
 in recognition failure, 33
creation of new words, by children, 385–88
creation of sentences, by children, 389
 past experience, 393
creativity
 in language, 385–89
 in problem solving, role of past experience, 250, 399
cues, retrieval, 67. *See also* recency cues and summary cues.
 category names, 15–16, 18–19
 cue-item relations, 15
 hierarchical organization, 15
cues in short-term memory
 recency, 9
 summary, 9–10

defining features, and abstraction, 107–9
 in pattern recognition, 115
depth cues, in pattern recognition, 95, 98
depth of encoding, 38–39
developmental psycholinguistics. *See* language development.
directed forgetting, 27–28
directive function of speech, 208, 212. *See also* speech and thought.
directive speech, 226. *See also* speech and thought.
 development, 227–29
 logic of self-direction, 230–32
 social factors, 227
 task difficulty, 227
discrimination learning and classification problems, 275–76
 hypotheses, 276
distractor, in short-term memory, 8
distractor task, as factor in forgetting, 5
dual process hypothesis, of recognition and recall, 25–32. *See also* recognition and recall.

egocentrism, 354–58. *See also* Piaget's theory.
 in child thought, critique, 354–58
 in communication, 383–84
encoding, 24–44
 depth, breadth, and elaborateness, 38–39
 imagery, 35

Subject index

encoding (*continued*)
    and imagination, 33
    implicit associative responses (IARs), 34 as memory for word, 32–41
    and recognition failure, 36
    recognition tests, 34
    referential encoding, 35
    structural vs semantic encoding and recall, 37–39
    and thinking, 42
    verbal encodings, 36
episodes, as groups of events, 177, 179
    in memory, 34
episodic and semantic memory, 67, 79
events, as basis for episodes in memory, 177, 179
    based on actions, 179
expectations
    in listening to sentences, 102
    in perception, 124–28
    in reading, 101–2
    in selective attention, 130–32
    in sentences, transition networks, 202
    in visual perception, 333–35
eye movements
    in pattern recognition, 92–95, 98
    in reading, 101–2
    in visual tracking, 331–35

facial recognition, orientation, 99
family resemblances, and concepts, 190–93, 220–21
feature analysis, in pattern recognition, 88
feature ring in pattern recognition, 93–95, 98
features
    as basis for concepts, 185
    defining in pattern recognition, 89–90
features of words in memory, 25
filter model
    bottom-up processing, 118
    and consciousness, 118
    and processing meaning, 119
    of selective attention, 116
    Treisman's reformulation, 120
fixation, in problem solving, 293, 296–99, 305. *See also* insight.
fixations
    in memory for pictures, 29
    in pattern recognition, 92–95, 98
first words
    functional concepts, 374–77
    semantic features, 369–73
fixed-action patterns (FAPs)
    and releasers in sensorimotor development, 404

    and releasers in species-specific behavior, 403–4
forgetting. *See also* memory, proactive interference, retroactive interference.
    directed, 27–28
    law of disuse, 19
    retention interval, 5
    role of distractor, 5
    role of time, 19
frames, in pattern recognition, 104. *See also* scripts.
free recall
    negative recency, 13
    recency, 12
    serial position curve, 12
functional concepts, as basis for first words, 374–77
functional fixation, in problem solving, 314–16
functional fixedness. *See* functional fixation
functional fixity. *See* functional fixation.

General Problem Solver (GPS) program, 80–81
general knowledge, and specific experiences, 80–81
generalization in sensorimotor development memory, 405–9
generate and test model, of recognition and recall, 26. *See also* recognition and recall.
generic images, and abstract ideas, 149–50
goals, and behavior, 411–13
Gomoku, as problem solving, 264–65
grammatical classes, and transition networks, 203

habit family hierarchy, in problem solving, 289
habituation, and thinking, 409
habituation of orienting reflex, role of knowledge, 407–9
hat rack problem, 309–10
hierarchical organization,
    in pattern recognition, 105–6
    in recall, 15
hierarchical structure of knowledge, 106
hypotheses
    in classification problems, 177–78. *See also* win-stay, lose-shift strategy.
    in discrimination learning, 176
hypothesis testing in problem solving, 282–85

ideas, as elements of thought, 187
ill- vs well-defined problems, 270–72

Subject index

imageless thought, Wurzburg, 152
imagery, 143–74
 and behaviorism, 153
 and consciousness, 171–72
 in early psychology (Titchener), 151
 in encoding, 33, 35
 and knowledge, 158, 205
 and memory, 153–58
 mind's eye, 167–68
 and pattern maps, 162
 and perception, 159–62
 in problem solving, 256
images
 and actions, 414–16
 generic, and abstract ideas, 149
 knowledge and recall, 162–65
 scanning, 165–70
 as symbols for thought, 144, 147–49, 171
 vs propositions as medium of thought, 170
images and abstract ideas, 147
 generic images, 150
 Locke vs Berkeley, 148–49
imagination. See imagery, images.
imagist theory of thought, 146
implicit associative responses in recognition, 34
infancy, cognitive development. See Piaget's theory.
inferences, based on concepts, 183
 in memory for sentences, 52
insight and fixation in problem solving, 305–16
insight, in problem solving, 248–49, 287–317
 vs trial and error, 289–92
interactive imagery and recall, 154–55, 162–65
interference
 in the development of general knowledge, 80–81
 in the development of the object concept, 338–40
 proactive, 19–21
  in object concept, 341–42
  in short-term memory, 5–7, 9–11
 retroactive, 21–22
internalization of thought, 409

judgments of recency, 72–76

knowledge and expectations
 imagery, 158, 205
 internalization of thought, 410
 hierarchical structure, 106
 in listening to sentences, 102
 in memory, 53–57

for sentences, 53, 57
 in orienting reflex, 129–32
 in pattern recognition and selective attention, 124–28
 in problem solving, 5–9, 258, 274
  chess master, 263–64
  classification problems, 285
  Gomoku, 265
  Selz's analysis, 265
 in recall, 18–19
  of categorized lists, 63–67
  chess master, 62–67
  of images, 162–65
  of verbal material, 60–61
  as result of abstraction, 187–88
 in short-term memory, 10

language games, 204
 reasoning, 205–6
 thinking, 208, 232–33
language
 and concepts, 209, 212, 216–17, 220–21
 deafness, 219
 perception, 217
language development, 368–97
 communication, 383–84
 creation of new words, 385–88
 creation of sentences, 389, 393
 first words, 369–77
 language in chimps, 397
 processing limitations, 395
 selective reinforcement, 394–95
 semantic relations, 380–81
 telegraphic speech, 390–93
 two-word utterances, 378–80
law of disuse in forgetting, 19
learning set, 300–1
letter recognition, vs words, 106
limited capacity
 consciousness, 134–38
 in language development, 391–93, 395–96
 in selective attention, 121–22
Locke vs Berkeley on abstract ideas, 110
 on images as abstract ideas, 148–49

manual search and object concept, 335–39
marking nodes in memory, 26
meaning
 and expectations in selective attention, 132–33
 in memory for sentences, 48, 50, 60–61
 and use, 204
meanings of words as concepts, 185
mediational theory of speech and thought, 214–16

medium of thought. *See* concepts, imagery, language, speech, propositions.
memory. *See also* proactive interference, retroactive interference, recall, recognition.
 in cognitive development, 405–9
 in development of conservation, 365–66
 interactive imagery, 156–58
 in operational thought, 365–66
 and perception, 64–67
 in problem solving, 252
 in telegraphic speech in children, 390
memory for sentences
 comprehension, 53–57
 inferences, 52
 meaning, 48–50
 meaning vs words, 60–61
 scripts, 53–57
 semantic integration, 51
memory for temporal order, 72–76
memory interference and object concept, 338–39
memory nodes, 25
 in recognition, 33
mental combination in cognitive development, 327. *See also* Piaget's theory.
mental actions and thinking, 400–1
mental representations, 42. *See also* images, imagery, concepts, speech and thought.
method of loci, 154–55
mind's eye, 167–68
missionaries and cannibals problem, 266
mnemonic methods based on imagery, 154–55
modality-specific interference, imagery, 159
move problems, 266–70
 problem space, 267
 problem-specific knowledge, 270

negative recency in free recall, 13
name, as stimulus for selective attention, 119–21, 123, 126, 128–32
nine-dot problem, 311
nodes in memory, 26
 in recognition, 33
nominalism
 concepts, 186–89
 family resemblances, 190
 studies of family resemblances, 191–93
novel patterns, recognition, 103

object concept, 328–30
 manual search, 335–39
 perseverative search, 340–43
 role of memory, 338–39, 341–43

 and visual tracking, 331–35
organization in recall, 18–19, 41
 categories, 15
 subjective, 16–17
orienting reflex
 habituation and knowledge, 407–9
 knowledge and expectations, 129–32
 and sensorimotor development, 407–9
orientation and recognition of faces, 99

paired associates, 20
pandemonium model, of pattern recognition, 90
parallel processing, in pattern recognition, 95, 98
paraphrase, based on concepts, 182
partial learning, in recognition, 31
partial reinforcement effect, in problem solving, 304–5
past experience
 creativity, 399
 in the creation of new sentences, 393
 in problem solving, 250
pattern maps
 imagery, 162–63
 pattern recognition, 94–95, 98, 104
pattern recognition, 88–115, 124–28
 abstract attributes, 113
 abstract ideas, 109–10
 abstract pattern maps, 109
 ambiguous figures, 99
 and attention, 124–28
 defining features, 89–90, 115
 depth cues, 95–98
 expectations and knowledge, 101–2
 eye movements, 92–95, 98
 feature analysis, 88–90
 feature ring, 93–95, 98
 frames, 104
 hierarchical organization of patterns, 105–6
 knowledge, 104
 knowledge and expectations, 101–2
 novel patterns, 103
 orientation and recognition, 99
 pandemonium model, 90
 parallel processing within fixations, 95, 98
 pattern maps, 94–95, 98, 104
 question of essences, 91
 resonance, 103
 scripts, 104
 sequential processes, 92
 templates, 88
 top-down vs bottom-up, 114–15
patterns and concepts, 114

Subject index

peg-wood mnemonic method, 155
perception. *See also* pattern recognition.
  action, 399
  in chess, 262
  imagery, 159–62
  language, 217
  role of expectations, 333–35
perceptual synthesis, as basis for selective attention, 122–23
perseverative search, and object concept, 340–43
Piaget's theory, 321–67
  accommodation, 321, 323–24
  animism, 350
  artificialism, 350
  assimilation, 321, 323–24
  centration of thought, 353
  conservation, 351–52
    critique, 359–65
  critical analysis, 354–58
  egocentrism, 354–58
  infancy, 321–45
  mental combinations, 327
  object concept, 328–43
  operational thought, 345–67
  primary circular reactions, 325–26
  reality, 348–50
  reflexes, 323–24
  reversibility of thought, 348, 353
  schemas, 323–24, 326
  schemas to operations, 346
  secondary circular reactions, 326
  sensorimotor development, 324–28
  symbolist view, 328
  tertiary circular reactions, 327
  thought as internal action, 327
  transitive inferences, 352–53
  understanding of relations, 347–48
picture recognition, 28–29
uniqueness, 30
pivot open grammars, two-word utterances, 378–80
Plato's forms, and concepts, 186
primary circular reactions, 325–26. *See also* Piaget's theory.
proactive interference
  amount of prior learning, 20
  and object concept, 341–3
  retention interval, 6
  retrieval failure, 11
  in short-term memory, 5–11
  similarity, 6
  storage vs retrieval, 11
  temporal factors, 20–1
problem solving
  candle problem, 251–60

  in chess, 261–64
  classification problems, 274–86
  computer simulation, 271–72
  creativity and past experience, 250
  familiar problems, 252
  functional fixation, 314–16
  general knowledge, 274
  Gomoku, 264–65
  habit family hierarchy, 289
  hat rack problem, 309–10
  hypotheses, 276
  hypothesis formation, 278
  hypothesis testing, 282–85
  insight, 290, 293
  insight and fixation, 305–16
  insight problems, 306–13
  insight vs trial and error, 288, 292
  Kohler's apes, 290
  learning set, 300–1
  move problems, 266–70
  new problems, 254–55
  nine-dot problem, 311
  partial reinforcement effect, 304
  radiation problem, 312–13
  reproductive vs productive thought, 292
  retrieval from memory, 252
  role of knowledge, 258–59
  role of speech, 226–29
  scripts, 297–99
  set and fixation, 296–99, 302–3
  similar problems, 254
  spontaneous restructuring, 293
  stages, 249
  stopping and thinking, 258–59
  subject's attitude, 299–300
  subject's interpretation, 296–99
  trial and error vs insight, 289–90
  triangles problem, 312
  two-string problem, 306–8
  unsolvable problems, 303–4
  water jars, 296–303
  well- vs ill-defined problems, 270–72
  win-stay, lose-shift, 277, 282–86
processing limitations, in language development, 395
  in telegraphic speech, 391–92
productive thinking, Selz's analysis, 265–66
productive vs reproductive thought in problem solving, 290
propositions, and concepts, 183
  as basis for knowledge, 183–84
  vs images as medium of thought, 170
prototype studies, 110–13
psycholinguistics. *See* language development, memory for sentences, sentence comprehension.

psychological state, in recall, 77–79
  in temporal judgments, 75–76
pure thought, 144

radiation problem, 312–13
reading
  expectations, 101–2
  eye movements, 101–2
realism
  concepts, 185
  in child thought, 349. See also Piaget's theory.
recall
  dual process hypothesis, 32
  organization and use of knowledge, 18
  and recognition, 26–28
  and reconstruction, 45–70
  rehearsal, 27, 31–32
recency
  in free recall, 13
  judgments, 72–76
  in recall, 8–13, 77–79
  in short-term memory, 8–10
recognition
  dual-process hypothesis, 32
  and recall, 25–28
  rehearsal, 31–32
recognition errors
  in memory for sentences, 48–50
recognition failure, 32–34
recognition
  of faces, orientation, 99
  lack of retrieval, 26
  of letters vs words, 106
  of novel patterns, 103
  partial learning, 31
  of pictures, 28–30
reconstruction and recall, 45–70
  chess masters, 62–67
  recall errors, 48–50
  schemas, 48–50
referential encoding, in memory, 35
reflexes in cognitive development, 323–24. See also Piaget's theory.
rehearsal
  in recognition and recall, 27, 31–32
  in short-term memory, 8
release from proactive interference in short-term memory, 7
representations, and actions, 176
resonance, in pattern recognition, 103, 124
retention interval
  factor in forgetting, 5
  in proactive interference in short-term memory, 6

retrieval cues, 67. See also cues, recency cues, summary cues.
  in encoding, 40
  in short-term memory, 10
retrieval failure in proactive interference, 11
retrieval vs storage in proactive interference in short-term memory, 11
retroactive interference, 21
  in short-term memory, 21–2
reversibility of thought, 348, 353. See also Piaget's theory.
revolution, in cognitive psychology, 368
rotation studies, of imagery, 160–62

scanning images, vs scanning objects, 165–70
schemas
  as basis for reconstruction, 48–50
  in cognitive development, 323–24
scripts
  in comprehension, 53–57
  in memory for sentences, 53–57
  in pattern recognition, 104
  in problem solving, 285, 297–99
  in recall of verbal material, 59
  and transition networks, 203
Sechenov
  on speech and thought, 210–11, 213–14
  on thought and behavior, 210–11, 398–99, 410
second signal system, 211
secondary circular reactions in cognitive development, 326. See also Piaget's theory.
selective attention
  analyzing meaning, 132
  and consciousness, 134–37
  filter model, 116, 118
  limited capacity, 121–22
  meaning and expectations, 133
  to one's name, 128–32
  perceptual synthesis, 122–23
  shadowing, 117
  and top-down models of pattern recognition, 123–28
selective reinforcement, in language development, 394–95
semantic and episodic memory, 67, 79–81
semantic conditioning, 217
semantic encoding
  and recall-organization, 41
  retrieval cues, 40
semantic features, as basis for first words, 369–73
semantic integration, in memory for sentences, 51

Subject index

semantic relations
  in two-word utterances, 380–81
semantic vs structural encoding and recall, 37–39
semantics. *See also* meaning.
  and transition networks, 202
sensorimotor period of cognitive development, 324–28. *See also* Piaget's theory.
sensorimotor development
  generalization, 405–9
  and the orienting reflex, 407–9
  selectivity, 402
  waning of responses, 407–9
sentence comprehension
  and concepts, 196
  models, 176
  transition networks, 201–2
sentence processing, expectations, 102
sentences
  inferences in memory, 52
  memory for meaning vs words, 60–61
  recognition errors, 48–50
  semantic integration, 51
  as symbols, 233
  wholistic ideas, 51
sequential processes
  in pattern recognition, 91–95, 124. *See also* pattern maps.
  in recall of images, 162–65
serial position curve, of free recall, 12
set and fixation, in problem solving, 296–303
shadowing task, processing rejected message, 117
short-term memory, 4–11, 21
  distractor, 8
  proactive interference, 8–11
  recency, 9
  rehearsal, 8
  retrieval cues, 10
  retroactive interference, 21
  role of knowledge, 10
  summary cues, 9
similarity
  in proactive interference, 6
  in retroactive interference, 22
species-specific behavior, 402–4
  fixed-action patterns and releasers, 403–4
speech, and consciousness, 234
speech and thought, 209. *See also* directive speech, speech for self.
  mediation, 214, 216
  Russian theorizing, 212
  Sechenov, 210–11, 213–14
  second signal system, 211
  transposition, 218
  Watson's view, 214

speech for self. *See also* directive speech, speech and thought.
  and capacity, 239–41
  and communication, 236
  masking, 235
  memory, 236
  overflow model, 237–41
speech muscles and thought, 209, 214, 222–25
stages in problem solving, 249
stickleback, 402–4
storage vs retrieval, in interference in short-term memory, 11
structural vs semantic encoding
  and recall, 37–39
  retrieval cues, 40
subjective organization
  cue-item relations, 17
  in recall, 16–17
summary cues
  cue-item relations, 15
  in recall, 14, 16
  in short-term recall, 9–10
switching attention, 129–32
symbolist view of thinking, 4, 328
symbolization
  images, 171
  thought, 143, 233

telegraphic speech, 390–93
  process limitations, 391–92
  role of memory, 390
templates, in pattern recognition, 88
temporal factors, in proactive interference, 7, 20–21
temporal judgments, psychological state, 75–76
temporal order in memory, 71, 81
tertiary circular reaction, in cognitive development, 327
thinking. *See also* concepts, imagery, Piaget's theory, problem solving, speech and thought.
  and behaving, 327, 398–99
  as behavior, central vs peripheral, 146
  and concepts, 400–1
  conscious vs unconscious, 145
  habituation, 409
  images, 144–74
  imagist theory in philosophy, 146
  as internal activity, 3
  as internal operations, 3
  mental actions, 400–1
  pure thought, 144
  role of speech muscles, 209, 214, 222–25
  two-thirds of a reflex, 410

thinking (*continued*)
   universals, 144
   verbalizations, 144
thought. *See* thinking.
thought and volition, 414–16
thoughts, as causes of actions, 414–16
time. *See also* recency, temporal factors.
   as the cause of forgetting, 19
Titchener on imagery and thought, 151
top-down models of pattern recognition and selective attention, 123–8
   Treisman's model, 120
   vs bottom-up processing, 114–15
TRANS, as basic action, 182
transition networks
   and expectations, 202
   and grammatical classes, 203
   as models of sentence comprehension, 201–2
   scripts, 203
   semantics, 202
transitive inferences, in child thought, 352–53. *See also* Piaget's theory.
transposition, and verbal responses, 218
trial and error
   in problem solving, 288–93
   vs insight in problem solving, 288–93
triangles problem, 312
Treisman's attenuation model of selective attention, 120
   dictionary units, 120
   top-down processing, 120

two-string problem, 306–8
two-word utterances
   pivot open grammars, 378–80
   semantic relations, 380–81
typicality, in concepts, 191–93

unconscious thought, vs conscious, 145
universals
   Plato's discussion, 186
   in thinking, 144
unsolvable problems, 303–4
use, and meaning, 204

verbal encodings, 36
verbal vs visual processing, 159
verbalizations, as symbols of thought, 144. *See also* speech and thought.
visual prototype studies, 110–13
visual tracking, and object concept, 331–35
visual vs verbal processing, 159
volition, and voluntary action, 414–16

war of the ghosts, 47
water jar problems, 294–303
   set and fixation, 296–99
Watson, on speech and thought, 214
well- vs ill-defined problems, 270–72
wholistic ideas, in memory for sentences, 51
win-stay, lose-shift strategy, 277, 282–85
wording, in memory for sentences, 61–62
words, as nodes in memory, 25–26

Copyrights and Acknowledgments:

Fig. 1.2: From Craik, F. I. M. The fate of primary memory items in free recall. *Journal of Verbal Learning and Verbal Behavior,* 1970, *9,* 143–148, fig. 2. **Fig. 1.3:** From Bower, G., Clark, M. C., Lesgold, A. M., and Winzenz, D. Hierarchical retrieval schemes in recall of categorical word lists. *Journal of Verbal Learning and Verbal Behavior,* 1969, *8,* 323–343, fig. 1. **Box 3.3:** From Bransford, J. D. and Johnson, M. K. Contextual prerequisites for understanding: Some investigations of comprehension and recall. *Journal of Verbal Learning and Verbal Behavior,* 1972, *11,* 717–726, fig. 1. **Fig. 5.5:** From Posner, M. I. Abstraction and the process of recognition. In Bower, G. H. and Spence, J. T. (Eds.) *The psychology of learning and motivation,* 1969, p. 63, fig. 4. **Box 8.1:** From Lindsay, P. and Norman, D. *Human information processing,* 1st Ed., 1972, p. 397, table 10.1. **Fig. 8.1:** From Lindsay, P. and Norman, D. *Human information processing,* 1st Ed., 1972, p. 390, fig. 10.6. **Fig. 8.2:** From Lindsay, P. and Norman, D. *Human information processing,* 1st Ed., 1972, p. 396, fig. 10.12. **Fig. 8.3:** From Lindsay, P. and Norman, D. *Human information processing,* 1st Ed., 1972, p. 398, fig. 10.14. **Fig. 8.4:** From Lindsay, P. and Norman, D. *Human information processing,* 1st Ed., 1972, p. 400, fig. 10.16. **Fig. 12.2:** From Lindsay, P. and Norman, D. *Human information processing,* 2nd Ed., 1977, p. 515, fig. 14.8. **Fig. 10.1:** From Weisberg, R. and Suls, J. An information-processing model of Duncker's candle problem. *Cognitive Psychology,* 1973, *4,* 255–276, fig. 1. **Fig. 10.3:** From Jeffries, R., Polson, P. G., Razran, L., and Atwood, M. A process model for missionaries, cannibals and other river-crossing problems. *Cognitive Psychology,* 1977, *9,* 412–440, fig. 1. **Table 15.1:** From Clark, E. V. What's in a word? On the child's acquisition of semantics in his first language. In Moore, T. E. (Ed.) *Cognitive development and the acquisition of language,* 1973, pp. 65–110, tables 1-4. Reprinted by permission of Academic Press and the individual authors.

Box 3.2: From Rumelhart, D. *Introduction to human information processing.* Copyright © 1977 by John Wiley & Sons, Inc. **Fig. 5.3:** From Hochberg, J. In the mind's eye. In Haber, R. N. (Ed.) *Contemporary theory and research in visual perception.* Copyright © 1968 by John Wiley & Sons, Inc. Reprinted by permission of John Wiley & Sons, Inc.

Table 5.1: From Restle, F. *Learning: animal behavior and human cognition,* 1975, p. 196, table 10.2. Reprinted by permission of McGraw-Hill Book Company, Inc.

Fig. 5.1: From Noton, D. and Stark, L. Eye movements and visual perception. *Scientific American,* 1972, *227,* 35–43. Copyright © 1972 by Scientific American, Inc. All rights reserved. **Fig. 12.7:** From Scheerer, M. Problem-solving. *Scientific American,* 1963, *208,* 118–128. Copyright © 1963 by Scientific American, Inc. All rights reserved.

Fig. 8.5: From *Explorations in Cognition* by Donald A. Norman, David E. Rumelhart, and the LNR Research Group. W. H. Freeman and Company. Copyright © 1975. Reprinted by permission.

Fig. 7.2: From Paivio, A. *Imagery and Verbal Processes.* Copyright © 1971 by Holt, Rinehart & Winston, p. 345, fig. 10-8. Reprinted by permission.

Fig. 7.3: From Shepard, R. N. and Metzler, B. Mental rotation of three-dimensional objects. *Science,* 19 February 1971, *171,* 701–703, fig. 1. Copyright © 1971 by the American Association for the Advancement of Science. Reprinted by permission of the publisher and authors.

Fig. 7.5: From Reed, S. K. and Johnsen, J. A. Detection of parts in patterns and images. *Memory & Cognition,* 1975, *3,* 569–575, figs. 1 and 2. Reprinted by permission of the Psychonomic Society and the author.

Copyrights and acknowledgments

Table 11.1: From Bourne, Jr./Ekstrand/Dominowski, *The Psychology of Thinking,* © 1971, p. 181. Reprinted by permission of Prentice-Hall, Inc., Englewood Cliffs, New Jersey.

Fig. 11.2: From Levine, M. Hypothesis behavior by humans during discrimination learning. *Journal of Experimental Psychology,* 1966, 71, 331–338, fig. 1. Copyright © 1966 by the American Psychological Association. **Fig. 15.1:** From Olson, D. Language and thought: aspects of a cognitive theory of semantics. *Psychological Review,* 1970, 77, 257–273, fig. 2. Copyright © 1970 by the American Psychological Association. Reprinted by permission.